Digital Multimedia Broadcasting

Digital Multimedia Broadcasting

Edited by
Liam Lopez

www.willfordpress.com

Published by Willford Press,
118-35 Queens Blvd., Suite 400,
Forest Hills, NY 11375, USA

ISBN: 978-1-68285-767-0

Cataloging-in-Publication Data

Digital multimedia broadcasting / edited by Liam Lopez.
    p. cm.
Includes bibliographical references and index.
ISBN 978-1-68285-767-0
1. Multimedia communications. 2. Digital communications. 3. Broadcasting--Technological innovations.
4. Digital audio broadcasting. 5. Communication and technology. I. Lopez, Liam.
TK5105.15 .D54 2020
006.7--dc23

For information on all Willford Press publications
visit our website at www.willfordpress.com

Contents

Preface

The method which is used to multicast multimedia content to portable devices by satellite or terrestrial services is referred to as digital multimedia broadcasting. The different examples of multimedia content which is broadcasted are text and audio, text and full motion video, animated graphics, images, etc. Mobile television is the most common and popular application of digital multimedia broadcasting. It enables the users to send and receive video clips, music and RSS feeds. This book elucidates the concepts and innovative models around prospective developments in the field of digital multimedia broadcasting. It strives to provide a fair idea about this subject and to help develop a better understanding of the latest advances within this field. Coherent flow of topics, student-friendly language and extensive use of examples make this book an invaluable source of knowledge.

Significant researches are present in this book. Intensive efforts have been employed by authors to make this book an outstanding discourse. This book contains the enlightening chapters which have been written on the basis of significant researches done by the experts.

Finally, I would also like to thank all the members involved in this book for being a team and meeting all the deadlines for the submission of their respective works. I would also like to thank my friends and family for being supportive in my efforts.

Editor

Individual Channel Estimation in a Diamond Relay Network using Relay-Assisted Training

Xianwen He, Gaoqi Dou, and Jun Gao

College of Electronic Engineering, Naval University of Engineering, Wuhan 430033, China

Correspondence should be addressed to Gaoqi Dou; hjgcqq@163.com

Academic Editor: Wanggen Wan

We consider the training design and channel estimation in the amplify-and-forward (AF) diamond relay network. Our strategy is to transmit the source training in time-multiplexing (TM) mode while each relay node superimposes its own relay training over the amplified received data signal without bandwidth expansion. The principal challenge is to obtain accurate channel state information (CSI) of second-hop link due to the multiaccess interference (MAI) and cooperative data interference (CDI). To maintain the orthogonality between data and training, a modified relay-assisted training scheme is proposed to migrate the CDI, where some of the cooperative data at the relay are discarded to accommodate relay training. Meanwhile, a couple of optimal zero-correlation zone (ZCZ) relay-assisted sequences are designed to avoid MAI. At the destination node, the received signals from the two relay nodes are combined to achieve spatial diversity and enhanced data reliability. The simulation results are presented to validate the performance of the proposed schemes.

1. Introduction

To combat the effects of multipath fading in wireless networks, relay cooperative communication is proposed to generate a virtual multiple-antenna network by sharing antennas [1, 2]. This topic has been the subject of intensive research due to its potential for providing spatial diversity and coverage extension without the limitation of hardware complexity [3]. The diamond relay network is one of the special cases of the multiple-relay networks. Specifically, with only two relays utilized, the diamond relay network can yield diversity benefits to combat fading and be simple enough to design the transmission protocol and efficient scheduling [4]. Moreover, as compared to three-node network with a single relay utilized, the most advantage of the diamond relay network is that different relays can transmit and receive at the same time, which in turn translates to gains due to spatial reuse [5]. Many applications practical in diamond relay network have been studied, for example, the optimal power allocation [6, 7], the optimal opportunistic relay scheme [8–11], and the optimal position selection of relays [4, 5]. In essence, a diamond relay network is a cascade of two single-hop links

consisting of the broadcast channel and the multiple-access channel. However, purely knowing the cascaded channel is insufficient to support the above optimal design in diamond relay network. As a result, channel estimation problems are generally more challenging in diamond relay networks than in three-node relay networks.

With regard to an amplify-and-forward- (AF-) based relay cooperation system, most research has focused on acquiring the cascaded channel state information (CSI). The authors in [12] designed a cyclic-orthogonal training sequence and presented a practical estimation algorithm for a cascaded channel. In [13], the authors derived necessary and sufficient conditions for a relay amplifying matrix in Multi-Input Multi-Output (MIMO) systems. However, the schemes presented in [12, 13] cannot be adopted for estimating an individual channel. For most applications, the CSI of an individual link is indispensable at the receiver to perform signal retrieving and system optimization [14, 15]. Recently, it has been shown in [16] that a multiuser receiver can be used to blindly estimate the channel matrices associated with both individual links. Unfortunately, it is difficult to obtain an instantaneous CSI. The subsequent work in [17] had expanded the superimposed training scheme presented in [18] to the area of multirelay networks. The authors derived optimal pilot symbol designs including both modification diagonal matrix and relay superimposed pilot symbol. Nevertheless, the orthogonal constraint among the source pilot, superimposed pilot, and the modification matrix demands an additional spending and a protocol to coordinate the relay-pilot sequence and modification matrix with the special form of orthogonality, which adds additional complexity to power allocation and joint optimization.

A typical example is the AF-based diamond relay network consisting of source node (SN), destination node (DN), and two AF half-duplex relay nodes with no direct link between the source and the destination [19]. In this paper, we consider an AF-based diamond relay network and propose a modified relay-assisted training strategy to estimate second-hop link. Our strategy is to transmit the source training and data in time-multiplexing (TM) mode from the SN, while each relay superimposes its specialized relay training over the amplified received data vectors. In this manner, the complex problem of a joint optimization design of source training and relay training is disassembled into two independent optimization design problems. In the work, two methods are employed to eliminate cooperative data interference (CDI) and multiaccess interference (MAI). Firstly, to remove the effects of the unknown cooperative information-induced interference on the estimator of second-hop links, some cooperative information-bearing data tones of the received signal at each relay node are discarded to accommodate relay training sequence to keep the orthogonality between data and training. Meanwhile, a simple iterative reconstruction method is employed to compensate the distortion at the DN. Secondly, we derive a couple of optimal zero-correlation zone (ZCZ) relay-assisted sequences designed to eliminate the MAI and minimize the MSE when estimating the second-hop ($\mathbb{R}_1 - \mathbb{D}$, $\mathbb{R}_2 - \mathbb{D}$) channel [20, 21]. At the DN, the received signals from each relay node are combined to achieve spatial diversity and enhance data reliability. The simulation results are presented to prove the performance of the proposed schemes.

The rest of the paper is organized as follows. In Section 2, we present the AF-based diamond relay network. The design of the training sequences at relay nodes is described in Section 3. The detection performance and iterative reconstruction method are introduced in Section 4. The simulations results are presented in Section 5 and conclusions are drawn in Section 6.

Notation 1. Superscripts H, T, and † denote the complex conjugate transpose, transpose, and pseudo-inverse, respectively. The $N \times N$ identity matrix is denoted by $\mathbf{I}$. The Discrete Fourier Transform (DFT) of the $N \times 1$ vector $\mathbf{x}$ is denoted by $\tilde{\mathbf{x}} = \mathbf{F}_N \mathbf{x}$, where $\mathbf{F}_N$ has (m, n) entry $1/\sqrt{N} e^{-j2\pi mn/N}$.

2. System Model

We consider a single-carrier transmission in the AF-based diamond relay network operating in a frequency-selective fading environment, where the data is transmitted from the SN to the DN through two relay nodes $\mathbb{R}_1$, $\mathbb{R}_2$ as shown in

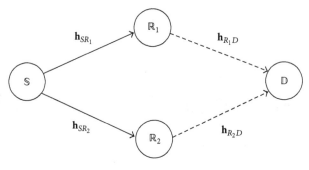

$\longrightarrow$ First slot
$--\rightarrow$ Second slot

FIGURE 1: Diagram for cooperative diversity with two relay nodes.

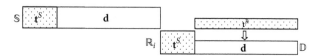

FIGURE 2: Structure of one frame with relay-assisted training.

Figure 1. The individual channel impulse response links are defined as $\mathbf{h}_{SR_i} = [h_{SR_i}(0), h_{SR_i}(1), \ldots, h_{SR_i}(L_{SR_i} - 1)]^T$, $\mathbf{h}_{R_iD} = [h_{R_iD}(0), h_{R_iD}(1), \ldots, h_{R_iD}(L_{R_iD} - 1)]^T$, $i = 1, 2$. Individual channel taps are independent and Rayleigh-distributed as $h_{SR_i}(l) \sim \mathscr{CN}(0, \sigma^2_{SR_i,l})$, $h_{R_iD}(l) \sim \mathscr{CN}(0, \sigma^2_{R_iD,l})$. The signal transmission between $\mathbb{S}$ and $\mathbb{D}$ can be partitioned into two time slots. We consider a cyclic prefix (CP) single-carrier transmission system and assume perfect synchronization for both transmission phases.

At the SN, we first design a frame consisting of the training block $\mathbf{t}^S = [t^S(0), t^S(1), \ldots, t^S(N - 1)]^T$ and the data block $\mathbf{d} = [d(0), d(1), \ldots, d(N - 1)]^T$, where N denotes the block length. To avoid interblock interference at both relay nodes and the DN, a CP of a length $L_{cp} \geq \max\{L_{SR_1} - 1, L_{SR_2} - 1\}$ is inserted into the front of each block before transmission and is removed after reception. During the first time slot, the SN transmits one data block to each relay nodes with average power of $E[(\mathbf{t}^S)^H \mathbf{t}^S] = E[\mathbf{d}^H \mathbf{d}] = NP_s$.

At the second time slot, $\mathbb{R}_1$ and $\mathbb{R}_2$ amplify the received signal and forward the signal to $\mathbb{D}$ with average power of $E[(\mathbf{z}_i^t)^H \mathbf{z}_i^t] = E[(\mathbf{z}_i^d)^H \mathbf{z}_i^d] = NP_r$, respectively. In our strategy, relay-assisted training is superimposed onto the top of the amplified data vector as illustrated in Figure 2. Due to MAI, $\mathbb{D}$ cannot identify the corresponding relay channels. Therefore, linear modification diagonal matrix is designed for training signal at each relay.

After the signal processing at each relay node, the retransmitted signal is given by, respectively,

$$\mathbf{z}_i^t = \beta_i^t \mathbf{\Lambda}_i \mathbf{r}_i^t = \beta_i^t \mathbf{\Lambda}_i \mathbf{H}_{SR_i} \mathbf{t}^S + \beta_i^t \mathbf{\Lambda}_i \mathbf{n}_{R_i}^t,$$

$$\mathbf{z}_i^d = \beta_i^d \mathbf{r}_i^d + \mathbf{t}^{R_i} = \beta_i^d \mathbf{H}_{SR_i} \mathbf{d} + \mathbf{t}^{R_i} + \beta_i^d \mathbf{n}_{R_i}^d,$$

$$(1)$$

where $\mathbf{H}_{SR_i}$ is an $N \times N$ circulant matrix, with the first columns $[(\mathbf{h}_{SR_i})^T, \mathbf{0}_{1\times(N-L_{SR_i})}]^T$, and $\mathbf{n}_{R_i}^t$, $\mathbf{n}_{R_i}^d$ are circular complex white Gaussian noise with zero mean and covariance matrix $\text{cov}(\mathbf{n}_{SR_i}^t) = \text{cov}(\mathbf{n}_{SR_i}^d) = \sigma_n^2\mathbf{I}$, γP_{r_i} that is allocated to the relay training, that is, $E[(t^{R_i})^H t^{R_i}] = \gamma N P_{r_i}$, and $(1 - \gamma)P_{r_i}$ is allocated to the amplified received data, where $0 < \gamma < 1$. The modification diagonal matrix $\Lambda_i = \text{diag}\{\Lambda_i(0), \Lambda_i(1), \ldots, \Lambda_i(N-1)\}$ is set, where $\Lambda_i(k) = e^{j2\pi(i-1)(k-1)/N}$ and the amplified factors are given by

$$\beta_i^t = \sqrt{\frac{P_{r_i}}{P_s\sigma_{h_{SR_i}}^2 + \sigma_n^2}},$$

$$\beta_i^d = \sqrt{\frac{(1-\gamma)P_{r_i}}{P_s\sigma_{h_{SR_i}}^2 + \sigma_n^2}}, \tag{2}$$

where $\sigma_{h_{SR_i}}^2 = \sum_{l=0}^{L_{SR_i}-1}\sigma_{h_{SR_i},l}^2$. The received signal at the DN can be expressed by

$$\mathbf{y}^t = \sum_{i=1}^{2}\mathbf{H}_{R_iD}\beta_i^t\Lambda_i\mathbf{r}_i^t + \mathbf{n}_D^t \tag{3}$$

$$= \beta_1^t\mathbf{H}_{R_1D}\Lambda_1\mathbf{H}_{SR_1}\mathbf{t}^S + \beta_2^t\mathbf{H}_{R_2D}\Lambda_2\mathbf{H}_{SR_2}\mathbf{t}^S + \mathbf{n}_Z^t,$$

$$\mathbf{y}^d = \sum_{i=1}^{2}\mathbf{H}_{R_iD}\beta_i^d\mathbf{r}_i^d + \mathbf{n}_D^d \tag{4}$$

$$= \left(\beta_1^d\mathbf{H}_{R_1} + \beta_2^d\mathbf{H}_{R_2}\right)\mathbf{d} + \mathbf{H}_{R_1D}\mathbf{t}^{R_1} + \mathbf{H}_{R_2D}\mathbf{t}^{R_2} + \mathbf{n}_Z^d,$$

where $\mathbf{H}_{R_iD}$ is an $N \times N$ circulant matrix, with the first columns $[(\mathbf{h}_{R_iD})^T, \mathbf{0}_{1\times(N-L_{R_iD})}]^T$, $\mathbf{n}_D^t$, $\mathbf{n}_D^d$ are circular complex white Gaussian noise, $\mathbf{H}_{R_i} = \mathbf{H}_{SR_i}\mathbf{H}_{R_iD}$, with $L_{R_i} = L_{SR_i} + L_{R_iD} - 1$, $L_S = \max\{L_{R_1}, L_{R_2}\}$. And $\mathbf{n}_Z^t = \sum_{i=1}^{2}\beta_i^t\Lambda_i\mathbf{n}_{R_i}^t + \mathbf{n}_D^t$, $\mathbf{n}_Z^d = \sum_{i=1}^{2}\beta_i^d\mathbf{n}_{R_i}^d + \mathbf{n}_D^d$, $\mathbf{n}_{R_i}^t$, $\mathbf{n}_{R_i}^d$ are also circular complex white Gaussian noise.

3. Design of the Relay Training Sequence

With the purpose of signal retrieving and obtaining diversity, individual channel estimation is required in a diamond relay network. From (4), the received data signal can be expressed as follows:

$$\mathbf{y}^d = \mathbf{\Phi}_{L_{R_1D}}\left[\mathbf{t}^{R_1}\right]\mathbf{h}_{R_1D}$$

$$+ \mathbf{\Phi}_{L_S}[\mathbf{d}]\left(\beta_1^d\mathbf{h}_{R_1} + \beta_2^d\mathbf{h}_{R_2}\right) + \mathbf{\Phi}_{L_{R_2D}}\left[\mathbf{t}^{R_2}\right]\mathbf{h}_{R_2D} + \mathbf{n}_Z^d, \tag{5}$$

$$\underbrace{\phantom{+ \mathbf{\Phi}_{L_S}[\mathbf{d}]\left(\beta_1^d\mathbf{h}_{R_1} + \beta_2^d\mathbf{h}_{R_2}\right) + \mathbf{\Phi}_{L_{R_2D}}\left[\mathbf{t}^{R_2}\right]\mathbf{h}_{R_2D} + \mathbf{n}_Z^d}}_{\mathbf{v}_d}$$

where $\mathbf{\Phi}_L[\mathbf{x}]$ is an $N \times L$ column-wise circulant matrix with the first column $\mathbf{x}$. It is noted that $\mathbf{v}_d$ includes the equivalent noise $\mathbf{n}_Z^d$ that is related to the specific realization of $\mathbf{h}_{R_iD}$, the extra CDI term $\mathbf{\Phi}_{L_S}[\mathbf{d}](\beta_1^d\mathbf{h}_{R_1} + \beta_2^d\mathbf{h}_{R_2})$, and the MAI term $\mathbf{\Phi}_{L_{R_2D}}[\mathbf{t}^{R_2}]\mathbf{h}_{R_2D}$. Assuming that the received data, training sequence, and noise in (5) are mutually independent, the covariance matrices of $\mathbf{v}_d$ can be written, respectively, as

$$\mathbf{C}_d = E\left(\mathbf{v}_d\mathbf{v}_d^H\right) = \left[\left(\beta_1^d\sigma_{h_{R_1}}^2 + \beta_2^d\sigma_{h_{R_2}}^2\right)P_s + \sigma_{h_{R_2D}}^2\gamma P_{r_2}\right.$$

$$\left. + \left(\beta_1^d\sigma_{h_{R_1D}}^2 + \beta_2^d\sigma_{h_{R_2D}}^2 + 1\right)\sigma_n^2\right]\mathbf{I}_N = \sigma_{v_b}^2\mathbf{I}_N, \tag{6}$$

where $\sigma_{h_{R_iD}}^2 = \sum_{l=0}^{L_{R_iD}-1}\sigma_{h_{R_iD},l}^2$, $\sigma_{h_{R_i}}^2 = \sum_{l=0}^{L_{SR_i}+L_{R_iD}-2}\sigma_{h_{R_i},l}^2$ with $\sigma_{h_{R_i},l}^2 = \sum_{j=0}^{l}\sigma_{h_{SR_i},j}^2\sigma_{h_{R_iD},(l-j)}^2$. Without loss of generality, we take the estimation of $\hat{\mathbf{h}}_{R_1D}$ as an example, and the traditional Least Square (LS) estimation of the second-hop channel is obtained by

$$\hat{\mathbf{h}}_{R_1D} = \mathbf{\Phi}_{L_{R_1D}}^{\dagger}\left[\mathbf{t}^{R_1}\right]\mathbf{y}^d = \mathbf{h}_{R_1D} + \mathbf{\Phi}_{L_{R_1D}}^{\dagger}\left[\mathbf{t}^{R_1}\right]$$

$$\cdot\left\{\mathbf{\Phi}_{L_S}[\mathbf{d}]\left(\beta_1^d\mathbf{h}_{R_1} + \beta_2^d\mathbf{h}_{R_2}\right) + \mathbf{\Phi}_{L_{R_2D}}\left[\mathbf{t}^{R_2}\right]\mathbf{h}_{R_2D} \tag{7}\right.$$

$$\left. + \mathbf{n}_Z^d\right\}.$$

The MSE of the LS estimator can be given by

$$\text{MSE}_{h_{R_1D}} = E\left\{\left\|\hat{\mathbf{h}}_{R_1D} - \mathbf{h}_{R_1D}\right\|\right\}$$

$$= \text{tr}\left(\mathbf{\Phi}_{L_{R_1D}}^{\dagger}\left[\mathbf{t}^{R_1}\right]\mathbf{C}_d\mathbf{\Phi}_{L_{R_1D}}^{\dagger H}\left[\mathbf{t}^{R_1}\right]\right) \tag{8}$$

$$= \sigma_{v_d}^2\text{tr}\left[\left(\mathbf{\Phi}_{L_{R_1D}}^{H}\left[\mathbf{t}^{R_1}\right]\mathbf{\Phi}_{L_{R_1D}}\left[\mathbf{t}^{R_1}\right]\right)^{-1}\right].$$

For an $N \times N$ positive definite matrix $\mathbf{M}$, we have $\text{tr}(\mathbf{M})\text{tr}(\mathbf{M}^{-1}) \geq N^2$, where the equality holds if and only if $\mathbf{M} = \lambda\mathbf{I}_N$ for some nonzero constant λ. Using this and the fact that the matrix $(\mathbf{\Phi}_{L_{R_1D}}^{H}[\mathbf{t}^{R_1}]\mathbf{\Phi}_{L_{R_1D}}[\mathbf{t}^{R_1}])^{-1}$ is positive definite, the optimal training for a fixed power γP_{r_1} must satisfy the following conditions:

$$\text{C1: } \mathbf{\Phi}_{L_{R_1D}}^{H}\left[\mathbf{t}^{R_i}\right]\mathbf{\Phi}_{L_{R_1D}}\left[\mathbf{t}^{R_i}\right] = \gamma N P_{r_i}\mathbf{I}_{L_{R_1D}} \tag{9}$$

and the Minimum Mean-Square Error (MSE) of the LS estimation is given by

$$\text{MSE}_{h_{R_1D}} = \frac{\sigma_{v_b}^2 L_{R_1D}^2}{\text{tr}\left(\mathbf{\Phi}_{L_{R_1D}}^{H}\left[\mathbf{t}^{R_1}\right]\mathbf{\Phi}_{L_{R_1D}}\left[\mathbf{t}^{R_1}\right]\right)} = \frac{L_{R_1D}\left[\left(\beta_1^d\sigma_{h_{R_1}}^2 + \beta_2^d\sigma_{h_{R_2}}^2\right)P_s + \sigma_{h_{R_2D}}^2\gamma P_{r_2} + \left(\beta_1^d\sigma_{h_{R_1D}}^2 + \beta_2^d\sigma_{h_{R_2D}}^2 + 1\right)\sigma_n^2\right]}{N\gamma P_{r_1}}. \tag{10}$$

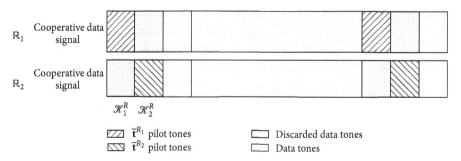

FIGURE 3: Sketch of the structure in the frequency domain for Scheme A.

The MSE of the second-hop channel in (10) consists of three terms. The first term is related to the CDI, the second term is related to the MAI, and the third term is related to the equivalent noise, all of which have serious effects on the estimate of the MSE.

(A) Cooperative Data Interference and Relay-Propagated Noise Cancellation. To eliminate the effects of the unknown CDI and relay-propagated noise on the estimator of the second-hop links, it is crucial to perform signal preprocessing at each relay node. Because relay-assisted training is periodic and its energy is concentrated only at the equispaced frequency pins, we discard some cooperative data tones of the received signal at each relay node so that the DFT at the specific frequency pins is identically zero. In this way, we construct an orthogonal structure between the cooperative data and the relay-assisted training. In fact, the discarded cooperative data tones include both the CDI and the relay-introduced noise terms. At each relay node, we subtract the vector $\mathbf{e} = \mathbf{J}_R \mathbf{r}_i^d$ from the received signal $\mathbf{r}_i^d$, where $\mathbf{J}_R = \mathbf{F}^H \widetilde{\mathbf{J}}_R \mathbf{F}$. Here, we define an $N \times N$ diagonal matrix in the frequency domain $\widetilde{\mathbf{J}}_R = \text{diag}\{\widetilde{J}_R(0), \widetilde{J}_R(1), \dots, \widetilde{J}_R(N-1)\}$ with

$$\widetilde{J}_R(k) = \begin{cases} 1 & k \in \mathcal{K}_1^R \\ 0 & k \notin \mathcal{K}_1^R \end{cases}. \tag{11}$$

Assume that the indices of the nonzero pilot tones corresponding to $\mathbf{t}^{R_1}$ and $\mathbf{t}^{R_2}$ belong to $\mathcal{K}_1^R$. The data signal at $\mathbb{R}_i$ can be refreshed as follows:

$$\begin{aligned} \mathbf{z}_i^d &= \beta_i^d \left(\mathbf{r}_i^d - \mathbf{e} \right) + \mathbf{t}^{R_i} \\ &= \beta_i^d \left(\mathbf{I} - \mathbf{J}_R \right) \mathbf{H}_{SR_i} \mathbf{d} + \beta_i^d \left(\mathbf{I} - \mathbf{J}_R \right) \mathbf{n}_{SR_i}^d + \mathbf{t}^{R_i} \\ &= \beta_i^d \left(\mathbf{H}_{SR_i} \mathbf{d} + \mathbf{n}_{SR_i}^d \right) - \beta_i^d \mathbf{J}_R \left(\mathbf{H}_{SR_i} \mathbf{d} + \mathbf{n}_{SR_i}^d \right) + \mathbf{t}^{R_i}. \end{aligned} \tag{12}$$

(B) Multiaccess Interference Cancellation. With the aim of minimizing the MSE of second-hop channel, the following constrained conditions $\mathbf{C}_2$ and $\mathbf{C}_3$ should be satisfied according to (7):

$$\begin{aligned} \mathbf{C}_2 &: \mathbf{\Phi}_{L_{R_1 D}}^H \left[\mathbf{t}^{R_1} \right] \mathbf{\Phi}_{L_{R_2 D}} \left[\mathbf{t}^{R_2} \right] = \mathbf{0}, \\ \mathbf{C}_3 &: \mathbf{\Phi}_{L_{R_2 D}}^H \left[\mathbf{t}^{R_2} \right] \mathbf{\Phi}_{L_{R_1 D}} \left[\mathbf{t}^{R_1} \right] = \mathbf{0} \end{aligned} \tag{13}$$

In Scheme A, a couple of relay training sequences ($\mathbf{t}^{R_1}$ and $\mathbf{t}^{R_2}$) with their energy concentrated at different frequency pins is designed. We assume that the indices of the nonzero pilot tones corresponding to $\mathbf{t}^{R_1}$ belong to $\mathcal{K}_1^R$, while the indices of the nonzero pilot tones corresponding to $\mathbf{t}^{R_2}$ belong to $\mathcal{K}_2^R$. The condition $\mathcal{K}_1^R \cap \mathcal{K}_2^R = \varnothing$ should be satisfied. With pilot tones occupying the disjoint frequency tones, the problem of MAI can be solved. However, it is necessary to perform signal preprocessing at each relay node. As a result, to maintain the orthogonality, it is indispensable that the frequency components of the received signal corresponding to both $\mathcal{K}_1^R$ and $\mathcal{K}_2^R$ should be removed to accommodate relay-pilot tones as illustrated in Figure 3. Clearly, the distortion of the received data would be doubled in Scheme A and the detection performance will be seriously degraded. Therefore, this is not an appropriate scheme to avoid MAI.

In Scheme B, a couple of relay training with autocorrelation and cross-correlation properties are designed. In the ZCZ sequence group $\{t^{R_1}(k), t^{R_2}(k)\}$, P denotes the period of the ZCZ sequence, Z denotes the length of the zero-correlation zone, and the condition $Z \geq \max\{L_{R_1 D} - 1, L_{R_2 D} - 1\}$ is required, where $N = PQ$ and Q is an integer. The autocorrelation and cross-correlation properties of the ZCZ sequence are stated as follows:

$$\begin{aligned} R_{i,j}(\tau) &= \sum_{k=0}^{P-1} t^{R_i}(k) t^{R_j}(k+\tau) \\ &= \begin{cases} P, & \text{if } \tau = 0, \ i = j \\ 0, & \text{if } 0 < \tau \leq Z, \ i = j \\ 0, & \text{if } 0 \leq \tau \leq Z, \ i \neq j, \end{cases} \end{aligned} \tag{14}$$

where $i, j = 1, 2$. The relay training sequences can satisfy the conditions $\mathbf{C}_2$ and $\mathbf{C}_3$ denoted in (13). Moreover, the indices of the nonzero pilot tones corresponding to the ZCZ sequence group including $\mathbf{t}^{R_1}$ and $\mathbf{t}^{R_2}$ both belong to $\mathcal{K}_1^R$. As a result, only the frequency components corresponding to $\mathcal{K}_1^R$ should be removed. This is the optimal scheme to avoid MAI. The structure of the data block in the frequency domain is illustrated in Figure 4.

At the DN, the decoupling of the two relay training sequences is easily realized. In essence, the complicated two-access channel estimation problem is decomposed into two

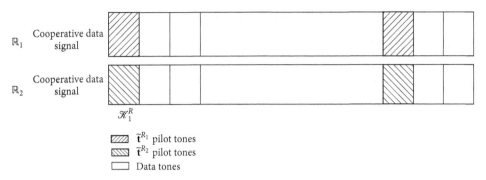

FIGURE 4: Sketch of the structure in the frequency domain for Scheme B.

independent channel estimation problems. According to (5) and (12), the received data signal at the DN can be refreshed as follows:

$$\mathbf{y}^d = \Phi_{L_{R_1D}}\left[\mathbf{t}^{R_1}\right]\mathbf{h}_{R_1D}$$

$$+ \Phi_{L_S}\left[(\mathbf{I}-\mathbf{J}_R)\mathbf{d}\right]\left(\beta_1^d\mathbf{h}_{R_1}+\beta_2^d\mathbf{h}_{R_2}\right) \quad (15)$$

$$+ \Phi_{L_{R_2D}}\left[\mathbf{t}^{R_2}\right]\mathbf{h}_{R_2D}+\overline{\mathbf{n}}_Z^d,$$

where $\overline{\mathbf{n}}_Z^d = \beta_1^d\Phi_{L_{R_1D}}[(\mathbf{I}-\mathbf{J}_R)\mathbf{n}_{SR_1}^d]\mathbf{h}_{R_1D} + \beta_2^d\Phi_{L_{R_2D}}[(\mathbf{I}-\mathbf{J}_R)\mathbf{n}_{SR_2}^d]\mathbf{h}_{R_2D}+\mathbf{n}_{RD}^d$. It is noted that the partial cooperative data vector [the second term in (15)] and the relay training vector [the third term in (15)] occupy the disjoint frequency tones, respectively. As a result, the cooperative data have no effect on the estimation of the second-hop channel. According to C1, the pseudo-inverse of $\Phi_{L_{R_1D}}[\mathbf{t}^{R_1}]$ can be denoted as

$$\Phi_{L_{R_1D}}^\dagger\left[\mathbf{t}^{R_1}\right]$$

$$= \left(\Phi_{L_{R_1D}}^H\left[\mathbf{t}^{R_1}\right]\Phi_{L_{R_1D}}\left[\mathbf{t}^{R_1}\right]\right)^{-1}\Phi_{L_{R_1D}}^H\left[\mathbf{t}^{R_1}\right] \quad (16)$$

$$= \frac{1}{\gamma NP_{r_1}}\Phi_{L_{R_1D}}^H\left[\mathbf{t}^{R_1}\right].$$

In the LS estimation, according to $\mathbf{C}_2$ and $\mathbf{C}_3$, the improved estimation of the second-hop channel is obtained by

$$\widehat{\mathbf{h}}_{R_1D} = \Phi_{L_{R_1D}}^\dagger\left[\mathbf{t}^{R_1}\right]\mathbf{y}^d = \mathbf{h}_{R_1D}+\frac{1}{\gamma NP_{r_1}}\Phi_{L_{R_1D}}^H\left[\mathbf{t}^{R_1}\right]$$

$$\cdot\left\{\Phi_{L_S}\left[(\mathbf{I}-\mathbf{J}_R)\mathbf{d}\right]\left(\beta_1^d\mathbf{h}_{R_1}+\beta_2^d\mathbf{h}_{R_2}\right)\right.$$

$$+ \Phi_{L_{R_2D}}\left[\mathbf{t}^{R_2}\right]\mathbf{h}_{R_2D}+\overline{\mathbf{n}}_Z^d\Big\} = \mathbf{h}_{R_1D}+\frac{1}{\gamma NP_{r_1}} \quad (17)$$

$$\cdot\Phi_{L_{R_1D}}^H\left[\mathbf{t}^{R_1}\right]\mathbf{n}_{RD}^d.$$

According to (17), the relay-propagated noise introduced from each relay node is removed thoroughly. As both the CDI

and MAI are removed, the minimum MSE of the improved LS estimation is given by

$$\text{MSE}_{h_{R_1D}} = \frac{L_{R_1D}\sigma_n^2}{\gamma NP_{r_1}}. \quad (18)$$

4. Diversity Combining and Iterative Reconstruction

With the purpose of signal retrieving and obtaining diversity, individual channel ($\mathbb{S}-\mathbb{R}_1$ and $\mathbb{S}-\mathbb{R}_2$) estimation is required in diamond relay networks. With the estimated second-hop channels $\widehat{\mathbf{h}}_{R_1D}$ and $\widehat{\mathbf{h}}_{R_2D}$, we employ the LS channel estimation in [12] to obtain estimated channels $\widehat{\mathbf{h}}_{SR_1}$ and $\widehat{\mathbf{h}}_{SR_2}$. After removing the contribution of the relay training sequences from $\mathbf{y}^d$ by simply computing $\mathbf{y}_{re}^d = (\mathbf{I}-\mathbf{J}_R)\mathbf{y}^d$, the DFT of $\mathbf{y}_{re}^d$ can be written as

$$\widetilde{\mathbf{y}}_{re}^d = \left(\beta_1^d\widetilde{\mathbf{H}}_{R_1D}\widetilde{\mathbf{H}}_{SR_1}+\beta_1^d\widetilde{\mathbf{H}}_{R_2D}\widetilde{\mathbf{H}}_{SR_2}\right)\left(\mathbf{I}-\widetilde{\mathbf{J}}_R\right)\widetilde{\mathbf{d}}$$

$$+ \left(\mathbf{I}-\widetilde{\mathbf{J}}_R\right)\widetilde{\mathbf{n}}_Z^d. \quad (19)$$

The equalized signal is given by

$$\widetilde{\mathbf{u}} = \Sigma_S^H\mathbf{R}_y^{-1}\widetilde{\mathbf{y}}_{re}, \quad (20)$$

where $\Sigma_S = \beta_1^d\widehat{\widetilde{\mathbf{H}}}_{SR_1}\widehat{\widetilde{\mathbf{H}}}_{R_1D}+\beta_2^d\widehat{\widetilde{\mathbf{H}}}_{SR_2}\widehat{\widetilde{\mathbf{H}}}_{R_2D}$, $\mathbf{R}_y = \Sigma_S\Sigma_S^H + [(\beta_1^d)^2\widehat{\widetilde{\mathbf{H}}}_{R_1D}\widehat{\widetilde{\mathbf{H}}}_{R_1D}^H + (\beta_2^d)^2\widehat{\widetilde{\mathbf{H}}}_{R_2D}\widehat{\widetilde{\mathbf{H}}}_{R_2D}^H + \mathbf{I}]\widehat{\sigma}_n^2$ in the case of Minimum Mean-Square Error (MMSE) equalization, $\widehat{\widetilde{\mathbf{H}}}_{SR_i}$, $\widehat{\widetilde{\mathbf{H}}}_{R_iD}$ are the DFT of the estimated channels $\widehat{\mathbf{h}}_{SR_i}$ and $\widehat{\mathbf{h}}_{R_iD}$, $\widetilde{\mathbf{n}}_Z^d$ is the DFT of equivalent noise $\mathbf{n}_Z^d$, and $\widehat{\sigma}_n^2 = (1-1/Q)(\beta_1^d\sigma_{h_{R_1D}}^2+\beta_2^d\sigma_{h_{R_2D}}^2+1)\sigma_n^2$. Because the data distortion is singular, $\mathbf{d}$ cannot be recovered linearly. As a result, we employ the symbol-to-symbol iterative detection scheme. The initial hard detector of $\mathbf{d}$ is given by

$$\widehat{\mathbf{d}}^{(0)} = \lfloor\mathbf{F}^H\widetilde{\mathbf{u}}\rfloor, \quad (21)$$

where $\lfloor\cdot\rfloor$ stands for the decision function. For subsequent iterations, the detected symbols are utilized to compute $\mathbf{J}_R\widehat{\mathbf{d}}$

TABLE 1: Binary ZCZ sequence group (0 for −1).

(P, Z)	Relay training	ZCZ sequences
(32, 4)	$\mathbf{t}^{R_1}$	{**1 1 0 1 1 1 0 1 0 0 0 1 0 0 0 1 0 0 1 0 1 1 0 1 1 1 1 0 0 0 0 1**}
	$\mathbf{t}^{R_2}$	{**0 0 1 0 1 1 0 1 1 1 1 0 0 0 0 1 1 1 0 1 1 1 0 1 0 0 0 1 0 0 0 1**}

TABLE 2: Various system parameters for different choices.

	Frame N_f	Training N_c	Data N_b	$\alpha = N_c/N_f$	BER at 20 dB
Case 1	496	48	448	0.1	0.003768
Case 2	640	64	576	0.1	0.00329

and compensate for the data loss. The detected symbols at the next iteration are given by

$$\hat{\mathbf{d}}^{(i)} = \left\lfloor \mathbf{F}^H \tilde{\mathbf{u}} + \mathbf{J}_R \hat{\mathbf{d}}^{(i-1)} \right\rfloor. \tag{22}$$

5. Simulation Results

In this section, we present the simulation results to evaluate performance of both the proposed scheme (denoted as "proposed" in figures) and the pilot-based scheme in [15] (denoted as "pilot-based scheme" in figures) in terms of bit error rate (BER) and normalized MSE of channel estimation. The channel is randomly generated and assumed to be uncorrelated Rayleigh fading with a length of $L_{SR_1} = L_{SR_2} = L_{R_1D} = L_{R_2D} = 4$. For ease of description, the block lengths are the same in this context. However, different lengths can be used based on the requirements. The equispaced and equipowered pilots are selected. The data symbols are extracted from the quadrature phase-shift keying constellation. The relay training is designed using $P = 32$, $Z = 4$ and the relay training sequences are set as shown in Table 1 according to [20, 21]. SNR of each link are assumed that $\text{SNR} = P_S/\sigma_n^2 = P_{R_1}/\sigma_n^2 = P_{R_2}/\sigma_n^2$, where $P_S = P_{R_1} = P_{R_2} = 1$. In the simulation, we employ various system parameters of frame (Case 1 and Case 2), respectively, as shown in Table 2.

To obtain the optimal design for the relay training sequences, we display the bit error rate (BER) performance versus γ for the proposed scheme under different signal-to-noise ratio (SNR) conditions in Figure 5. Clearly, the BER performance improves when γ increases. This occurs because more power is allocated to the superimposed relay training, while less power is allocated to the data sequence. It is evident that the optimal γ remains at the minimum value when the SNR is 10, 15, and 20, respectively. As a result, we adopt $\gamma = 0.1$ as the approximately optimal value.

Figure 6 shows the MSE performance of channel estimation with different schemes for Case 1. The estimation performance of the $\mathbb{S} - \mathbb{R}_i$ link is worse than that of the $\mathbb{R}_i - \mathbb{D}$ link because the former link is affected by both the propagated noise introduced from the relay nodes and the estimation error of the second-hop link. Moreover, the performance

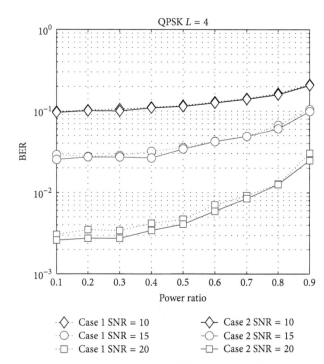

Case 1 SNR = 10, Case 1 SNR = 15, Case 1 SNR = 20, Case 2 SNR = 10, Case 2 SNR = 15, Case 2 SNR = 20

FIGURE 5: BER versus γ for different SNR conditions.

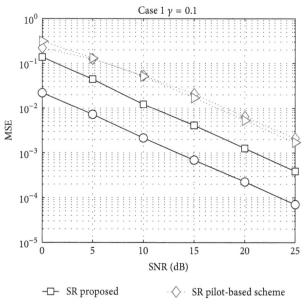

SR proposed, RD proposed, SR pilot-based scheme, RD pilot-based scheme

FIGURE 6: MSE performance with different schemes for Case 1.

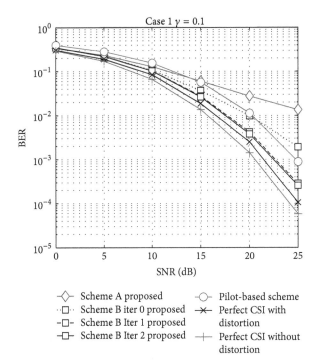

FIGURE 7: BER performance with different schemes for Case 1.

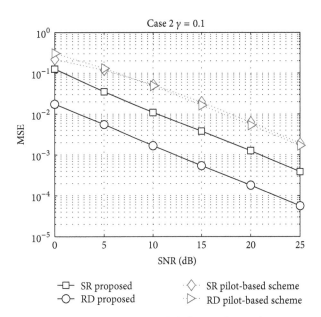

FIGURE 8: MSE performance with different schemes for Case 2.

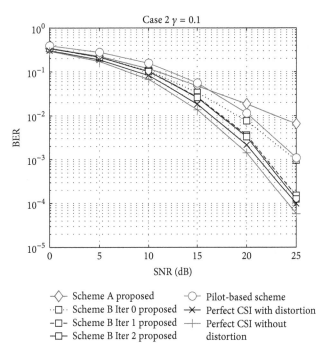

FIGURE 9: BER performance with different schemes for Case 2.

of the proposed scheme is superior to that of the pilot-based scheme described in [17]. The pilot-based scheme aims to superimpose the relay-assisted training onto the source training signal with a special orthogonal constraint. With the same average power and different block length, the total energy of the relay-assisted training in the scheme [17] is reduced compared to the proposed scheme. Moreover, the relay-propagated noise has a serious impact on the estimation of the $\mathbb{R}_i - \mathbb{D}$ link in the scheme [17]. As a result, the proposed estimation scheme is superior to the scheme [17].

Figure 7 shows the BER performance with different schemes for Case 1. In the proposed Scheme B, the performance improvement via the first iteration is distinct but negligible with additional iterations. It can be observed that the BER performance of the Scheme B is much better than that of Scheme A and for the scheme described in [17]. It is noted that a double distortion is induced in Scheme A and the inferior channel estimation of the pilot-based scheme clearly results in a degradation in BER. It can be predicted that a symbol error floor will occur in both Scheme A and the scheme described in [17] with an increasing SNR. After two iterations, the detection performance in Scheme B can approach that with perfect CSI, which means the channel estimation satisfies the need of the cooperative system. The performance reduction caused by the distortion can be judged in terms of the BER loss in the figure.

Figures 8 and 9 show the MSE performance and BER performance with different schemes for Case 2. We obviously observe that the estimation performance is almost the same for Case 1 and Case 2. Moreover, the BER performance for the pilot-based scheme would remain the same with various system parameters of frame. However, with the length of data

block (N_b) increasing, the BER performance in the proposed scheme get a certain improvement. It is because that the distortion on every symbol is reduced with N_b increasing, when the fixed distortion is scattered throughout the data block. As a result, when we employ the system parameter of larger frames, the proposed scheme is more competitive.

6. Conclusions

In the AF-based diamond relay network, a novel relay-assisted training strategy is proposed to acquire the individual

CSI. In our strategy, each relay node superimposes its own special training sequence over the amplified received data, which can be used to acquire the second-hop CSI. To solve the interference problems of unknown cooperative data, we discarded some cooperative data at each relay to accommodate the relay-pilot tones. Meanwhile, we derive a couple of relay training with autocorrelation and cross-correlation properties to decouple the combined relay training sequences. The simulations show that the channel estimation performance of the proposed scheme is superior to that of the pilot-based scheme described in [17]. Moreover, the detecting performance improvement via the iteration reconstruction is distinct.

Acknowledgments

This work was supported by the National Natural Science Foundation of China (Grant no. 61302099) and China Postdoctoral Science Foundation (Grant no. 2015T81107).

References

[1] W. Zhuang and M. Ismail, "Cooperation in wireless communication networks," *IEEE Wireless Communications Magazine*, vol. 19, no. 2, pp. 10–20, 2012.

[2] G. J. Foschini and M. J. Gans, "On limits of wireless communications in a fading environment when using multiple antennas," *Wireless Personal Communications*, vol. 6, no. 3, pp. 311–335, 1998.

[3] J. N. Laneman, D. N. Tse, and G. W. Wornell, "Cooperative diversity in wireless networks: efficient protocols and outage behavior," *IEEE Transactions on Information Theory*, vol. 50, no. 12, pp. 3062–3080, 2004.

[4] Q. Wang, P. Fan, M. R. McKay, and K. Ben Letaief, "On the position selection of relays in diamond relay networks," *IEEE Transactions on Communications*, vol. 59, no. 9, pp. 2515–2527, 2011.

[5] C. Huang and S. Cui, "On the alternative relaying gaussian diamond channel with conferencing links," *IEEE Transactions on Wireless Communications*, vol. 12, no. 2, pp. 758–768, 2013.

[6] A. Reznik, S. R. Kulkarni, and S. Verdú, "Degraded Gaussian multirelay channel: capacity and optimal power allocation," *IEEE Transactions on Information Theory*, vol. 50, no. 12, pp. 3037–3046, 2004.

[7] S. Zhang, F. Gao, C. Pei, and X. He, "Segment training based individual channel estimation in one-way relay network with power allocation," *IEEE Transactions on Wireless Communications*, vol. 12, no. 3, pp. 1300–1309, 2013.

[8] G. Yuan, M. Peng, and W. Wang, "Opportunistic user cooperative relaying in TDMA-based wireless networks," *Wireless Communications and Mobile Computing*, vol. 10, no. 7, pp. 972–985, 2010.

[9] A. Bletsas, H. Shin, and M. Z. Win, "Cooperative communications with outage-optimal opportunistic relaying," *IEEE Transactions on Wireless Communications*, vol. 6, no. 9, pp. 3450–3460, 2007.

[10] Y. Jing and H. Jafarkhani, "Single and multiple relay selection schemes and their achievable diversity orders," *IEEE Transactions on Wireless Communications*, vol. 8, no. 3, pp. 1414–1423, 2009.

[11] M. Elfituri, A. Ghrayeb, and W. Hamouda, "Antenna/relay selection for coded cooperative networks with AF relaying," *IEEE Transactions on Communications*, vol. 57, no. 9, pp. 2580–2584, 2009.

[12] M. Lei, M. Zhao, J. Zhong, and Z. Zhang, "Channel estimation based on cyclic orthogonal training sequence for relay-assisted cooperative communication system," in *Proceedings of the International Conference on Computer, Information and Telecommunication Systems (CITS '12)*, Amman, Jordan, May 2012.

[13] J. Ma, P. Orlik, J. Zhang, and G. Y. Li, "Pilot matrix design for estimating cascaded channels in two-hop MIMO amplify-and-forward relay systems," *IEEE Transactions on Wireless Communications*, vol. 10, no. 6, pp. 1956–1965, 2011.

[14] O. Munoz-Medina, J. Vidal, and A. Agustin, "Linear transceiver design in nonregenerative relays with channel state information," *IEEE Transactions on Signal Processing*, vol. 55, no. 6, part 1, pp. 2593–2604, 2007.

[15] D. Qin, Z. Ding, and S. Dasgupta, "On forward channel estimation for MIMO precoding in cooperative relay wireless transmission systems," *IEEE Transactions on Signal Processing*, vol. 62, no. 5, pp. 1265–1278, 2014.

[16] H. Xi and A. L. F. de Almeida, "Multiuser receiver for joint symbol/channel estimation in dual-hop relaying systems," *Wireless Personal Communications*, vol. 83, no. 1, pp. 17–33, 2015.

[17] B. Zahedi, M. Ahmadian, K. Mohamed-Pour, M. Peyghami, M. Norouzi, and S. Salari, "Pilot-based individual forward and backward channel estimation in amplify-and-forward OFDM relay networks," in *Proceedings of the IFIP Wireless Days (WD '11)*, Niagara Falls, Canada, October 2011.

[18] F. Gao, B. Jiang, X. Gao, and X. Zhang, "Superimposed training based channel estimation for OFDM modulated amplify-and-forward relay networks," *IEEE Transactions on Communications*, vol. 59, no. 7, pp. 2029–2039, 2011.

[19] R. Simoni, V. Jamali, N. Zlatanov, R. Schober, L. Pierucci, and R. Fantacci, "Buffer-Aided Diamond Relay Network With Block Fading and Inter-Relay Interference," *IEEE Transactions on Wireless Communications*, vol. 15, no. 11, pp. 7357–7372, 2016.

[20] W. N. Yuan, P. Wang, and Z. P. Fan, "Enhanced performance for MIMO channel estimation based on implicit ZCZ training sequences," *ACTA Electronica Sinica*, vol. 38, no. 1, pp. 74–78, 2010.

[21] P. Z. Fan, N. Suehiro, N. Kuroyanagi, and X. M. Deng, "A class of binary sequences with zero correlation zone," *IEEE Electronics Letters*, vol. 35, no. 10, pp. 777–779, 1999.

Research of Simulation in Character Animation based on Physics Engine

Yang Yu,[1] Jucheng Yang,[1] Xiaofei Zan,[2] Jiangang Huang,[1] and Xiangbo Zhang[1]

[1]*College of Computer Science and Information Engineering, Tianjin University of Science and Technology, Tianjin, China*
[2]*School of Computer and Information Technology, Beijing Jiaotong University, Beijing, China*

Correspondence should be addressed to Jiangang Huang; huangjg@tust.edu.cn

Academic Editor: Jenq-Neng Hwang

Computer 3D character animation essentially is a product, which is combined with computer graphics and robotics, physics, mathematics, and the arts. It is based on computer hardware and graphics algorithms and related sciences rapidly developed new technologies. At present, the mainstream character animation technology is based on the artificial production of key technologies and capture frames based on the motion capture device technology. 3D character animation is widely used not only in the production of film, animation, and other commercial areas but also in virtual reality, computer-aided education, flight simulation, engineering simulation, military simulation, and other fields. In this paper, we try to study physics based character animation to solve these problems such as poor real-time interaction that appears in the character, low utilization rate, and complex production. The paper deeply studied the kinematics, dynamics technology, and production technology based on the motion data. At the same time, it analyzed ODE, PhysX, Bullet, and other variety of mainstream physics engines and studied OBB hierarchy bounding box tree, AABB hierarchical tree, and other collision detection algorithms. Finally, character animation based on ODE is implemented, which is simulation of the motion and collision process of a tricycle.

1. Research Background and Significance

The mainstream animation production technologies are key frame technology based on artificial production and motion capture technology based on capture equipment. Key frame technology based on artificial production is the original animation combination technology. It depends on the key frame production and the interpolation between key frames to drive the continuous animation playing. The technology allows designers to create animation by their own will with the greatest degree of freedom, but the products of the technology are not very good in terms of natural performance; moreover, the process of production is quite complicated [1]. Since the motion capture equipment appeared, it can be used to capture the motion data as the information source of animation production, so that the efficiency of producing character animation and the reality sense of character animation can be greatly improved. However, since the technology needs the genuine characters to take part in the process of capturing

the motion information, its application scope becomes quite limited. When using this technology, it is not allowed for the genuine actors to take some dangerous actions. Furthermore, the high cost of this kind of equipment will also restrict the wide use of the technology.

In the background of growing industrial demand, increased user experience requirement, and fast developing of computer-related technologies, the above-mentioned two kinds of common traditional animation production methods are becoming less and less possible to satisfy the requirements of design and use. The root cause is that the two kinds of technologies use the offline way during the process of animation combination and storage and then for the post-production use; thus, the animation will be charged with the corresponding huge data storage space considering its high quality and long duration. Moreover, the biggest issue of this method is the poor rate in terms of real-time and self-adaption performance, so that the animation, which has cost plenty of time and money, can be just used for the specific circumstance for once. All of these issues do not fit into the current trend of fast increase of computer processing and user experience [2].

This article, in order to deal with the issues of poor real-time performance, low utilization rate, and complicated procedure, existing during the process of producing character animation, does research on the character animation simulation method based on physics engine and uses an example to implement the method.

2. Foundation of Related Researches

Nowadays, character animation is always the focus and difficulty in the computer graphics research. In the research, there are various animation production methods, which can be categorized as follows [3]:

(i) The animation production method based on kinematics

(ii) The animation production method based on dynamics

(iii) The animation production method based on motion data

A brief introduction of the above three kinds of character animation is next.

2.1. Principle of Character Animation Production Based on Kinematics.
Kinematics is a very important branch in physics mechanics. During the research, the object is abstracted as a rigid body model and a particle model [4]. These models are used to study the motion of objects. The key point of the rigid body model is to research the rigid body's angular velocity, rotary motion, linear velocity, and so forth. The focus of the research on the particle model is on the velocity, acceleration, deceleration, and motion equation of the particle in the specified reference system. In addition, it is not necessary to consider the influence factors of dynamics, such as quality and force.

The kinematics method is divided into forward kinematics and inverse kinematics.

2.1.1. Forward Kinematics Method [5].
In a simple kinematic system, there are often two ends. They are free end and fixed end. Forward kinematics describes the motion of the free end with the fixed end of the system as the starting point. Forward kinematics method: the first step is to establish the hierarchical structure of the object and then to establish the rotation and position of each object in the hierarchy.

2.1.2. Inverse Kinematics Method.
Another simulation technique based on kinematics is the inverse kinematics method [5]. Inverse kinematics is just opposite to forward kinematics. The inverse kinematics is the motion of which the fixed end drove by the free end.

Use the following formula to express the basic principles of the inverse kinematics [6]:

$$\Delta X = J\Delta\theta. \tag{1}$$

Formula (1) is the basic formula of the inverse kinematics, in which ΔX is the displacement of the end of the joint chain, $\Delta\theta$ is the rotate angle of the end of the joint chain, and J is the Jacobian matrix. By the formula above, the displacement of joint is equal to a product, the rotation angle of joint chain ends, and the Jacobian matrix. But formula (2) is frequently used in inverse kinematics [6]:

$$\Delta\theta = J^{+}\Delta X + \alpha\left(I - J^{+}J\right)\Delta z. \tag{2}$$

In the formula, ΔX and $\Delta\theta$ are similarly found in formula (1). J^{+} is pseudo-inverse matrix of the Jacobian matrix in linear algebra. I is a unit matrix. α is optimization constant. Δz is the energy consumption of joints in minimizing motion. The inverse kinematics is calculated from the end of the entire joint chain. Compared with the forward kinematics, inverse kinematics is more suitable for the creation of more complex motion and easier to enable the flip of the object in the animation. However, the inverse kinematics is not universal. Some problems which are suitable for forward kinematics are not suitable for inverse kinematics.

2.2. Principle of Animation Production Based on Dynamics.
Dynamics is also a very important branch of physics, which researches the relationship between force and motion. The basic theory of kinetic research is Newton's law of motion. The object of the dynamics study is a macroscopic object that is far lower than the speed of light. The animation produced by this method has a strong physical reality, because it is based on the laws of physics.

In the simulation of character animation, kinematics method is to calculate the position and rotate angle of each joint for the characters, and the key frames are composed of two kinds of data.

In the simulation of character animation, the dynamic method first gives the object to the physical properties and exerts various forces and then uses Newton's law of motion to calculate the state of the character. The essence of this method is to calculate the acceleration of an object by force. In dynamics, the type of force can be divided into two types: point force and field force [7].

In addition to the force, the collision is also an important factor affecting the movement of the character. In the real world, when two objects collide, they collide, but they do not penetrate each other. When the collision occurs, the interaction force will change the original state of the two objects, such as position, trajectory, and direction. Therefore, in the simulation of the character animation, if the collision is between objects, the original motion state of the character will be changed because of the interaction force.

2.3. Principle of Character Animation
Production Based on Motion Data

2.3.1. Motion Capture. The animation methods mentioned above are realized by the use of mechanics, biomechanics, and daily life experience. In motion capture technology, data is originated from the real actor performance, through motion capture equipment to obtain action data. Because the processed data is produced by human beings, the motion capture technology can make the animation more real and natural. There was no artificial data from capture and processing. But, motion capture equipment is very expensive and complicated to operate. During the data collection, the motion model's limb, body, and head commonly set sensors point, and those collective data are a very important part in whole motion capture technology [8].

The dynamic and kinematics techniques introduced in this paper are used to animate the physical laws of motion. However, the complexity of human motion with physical laws, especially in terms of human motion coordination mechanism, makes simulation work very difficult, thus leading to the produced animation being not realistic and the lack of rich detailed information of actual human body movement. In recent years, the motion capture technology has entered the line of sight; it overcomes the shortcomings of the above two methods of animation and has become one of the most promising technologies in human animation.

2.3.2. Motion Blend. The motion blending technology is a technology based on special motion database and algorithm. To use this technique to deal with animation, we generally need to use interpolation algorithm and interpolation parameters.

The main advantage of motion blend technology is its low computational complexity. And it is based on motion capture data, to maintain the original dynamic motion. Its main drawback is that, for example, tension, worry, and other acts are too dependent on the existing operating data, and the amount of data increases. If a character is walking in a gait that is not too tired or tired, it is necessary to have a normal walking gait data and also to have a very tired walking data. In the interpolation process, the producers usually deal with the transition and transformation between the collection of parameters by the persistent and linear default views [9].

2.3.3. Motion Deformation. Motion deformation is the technology to modify and use the existing motion information. Popoivc and Witkin use interactive methods to shift and scale the selected key frames to modify the existing data. Compared with the trajectory in the time domain, Williams and Bruderlin are used to adjust, modify, and reuse the existing animation data in the frequency domain. Compared with moving animation technology and process animation technology, the advantage of motion mixing technology is that it can use the existing real capture data for animation generation. Moreover, this technology gives the animation creator and key frame animation compatible with a tool that will be very convenient to deal with.

Compared with kinematics animation technology and process animation technology, the advantage of the motion blending technology, which belongs to the process animation technology, is that it can make use of the existing real capture data to generate animation [10]. Moreover, this technology is compatible with key frame animation technology.

3. The Physics Engine Related Research

Generally, there are two types of physics engines: open source physics engine and commercial physics engine.

Commonly used professional physics engines include ODE, PhysX, Bullet, Havork, Newton, and Vortex. These physics engines are widely used in the domains as graphics modeling tools, game development, virtual reality systems, and so on.

Collision detection is the technical core of physics engine, so most of the research on physics engine is the research on the collision detection algorithm. In real life, some reactions occur naturally at and after the collision of objects [11]. However, in the virtual world, the collision issue needs some algorithms to be solved. Collision detection is the important part of the domains like Robot, VR, and so on. Its main purpose is to determine whether two or more objects will penetrate or contact. The research of collision detection is, through a certain algorithm, to enable two or more objects not to occupy the same spatial area at the same time, without damaging the objects.

At present, there are two major categories of research on collision detection worldwide: spatial decomposition method and bounding box method. The bounding box method simulates a complexly shaped object into an approximate simple three-dimensional space. The hierarchical bounding box method of the bounding box method is suitable for the collision detection in complex environment.

The ODE (Open Dynamics Engine) is an open source library of rigid body dynamics that is often used in the simulation of joint connections. ODE can be applied to simulate the moving objects in the VR environment, legged creatures, and vehicles on the ground. It is robust, flexible, and fast. Flexibility is reflected in the portability; Unix/Linux, Windows, and MacOS can be used. And it has a built-in collision detection system.

4. Research and Design of Character Animation Simulation Based on ODE

4.1. Dynamics Modeling of Simulated Vehicle Based on ODE. In ODE, there is a special type of joint as shown in Figure 1.

Hinge-2 joint is made up of two noncoaxial hinges. The utility model comprises two rotating shafts and a supporting point. Among them, Axis 2 can only rotate around the axis; however, Axis 1 not only can rotate around the axis but also can limit the scope of its rotation.

The car model consists of body and wheels. According to the joint type of Hinge-2, Body 1 can represent the body and Body 2 can represent the wheel; similarly, Axis 1 can represent the steering wheel of the wheel and Axis 2 can represent the

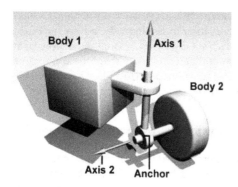

FIGURE 1: Hinge-2 joints [20].

wheel rolling shaft. In the dynamics design of the ODE system, ODE rigid object with the quality and position is generated, and ODE geometry corresponding to the rigid body is created at the same time. Finally, the body and the wheels are connected by Hinge-2 joint. A simple car model has been built.

4.2. Simulation of Character Collision Based on ODE. The simulation process of character collision based on ODE is as follows.

4.2.1. Spatial Initialization in Collision Simulation. At this stage, it is necessary to set the type of collision space and the relevant properties of the contact surface, such as flexibility, elasticity, and friction.

4.2.2. Data Initialization in Collision Simulation. At this stage, it is necessary to do some work on the initialization and cleanup of the data before the collision simulation [12].

Collision Data Cleaning. Clear all kinds of collision information, including clearing collision data, clearing contact group, and destroying the current collision space. Then, reset all the properties of the contact surface to comply with the needs of the user.

According to user needs, create four-fork tree space, hash space, and simple space. These three new types of collision space use different collision detection algorithms and different data structures. Different geometries are stored using different data structures.

Collision Data Detection. Collision data is a custom variable that stores all the data needed for a collision geometry. The character object is the source of the data. Prior to the crash simulation, you need to set up a collision data for each collision object and add the data to a list of collisions. Finally, the collision information is transferred to the collision function when the collision simulation is performed.

4.2.3. Collision Simulation Start. The simulation process takes the time step as a unit. With the ODE simulator, simulation to complete a time step for the unit collision effect

needs to use the current state before the impact and role of the data and then the collision effect exerted on the role of the body [13, 14]. This link needs to call the existing space collision function in ODE. Finally, according to the data of the contact nodes generated by the two contact rigid bodies in the collision, the ODE completes the collision [15]. The space collision function is a very important function in this link. Its function prototype is

> Void dSpaceCollide (dSpaceID space, void *data, dNearCallback *callback).

This function determines which geometries are likely to occur in space and then calls the callback function to handle the pair of geometries and finally completes the collision.

Callback's function type is dNearCallback, defined as follows:

> Typedef void dNearCallback (void *data, dGeomID $o1$, dGeomID $o2$)

Among them, data is user-defined parameters, directly from the dSpaceCollide pass. A pair of geometries that detect a possible collision are represented by parameters $o1$ and $o2$ [16]. This callback function then uses dCollide to generate the contact point between the geometries. Then, these contact points will be added to the simulation process as a contact joint.

The following operation will occur inside the callback [17]:

  (i) Use the dCollide function to generate the selected contact points between the geometries, while returning the number of contact points.

  (ii) Based on all the collision data in the previous link, for each contact point, two eligible collision data points are searched.

  (iii) ODE completes the collision effect according to the contact joint information contained in these two collisions and shows the picture again.

4.2.4. Collision Simulation End. With the end of the ODE simulation, the collision simulation also acts as a driving force to stop the character of force. This link will do some related data cleanup work, which is conducive to the next simulation.

5. Implementation and Testing of Character Animation Simulation

5.1. Creating an Example in the Character Animation. Open the physics engine software and edit and run the C language program to get the scenario shown in Figure 2.

In Figure 2, you can see the basic elements of the scene, including the sky, the ground, the car, and the obstacles.

The simulation example consists of simple elements: the power of vehicle comes from the motor; the power output and the steering are set in the front wheel; the wheel and the vehicle body joint through the hinge; the vehicle may have interaction forces when touching any object of the scenario; there is a collision detection device in the vehicle.

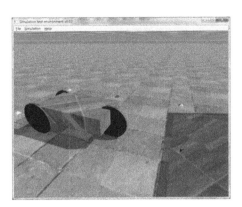

FIGURE 2: Scenario picture.

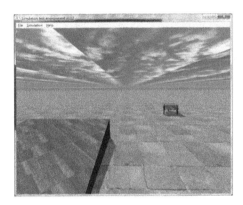

FIGURE 3: Forward, backward, acceleration, and deceleration of the vehicle model.

5.2. Testing. By setting the power of the vehicle, the interaction force between the vehicle and the objects in the scenario, as well as the ground slip rate, the simulation of the vehicle motion, and collision process can be implemented.

The performance testing is shown in Figures 3, 4, and 5.

In the course of the testing, change the vehicle or the various parameters of the surrounding environment and observe whether the character change in the pictures conforms to the kinetic principle.

5.2.1. Friction Testing. When the vehicle has contact with the ground, change the Coulomb friction coefficient mu from the original dInfinity (there will not be sliding contact) to 0 (no friction contact). This coefficient must be set. And the testing result is that the wheel is idling. At this time, the front wheel as the power output can only be idling, since there is no friction, so the vehicle cannot move [18].

5.2.2. Penetration Testing. When the vehicle is in contact with the ground, soft_cfm is the contact normal flexibility parameter, which is used to adjust the flexibility of the object. Enlarging the soft_cfm value, from the original 0.3 to 1, indicates that there will be very obvious object penetration

phenomenon; the testing result is shown in Figure 6; there appears very obvious penetration phenomenon between the wheel and the ground [18].

5.2.3. Slide Coefficient Testing. Set the FDS (Force Dependent Slip factor) to zero. After the vehicle model rolls over, continue to give power to the vehicle, and the vehicle has no side slide but has been static. (FDS indicates the lateral slide phenomenon due to the lateral external force when the object is moving, and the sliding distance is proportional to the moving speed of the object and the external force, so FDS is also called lateral force slide coefficient [18, 19].)

If the FDS slide coefficient of friction is set to 0.1, continue to give power to the vehicle after its rollover, and the vehicle can still move laterally. The testing result is shown in Figure 7.

When the world is created, the z-axis direction of gravity acceleration that is set to 0 can be obtained as in Figure 8.

From the test results, due to the acceleration of gravity of 0, there is simulation of the suspension in the vehicle.

Through the simulation of the car and the surrounding environment of various parameters set, you can carry out a variety of physics engine-based animation*a* simulation.

6. Summary

Regarding the research on the simulation of character animation, there have been many achievements at home and abroad. On the basis of studying and researching the existing scientific research achievements, this article has done the following works: in-depth research on the mainstream computer character animation production technologies; in-depth analysis and research on the mainstream physics engines; in-depth research on the related collision detection algorithms; designing and building the simulation architecture, to make the character animation simulation feasible by using ODE engine; building the simulation experiment platform and successfully operating examples

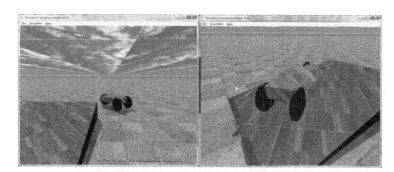

FIGURE 4: Turning and climbing of the vehicle model.

FIGURE 5: The vehicle model has high-speed collision with obstacle and rollover, due to high-speed turning and rushing out of the ramp.

FIGURE 6: Comparison between preadjusted and adjusted penetration effects.

FIGURE 7: Horizontal movement.

to implement the ODE-based character animation simulation; and carrying out the test and analysis with different parameters.

The focus for next research includes the following: from the vehicle motion model upgrading to the more complex human body motion model, simulating the more complex and precise movements of human body; establishing different controllers for different character models and motion states and implementing more efficient and more realistic simulation through more intelligent controllers; enabling the natural switch-off states of character through animation blending technology.

FIGURE 8: Vehicle suspension.

References

[1] B. Dai, *Research and Implementation of Role Based Animation Simulation*, University of Electronic Science and Technology of China, 2012.

[2] C. K. Liu, A. Hertzmann, and Z. Popović, "Composition of complex optimal multi-character motions," in *Proceedings of the ACM SIGGRAPH/Eurographics Symposium on Computer Animation (SCA '06)*, pp. 215–222, ACM, Vienna, Austria, September 2006.

[3] H. Duan, *Research and Application of Key Technologies of Physics Engine in Virtual Reality*, Shandong University of Science and Technology, 2010.

[4] http://baike.baidu.com/view/85895.htm.

[5] S. Gao, *Design and Implementation of Driving Simulation System Based on OGRE and ODE*, Wuhan University of Technology, 2006.

[6] V. B. Zordan and J. K. Hodgins, "Motion capture-driven simulations that hit and react," in *Proceedings of the ACM SIGGRAPH/Eurographics Symposium on Computer Animation (SCA '02)*, pp. 89–96, ACM, July 2002.

[7] Z. Wang, H. Jiazhen, and H. Yang, "Summary of research on the collision detection problem," *Journal of Software*, no. 5, 1999.

[8] T. Larsson and T. A. Moiler, "Collision detection for continuously deforming bodies," in *Proceedings of the Eurographi cs'*, 2001.

[9] Z. Popović, "Controlling physics in realistic character animation," *Communications of the ACM*, vol. 43, no. 7, pp. 51–58, 2000.

[10] M. Zhang, *Research on Dynamic Fault Diagnosis Method for Vehicle Mounted Track*, North Central University, 2014.

[11] T. Zhang, *Research on Automobile Virtual Driving Training System Based on Quest 3D*, Henan Polytechnic University, 2012.

[12] X. Yang, *Improvement and Optimization of Collision Detection Module for Space Desktop System*, Capital Normal University, 2011.

[13] T. Wang, "Adaptive stochastic collision detection between deformable objects using particle swarm optimization," in *Proceedings of the EvoWorkshops (EvoIASP '06)*, 2006.

[14] F. A. Madera, A. M. Day, and S. D. Laycock, "A hybrid bounding volume algorithm to detect collisions between deformable objects," in *Proceedings of the 2nd International Conferences on Advances in Computer-Human Interactions (ACHI '09)*, pp. 136–141, IEEE, Cancún, Mexico, February 2009.

[15] Y. Zou, G. Ding, M. Xu, and Y. He, "Overview of real time collision detection algorithm," *Computer Application Research*, no. 1, 2008.

[16] J. T. Klosowski, M. Held, J. S. B. Mitchell, H. Sowizral, and K. Zikan, "Efficient collision detection using bounding volume hierarchies of k-DOPs," *IEEE Transactions on Visualization and Computer Graphics*, vol. 4, no. 1, pp. 21–36, 1998.

[17] R. Smith, "Open Dynamics Engine v0.5 User Guide," 2006, http://www.ode.org/ode-latest-userguide.html.

[18] T. Geijtenbeek and N. Pronost, "Interactive Character Animation using Simulated Physics," Games and Virtual Worlds, 2011.

[19] M. Wang, *Research and Practice of Virtual Reality Art in Engineering*, Harbin Engineering University, 2010.

[20] P. Jiménez, F. Thomas, and C. Torras, "3D collision detection: A survey," *Computers & Graphics*, vol. 25, no. 2, pp. 269–285, 2001.

3

Real-Time QoE Monitoring System for Video Streaming Services with Adaptive Media Playout

Mingfu Li ⓘ,[1,2] Chien-Lin Yeh,[1] and Shao-Yu Lu[1]

[1]*Department of Electrical Engineering, School of Electrical and Computer Engineering, College of Engineering, Chang Gung University, Guishan District, Taoyuan City 33302, Taiwan*
[2]*Neuroscience Research Center, Chang Gung Memorial Hospital, Linkou, Guishan District, Taoyuan City 33305, Taiwan*

Correspondence should be addressed to Mingfu Li; mfli@mail.cgu.edu.tw

Academic Editor: Miroslav Voznak

Quality of Experience (QoE) of video streaming services has been attracting more and more attention recently. Therefore, in this work we designed and implemented a real-time QoE monitoring system for streaming services with Adaptive Media Playout (AMP), which was implemented into the VideoLAN Client (VLC) media player to dynamically adjust the playout rate of videos according to the buffer fullness of the client buffer. The QoE monitoring system reports the QoE of streaming services in real time so that network/content providers can monitor the qualities of their services and resolve troubles immediately whenever their subscribers encounter them. Several experiments including wired and wireless streaming were conducted to show the effectiveness of the implemented AMP and QoE monitoring system. Experimental results demonstrate that AMP significantly improves the QoE of streaming services according to the Mean Opinion Score (MOS) estimated by our developed program. Additionally, some challenging issues in wireless streaming have been easily identified using the developed QoE monitoring system.

1. Introduction

Internet Protocol Television (IPTV) services [1] have been becoming increasingly popular among telecommunication companies. Network/service providers are concerned with not only the cost of constructing an IPTV service system [2] but also its service quality [3, 4]. In the past, Quality of Service (QoS) of network services is the main concern. However, QoS cannot accurately characterize the users' perception. Therefore, the concept of Quality of Experience (QoE) was proposed and studied recently [5–13].

The most accurate method to obtain QoE is doing subjective tests [14] that are time-consuming and costly. Therefore, we proposed a cost-effective and real-time QoE evaluation method in [5], where a hybrid QoE assessment scheme was employed. In the hybrid QoE assessment, subjective tests only need be performed occasionally for updating the parameters of QoS-QoE mapping functions. Hence, the cost of a hybrid QoE assessment scheme reduces significantly. In [7], the QoE measurement for P2P-based IPTV services was studied. Another paper [8] proposed a QoS/QoE

mapping and adjustment model for the cloud-based multimedia infrastructure. Additionally, since streaming services over wireless networks have been becoming popular, the QoE enhancement algorithms, protocols, and evaluation methods for wireless streaming services were proposed [9–12]. In [13], Chen et al. presented a comprehensive survey of the evolution of video quality assessment methods and analyzed their characteristics, advantages, and drawbacks.

Since the QoE evaluation for streaming services becomes more and more important, several QoE evaluation or monitoring tools were developed [15–19]. A QoE monitoring tool for multimedia quality assessment in NS-3 network simulator was presented in [15]. However, since the objective and full-reference QoE assessment method is used in [15], it is costly and cannot accurately indicate the users' perception in a real commercial video streaming system. The paper [16] developed a testbed, which allows obtaining conclusive results regarding QoE in video-mediated group communication, for controlled experiments. In [17], Jeong and Ahn designed the QoE monitoring function for video services by extending ITU-T IPTV QoS/QoE metrics and integrating to OMA-DM protocol agent. Although the monitoring service can improve the user experience, the presented QoE factors are still not good enough. In [18], the proposed concept, Monitoring of Audio Visual Quality by Key Performance Indicators (MOAVI), is able to isolate and focus investigation, set up algorithms, increase the monitoring period, and guarantee better prediction of perceptual quality. In [19], Ickin et al. added functionality to the VideoLAN Client (VLC) media player [20] to record a set of metrics from the user interface, application-level, network-level, and the available sensors of the device. Based on these metrics, the proposed VLQoE, a QoE instrumentation for video streaming, can infer the QoE of streaming services on a smartphone.

To improve the playout quality of video streaming services, Adaptive Media Playout (AMP) schemes [21, 22] have been used. In this work, an AMP playout system is implemented into the VLC media player, which is a free and open source cross-platform multimedia player. Since the playout rate of the AMP system can be dynamically adjusted during video playback, the effects of AMP on QoE must be considered as well. However, almost all the developed QoE monitoring tools in the literature [15–19] did not take the effects of AMP on QoE into account. Thus, in [23] we proposed the QoE monitoring system that takes the effects of AMP on QoE into consideration. Additionally, the most important feature of our proposed QoE monitoring system is that it can derive an overall QoE for several QoS metrics using the product form presented in [5]. Our previous work [5] has shown that the product form performs much better than the conventional averaging techniques in deriving an overall QoE of multiple QoS metrics. Using the developed QoE monitoring program, network providers can identify network troubles and fix them in real time to improve the system performance and qualities.

The novelties and contributions of this paper are summarized as follows. First, the implemented QoE monitoring system takes the effects of AMP on QoE into consideration. Second, the developed QoE monitoring system derives an overall QoE from several QoS metrics such as the initial playout delay, packet loss rate, underflow time ratio, and normalized playout rate. Thirdly, we implement the AMP scheme, which was proposed in [22], into the VLC media player. Finally, the Group of Pictures- (GOP-) based cumulative average jitter J_n, which is used to determine the playback threshold P_n of the proposed AMP, is proposed to eliminate the effect of diverse frame sizes on the estimation of network jitter.

The rest of this paper is organized as follows. Section 2 describes the implementation of the AMP playout system. Implementation of the QoE monitoring system is then introduced in Section 3. Section 4 conducts several experiments and evaluates the QoE performance of video streaming services using the developed programs. Finally, the concluding remarks are given in Section 5.

2. Implementation of AMP

This section first describes the principles of AMP in Section 2.1. Then the implementation schemes, available

programming tools, and some challenging issues on measurements or estimations of key parameters are addressed in Section 2.2.

2.1. Principles of Proposed AMP. In this work, we employ the freeware VLC media player to realize the AMP. The AMP is implemented according to our proposed scheme [22] whose principle is described briefly as follows. In addition to the conventional slowdown threshold L, a dynamic playback threshold P_n and a speedup threshold H are designed. If the buffer fullness is below L, the playout rate is reduced to avoid buffer underflow. When the buffer fullness exceeds the speedup threshold H, the playout rate is increased to reduce the buffer fullness for avoiding buffer overflow. The Dynamic Playback Threshold Algorithm (DPTA) in [22] is designed to dynamically adjust the playback threshold P_n, which affects the initial playout delay, under various network conditions. Whenever the current buffer fullness n surpasses or equals P_n, the playback starts immediately with the proper playout rate $\mu(i, n)$ which is determined by the following equation:

$$\mu(i, n) = \begin{cases} R_L(n) & \text{if } n < L, \\ R_S(i) & \text{if } L \le n \le H, \\ R_H(n) & \text{if } n > H, \end{cases} \tag{1}$$

where $R_S(i)$ is a random process and is estimated by the Arrival Process Tracking Algorithm (APTA) presented in [22]. That is, $R_S(i)$ depends on the frame arrival process at the client buffer and is limited between $(1 - r)\mu_0$ and $(1 + r)\mu_0$, as shown in Figure 1. Anyone interested in the detailed derivation of $R_S(i)$ and P_n can refer to [22]. The quadratic playout rate functions $R_H(n)$ and $R_L(n)$ in [22] are defined as follows:

$$R_H(n) = (1 + r_2)\mu_0 - \left(\frac{N - \min\{n, N\}}{N - H}\right)^2 (r_2 - r)\mu_0,$$

$$R_L(n) = (1 - r_1)\mu_0 + \left(\frac{n}{L}\right)^2 (r_1 - r)\mu_0, \tag{2}$$

where N is the uppermost threshold correlated to the buffer size at the client. Notably, the playout rate must be limited such that rate variations are unnoticeable or acceptable by users. The perception of a slowdown video is usually different from that of a speedup video for users. Therefore, two different restricted deviation ratios, denoted by r_1 and r_2 for $R_L(n)$ and $R_H(n)$, respectively, are set for playout rates. The corresponding playout rate function of the proposed AMP is given by Figure 1. Numerical results in [22] have shown that the proposed AMP with quadratic playout rates performs much better than several conventional playout systems with linear playout rates and can adapt to different network load conditions for reducing the initial playout delay.

2.2. Realization of AMP. VLC media player provides a useful VLC ActiveX package whose architecture is given in Figure 2. The main component of VLC ActiveX package is LibVLC which supports several properties such as *input,*

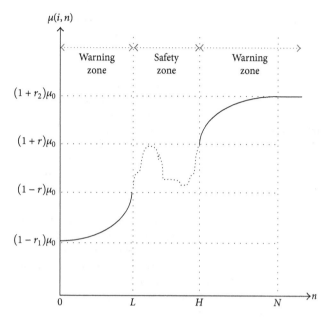

FIGURE 1: Playout rate function of the proposed AMP [22].

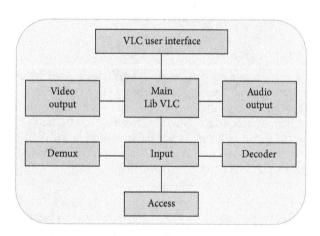

FIGURE 2: Architecture of VLC ActiveX package.

TABLE 1: Receiving parameters in VLC *input.item():stats()*.

Parameters	Meaning
demux_read_packets	Number of packets received
demux_read_bytes	Number of bytes received
demux_bitrate	Bit rate of the video stream
average_demux_bitrate	Average bit rate of the video stream
demux_corrupted	Number of corrupted frames
decoded_audio	Number of audio frames decoded
decoded_video	Number of video frames decoded
lost_pictures	Number of frames lost

a new MPEG-2 TS video frame is arriving. Hence, the buffer fullness n can be computed by the following equation:

$$n = demux\_frames - decoded\_video. \qquad (3)$$

After deriving the buffer fullness n, the playout rate of the AMP media player can be dynamically adjusted according to (1). The command to dynamically set the playout rate of the VLC media player is defined by the function *var.set(input,* *"rate", $\mu(i,n)$)*. Although the currently developed program is designed for the MPEG-2 TS format, there is no difficulty to include other advanced video encoding technologies such as the H.264/AVC and H.265/HEVC [24] in the future.

The dynamic playback threshold P_n [22] is determined by

$$P_n = L_0 + (L - L_0) \cdot \min\left\{1, \frac{J_n}{cT}\right\}, \qquad (4)$$

where L_0 and c are design parameters and $T = 1/\mu_0$ is the average frame interarrival time. J_n is the cumulative average jitter and is defined by

$$J_n = \left(1 - \frac{1}{n-1}\right)J_{n-1} + \frac{|X_{n-1} - T|}{n-1}, \quad \text{for } n > 1, \qquad (5)$$

where X_{n-1} is the frame interarrival time between the $(n-1)$-st and the nth frames. However, video frames are categorized into I, B, and P frames and different types of frames usually have very different frame sizes. For example, the frame size of an I frame is usually much larger than that of a B or P frame. Hence, the frame interarrival time between two successive I and B (or P) frames may become relatively large because of the long transmission time of an I frame, compared with that between two successive B and P frames. Such variance of frame interarrival times maybe is not due to the network jitter but the diversity of frame sizes. To reduce the impact of frame size variation on the estimation of network jitter J_n and estimate J_n more accurately, in this work the average frame interarrival time within a GOP is used. Hence, the variable X_{n-1} in (5) is replaced by Y_{k-1}/G, where $k = \lfloor n/G \rfloor$, G is the number of frames in a GOP, and Y_{k-1} is the interarrival time between the I frames of the $(k-1)$-st and the kth GOPs.

3. Implementation of QoE Monitoring System

The procedures to implement the QoE monitoring system are described as follows. First, we propose an architecture

audio output, and *video output*. The *input* property collects all related parameters of the received video stream from the Network Interface Card (NIC) *(Access)*, the network demultiplexer *(Demux)*, and the video decoder *(Decoder)*, as shown in Figure 2. Several useful statistical parameters in *input.item():stats()* are listed in Table 1. Based on these collected parameters from the *input* property, one can set and control the playout rate of the VLC media player to realize the AMP function.

According to the descriptions in Section 2.1, the playout rate mainly depends on the buffer fullness n (in frames). To accurately measure the number *demux_frames* of demultiplexed video frames, one can directly analyze the packets arriving at the NIC card. By reading the "payload unit start indicator" bit in the header of each 188-byte MPEG-2 TS (Transport Stream) packet, as shown in Figure 3, one can easily calculate the number *demux_frames* of video frames received. When the "payload unit start indicator" bit equals 1,

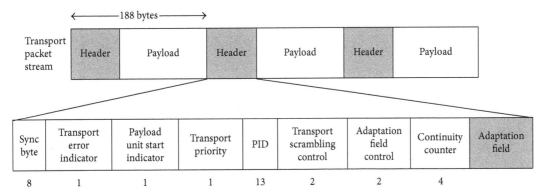

FIGURE 3: MPEG-2 TS packet format.

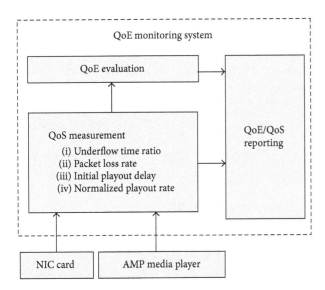

FIGURE 4: Architecture of the QoE monitoring system.

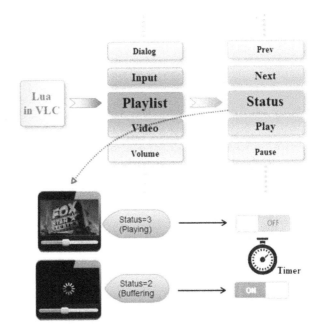

FIGURE 5: Buffering mechanism in VLC player.

for the QoE monitoring system. Next, several network-based QoS metrics are defined and their measurement methods are presented. Finally, the overall QoE evaluation method for the QoE monitoring system is introduced.

3.1. Architecture of QoE Monitoring System. The architecture of our proposed QoE monitoring system is plotted in Figure 4. It includes the QoS measurement engine, QoE evaluation function, and performance reporting window. The QoS measurement engine is designed to collect the QoS metrics from the media player and the NIC card. These obtained QoS metrics are used by the QoE evaluation function for producing the overall QoE of video streaming services. All instantaneous QoS metrics and QoE results are reported in real time and the curve of overall QoE versus time is also displayed with a chart in the Graphic User Interface (GUI) for the monitoring purpose.

3.2. Measurements of QoS Parameters. In the proposed QoE monitoring system, the considered QoS metrics include underflow time ratio QoS_u, packet loss rate QoS_l, initial

playout delay QoS_d, and normalized playout rate QoS_r. The measurements of these parameters are described as follows.

(a) Underflow time ratio QoS_u: whenever an underflow event occurs, the underflow time starts to accumulate until the playback restarts again. At the same time, the number of underflow events is increased by 1. The underflow time ratio equals the ratio of accumulated underflow time to the total playback time duration. The accumulated underflow time can be computed according to the value of *Status()* provided by VLC Lua extension program, as shown in Figure 5. When the value of *Status()* changes into 2, the underflow timer turns ON until the value of *Status()* becomes 3. The sojourn time at the state with *Status()* = 2 is the underflow time. Whenever the underflow timer turns OFF, the accumulated underflow time is updated.

(b) Packet loss rate QoS_l: the packet loss rate is obtained by analyzing the number of receiving packets at the

NIC card or using the network protocol analyzer such as Wireshark.

(c) Initial playout delay QoS_d: initial playout delay strongly depends on the buffering time set in VLC media player. However, in our implemented AMP this parameter is directly determined by the DPTA algorithm proposed in [22].

(d) Normalized playout rate QoS_r: whenever the playout rate is adjusted, the normalized playout rate is computed and saved. However, within each minute only the maximum and minimum normalized playout rates are used in our design [5]. That is, the corresponding QoE of QoS_r during every minute equals the mean of these two individual QoEs resulting from the maximum and minimum normalized playout rates.

3.3. Overall QoE Evaluation Function. The overall QoE evaluation function adopts the integrated multivariate QoE function $f_I(QoS_u, QoS_l, QoS_d, QoS_r)$ and the individual QoS-QoE mapping functions $f_u(x)$, $f_l(x)$, $f_d(x)$, and $f_r(x)$ proposed in [5] to derive the overall QoE. Based on the results of [5], they are given as follows:

$$f_I(QoS_u, QoS_l, QoS_d, QoS_r)$$

$$= 5 \cdot \frac{f_u(QoS_u)}{5} \cdot \frac{f_l(QoS_l)}{5} \cdot \frac{f_d(QoS_d)}{5} \qquad (6)$$

$$\cdot \frac{f_r(QoS_r)}{5},$$

$$f_u(x) = 5e^{-5.71x}, \qquad (7)$$

$$f_l(x) = 5e^{-1.607x}, \qquad (8)$$

$$f_d(x) = 5e^{-0.0416x}, \qquad (9)$$

$$f_r(x) = 5x^{8.94}e^{-8.94(x-1)}. \qquad (10)$$

The scheme used in [5] consists of three steps to be done beforehand. First, several Key Performance Indicators (KPIs) or QoS metrics, such as the initial playout delay, packet loss rate, underflow time ratio, and playout rate, were selected. Then several distorted videos were generated based on these selected QoS metrics. Second, subjective tests were conducted using human observers to rate the distorted videos in terms of Mean Opinion Score (MOS) [25]. The ACR subjective test method was adopted in [5]. However, the length of each distorted video clip is about 64 s rather than 10 s. Each distorted video clip was viewed and rated by no less than 30 viewers. The title of the used video clip, which is with the frame rate 30 fps, resolution 1920 × 1080 p, and video codec MPEG-2, is "Avatar." Thirdly, using the regression approach, the QoS-QoE mapping functions for individual QoS metrics were obtained. Finally, the product form of individual QoS-QoE mapping functions [5, 6] is used to derive the overall QoE of a video streaming service. Notably, although only four QoS metrics are considered in

Figure 6: VLC media player and Lua program.

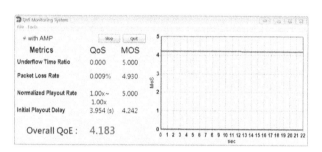

Figure 7: QoE/MOS monitoring program.

(6), the number of QoS metrics can be arbitrarily extended as needed.

4. Experimental Results

In this section, we first briefly introduce the GUIs and functions of developed AMP and QoE monitoring programs. Subsequently, using the developed QoE monitoring program, several experiments are conducted to demonstrate the performance of AMP. Finally, we use the QoE monitoring program to identify some challenging issues of wireless streaming.

4.1. QoE Monitoring System. The developed AMP is based on the VLC media player and its add-ons such as the Lua extension. Figure 6 shows the VLC media player and its Lua extension program. One can directly set the multicast IP of the streaming source and activate the AMP function on the VLC Lua extension program. Although in this paper the AMP is implemented into the VLC media player, there is no difficulty to implement it into other popular media players such as the MS Windows Media Player or YouTube Player. The QoE monitoring program, which is developed using the C++ Builder and is shown in Figure 7, evaluates and displays the overall QoE. The measured QoS and synthetic QoE/MOS are displayed in real time on the monitoring window, as shown in Figure 7. The corresponding QoEs of individual QoSs are displayed on the left side of the monitoring window while the curve of the overall QoE versus time is displayed on the right side of the monitoring window, as shown in Figure 7. By clicking the "Tools" on the menu bar of the QoE monitoring program, other detailed QoS metrics

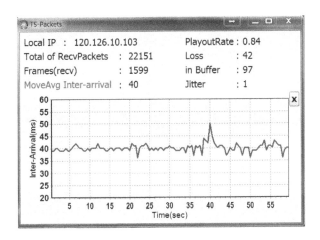

FIGURE 8: Monitoring tools for video packets at the client.

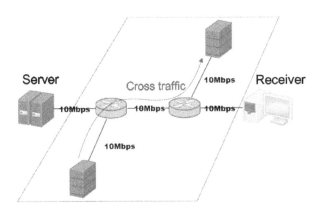

FIGURE 9: Experimental network scenario 1.

TABLE 2: Information of test video 1.

Parameter	Value
Video title	The Big Bang Theory
Length	593 sec
Resolution	352 × 288 pixels
Encoding scheme	MPEG-2 TS
Bit rate	1406 kbps
Frame rate	25 fps
GOP size	15
Content size	99.5 MB

such as the interarrival time of video frames, normalized playout rate, number of packet losses, buffer fullness, and the jitter observed at the client can be displayed, as shown in Figure 8. By clicking the interested QoS parameter, such as the "MoveAvg Interarrival," the curve of the QoS versus time is immediately displayed on the monitoring window of Figure 8.

4.2. Performance Evaluation of AMP. In order to demonstrate our AMP design and QoE monitoring system, the first experimental network scenario is constructed, as shown in

Figure 9. The server pumps the video stream into the first router, followed by a bottleneck link and the second router. Finally, the disturbed video stream arrives at the receiver. All link capacities in Figure 9 are set to be 10 Mbps. The Pareto ON-OFF cross-traffic is injected into the bottleneck link using the Distributed Internet Traffic Generator (D-ITG) tool [26]. Therefore, the video stream is disturbed by the cross-traffic in the bottleneck link and thus packet losses and jitters may occur. The video is encoded into the MPEG-2 TS at the streaming server and the RTP/UDP streaming protocol is employed. Table 2 lists the detailed information of the first test video and Table 3 lists the parameters of AMP. The other parameters not mentioned here are set the same as those in [22].

First, the QoEs of two media playout systems with and without AMP are compared. The video server pumps a multicast stream into the network and two independent clients simultaneously receive the same multicast stream at the remote side. One client uses the media player with AMP, while the other one adopts the media player without AMP. The observed QoEs of these two systems with and without AMP under different cross-traffic rates 0, 4, and 8 Mbps are given in Figure 10. When the cross-traffic rate is not larger than 4 Mbps, the overall QoE is almost over 4, no matter whether the AMP is enabled or not. This is because the jitter, burstiness, and losses of video packets are very small under a low cross-traffic rate. Additionally, under a low cross-traffic rate the observed QoE on the media player without AMP remains very stable while the QoE on the media player with AMP slightly oscillates in the first minute. The reason is explained as follows. The media player without AMP can start playback only when the buffer fullness exceeds $L = 100$, yielding the initial playout delay about 4 s, and always plays the video with the normal playout rate. However, the media player with AMP can start playback earlier but with a lower initial playout rate. Since the initial playout rate of the media player with AMP is smaller than the normal playout rate, the observed QoE on the media player with AMP is slightly degraded in the first minute, as shown in Figure 10. Table 4 shows the measured initial playout delays QoS_d of the media players with and without AMP. Because the initial playout delay in the media player with AMP is much smaller than that without AMP, the corresponding QoE of QoS_d of the media player with AMP becomes better. When the cross-traffic rate becomes 8 Mbps, the video stream is seriously disturbed by the cross-traffic so that the observed QoE at the client becomes unacceptable (MOS < 3). The serious QoE degradation is mainly due to the increase of the number of underflow events and underflow time. However, the observed QoE on the media player with AMP is still much better than that without AMP, as shown in Figure 10.

The corresponding buffer fullness and the playout rate at the client under the cross-traffic rate 6 Mbps are shown in Figure 11. According to Figure 11, the buffer fullness of the system with AMP is more stable than that of the system without AMP. For the media player with AMP, the underflow events never happen because the buffer fullness never drops to an unacceptable low level after the playback. Although the playout rate of the media player with AMP varies, the

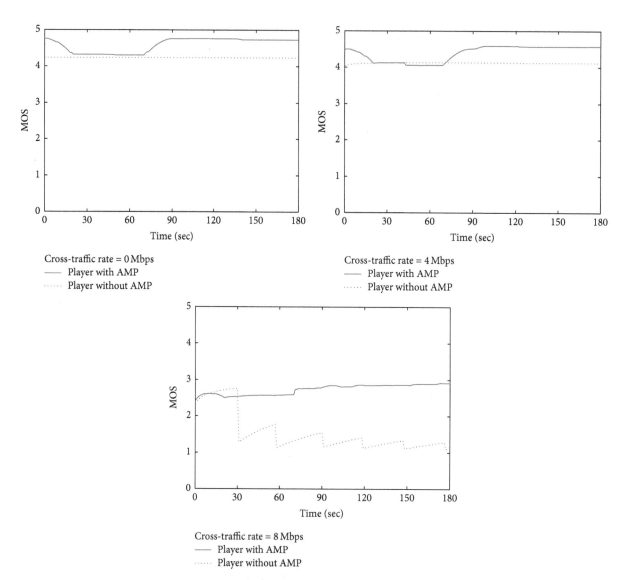

FIGURE 10: Comparison of synthetic MOSs/QoEs between the systems with and without AMP under various cross-traffic rates.

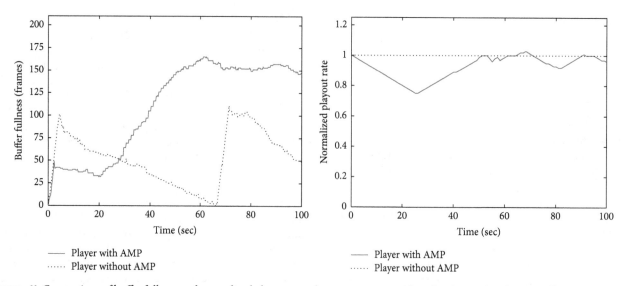

FIGURE 11: Comparison of buffer fullness and normalized playout rates between systems with and without AMP (cross-traffic rate = 6 Mbps).

TABLE 3: Parameters setting in AMP.

Parameter	L_0	L	H	N	c	r	r_1	r_2
Value	30	100	200	500	0.4	0.15	0.3	0.3

TABLE 4: Initial playout delay QoS_d and corresponding QoE.

Cross-traffic rate (Mbps)	Player with AMP QoS_d/QoE	Player without AMP QoS_d/QoE
0	1.124 sec/4.776	4.001 sec/4.233
4	1.656 sec/4.667	4.250 sec/4.189
8	3.876 sec/4.255	4.756 sec/4.102

TABLE 5: Information of test video 2.

Parameter	Value
Video title	Call Me Maybe (MV)
Length	199 sec
Resolution	720×480 pixels
Encoding scheme	MPEG-2 TS
Bit rate	1936 kbps
Frame rate	30 fps
GOP size	15
Content size	46 MB

deviation of the playout rate is never over 25% so that the QoE degradation resulting from it is still acceptable. However, for the media player without AMP, the buffer fullness during the time interval (10 s, 66 s) decreases almost linearly to zero and leads to an underflow event, yielding a significant QoE degradation. All results in Figures 10 and 11 demonstrate that the AMP significantly improves the QoE of streaming services.

4.3. Performance Monitoring for Wireless Streaming. Video streaming over wireless networks has become very popular recently. However, it is still challenging to offer streaming services over wireless networks. To clearly identify the challenging issues of wireless streaming services, in this subsection the AMP function is not enabled in the media players of all receivers. To evaluate the QoE of wireless streaming services, the second network scenario shown in Figure 12 is considered and the first test video given in Table 2 is used. The video stream is multicast to two independent receivers at the last hop: via the IEEE 802.11n wireless link to Receiver 1 and via the wired link to Receiver 2. Receiver 1 is away from the WiFi AP by 2 m and no obstacle between them. Figure 13 shows the observed synthetic MOSs at Receivers 1 and 2 under different cross-traffic rates, using the QoE monitor program developed in this paper. By Figure 13, the QoE at Receiver 2 using a wired link is better than that at Receiver 1 using a wireless link. Even though no cross-traffic exists, the MOS of the video streaming service at Receiver 1 via the wireless link is less than 4. According to the QoS parameters measured at Receivers 1 and 2, the difference of QoE between them is mainly due to a higher packet loss rate in the wireless link.

Subsequently, to compare the performance of multicast and unicast, the network scenario 3 shown in Figure 14 is considered. The second video clip with the resolution 720 × 480 p and bit rate 1936 kbps is used, as shown in Table 5. Different numbers of similar unicast streams are pumped from the video server to the receivers using a wireless link at the last hop. The synthetic MOS of the streaming service at the receivers decreases significantly as the number of unicast streams increases, as shown in Figure 15. This is because the jitter, burstiness, and packet loss rate increase as the number of unicast streams in the network grows, yielding the QoE degradation at the receivers. Note that if the multicast scheme

is used, only one video stream is required to be pumped into the network no matter how many receivers exist. That is, the QoE of video streaming services is irrelevant to the number of receivers if the multicast scheme is employed. Obviously, under the scenario that multiple users watch the same video stream, the multicast scheme performs much better than the unicast one in terms of QoE.

Finally, to investigate the impact of transmission distance and obstacles on the QoE of wireless streaming services, the wireless network scenario 4 plotted in Figure 16 is considered and the second test video given in Table 5 is used. The video stream is multicast to several wireless receivers at different positions in our labs. No cross-traffic is injected into the network. No obstacles exist between the wireless AP and the receivers at Locations 1 and 2. However, the receiver at Location 1 is much closer to the AP than the receiver at Location 2 is. There are cupboards and a wall between the AP and the receiver at Location 3. The receiver at Location 4 is outside the door of our lab and is isolated from the AP by a wall. The other receiver at Location 5 is also isolated from the AP by a wall and cupboards. All receivers receive the same multicast stream simultaneously and their individual MOSs are estimated using the developed QoE monitoring program. The results are shown in Figure 17, where the MOSs of the receivers located at Locations 1 and 2 are the best because no obstacle blocks the wireless signals for them, while the MOSs of the receivers located at Locations 4 and 5 are the worst because there exist cupboards and a wall between them and the AP. The MOS of the receiver located at Location 3 is better than those located at Locations 4 and 5 because the receiver at Location 3 is much closer to the AP than those at Locations 4 and 5 are. Accordingly, the distance and the number of obstacles between the WiFi AP and the receivers strongly affect the QoE of wireless streaming services.

5. Conclusions

In this work, an AMP and a real-time QoE monitoring system for video streaming services are realized. The AMP design is

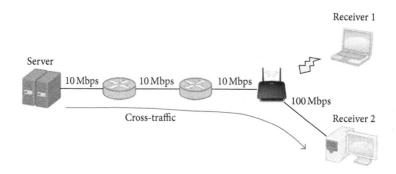

FIGURE 12: Experimental network scenario 2.

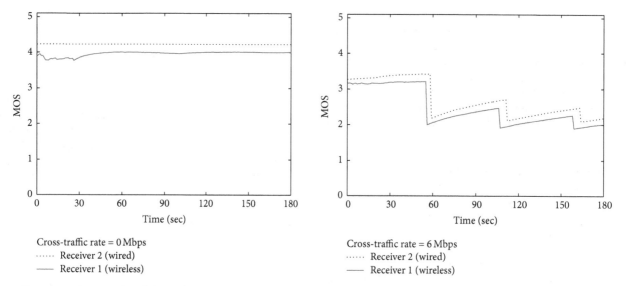

Cross-traffic rate = 0 Mbps
····· Receiver 2 (wired)
— Receiver 1 (wireless)

Cross-traffic rate = 6 Mbps
····· Receiver 2 (wired)
— Receiver 1 (wireless)

FIGURE 13: Comparison of QoEs of streaming services between wired and wireless receivers under different cross-traffic rates.

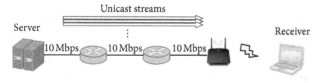

FIGURE 14: Experimental network scenario 3.

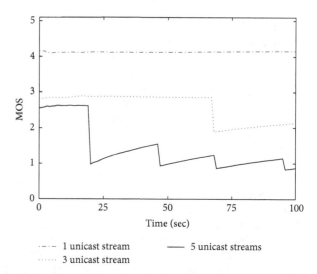

-·-· 1 unicast stream   — 5 unicast streams
····· 3 unicast stream

FIGURE 15: Impact of number of unicast streams on MOS of wireless receivers.

implemented into the freeware VLC media player. The QoE monitoring system can measure several key QoS metrics such as the packet loss rate, underflow time ratio, initial playout delay, and the playout rates of a video streaming service and derive the overall QoE in real time. Several experiments are conducted in various scenarios including wired and wireless networks. All numerical results demonstrate that the QoE monitoring system works well and the proposed AMP significantly improves the QoE of video streaming services. Using the real-time QoE monitoring system, network/content providers can find the network troubles and resolve them timely to maintain good QoEs for users. In the future, more advanced video codecs such as H.264/AVC and H.265/HEVC will be implemented into the developed system.

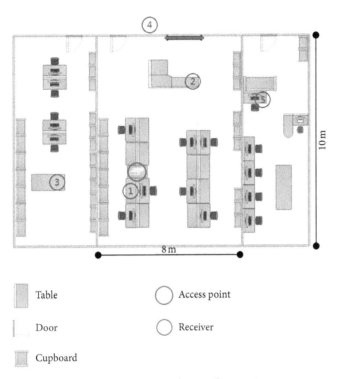

FIGURE 16: Experimental network scenario 4.

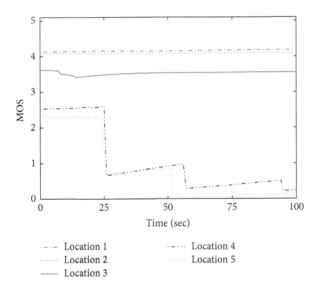

FIGURE 17: Impact of transmission distances and obstacles on QoE of wireless streaming services.

Acknowledgments

This work was supported by Ministry of Science and Technology of Taiwan under Grant NSC101-2221-E-182-004 and Grant MOST106-2221-E-182-012-MY2.

References

[1] Y. Xiao, X. Du, J. Zhang, F. Hu, and S. Guizani, "Internet protocol television (IPTV): the killer application for the next-generation internet," *IEEE Communications Magazine*, vol. 45, no. 11, pp. 126–134, 2007.

[2] M. Li and C.-H. Wu, "A cost-effective resource allocation and management scheme for content networks supporting IPTV services," *Computer Communications*, vol. 33, no. 1, pp. 83–91, 2010.

[3] S. Park and S.-H. Jeong, "Mobile IPTV: Approaches, challenges, standards, and QoS support," *IEEE Internet Computing*, vol. 13, no. 3, pp. 23–31, 2009.

[4] G. Gardikis, G. Xilouris, E. Pallis, and A. Kourtis, "Joint assessment of Network- and Perceived-QoS in video delivery networks," *Telecommunication Systems*, vol. 49, no. 1, pp. 75–84, 2012.

[5] M. Li and C.-Y. Lee, "A cost-effective and real-time QoE evaluation method for multimedia streaming services," *Telecommunication Systems*, vol. 59, no. 3, pp. 317–327, 2015.

[6] M. Li, "QoE-based performance evaluation for adaptive media playout systems," *Advances in Multimedia*, vol. 2013, Article ID 152359, 2013.

[7] M. Mu, J. Ishmael, W. Knowles et al., "P2P-based IPTV services: Design, deployment, and QoE measurement," *IEEE Transactions on Multimedia*, vol. 14, no. 6, pp. 1515–1527, 2012.

[8] W.-H. Hsu and C.-H. Lo, "QoS/QoE mapping and adjustment model in the cloud-based multimedia infrastructure," *IEEE Systems Journal*, vol. 8, no. 1, pp. 247–255, 2014.

[9] Y. Ju, Z. Lu, D. Ling, X. Wen, W. Zheng, and W. Ma, "QoE-based cross-layer design for video applications over LTE," *Multimedia Tools and Applications*, vol. 72, no. 2, pp. 1093–1113, 2014.

[10] J. Lloret, A. Canovas, J. Tomas, and M. Atenas, "A network management algorithm and protocol for improving QoE in mobile IPTV," *Computer Communications*, vol. 35, no. 15, pp. 1855–1870, 2012.

[11] M. A. Hoque, M. Siekkinen, J. K. Nurminen, M. Aalto, and S. Tarkoma, "Mobile multimedia streaming techniques: QoE and energy saving perspective," *Pervasive and Mobile Computing*, vol. 16, pp. 96–114, 2015.

[12] L. Qian, H. Chen, and L. Xie, "SVM-based QoE estimation model for video streaming service over wireless networks," in *Proceedings of the IEEE International Conference on Wireless Communications Signal Processing (WCSP)*, Nanjing, China, 2015.

[13] Y. Chen, K. Wu, and Q. Zhang, "From QoS to QoE: A tutorial on video quality assessment," *IEEE Communications Surveys & Tutorials*, vol. 17, no. 2, pp. 1126–1165, 2015.

[14] ITU-T Rec. P.910, "Subjective video quality assessment methods for multimedia applications," 2008.

[15] D. Saladino, A. Paganelli, and M. Casoni, "A tool for multimedia quality assessment in NS3: QoE Monitor," *Simulation Modelling Practice and Theory*, vol. 32, pp. 30–41, 2013.

[16] M. Schmitt, S. Gunkel, P. Cesar, and P. Hughes, "A QoE testbed for socially-aware video-mediated group communication," in *Proceedings of the 2nd International Workshop on Socially-Aware Multimedia, SAM 2013 - Co-located with ACM Multimedia 2013*, pp. 37–41, Spain, October 2013.

[17] S. Jeong and H. Ahn, "Mobile IPTV QoS/QoE monitoring system based on OMA DM protocol," in *Proceedings of the 2010 International Conference on Information and Communication Technology Convergence, ICTC 2010*, pp. 99-100, Republic of Korea, November 2010.

[18] M. Leszczuk, M. Hanusiak, M. C. Q. Farias, E. Wyckens, and G. Heston, "Recent developments in visual quality monitoring by key performance indicators," *Multimedia Tools and Applications*, vol. 75, no. 17, pp. 10745–10767, 2016.

[19] S. Ickin, M. Fiedler, K. Wac, P. Arlos, C. Temiz, and K. Mkocha, "VLQoE: Video QoE instrumentation on the smartphone," *Multimedia Tools and Applications*, vol. 74, no. 2, pp. 381–411, 2014.

[20] VideoLAN- VLC medial player official site, http://www.videolan.org/.

[21] J. Yang, H. Hu, H. Xi, and L. Hanzo, "Online buffer fullness estimation aided adaptive media playout for video streaming," *IEEE Transactions on Multimedia*, vol. 13, no. 5, pp. 1141–1153, 2011.

[22] M. Li, T.-W. Lin, and S.-H. Cheng, "Arrival process-controlled adaptive media playout with multiple thresholds for video streaming," *Multimedia Systems*, vol. 18, no. 5, pp. 391–407, 2012.

[23] M. Li, C.-L. Yeh, and S.-Y. Lu, "Realization of intelligent media player and QoE monitoring system for multimedia streaming services," *IEEE ICCP & HSIC*, pp. 1–4, 2013.

[24] P. Seeling and M. Reisslein, "Video traffic characteristics of modern encoding standards: H.264/AVC with SVC and MVC extensions and H.265/HEVC," *The Scientific World Journal*, vol. 2014, Article ID 189481, 16 pages, 2014.

[25] ITU-T Rec. P.800, "Mean opinion score (MOS) terminology," 2003.

[26] A. Botta, A. Dainotti, and A. Pescapé, "A tool for the generation of realistic network workload for emerging networking scenarios," *Computer Networks*, vol. 56, no. 15, pp. 3531–3547, 2012.

4

Visual Three-Dimensional Reconstruction of Aortic Dissection based on Medical CT Images

Xiaojie Duan,[1] **Dandan Chen,**[1] **Jianming Wang,**[1] **Meichen Shi,**[1] **Qingliang Chen,**[2] **He Zhao,**[1] **Ruixue Zuo,**[1] **Xiuyan Li,**[1] **and Qi Wang**[1]

[1]*Tianjin Key Laboratory of Optoelectronic Detection Technology and Systems, School of Electronics and Information Engineering, Tianjin Polytechnic University, Tianjin 300387, China*
[2]*Tianjin Chest Hospital, Tianjin 300000, China*

Correspondence should be addressed to Jianming Wang; wangjianming@tjpu.edu.cn

Academic Editor: Zhijun Fang

With the rapid development of CT technology, especially the higher resolution of CT machine and a sharp increase in the amount of slices, to extract and three-dimensionally display aortic dissection from the huge medical image data became a challenging task. In this paper, active shape model combined with spatial continuity was adopted to realize automatic reconstruction of aortic dissection. First, we marked aortic feature points from big data sample library and registered training samples to build a statistical model. Meanwhile, gray vectors were sampled by utilizing square matrix, which set the landmarks as the center. Posture parameters of the initial shape were automatically adjusted by the method of spatial continuity between CT sequences. The contrast experiment proved that the proposed algorithm could realize accurate aorta segmentation without selecting the interested region, and it had higher accuracy than GVF snake algorithm (93.29% versus 87.54% on aortic arch, 94.30% versus 89.25% on descending aorta). Aortic dissection membrane was extracted via Hessian matrix and Bayesian theory. Finally, the three-dimensional visualization of the aortic dissection was completed by volume rendering based on the ray casting method to assist the doctors in clinical diagnosis, which contributed to improving the success rate of the operations.

1. Introduction

Aortic dissection (AD) is a cardiovascular disease that is a dangerous threat to human health, which can quickly lead to death [1]. The main reason for this disease is that tissue weakness and high blood pressure lead to one or more aortic tissues perforation(s), blood flow along the intimae resulting in two separate blood flow channels: the true lumen (the primary aorta bed of blood flow) and the false lumen (a channel entirely within the media which appears during an aortic dissection) [2], as shown in Figure 1.

At present, the main separation therapy of aortic dissection is the lumen isolation technique requiring that the clinicians can clearly know the crevasse position, range, quantity, severity, and so on before surgery. In order to improve positive rate of aortic dissection, realize automation guidance to interventional treatment, and achieve precise surgery or postoperative evaluation, the aortic dissection 3D

reconstruction system is indispensable. The key technology is to achieve aortic segmentation. Threshold-based methods of image segmentation are challenged by intensity gradients within the image volume [3].

And edge detection methods are challenged by poor contrast in the medical images. Methods based on specific theory introduce mathematical models into image segmentation areas, and active shape model (ASM) belongs to the strategy of "top-down"; it combines the prior knowledge of top floor with information at the bottom of the image characteristics and is able to achieve accurate segmentation of complex medical images [4]. In three-dimensional space, there is continuity between CT image sequences; the thicker the slice is, the robuster the continuity is kept between CT slices. Based on the above methods, this paper adopts the method that combines active shape model with spatial continuity to extract aorta area quickly and accurately, which eliminates

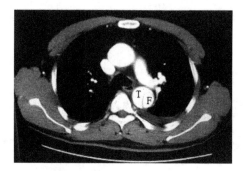

FIGURE 1: The true and the false lumen.

the interference of other organs by shape constraints in the process of extracting the aorta. Then extract aortic dissection membrane using Hessian matrix. And finally, we make use of volume rendering based on ray casting algorithm to perform three-dimensional reconstruction of the aortic dissection. Moreover, we set the transparency and colors of aortic dissection 3D model to make aortic dissection more intuitive; the location and the size of the intimae crevasse can be easily obtained.

2. Principle of System

The principle framework of the proposed three-dimensional reconstruction system is shown in Figure 2, via segmentation, extraction, and reconstruction of aortic dissection patients' CT images, to realize three-dimensional visualization of aortic dissection. Firstly, we preprocess the original CT images in order to eliminate noise and adjust the images' brightness for subsequent processing. Secondly, the active shape model is used to segment the aorta region, combined with the spatial continuity of the huge number of CT image sequences, automatically adjusting the posture parameters of the initial shape of each layer to improve the degree of automation and precision of the segmentation algorithm. Next, use gray gradient changes between aortic wall and membrane to extract the aortic dissection membrane by Hessian matrix and continuity a priori model. Finally, three-dimensionally reconstruct the aorta structure by volume rendering and set the transparency and colors of the aortic dissection three-dimensional model to make the interval more intuitive and clear. Ultimately, the system can provide help for clinical diagnosis and measures.

3. Implementation Method

3.1. Aorta Segmentation. Due to the complexity of the three-dimensional structure of the aorta, especially the aortic arch and descending aorta shape big differences, we need to set up aortic arch and descending aorta training set, respectively. In this paper, the training set of the aortic arch and descending aorta are composed of a quantity of samples extracted by equal interval from the aortic dissection patients' CT sequence which contain all the changes in the shape. The two training sets can reflect all the patterns of shape

change. We select multiple typical aortic dissection patients' CT images from the Tianjin chest hospital to build the aortic arch and descending aorta model library; different patients have different aortic CT sequence numbers, in the range of about 700~1000 on average. In order to model a shape, we represent it by a set of landmark points. This must be done for each shape in the training set and must be done correctly and accurately [5]. The number of feature points on each CT image must be consistent. The labeling is important, and each label represents a particular part of the aorta or its boundary [6, 7]. In general, we choose points marking parts of the object with particular application-dependent significance, points marking application-dependent things, and other points that can be interpolated from points of types above [8]. Aortic arch and descending aorta landmark points obtained by the expert are shown in Figure 3, and after marking feature points in each CT image we pick up the aortic arch and descending aorta training sample sets are derived, respectively.

According to landmark points, we build aorta big data model library. There is a big deviation in shape and position of different samples, so before modeling, we need to normalized registration shape vectors of two training sets, so as to realize the model building of the aorta [9]. Firstly, select one CT image, respectively, as a benchmark sample from two groups of big data training set, and then scale, rotate, and translate other samples in the library to align them with the benchmark sample; while all the differences between those samples and the reference sample are less than the setting threshold, registration is completed. Registration results of two groups of training set, respectively, are shown in Figure 4, and the horizontal ordinate represents the pixel coordinates in CT image.

Aortic model building is a high-dimensional data processing. In order to simplify calculation process, this paper applies Principal Component Analysis (PCA) approach to reduce dimensionality of the training set which involves all shape vectors to determine the main components [10]. The mean shape vector of the aortic training sample set is calculated by

$$\overline{X} = \frac{1}{N}\sum_{i=1}^{N}X_i,$$

$$X_i = \left(x_{i1}, y_{i1}, x_{i2}, y_{i2}, \ldots, x_{in}, y_{in}\right)^T, \quad (1)$$

where N is the number of the samples of the training set; X_i represents the shape vector by stacking n landmark points; then calculate the covariance matrix S by

$$S = \frac{1}{N-1}\sum_{i=1}^{N}\left(X_i - \overline{X}\right)\left(X_i - \overline{X}\right)^T. \quad (2)$$

Calculate the eigenvectors ϕ_i corresponding to the eigenvalues λ_i, arrange the eigenvalues in descending order, and choose k eigenvectors which are relative to k bigger eigenvalues, several changing patterns that describe the observed

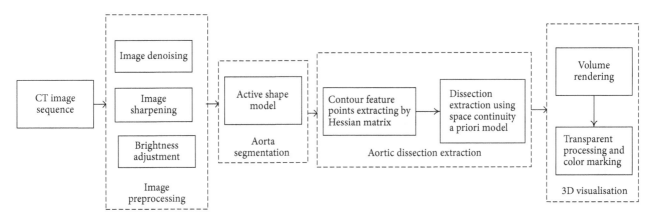

FIGURE 2: The framework of the three-dimensional reconstruction system.

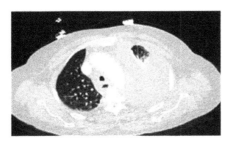

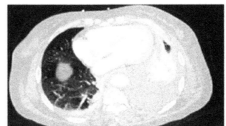

(a) Aortic arch landmark points

(b) Descending aorta landmark points

FIGURE 3: Landmark points marking.

variation of the training set; at the same time, k eigenvalues need to satisfy the formula as follows:

$$\sum_{i=1}^{k}\lambda_i \geq \rho \sum_{i=1}^{2n}\lambda_i, \tag{3}$$

where $\rho = 0.72$ [11]; the search accuracy can reach the highest by the principal components of 72%, and for the general value of 98%, too many constraints will appear when searching. Ultimately, the shape model can be approximated by

$$X = \overline{X} + \Phi B, \tag{4}$$

where Φ is the first k eigenvectors, $\Phi = (\phi_1, \phi_2, \ldots, \phi_k)$, and B is the projection coefficient on the principal component of the shape vector which is calculated as $B = (b_1, b_2, \ldots, b_k)^T$; suitable limits of b_i are typically determined in the range of $(-3\sqrt{\lambda_i}, 3\sqrt{\lambda_i})$, to make sure the active shape model changes within a small range.

The gray-scale texture model is established to match and search target contour at the time that the shape statistical model is built. In this paper, the gray-scale texture model for each landmark is carried out by putting the point as the center of the square of gray sampling, avoiding the traditional method using only the vertical direction information, leading to incomplete search and error convergence. Each landmark

gray vector g_{ji} mean and covariance of vector in the training sample can be approximated by

$$\overline{g}_j = \frac{1}{N}\sum_{i=1}^{N}g_{ji}, \quad j = 1, 2, \ldots, n,$$
$$S_j = \frac{1}{N}\sum_{i=1}^{N}\left(g_{ji} - \overline{g}_j\right)\left(g_{ji} - \overline{g}_j\right)^T, \quad j = 1, 2, \ldots, n. \tag{5}$$

We minimize the Mahalanobis distance between a new profile and the model in the subsequent matching search process as a standard; the matching function is expressed as

$$f\left(G_j\right) = \left(G_j - \overline{g}_j\right)^T S_j^{-1}\left(G_j - \overline{g}_j\right), \tag{6}$$

where G_j is the gray vector of the jth feature point of the matching image; we get the best matching point when the matching function takes the minimum, and when we find all the matching points, the new profile is obtained.

In order to improve the efficiency and robustness of the model, multiresolution search strategy is adopted [12]. 1 mm thickness at the time of CT scanning is used; therefore a complete set of aorta CT image sequences can be seen continuous, and based on CT image sequence space continuity, by adjusting the initial shape parameters to make the contour close to the target area, the target contour parameters, which are derived from the former image, are used to adjust the current layer, by repeating the above operation between

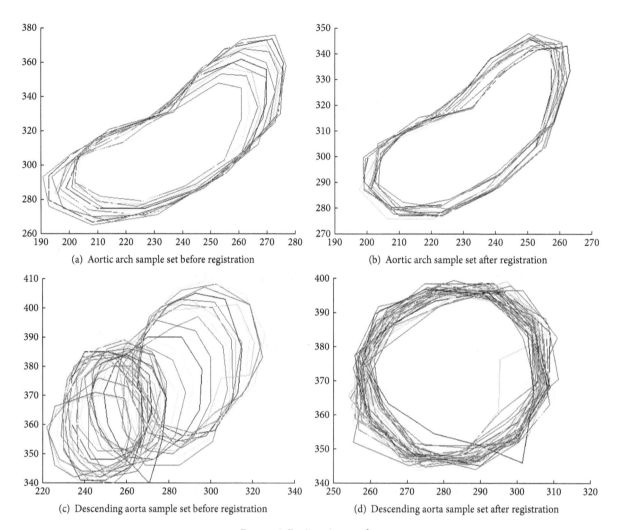

(a) Aortic arch sample set before registration

(b) Aortic arch sample set after registration

(c) Descending aorta sample set before registration

(d) Descending aorta sample set after registration

FIGURE 4: Registration results.

layers. High efficient and accurate segmentation of CT images can be realized; the algorithm is of high degree automation. Figure 5 shows the final segmentation results after iteration convergence.

3.2. Aortic Dissection Extraction and Three-Dimensional Reconstruction. In this paper, we propose a detection algorithm combining Hessian matrix and spatial continuity a priori model. The Hessian matrix can be used to extract the pixels on the dissection and aortic boundary [13], the result is shown in Figure 6(a), and then use the Bayesian theory of spatial continuity model to remove other nontarget pixels, that is, only the dissection membrane pixels extracted; the result is shown in Figure 6(b). This algorithm makes full use of the continuity between the CT images of each layer and limits the offset error of the interlayer membrane to a very small range and realizes the accurate extraction of the interlayer membrane.

After the aorta segmentation and dissection membrane extraction are complete, the ray casting is carried out to reconstruct the structure. The ray casting method is a direct

volume rendering algorithm based on the image sequence [14]. The specific reconstruction process is as follows.

(1) Read the three-dimensional discrete data field; set different opacity values and color values according to the size of the voxels' pixel values of vertices.

(2) A ray is emitted from each point of the screen based on the direction of the line of sight so that the rays pass through the data field space and k samples are selected equidistantly across all the rays.

(3) The opacity value and the color value of each sampling point are calculated by the trilinear interpolation algorithm using the data values of the eight vertices nearest to the sampling point.

(4) Calculate the opacity and color values for all pixels on the screen based on the cumulative order from front to back.

(5) The opacity value and the color value of each pixel obtained are projected onto the imaging screen to generate the final three-dimensional image.

(a) Descending aorta from segmentation

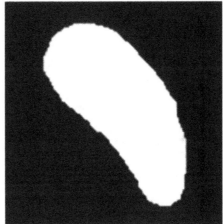

(b) Aortic arch from segmentation

FIGURE 5: Final result after iteration convergence.

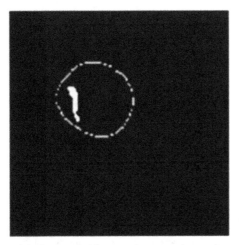

(a) Contour pixel feature points extraction result

(b) Aortic dissection results

FIGURE 6: Aortic dissection extraction result.

The final 3D reconstruction of a group of aortic region is as shown in Figure 7. By setting the aorta transparency and color, the interlayer is shown in red to give the final reconstruction results, as shown in Figure 8.

4. Experimental Results and Discussions

4.1. Experimental Results. Figure 9 shows a three-dimensional model of the aortic dissection of the other two patients reconstructed by the above method. It is clear from the three-dimensional reconstructed images that the dissection membrane occurs in the entire aortic cavity in the first set of models, and the dissection membrane of the second group appears in the aortic arch away from the heart. The results of the two groups intuitively and clearly show the location and extent of the break, so the method provides much more space relationship information of the aortic dissection to the

attending physician for the diagnosis of the diseases, surgery, and postoperative evaluation to provide assistance.

4.2. Segmentation Accuracy. In order to verify the algorithm for segmentation of CT image sequence aortic extraction effect, compare the aortic arch and descending aorta extraction results on this proposed method with those based on GVF snake algorithm. To test and verify the reliability of above two algorithms, we compare the extraction results by algorithms above with the manual results by doctor of rich clinical experience and calculate the overlapping rate to test the reliability of the algorithm in this paper; the extraction results by three methods are shown in Figure 10.

We can obtain that, for descending aorta, the segmentation results by both GVF snake model and the proposed segmentation algorithm are close to the real target contour. While for the aortic arch the GVF snake algorithm has certain errors, because of the absence of shape constraints, the

TABLE 1: Two segmentation algorithms' overlap ratio.

	GVF snake method (aortic arch)	Our proposed method (aortic arch)	GVF snake method (descending aorta)	Our proposed method (descending aorta)
Sample 1	84.52%	92.32%	89.75%	95.59%
Sample 2	86.51%	92.97%	88.16%	94.98%
Sample 3	87.63%	93.09%	90.03%	93.26%
Sample 4	89.95%	94.65%	89.80%	93.76%
Sample 5	88.02%	93.23%	88.70%	94.07%
Sample 6	88.63%	93.45%	89.04%	94.12%

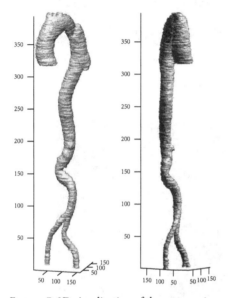

FIGURE 7: 3D visualization of the aorta region.

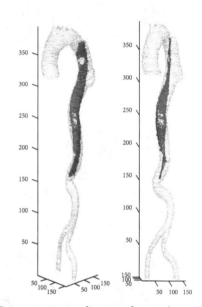

FIGURE 8: 3D visualization of aortic dissection.

curve is vulnerable to the interference of other organizations around the outline in the process of evolution, which is shown in Figure 11(a); curve 1 is the initial curve, and curve 2 is the end evolution of the curve. In order to avoid impact from other groups' contour in the curve evolution, the GVF snake model firstly determines the aorta interested area which involves complete aorta area but as far as possible to introduce the interference of other organizations [15, 16]. Generally speaking, fixed location areas or template matching methods are chosen, which are with low repeatability and adaptability, and the selecting accuracy directly affects the subsequent partitioning extraction results. However we can achieve the aorta automatic segmentation result after directly inputting one CT image with our proposed method. Figure 11(b) shows the iteration results by our proposed method. And this algorithm is of higher degree of automation and stronger robustness than GVF snake model.

In order to quantitatively describe the accuracy of the algorithm in this paper, using the overlap rate as evaluation indexes,

$$\text{Overlap} = \frac{A_{ab}}{A_a + A_b - A_{ab}};\qquad(7)$$

A_a and A_b, respectively, represent the proportion of the target area from the two images' segmentation; A_{ab} is the proportion of the target zone overlapping. With thoracic hospital doctors manual segmentation result as the gold standard, our experiment selects large number of images from groups of patients' CT images and then calculates the two algorithms' overlap, respectively, and some samples results of those all are displayed in Table 1.

For extraction accuracy, the proposed method is obviously of higher overlap ratio than the GVF snake method from the table (93.29% versus 87.54% on aortic arch, 94.30% versus 89.25% on descending aorta).

5. Conclusions

This paper introduces a kind of medical CT image processing method to rapidly and accurately obtain aortic dissection characteristic from huge CT image data and to three-dimensionally reconstruct the structure for doctors in clinical diagnosis. The algorithm of this paper has been improved on the basis of the traditional ASM algorithms; not only is the statistical model more accurately constructed and the accuracy of the model matching improved, but also the initialization process combined with the continuity of the

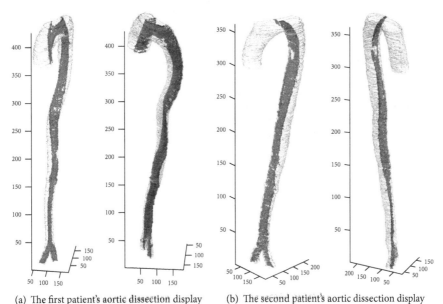

(a) The first patient's aortic dissection display   (b) The second patient's aortic dissection display

FIGURE 9: 3D visualization model of another two patients with aortic dissection.

(a) Aortic arch and descending aorta manual segmentation results

(b) Segmentation results by GVF snake method

(c) Segmentation results by this proposed method

FIGURE 10: Aortic arch and descending aorta segmentation results by three methods.

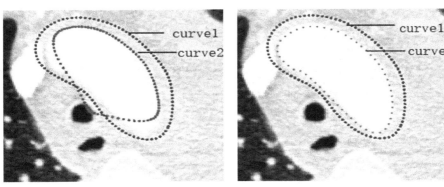

(a) Iteration result based on GVF snake method   (b) Iteration result based on the proposed method

FIGURE 11: Iteration results based on two methods.

CT sequence is simplified and the algorithm effectiveness is improved. Compared to GVF snake algorithm, the experiment can be a strong proof that our algorithm can effectively improve the accuracy of aorta segmentation. This method of this paper can effectively make up for the inadequacy of existing hospital equipment function, so that the attending physicians and patients can deeply understand and grasp the state of the illness. At the same time, for other cardiovascular diseases' diagnosis and treatment, this method is of great significance.

Acknowledgments

This work is supported by the National Natural Science Foundation of China (NSFC) (61405143, 61373104, and 61402330) and Key Projects in the National Science and Technology Pillar Program (2013BAF06B00) under Tianjin Key Laboratory of Optoelectronic Detection Technology and Systems, Tianjin Polytechnic University, China.

References

[1] N. Fetnaci, P. Lubniewski, B. Miguel, and C. Lohou, "3D segmentation of the true and false lumens on CT aortic dissection images," in *Proceedings of the Three-Dimensional Image Processing (3DIP) and Applications 2013*, Burlingame, CA, USA, February 2013.

[2] C. Lohou, N. Fetnaci, P. Lubniewski, B. Miguel, P. Chabrot, and L. Sarry, "Intimai flap segmentation on CTA aortic dissection images based on mathematical morphology," in *Proceedings of the 2013 6th International Conference on Biomedical Engineering and Informatics, BMEI 2013*, pp. 143–147, Hangzhou, China, December 2013.

[3] M. Deeley A, A. Chen, R. Datteri et al., "Comparison of manual and automatic segmentation methods for brain structures in the presence of space-occupying lesions: a multi-expert study," *Physics in Medicine and Biology*, vol. 56, no. 14, p. 4557, 2011.

[4] T. F. Cootes and C. J. Taylor, "Statistical models of appearance for medical image analysis and computer vision," in *Proceedings of the Medical Imaging 2001 Image Processing*, pp. 236–248, San Diego, Calif, USA, February 2001.

[5] C. Je, W. Jo, and H.-M. Park, "Mouth map-assisted localisation of ASM lip landmarks," *Imaging Science Journal*, vol. 64, no. 8, pp. 419–424, 2016.

[6] Z. Zheng, J. Jiong, D. Chunjiang, X. Liu, and J. Yang, "Facial feature localization based on an improved active shape model," *Information Sciences*, vol. 178, no. 9, pp. 2215–2223, 2008.

[7] G. Gill, M. Toews, and R. R. Beichel, "Robust initialization of active shape models for lung segmentation in CT scans: A feature-based atlas approach," *International Journal of Biomedical Imaging*, vol. 2014, Article ID 479154, 2014.

[8] T. Cootes, C. Taylor J, and A. Lanitis, "Active shape models: evaluation of a multi-resolution method for improving image search," in *Proceedings of the British Machine Vision Conference*, pp. 327–336, 2010.

[9] H. Sun, X. Lu, and H. Liu, "A segmentation method of aorta in ct image," *Modern Scientific Instruments*, no. 02, pp. 45–48, 2013.

[10] J. Wang and C. Shi, "Automatic construction of statistical shape models using deformable simplex meshes with vector field convolution energy," *Biomedical Engineering Online*, vol. 16, article 49, no. 1, 2017.

[11] S. Kurugol, R. San Jose Estepar, J. Ross, and G. R. Washko, "Aorta segmentation with a 3D level set approach and quantification of aortic calcifications in non-contrast chest CT," in *Proceedings of the 34th Annual International Conference of the IEEE Engineering in Medicine and Biology Society (EMBS '12)*, pp. 2343–2346, IEEE, San Diego, Calif, USA, September 2012.

[12] C.-Y. Tsai, C.-H. Huang, and A.-H. Tsao, "Graphics processing unit-accelerated multi-resolution exhaustive search algorithm for real-time keypoint descriptor matching in high-dimensional spaces," *IET Computer Vision*, vol. 10, no. 3, pp. 212–219, 2016.

[13] R. Lakemond, C. Fookes, and S. Sridharan, "Affine adaptation of local image features using the Hessian matrix," in *Proceedings of the 6th IEEE International Conference on Advanced Video and Signal Based Surveillance, AVSS 2009*, pp. 496–501, Genova, Italy, September 2009.

[14] J. Sun, H. Li, P. Gao, and L. Wu, "Research on high efficient ray casting algorithm based on VTK," in *Proceedings of the 7th International Conference on Information Technology in Medicine and Education, ITME 2015*, pp. 212–214, Huangshan, China, November 2015.

[15] T. Guan, D. Zhou, and Y. Liu, "Accurate segmentation of partially overlapping cervical cells based on dynamic sparse contour searching and GVF snake mode," *Journal of Biomedical and Health Informatics*, vol. 19, no. 4, pp. 1494–1504, 2015.

[16] F. Zhang, X. Zhang, K. Cao et al., "Contour extraction of gait recognition based on improved GVF Snake model," *Computers & Electrical Engineering*, vol. 38, no. 4, pp. 882–890, 2012.

5

Small Object Detection with Multiscale Features

Guo X. Hu,[1,2] **Zhong Yang** ⓘ,[1] **Lei Hu,**[3] **Li Huang,**[4] **and Jia M. Han**[1]

[1]*College of Automation Engineering, Nanjing University of Aeronautics and Astronautics, Nanjing 211106, China*
[2]*School of Software, Jiangxi Normal University, Nanchang 330022, China*
[3]*School of Computer Information Engineering, Jiangxi Normal University, Nanchang 330022, China*
[4]*Elementary Education College, Jiangxi Normal University, Nanchang 330022, China*

Correspondence should be addressed to Zhong Yang; yz.nuaa@163.com

Guest Editor: Wei Quan

The existing object detection algorithm based on the deep convolution neural network needs to carry out multilevel convolution and pooling operations to the entire image in order to extract a deep semantic features of the image. The detection models can get better results for big object. However, those models fail to detect small objects that have low resolution and are greatly influenced by noise because the features after repeated convolution operations of existing models do not fully represent the essential characteristics of the small objects. In this paper, we can achieve good detection accuracy by extracting the features at different convolution levels of the object and using the multiscale features to detect small objects. For our detection model, we extract the features of the image from their third, fourth, and 5th convolutions, respectively, and then these three scales features are concatenated into a one-dimensional vector. The vector is used to classify objects by classifiers and locate position information of objects by regression of bounding box. Through testing, the detection accuracy of our model for small objects is 11% higher than the state-of-the-art models. In addition, we also used the model to detect aircraft in remote sensing images and achieved good results.

1. Introduction

Object detection, which not only requires accurate classification of objects in images but also needs accurate location of objects is an automatic image detection process based on statistical and geometric features. The accuracy of object classification and object location is important indicators to measure the effectiveness of model detection. Object detection is widely used in intelligent monitoring, military object detection, UAV navigation, unmanned vehicle, and intelligent transportation. However, because of the diversity of the detected objects, the current model fails to detect objects. The changeable light and the complex background increase the difficulty of the object detection especially for the objects that are in the complex environment.

The traditional method of image classification and location by multiscale pyramid method needs to extract the statistical features of the image in multiscale and then classify the image by a classifier [1–3]. Because different types of images are characterized by different features, it is difficult to use one or more features to represent objects, which do

not achieve a robust classification model. Those models failed to detect the objects especially that there are more detected objects in an image.

Since deep learning has been a great success in the field of object detection, it has become the mainstream method for object detection. These methods (e.g., RCNN [4], Fast-RCNN [5], Faster-RCNN [6], SPP-Net [7], and R-FCN [8]) have achieved good results in multiobject detection in images. But most of these object detection algorithms are based on PASCAL VOC dataset [9] for training and testing. PASCAL VOC dataset, which provides a standard evaluation system for detection algorithms and learning performance, is the most widely used standard dataset in the field of object classification and detection. The dataset consists of 20 catalogues closely related to human life, including human and animal (bird, cat, cattle, dog, horse, and sheep), vehicle (aircraft, bicycle, ship, bus, car, motorcycle, and train), and indoor item (bottle, chair, table, potted plants, sofa, and television). From the above object category, we can find that the actual size of most objects in the dataset is large object. Even if there are some small objects, such as bottles, these small objects

FIGURE 1: Small object dataset.

display very large objects in the image because of the focal length. Therefore, the detection model based on the dataset composed of large objects will not be effectively detected for the small objects in reality [10].

Based on this problem, we mainly study automatic detection of small object. For small object, we define it as two types: one is a small object in the real world, such as mouse and telephone. And the other is small objects; those are large objects in the real world, but they are shown in the image as small objects because of the camera angle and focal length, such as objects detection in aerial images or in remote sensing images. The small object dataset is shown in Figure 1.

Usually, since small objects have low resolution and are near large objects, small objects are often disturbed by the large objects and it leads to failure in being detected in the automatic detection process. As the mouse in Figure 1 is often placed next to the monitor, the common saliency detection model [11, 12] usually focuses on more significant monitor and ignores the mouse. In addition, we not only find the

detected objects in the image but also need to accurately mark object location for object detection. Because the big detected objects have many pixels in the image, they can accurately locate their location. But, it is just the opposite for the small objects that have low resolution and few pixels. Even more, because the small objects have fewer pixels and the finite pixels contain few object features, it is difficult to detect the small objects by the conventional detection model. In addition, there are few studies, references, and also no standard dataset on automatic detection of small objects.

In order to solve these problems, we propose a multiscale deep convolution detection network to detect small objects. The network is based on the Faster-RCNN detection model. We firstly combine the features of the 3th, 4th, and 5th convolution layers for the small objects to a multiscale feature vector. Then, we use the vector to detect the small objects and locate the bounding box of objects. In order to train small objects, the paper also uses the method [13] to build a dataset focusing on small objects. Finally, by comparing the proposed detection model with the state-of-the-art detection model, we find that the accuracy of our method is much better than that of Faster-RCNN.

The paper is organized as follows. In Section 2, we introduce related works. Thereafter in the Section 3, we demonstrate the detection model. Experiments are presented in Section 4. We conclude with a discussion in Section 5.

2. Related Works

Object detection is always a hot topic in the field of machine vision. The conventional detection method based on sliding window needs to decompose images in multiscale images. Usually, one image is decomposed into lots of subwindows of several million different locations and different scales. The model then uses a classifier to determine whether the detected object is contained in each window. The method is very inefficient because it needs exhaustive search. In addition, different classifiers also affect the detection accuracy of objects. In order to obtain robust classifier, the classifiers are designed according to the different kinds of detected objects. For example, the Harr feature combined with Adaboosting classifier [14] is availability for face detection. For pedestrian detection, we use the HOG feature (Histogram of Gradients) combined with support vector machine [15] and the HOG feature combined with DPM (Deformable Part Model) [16, 17] is often used in the field of the general object detection. However, if there are many different kinds of detected objects in an image, those classifiers will fail to detect the objects.

Since 2014, Hinton used deep learning to achieve the best classification accuracy in the year's ImageNet competition, and then the deep learning has become a hot direction to detect the objects. The model of object detection based on the deep learning is divided into two categories: the first that is widely used is based on the region proposals [18–20], such as RCNN [4], SPP-Net [7], Fast-RCNN [5], Faster-RCNN [6], and R-FCN [8]. The other method does not use region proposals but directly detects the objects, such as YOLO [21] and SSD [22].

For the first method, the model firstly performs RoIs selection during the detection; i.e., multiple RoIs are generated by selective search [23], edge box [24], or RPN [25]. Then the model extracts features for each RoIs by CNN, classifies objects by classifiers, and finally obtains the location of detected objects. RCNN [4] uses selective search [23] to produce about 2000 RoIs for each picture and then extracts and classifies the convolution features of the 2000 RoIs, respectively. Because these RoIs have a large number of overlapped parts, the large number of repeated calculations results in the inefficient detection. SSP-net [7] and Fast-RCNN [5] propose a shared RoIs feature for this problem. The methods extract only a CNN feature from the whole original image, and then the feature of each RoI is extracted from the CNN feature by RoI pooling operation independently. So the amount of computing of extracting feature of each RoI is shared. This method reduces the CNN operation that needs 2000 times in RCNN to one CNN operation, which greatly improves the computation speed.

However, whether it is SSP-net or Fast-RCNN, although they reduce the number of CNN operations, its time consumption is far greater than the time of the CNN feature extraction on GPU because the selection of the bounding box of each object requires about 2 seconds/image on CPU. Therefore, the bottleneck of the object detection lies in region proposal operation. Faster-RCNN inputs the features extracted by CNN to the RPN (Region Proposal Network) network and obtains region proposal by the RPN network, so it can share the image features extracted by CNN and thereby it reduces the time of selective search operation. After RPN, Faster-RCNN classifies the obtained region proposal through two fully connected layers and the regression operation of the bounding box. Experiments prove that not only is this speed faster, but also the quality of proposal is better. R-FCN thinks that the full connection classification for each RoI by Faster-RCNN is also a very time-consuming process, so R-FCN also integrates the classification process into the forward computing process of the network. Since this process is shared for different RoI, it is much faster than a separate classifier.

The other type is without using region proposal for the object detection. YOLO divides the entire original image into the $S*S$ cell. If the center of an object falls within a cell, the corresponding cell is responsible for detecting the object and setting the confidence score for each cell. The score reflects the probability of the existence of the object in the bounding box and the accuracy of IoU. YOLO does not use region proposal, but directly convolution operations on the whole image, so it is faster than Faster-RCNN in speed, but the accuracy is less than Faster-RCNN. SSD also uses a single convolution neural network to convolution the image and predicts a series of boundary box with different sizes and ratio of length and width at each object. In the test phase, the network predicts the possibility of each class of objects in each bounding box and adjusts the boundary box to adapt to the shape of the object. G-CNN [25] regards object detection as a problem of changing the detection box from a fixed grid to a real box. The model firstly divides the entire image with different scale to obtain the initial bounding box and extracts the features from the whole image by the convolution operation. Then the feature image encircled by an initial bounding box is adjusted to a fixed size feature image by the method Fast-RCNN mentioned. Finally we can obtain a more accurate bounding box by regression operation. The bounding box will be the final output after several iterations.

In short, for the current mainstream there are two types of object detection methods, the first will have better accuracy, but the speed is slower. The accuracy of the second one is slightly worse, but faster. No matter which way to carry out the object detection, the feature extraction uses multilayer convolution method, which can obtain the rich abstract object feature for the target object. But this method leads to a decrease in detection accuracy for small target objects because the features extracted by the method are few and can not fully represent the characteristics of the object.

In addition, the PASCAL VOC dataset is the main dataset for object detection and it is composed of 20 categories of object, e.g., cattle, buses, and pedestrians. But all of these objects in the image are large objects. Even in the PASCAL VOC, there are also some small objects, e.g., cup, but these small objects display very large objects in the image because of the focal length. So, the PASCAL VOC is not suitable for the detection of small objects.

Microsoft COCO dataset [26] is a standard dataset built by Microsoft team for object detection, image segmentation, and other fields. The dataset includes various types of small objects with the complexity of the background, so it is suitable for small objects detection. The SUN dataset [27] consists of 908 scene categories and 4479 object categories and a total of 131067 images that also contain a large number of small objects.

In order to get the rich small object dataset, the paper [13] adopted two standards to build the dataset. The first is that the actual size of the objects is not more than 30 centimeters. Another criterion is that the area occupied of the objects is not more than 0.58% in the image. The author also gives the mAP of RCNN based on the dataset and it has only 23.5% detection rate.

3. Model Introduction

3.1. Faster-RCNN. The RCNN model proposed by Girshick in 2014 is divided into four processes during the object detection. First, 2000 proposal regions in the image are obtained by region proposal algorithm. Second, it extracts the CNN features of the two thousand proposal regions separately and outputs the fixed dimension features. Third, the objects are classified according to the features. Finally, in order to get the precise object bounding box, RCNN accurately locate and merge the foreground objects by regression operation. The algorithm has achieved the best accuracy of the year. But it requires an additional expense on storage space and time because RCNN needs to extract the features of 2000 proposal regions in each image. Later, Fast-RCNN is proposed by Girshick based on RCNN, the model, which maps all proposal regions into one image and has only one feature extraction. So Fast-RCNN greatly improves the speed of detection and training. However, Fast-RCNN still needs to extract the proposal regions which is the same as RCNN. The proposal regions extracted lead to inefficiency. Faster-RCNN integrates the generation of proposal region, extracting feature of proposal region, detection of bounding box, and classification of object into a CNN framework by the RPN network (region proposal network). So it greatly improves the detection efficiency. The RPN network structure diagram is shown in Figure 2. The core idea of Faster-RCNN is to use the RPN network to generate the proposal regions directly and to use the anchor mechanism and the regression method to output an objectness score and regressed bounds for each proposal region; i.e., the classification score and the boundary of the 3 different scales and 3 length-width ratio for each proposal region are outputted. Experiments show that the VGG-16 model takes only 0.2 seconds to detect each image. In addition, it has been proved that the detection precision will be reduced if the negative sample is very high in the dataset. The RPN network generates 300 proposal regions for each image by multiscale anchors, which are less than 2000

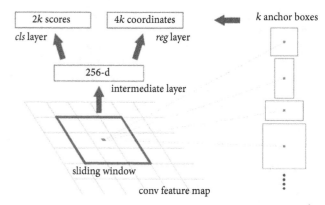

FIGURE 2: RPN network structure.

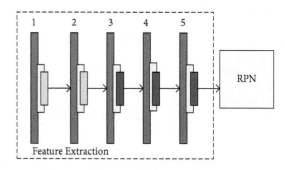

FIGURE 3: Faster-RCNN network structure.

proposal regions of Fast-RCNN or RCNN. So the accuracy is also higher than them.

Faster-RCNN only provides a RPN layer improvement compared to the Fast-RCNN network and does not improve the feature mapping layer compared to the Fast-RCNN network. Faster-RCNN network structure is shown in Figure 3. Faster-RCNN performs multiple downsampling operations in the process of feature extraction. Each sampling causes the image to be reduced by half. The output image in the fifth layer is the 1/16 of the original object for Faster-RCNN; i.e., only 1 byte feature is outputted on the last layer if the detected object is smaller than 16 pixels in the original image. The objects failed to be detected because little feature information can not sufficiently represent the characteristics of the object.

Although Faster-RCNN has achieved very good detection results on the PASCAL VOC, the PASCAL VOC is mainly composed of large objects. The detection precision will fall if the dataset is mainly composed of small objects.

3.2. Multiscale Faster-RCNN. In reality, the detected objects are low in resolution and small in size. The current model (e.g., Faster-RCNN) which has good detection accuracy for large objects can not effectively detect small objects in the image [28]. The main reason is that those models based on deep neural network make the image calculated with convolution and downsampled in order to obtain more abstract and high-level features. Each downsampling causes the image to be reduced by half. If the objects are similar to the size of the objects in the PASCAL VOC, the object's detail features can be obtained through these convolutions and

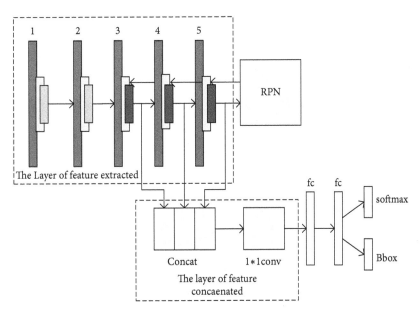

FIGURE 4: Our model structure.

downsampling. However, if the detected objects are the very small scale, the final features may only be left 1-2 pixels after multiple downsampling. So few features can not fully describe the characteristics of the objects and the existing detection method can not effectively detect the small target object.

The deeper the convolution operation, the more abstract the object features which can represent the high-level features of objects are. The shallow convolution layer can only extract the low-level features of objects. But for small objects, the low-level features can ensure rich object characteristics. In order to get high-level and abstract object features and ensure that there are enough pixels to describe small objects, we combine the features of different scales to ensure the local details of the object. At the same time, we also pay attention to the global characteristics of the object based on the Faster-RCNN. This model will have more robust characteristics. The model structure is shown in Figure 4.

The model is divided into four parts: the first part is the feature extraction layer which consists of 5 convolution layers (red part), 5 ReLU layers (yellow parts), 2 pooling layers (green parts), and 3 RoI pooling layers (purple part). We normalize the output of the 3th, 4th, and 5th convolution, respectively. Then the normalized output is sent to the RPN layer and the feature combination layer for the generation of proposal region and the extracted multiscale feature, respectively. The second part is the feature combination layer that combines the different scales features of third, fourth, and fifth layer into one-dimension feature vector by connection operation. The third part is the RPN layer which mainly realizes the generation of proposal regions. The last layer, which is used to realize classification and bounding box regression of objects that are in proposal regions, is composed of softmax and BBox.

3.3. L2 Normalization. In order to obtain the combinatorial feature vectors, we need to normalization the feature vectors

of different scales. Usually the deeper convolution layer outputs the smaller scale features. On the contrary, the lower convolution layer outputs the larger scale features. The feature scales of different layers are very different. The weight of large-scale features will be much larger than that of small scale features during the network weight which is tuned if the features of these different scales are combined, which leads to the lower detection accuracy.

To prevent such large-scale features from covering small scale features, the feature tensor that is outputted from different RoI pooling should be normalized before those tensors are concatenated. In this paper, we use L2 normalization. The normalization operation, which is used to process every feature vector that is pooled, is located after RoI pooling. After normalization, the scale of the feature vectors of the 3th,4th, and 5th layer will be normalized into a unified scale.

$$\widehat{X} = \frac{X}{\|X\|_2}, \tag{1}$$

$$\|X\|_2 = \left(\sum_{i=1}^{d} |x_i| \right)^{1/2}, \tag{2}$$

where X is the original vector from the 3th, 4th, and 5th layer, $\widehat{X}$ is normalized feature vector, and D is the channel number of each RoI pooling.

The vector X will be uniformly scaled by scale facto; i.e.,

$$Y = \gamma \widehat{X}, \tag{3}$$

where $Y = [y_1, y_2, \ldots, y_d]^T$.

In the process of error back propagation, we need to further adjust the scale factor γ and input vector X. The specific definition is as follows:

$$\frac{\partial l}{\partial \widehat{X}} = \gamma \frac{\partial l}{\partial y}, \tag{4}$$

TABLE 1: The process of model training.

Training process
Input: VGG_CNN_M_1024 and image
Output: detection model
Step 1 Initialize the ImageNet pre training model VGG_CNN_M_1024 and train the RPN network.
(1) Initialize network parameters using pre training model parameters
(2) Initialization of caffe
(3) Prepare for roidb and imdb
(4) Set output path to save the caffe module of intermediate generated.
(5) Training RPN and save the weight of the network
Step 2 Using the trained RPN network in step 1, we generate the ROIs information and the probability distribution of the foreground objects in the proposal regions.
Step 3 First training Fast RCNN network
(1) The proposal regions got from step 2 are sent to the ROIs
(2) The probability distribution of foreground objects is sent to the network as the weight of the objects in the proposal regions
(3) By comparing the size of Caffe blob, we get the weight of objects outside the proposal regions
(4) The loss-cls and loss-box loss functions are calculated, classify and locate objects, obtain the detection models.
Step 4 Replace the detection model obtained in step 3 with the ImageNet network model in step 1, repeat steps 1 to 3, and the final model is the training model.

$$\frac{\partial l}{\partial X} = \frac{\partial l}{\partial \widehat{X}} \left(\frac{I}{\|X\|_2} - \frac{XX^T}{\|X\|_2^3} \right), \tag{5}$$

$$\frac{\partial l}{\partial \gamma} = \sum_y \frac{\partial l}{\partial y} \widehat{X}. \tag{6}$$

3.4. Concat Layer. After the features of the third, fourth, and fifth layer are L2 normalized and RoI pooled, output vectors need to be concatenated. The concatenation operation consists of four tuples (i.e., number, channel, height, and weight), where number and channel represent the concatenation dimension and height and weight represent the size of concatenation vectors. All output of each layer will be concatenated into a single dimension vector by concatenation operations. In the initial stage of model training, we set a uniform initial scale factor of 10 for each RoI pooling layer [11] in order to ensure that the output values of the downstream layers are reasonable.

Then in order to ensure that the input vector of the full connection has the same scale as the input vector of the Faster-RCNN, an additional 1∗1 convolution layer is added to the network to compress the channel size of the concatenated tensor to the original one, i.e., the same number as the channel size of the last convolution feature map (conv5).

3.5. Algorithmic Description. Faster RNN provides two training methods with end-to-end training and alternate training and also provides three pretraining networks of different sizes with VGG-16, VGG_CNN_M_1024, and ZF, respectively. The large network VGG-16 has 13 convolutional layers and 3 fully connected layers. ZF net that has 5 convolutional layers and 3 fully connected layers is small network and the VGG_CNN_M_1024 is medium-sized network. Experiment shows that the detection accuracy of VGG-16 is better than

the other two models, but it needs more than 11G GPU. In order to improve the training speed of the model, we use the VGG_CNN_M_1024 model as a pretraining model and use the alternation training as a training method. The main process of training is shown in Table 1.

4. Experimental Analysis

4.1. Dataset Acquisition. At present, the dataset commonly used in target detection is PASCAL VOC, which is made up of larger objects or the objects whose size is very small but the area of the objects in the image is very large because of the focal length. Therefore, PASCAL VOC is not suitable for small object detection. There is no dataset for small target objects. In order to test the detection effect of the model on small objects, the paper will establish a small object dataset for object detection based on Microsoft COCO datasets and SUN datasets.

In the process of building small object dataset, we refer to the two criteria mentioned in [18]. The first criterion is that the actual size of the detected object is not more than 30 centimeters. The second criterion is that all the small objects in the image occupy 0.08% to 0.58% of the area in the image; i.e., the pixels of the object are between 16∗16 and 42∗42 pixels. The small objects in the PASCAL VOC occupy 1.38% and 46.40% of the area in the image, so it is not suitable for small object detection. The statistics table is shown in Table 2 [18].

Based on the above standards, we select 8 types of objects to make up a dataset, including mouse, telephone, outlet, faucet, clock, toilet paper, bottle, and plate. After filtering COCO and SUN dataset, we finally select 2003 images that include a total of 3339 objects. The 358 mouse are distributed in 282 images, and the other objects, e.g., toilet paper, faucet, socket panel, and clock, are shown in Table 3.

TABLE 2: PASCAL VOC object area account table. Unit: %.

category	cat	sofa	train	dog	table	motorbike	horse
area ratio	46. 40	33.87	32.33	30.96	23.73	23.69	23.15
category	bus	plane	bicycle	person	bird	cow	chair
area ratio	23.04	22.83	14.38	8.14	8.03	6.68	6.09
category	TV	boat	sheep	plant	car	bottle	
area ratio	5.96	3.82	3.34	2.92	2.79	1.38	

TABLE 3: The small object dataset.

category	Mouse	Telephone	Outlet	Faucet	Clock	Toilet paper	bottle	plate
Number of images	282	265	305	423	387	245	209	353
Number of objects	358	332	477	515	422	289	371	575

TABLE 4: The comparison of accuracy between our model and Faster-RCNN. (40000,20000).

model	mAP	Mouse	Telephone	Outlet	Faucet	Clock	Toilet paper	bottle	plate
Faster RCNN	0.479	0.360	0.409	0.519	0.392	0.643	0.350	0.485	0.676
Our model	0.589	0.402	0.482	0.600	0.506	0.687	0.641	0.585	0.806

TABLE 5: The comparison of accuracy between our model and Faster-RCNN (60000,30000).

model	mAP	Mouse	Telephone	Outlet	Faucet	Clock	Toilet paper	bottle	plate
Faster RCNN	0.491	0.447	0.449	0.549	0.424	0.604	0.309	0.428	0.719
Our model	0.587	0.371	0.564	0.572	0.561	0.690	0.546	0.514	0.880

The small object dataset established in this paper is based on COCO and SUN. Because the data in COCO and SUN are mainly based on the scenes of everyday life, the complexity of image background in our dataset is much larger than that in PASCAL VOC. In addition, there are more objects in single image compared with the PASCAL VOC, and most of these objects are not in the image center. These make the object detection based on the small object dataset more difficult than that based on the PASCAL VOC.

During the experiment, we randomly select 300 images as a test set and 600 as a validation set from the small dataset, and all the remaining images are trained as a training set.

4.2. Experimental Comparison. The paper compares our model with the state-of-the-art detection model Faster-RCNN for small object detection. In the process of model training, our model and Faster-RCNN model use the alternate training method. Firstly, we train the RPN network and use the RPN network as a pretraining network to train the detection network. Then we repeat the above steps to get the final detection model. In the training process, we have 40000 iterations for the RPN network and 20000 iterations for the detection network. The final accuracy of the detection is shown in Table 4.

With the increase in the number of iterations of the training network, different models will show different detection results. In the experiment, we also try to increase the number of iterations; that is, the RPN network iterates 60000 times

and the detection network iterates 30000 times. The results obtained are shown in Table 5.

We can find that the detection accuracy is stable when the number of iterations of RPN network is 40000 and the number of iterations of detection network is 20000 from the above experiments. The accuracy of our model is better than that of Faster-RCNN for all types of objects. The part renderings of the objects detection are shown in Figure 5.

In order to further detect the robustness of the model, we also detect the remote sensing images in real environment. The remote sensing image dataset comes from the Google map and the insulators of the field transmission line are photographed by the UAV (unmanned aerial vehicle). Because the images in real environment have the characteristics of changeable light, complex background, and incomplete objects, we try to take all the special cases into consideration during the building the dataset. Experiments show that our proposed detection model has better detection results in small objects detection in real environment. The part renderings of the objects detection are shown in Figure 6.

5. Conclusions

Small objects are very difficult to detect because of their lower resolution and larger influence of the surrounding environment. The existing detection models based on deep neural network are not able to detect the small objects because the features of objects that are extracted by many convolution and pooling operations are lost. Our model not

FIGURE 5: The detection renderings.

FIGURE 6: Effect of remote sensing image detection.

only ensures the integrity of the feature of the large object but also preserves the full detail feature of the small objects by extracting the multiscale feature of the image. So it can improve the accuracy of the detection of the small objects.

The GANs (Generative Adversarial Nets) have been widely applied to the game area and achieved good results [29]. For future work we believe that investigating more sophisticated techniques for improving the accuracy of small object detection, including the Generative Adversarial Nets, will be beneficial. Existing object detection usually detects small objects through learning representations of all the objects at multiple scales. However, the performance is usually limited to pay off the computational cost and the representation of the image. In the future, we address the small object detection problem that internally lifts representations of small objects to "super-resolved" ones, achieving similar characteristics as large objects and thus being more discriminative for detection. And finally, we use the adversarial network to train the detection model.

Acknowledgments

This work was supported by the National Natural Science Foundation of China under Grants nos. 61662033 and 61473144, Aeronautical Science Foundation of China (Key Laboratory) under Grant no. 20162852031, and the Special Scientific Instrument Development of Ministry of Science and Technology of China under Grant no. 2016YFF0103702.

References

[1] P. Viola and M. Jones, "Rapid object detection using a boosted cascade of simple features," in *Proceedings of the IEEE Computer Society Conference on Computer Vision and Pattern Recognition*, pp. 1511–1518, Kauai, Hawaii, USA, December 2001.

[2] R. Lienhart and J. Maydt, "An extended set of Haar-like features for rapid object detection," in *Proceedings of the International Conference on Image Processing (ICIP '02)*, pp. I/900–I/903, Rochester, NY, USA, September 2002.

[3] P. Viola, J. C. Platt, and C. Zhang, "Multiple Instance boosting for object detection," in *Proceedings of the Annual Conference on Neural Information Processing Systems (NIPS '05)*, vol. 18, pp. 1417–1424, Vancouver, British Columbia, Canada, December 2005.

[4] R. Girshick, J. Donahue, T. Darrell, and J. Malik, "Rich feature hierarchies for accurate object detection and semantic segmentation," in *Proceedings of the 27th IEEE Conference on Computer Vision and Pattern Recognition (CVPR '14)*, pp. 580–587, Columbus, Ohio, USA, June 2014.

[5] R. Girshick, "Fast R-CNN," in *Proceedings of the 15th IEEE International Conference on Computer Vision (ICCV '15)*, pp. 1440–1448, Santiago, Chile, December 2015.

[6] S. Ren, K. He, R. Girshick, and J. Sun, "Faster R-CNN: towards real-time object detection with region proposal networks," *IEEE Transactions on Pattern Analysis and Machine Intelligence*, vol. 39, no. 6, pp. 1137–1149, 2017.

[7] K. He, X. Zhang, S. Ren, and J. Sun, "Spatial pyramid pooling in deep convolutional networks for visual recognition," *IEEE Transactions on Pattern Analysis and Machine Intelligence*, vol. 37, no. 9, pp. 1904–1916, 2015.

[8] J. F. Dai, Y. Li, K. M. He et al., "R-FCN: Object Detection via Region-based Fully," in *Proceedings of the 30th Conference on Neural Information Processing Systems (NIPS 2016)*, Barcelona, Spain, 2016.

[9] M. Everingham, L. van Gool, C. K. I. Williams, J. Winn, and A. Zisserman, "The pascal visual object classes (VOC) challenge," *International Journal of Computer Vision*, vol. 88, no. 2, pp. 303–338, 2010.

[10] Y. Ren, C. Zhu, and S. Xiao, "Small object detection in optical remote sensing images via modified faster R-CNN," *Applied Sciences*, vol. 8, no. 5, article 813, 2018.

[11] L. Itti, C. Koch, and E. Niebur, "A model of saliency-based visual attention for rapid scene analysis," *IEEE Transactions on Pattern Analysis and Machine Intelligence*, vol. 20, no. 11, pp. 1254–1259, 1998.

[12] M.-M. Cheng, N. J. Mitra, X. Huang, P. H. S. Torr, and S.-M. Hu, "Global contrast based salient region detection," *IEEE Transactions on Pattern Analysis and Machine Intelligence*, vol. 37, no. 3, pp. 569–582, 2015.

[13] C. Chen, M. Y. Liu, O. Tuzel et al., "R-CNN for small object detection," in *Asian Conference on Computer Vision*, vol. 10115 of *Lecture Notes in Computer Science*, pp. 214–230, 2016.

[14] J. S. Lim and W. H. Kim, "Detection of multiple humans using motion information and adaboost algorithm based on Harr-like features," *International Journal of Hybrid Information Technology*, vol. 5, no. 2, pp. 243–248, 2012.

[15] R. P.Yadav, V. Senthamilarasu, K. Kutty, and S. P. Ugale, "Implementation of Robust HOG-SVM based Pedestrian Classification," *International Journal of Computer Applications*, vol. 114, no. 19, pp. 10–16, 2015.

[16] L. Hou, W. Wan, K.-H. Lee, J.-N. Hwang, G. Okopal, and J. Pitton, "Robust Human Tracking Based on DPM Constrained Multiple-Kernel from a Moving Camera," *Journal of Signal Processing Systems*, vol. 86, no. 1, pp. 27–39, 2017.

[17] A. Ali and M. A. Bayoumi, "Towards real-time DPM object detector for driver assistance," in *Proceedings of the 23rd IEEE International Conference on Image Processing, ICIP 2016*, pp. 3842–3846, Phoenix, Ariz, USA, September 2016.

[18] S. Bell, C. L. Zitnick, K. Bala, and R. Girshick, "Inside-outside net: Detecting objects in context with skip pooling and recurrent neural networks," in *Proceedings of the 2016 IEEE Conference on Computer Vision and Pattern Recognition, CVPR 2016*, pp. 2874–2883, Las Vegas, Nev, USA, July 2016.

[19] T. Kong, A. Yao, Y. Chen, and F. Sun, "HyperNet: towards accurate region proposal generation and joint object detection," in *Proceedings of the 2016 IEEE Conference on Computer Vision and Pattern Recognition (CVPR)*, pp. 845–853, Las Vegas, Nev, USA, June 2016.

[20] F. Yang, W. Choi, and Y. Lin, "Exploit all the layers: fast and accurate CNN object detector with scale dependent pooling and cascaded rejection classifiers," in *Proceedings of the 2016 IEEE Conference on Computer Vision and Pattern Recognition, CVPR 2016*, pp. 2129–2137, Las Vegas, Nev, USA, July 2016.

[21] J. Redmon, S. Divvala, R. Girshick, and A. Farhadi, "You only look once: Unified, real-time object detection," in *Proceedings of the 2016 IEEE Conference on Computer Vision and Pattern*

Recognition, CVPR 2016, pp. 779–788, Las Vegas, Nev, USA, July 2016.

[22] W. Liu, D. Anguelov, D. Erhan et al., "SSD: single shot multibox detector," in *European Conference on Computer Vision*, vol. 9905 of *Lecture Notes in Computer Science*, pp. 21–37, Springer, Cham, Switzerland, 2016.

[23] J. R. R. Uijlings, K. E. A. Van De Sande, T. Gevers, and A. W. M. Smeulders, "Selective search for object recognition," *International Journal of Computer Vision*, vol. 104, no. 2, pp. 154–171, 2013.

[24] C. L. Zitnick and P. Dollár, "Edge boxes: locating object proposals from edges," in *European Conference on Computer Vision*, pp. 391–405, Springer, Cham, Switzerland, 2014.

[25] M. Najibi, M. Rastegari, and L. S. Davis, "G-CNN: An iterative grid based object detector," in *Proceedings of the 2016 IEEE Conference on Computer Vision and Pattern Recognition, CVPR 2016*, pp. 2369–2377, Las Vegas, Nev, USA, July 2016.

[26] T.-Y. Lin, M. Maire, S. Belongie et al., "Microsoft COCO: Common objects in context," in *European Conference on Computer Vision*, vol. 8693 of *Lecture Notes in Computer Science*, pp. 740–755, Springer, Cham, Switzerland, 2014.

[27] http://groups.csail.mit.edu/vision/SUN/.

[28] T. H. N. Le, Y. Zheng, C. Zhu, K. Luu, and M. Savvides, "Multiple scale faster-RCNN approach to driver's cell-phone usage and hands on steering wheel detection," in *Proceedings of the 29th IEEE Conference on Computer Vision and Pattern Recognition Workshops, CVPRW 2016*, pp. 46–53, Las Vegas, Nev, USA, July 2016.

[29] X. Wu, K. Xu, and P. Hall, "A survey of image synthesis and editing with generative adversarial networks," *Tsinghua Science and Technology*, vol. 22, no. 6, pp. 660–674, 2017.

6

PO-MPTCP: Priorities-Oriented Data Scheduler for Multimedia Multipathing Services

Wei Lu[1], Dandan Yu,[1] Minghe Huang,[1] and Bin Guo[2]

[1]School of Software, Jiangxi Normal University, Nanchang 330022, China
[2]Information Office, Jiangxi Normal University, Nanchang 330022, China

Correspondence should be addressed to Wei Lu; weilu@jxnu.edu.cn

Guest Editor: Jiyan Wu

With the diversified wireless network access technology and large-scale equipment of multinetwork interface devices expanding, network transmission performance for multi-homed terminals has been widely concerned by academic circles. More and more scholars have paid attention to Multipath Transmission Control Protocol (MPTCP) as one of the representative methods for studying path transmission performance. However, their studies ignore the impact of dynamic network environments on data transmission performance and seldom consider the priority of data transmission. Undoubtedly, not prioritizing packets will have a dramatic effect on the users experience in the heterogeneous networks. In this paper, we propose a novel priority-aware streaming media multipath data scheduler mechanism (PO-MPTCP) to achieve the following goals: (1) detecting the priority of all streaming media data; (2) achieving multiattribute-aware path evaluation and switching mechanism; (3) introducing a path-quality priority-driven data distribution mechanism to improve streaming multipath transmission performance. The simulation experiment shows that PO-MPTCP proposed by this paper improves the transmission performance of streaming media and reduces the transmission delay. For the result of simulation experiment, it is easy for us to find that PO-MPTCP is more efficient in data delivery than the standard MPTCP mechanism.

1. Introduction

Under the background of establishment of various wireless access technologies (i.e., WiFi, 4G, Bluetooth, etc.), the number of mobile terminals equipped with several different standard network interfaces is increasing year by year. Multi-homed devices can use multiple network interfaces to transmit data in parallel, effectively improving network transmission throughput [1]. Due to the growing demands for bandwidth requirement and transmission rate requirement of real-time streaming applications (i.e., Facebook [2], WeChat [3], YouTube [4], etc.), traditional single-path Transmission Control Protocol (TCP) [5] cannot utilize the characteristics of the terminals multinetwork interfaces; thus the Internet Engineering Task Force (IETF) proposes Multipath TCP (MPTCP) to be compatible with the current application layer based on traditional TCP [6, 7].

As an extension of TCP, MPTCP is compatible with applications, and it never needs to make too many modifications

for traditional TCP sockets to achieve application layer transparency. MPTCP's main idea is that data streams would be parallel distributed to multiple links, and it will improve the performance of data transmission (i.e., improving network throughput, reducing transmission delay, maximizing the utilization of the network, etc.) [8]. From Figure 1, we can see the MPTCP-based multimedia multipath transmission in wireless network. It simply illustrates that mobile devices use three paths (Paths A, B, and C) to correspond to the MPTCP-based media server.

By adopting a multi-homing structure, MPTCP is considered to be a promising transmission technology, which can meet the requirements for specific Quality of Services (QoS) and balance real-time task utilization rate in network resources [9, 10]. However, most MPTCP data scheduling algorithms and congestion control algorithms only consider transmission efficiency and fairness [7–9] and ignored the priority difference of data transmission caused by the complexity of data types [11].

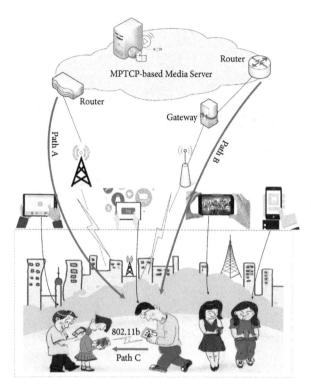

FIGURE 1: MPTCP-based multimedia multipath transmission in wireless network.

Inspired by the above considerations, this paper presents a priorities-oriented data scheduler for multimedia multi-pathing mechanism that allows applications to distinguish the relatively prioritized data, ensure higher-priority data can be transmitted via a good quality path, improve the transmission performance of higher-priority data, reduce the transmission delay, and enhance the overall transmission performance for real-time streaming media services. The simulation results confirm that this mechanism can effectively improve the transmission efficiency. PO-MPTCP's fundamental contributions are as follows:

(1) It gives MPTCP the ability to perceive the priority of streaming media data and the ability to know when and how to call priority scheduling services.

(2) It designs a multiattribute perceptual mechanism to estimate path qualities and design a multiattribute cooperative path switching algorithm.

(3) It introduces a data-priority-driven distribution strategy based on path quality.

The remainder of this paper is structured as follows. In Section 2, we briefly introduce the relevant works of our PO-MPTCP. Section 3 introduces the details of PO-MPTCP. In Section 4, we evaluate and analyze the performance of PO-MPTCP based on the experimental results. Section 5 gives summaries of this paper and our future work.

2. Related Work

MPTCP is defined as a development of the TCP that can be compatible with existing Internet devices and application interfaces and which still receives great attention from academic circles. Many scholars are devoted to optimizing the data scheduling algorithm of MPTCP. Cao et al. [12] proposed a receiver-driven data scheduling strategy based on MPTCP, and the purpose is to transfer some operations (e.g., data scheduling and path selection) from the sending end to the receiving end and balance the load of sender and receiver. Marikoshi et al. [13] introduced an improved method for rapidly received ACK based on MPTCP which applies the available increase of ACK to enhance throughput. Kim et al. [14] proposed a method for managing MPTCP (RBPM) based on the size of the receive buffer. The main operation is to estimate the disorder packets by using the available receiving buffer size and multipath dissimilar characteristics; that is, if congestion occurs, RBPM would immediately stop the bad transmission path. Due to capturing the quality of the path correctly, Chung et al. [15] described a new path management scheme on the basis of Machine Learning on MPTCP (MPTCP-ML), which used signal strength, throughput, and interfering APs number to estimate path quality. Kimura et al. [16] discussed three data scheduling mechanisms: (1) data scheduling based on the highest sending rate, (2) data scheduling based on the largest sending window, and (3) data scheduling based on the lowest sending delay.

At the same time, the optimization problem of streaming media data distribution with MPTCP has caused widespread exploration in the academic community. Hayes B et al. [17] used HyperText Transfer Protocol 2.0 adaptive bitrate video transmission based on the MPTCP architecture to eliminate network bandwidth and estimate buffer status by using three modular push strategies for MPTCP. The goal is to improve the transmission of video content in a loss environment, enabling the delivery of adaptive bit rate video. Xu et al. [18] extended the partial reliability protocol of MPTCP to provide a flexible QoS trade-off for multimedia applications in real-time and reliability. Cao et al. [19] introduced the concepts of partial reliability and real-time constraints in MPTCP and discussed the real-time constraints of multimedia streams and the partial reliability of TCP.

In many current MPTCP researches, we found that the focus of scholars research has begun to shift from improving data schedules and congestion control algorithms [20–23] to optimizing real-time streaming media services. But these optimizations do not take into account the priority of real-time streaming applications for different types of transmission data, and the existing literature on data-priority scheduling is almost limited to the network layer and wireless sensor network. As described in [24], a Markov model is used to control the flow of different priorities on sensor nodes. Therefore, we propose a priority-oriented streaming media multipath data transmission mechanism for developing future mobile streaming media applications and providing attractive benefits including transfer performance improvement and high-quality users experience provisioning.

3. PO-MPTCP Detail Design

As an extension of TCP, MPTCP has many attractive benefits for content-rich real-time multi-stream media in terms

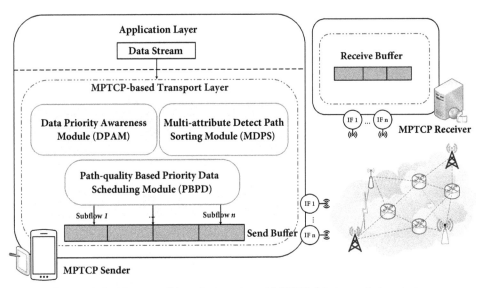

FIGURE 2: Architecture of the priority-oriented MPTCP data transmission strategy.

of performance improvement, bandwidth aggregation, and users experience. But these performances might be affected by many factors, such as path characteristics and data scheduling strategies, when the limited receive buffer with a strict sorting. Every wrong grievance is assumed to result in buffer congestion or serious MPTCP performance decline. In order to meet bandwidth requirements and transmit rate for the services of bandwidth-intensive and real-time-content-rich streaming, we discuss the theory about adding priority to MPTCP data scheduling which offers good probabilities including data scheduling dispatch, throughput improvement, and important data transmission-quality assurance.

In this paper, we define the priority of the data subflow as an additional service for the application, and the scheduling policy takes into account real needs of the network environment. According to the data submission order and currently available network bandwidth, the scheduling policy can allow application to determine the data priority and deliver other data sequentially; that is, the vital data should be prioritized and transmitted using the best quality link path. In this data scheduling strategy, it still guarantees relatively important data to be given priority for submitting, reduces transmission delays, and increases the efficiency of whole application when the network service quality is poor.

Figure 2 shows the system architecture for the priority-oriented MPTCP data transmission strategy, which mainly includes MPTCP's sender, MPTCP's receiver, and multipath heterogeneous wireless network. The sender includes three modules: (1) Data Priority Awareness Module (DPAM), (2) Multiattribute Detect Path Sorting Module (MDPS), and (3) Path-quality Based Priority Data scheduling Module (PBPD). If application layer has data to send, a module of sender is similar to SCTP multiflow buffer module which transfers data from application layer to transport layer, and it uses DPAM to detect and record the priority information for the delivery data, utilize MDPS to determine the status of each subpath based on the RTT and CWND values, and sort the paths according to the quality of each path. Priorities-oriented data

scheduler for multimedia multipathing services will dispatch data packets according to data priorities and path qualities; it also transmits information to network layer and finally gets to the receiver. In this way, when the receiver gets the data packets, it will restructure them in sequence, transfer them to the upper layer of the receiver, and feedback the SACK to the sender.

3.1. Data Priority Awareness Module (DPAM). In mobile Internet, data is developing to large scale and diversity which leads to multimedia applications demands for network bandwidth and data specialization is increasing. While the traditional MPTCP transmission method neglects the application's priority for messages, it just treats information equally as byte streams and results in data transmission blindness. Therefore, we have to establish a module to detect the data priorities.

In order to differentiate the data priorities, we will mark the different priority missions in the network. When the sender starts to transmit data, DPAM will be through the cross-layer cooperative communication [25], retrieve priority values corresponding to each stream, and store them in the status list (denoted by PO_{list}). Each element of PO_{list} is composed of a doublet (i.e., index of subflow i, priority of subflow PO_{D_i}). Algorithm 1 shows pseudocode of DPAM.

3.2. Multiattribute Detect Path Sorting Module (MDPS). The data stream transmission efficiency is proportional to the path quality in the ideal case, but the current environment of the heterogeneous network is very complex, so we hope all of data can choose a relatively good quality subpath for transmitting. In the priority-oriented data transmission protocol introduced by this paper, we assume that relatively important data will have a higher priority that can be transmitted through a relatively reliable path, which can reduce the loss probability of important packet. In addition, we propose a Multiattribute Detect Path Sorting Module (MDPS) which can determine the status of each subpath based on the RTT

```
Definition:
    D_i: the ith data stream within the MPTCP session.
    PO_{D_i}: the priority value of data stream D_i
    PO_{list}: the status list for each stream
When there are some data stream need to send,
(1)    for all data stream D_i within a MPTCP session do
(3)        PO_{list} = (i, PO_{D_i})
(4)    end for
```

ALGORITHM 1: DPAM-based priority information collection algorithm.

and CWND values and sort the path according to the quality of the path.

To deliver the prepared data, we assume that there are n available paths in an MPTCP, MDPS can record the qualities of each available path (RTT and CWND) according to the MPTCP connection quality, and uniformly storage is estimated in the set list (denoted by Q_{list}). According to the estimates of RTT and CWND in the Q_{list}, MDPS will give priority to supporting the lowest RTT and sort paths in ascending order based on the RTT values (except that the path's RTT values are the same, it will be followed by the descending order of the CWND values). MDPS will sort all available paths by quality which is used for MPTCP data scheduler. The pseudocode of MDPS is shown in Algorithm 2.

3.3. Path-Quality Based Priority Data Scheduling Module (PBPD). On the basis of DPAM and MDPS, PBPD will try to support that packets arrived in order. When the sending window is idle and n packets would be sent, we prefer to use the subpath with a good path quality to schedule important data. That is, as long as there is important data with prior in queue, it would be quickly removed from queue and utilize good priority subpath for transmission. It ensures that high-priority data in the queue can be transmitted by the best-quality path and achieve the lowest delay at the same time. When the sending window is idle and n data packets would be sent, PDPB will implement steps as follows:

(a) According to PO_{list} (priority collection of data) produced by DPAM, PDPB will determine whether the current data packet needs priority scheduling. If PO_{S_i} is NULL, the standardized MPTCP will be used for data distribution. Otherwise, it indicates that the application has priority packet, then PBPD would be dispatched.

(b) According to the sort path formed by the MDPS module, PBPD will use the first path of P_{list} set as the candidate path to be given priority to important data.

(c) PDPB will take the next path of P_{list} as the candidate path when the path *cwnd* is full.

(d) Repeat all above three steps until there is no available sending window on the sender; that is, n data have already been sent. Algorithm 3 shows the pseudocode for PBPD.

TABLE 1: Path configuration used in the simulation.

Network Parameters	Path A	Path B
Wireless technology	WiFi/IEEE 802.11b	WiMax/IEEE 802.16
Access link bandwidth	11Mbps	10Mbps
Access link queue type	Droptail	Droptail
Uniform loss rate	0-5%	0-5%

4. Performance Evaluation

4.1. Simulation Topology. In this section, we utilize the popular network simulator NS-2 [26, 27] to verify and evaluate the performance for our proposed priorities-oriented data scheduler algorithm and compare with classical MPTCP. In order to build a real and reliable MPTCP simulation environment, we embed MPTCP patch into NS-2 and then apply PO-MPTCP algorithm to the current MPTCP's simulator.

According to our previous work [6], we can find that the total Internet traffic is made up by 80%-83% of TCP traffic and 17%-20% of UDP, and the suddenness of the network background traffic increases the difficulty for deployment of MPTCP in the network. For simulating a more real network environment we will configure four TCP traffic generators and one UDP traffic generator in every router to get the 80% of TCP traffic and 20% of UDP traffic. The details are shown in Figure 3.

In Figure 3, the simulation topology forms MPTCP's sender and MPTCP's receiver, and it simultaneously fits two links together (denoted by Paths A and B) that have their own corresponding network parameters, as shown in Table 1. For simulating loss-of-frame at the network link layer, a random unified model is used for each path to set the packet loss rate which is caused by random connection competition or radio interference. At present, the bandwidth of Paths A and B is set to 11 Mbps and 10 Mbps, respectively, and Path A adopts the standard interface WiFi/IEEE802.11b, while Path B uses WiMax/IEEE 802.16 interface. In addition, the network simulation time of each path is set to 60s, and other experimental parameters are default as the values of NS-2 network simulator.

4.2. Simulation Analysis. For convenience, we denote the data result of the standard MPTCP transmission mechanism as "MPTCP" and define priority-oriented data multipath streaming media transmission mechanism proposed by us as "PO-MPTCP". In this section, we use a random unified model to uniform loss errors and take 0%-5% as the lossy rate of each path for analyzing the average throughput, average delay, jitter, and peak signal-to-noise ratio (PSNR) changes in the packet loss rate experiment.

(1) Average Throughput. In Figure 4, we can see the average throughput of standard MPTCP and PO-MPTCP at different packet loss rates. In lossy heterogeneous wireless environment, four simulation results show the influence of different packet loss rates on multimedia stream throughput, and PO-MPTCP can achieve a more reliable data transmission. When setting the same packet loss rate, PO-MPTCP achieves

```
Definition:
        PA_i: the ith path within the MPTCP session.
    RRT_{PA_i}: the RTT estimation value of path PA_i
  CWND_{PA_i}: the CWND estimation value of path PA_i
        S_i: the status information for ith path.
        Q_{list}: the quality list for each path
        P_{list}: a preferred path list selected by MDPS
(1)    for all path PA_i within a MPTCP session do
(3)        S_i = (i, RRT_{PA_i}, CWND_{PA_i})
(4)        put S_i into Q_{list}
(6)    end for
(7)    for all paths S_i within the Q_{list} do
(8)        all paths are sorted by RRT_{PA_i} values in an ascending order
(9)        if their RRT_{PA_i} values are same then
(10)            sort the paths in a descending order basing on their CWND_{PA_i} values
(11)        end if
(12)        set k = S_i ⟶ subflow index
(13)        put P_k into P_{list}
(14)        k = k + 1
(15)    end for
```

ALGORITHM 2: MDPS-based path information collection and sorting algorithm.

```
Definition:
        PO_{list}: the priority of data stream list perceived by DPAM
        PO_{D_i}: the priority information for ith data stream
        P_{list}: a preferred path list obtained by MDPS
    P_{list}(0): the first path of P_{list}
        P_{send}: a candidate path used for prioritized data delivery
When the send buffer is idle and can send packets,
(1)    for all PO_{D_i} within the PO_{list} do
(2)        if PO_{D_i} == 1 then
(3)            there is a prioritized packet to send
(4)            set P_{send} = P_{list}(0)
(5)            while the cwnd of P_{list}(0) is full do
(6)                set P_{send} = P_{list}(0) ⟶ next
(7)            end while
(8)        else then
(9)            using standard MPTCP data schedule to distribute
(10)        end if
(11)        schedule the packet over P_{send}
(12)    end for
```

ALGORITHM 3: PBPD-based data scheduling algorithm.

better average throughput than standard MPTCP with 2.28%, 8.18%, 2.69%, and 8.04% improvements, respectively. The standard MPTCP does not consider two factors: (1) the requirements of specific QoS on multimedia application; (2) the priorities of the application data and the qualities of different transmission paths in the heterogeneous network. These factors cause earlier packets which are in the MPTCP receiver buffer out of order. With the increase in the number of packets, it can cause buffer congestion and network transmission throughput reduction. Our proposed PO-MPTCP considers the data priorities and the path qualities and selects the best link to transmission;

it effectively improves the transmission performance of MPTCP.

(2) Average Delay. As an important parameter for measuring network performance, average delay is often used by researchers to determine the transmission rate of a path when it comes to researching related network protocols. Aiming to highlight the advantage for the PO-MPTCP, Figure 5 compares the average delay of PO-MPTCP and standard MPTCP with 0-5% packet loss rate. For the purpose of conveniently displaying the end-to-end transmission delay, we take the packet loss rate as an example of 0.01, as shown

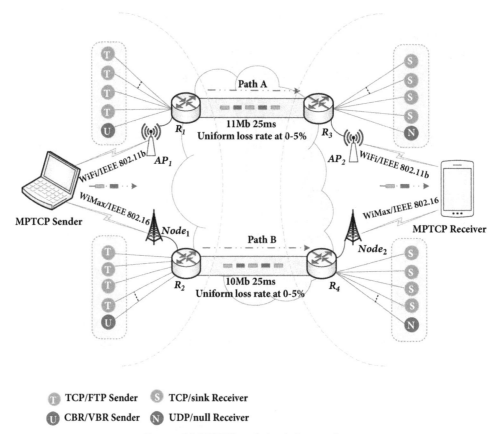

	TCP/FTP Sender		TCP/sink Receiver
	CBR/VBR Sender		UDP/null Receiver

FIGURE 3: MPTCP-based simulation topology.

in Figure 6, which shows PO-MPTCP is better than the standard MPTCP. Therefore, PO-MPTCP can improve the transmission performance and reduce the transmission delay through priority-aware data scheduling policies and link sequencing.

(3) Jitter. As far as we know, jitter is an important indicator for predicting the stability of streaming media packets, and it is usually achieved by measuring the last value of delay and the function value of packet length. We take the loss rate of 0.02 to explore the change of jitter within 60 seconds. Figure 7 illustrates that the standard MPTCP generates out-of-order packets more frequently than PO-MPTCP. PO-MPTCP can dynamically be aware of data's priority and adaptive switching path, which can better improve the transmission performance of streaming media and ensure the stability of multimedia streaming.

(4) Peak Signal-to-Noise Ratio. Streaming media services will become the core business of the future mobile Internet. So we studied the transmission performance of multimedia in the heterogeneous streaming media simulation. The performance is measured by PSNR [28] value which translates network transmission throughput and loss rate into user-perceived quality through the following equation.

$$PNSR = 20 \log_{10}\left(\frac{MAX\_Rbit}{\sqrt{(E\_Th - A\_Th)^2}}\right), \quad (1)$$

where MAX_Rbit represents the rate of the multimedia sub-flow transmission. E_Th denotes expected average throughput in network while A_Th is actual average throughput.

Figure 8 demonstrates that the PNSR of PO-MPTCP is 3.7% higher than the standard MPTCP in the heterogeneous wireless network. By analyzing the user quality experience with PSNR, PO-MPTCP can achieve a better transmission quality of streaming media and the PSNR fluctuation is more stable. Hence, compared to the existing mechanisms, PO-MPTCP can improve the user experience.

5. Conclusion

This paper presents PO-MPTCP which is a priorities-aware packet scheduler solution for multimedia multipathing services. It makes full use of its ability to identify packet priority and estimate and switch the path based on the multiattribute perception. In addition, PO-MPTCP provides a priority-driven data distribution strategy to distinguish data priority and ensure that high priority data is transmitted on the best quality path. PO-MPTCP improves the efficiency data delivery by utilizing the path-based priority-aware method. Simulation results show that PO-MPTCP provides attractive benefits in comparison with classical MPTCP including multimedia average throughput improvement, end-to-end delay reduction, and higher-stability multimedia transmission. In particular, we utilize PSNR to analyze the users service experience of PO-MPTCP, which shows that PO-MPTCP

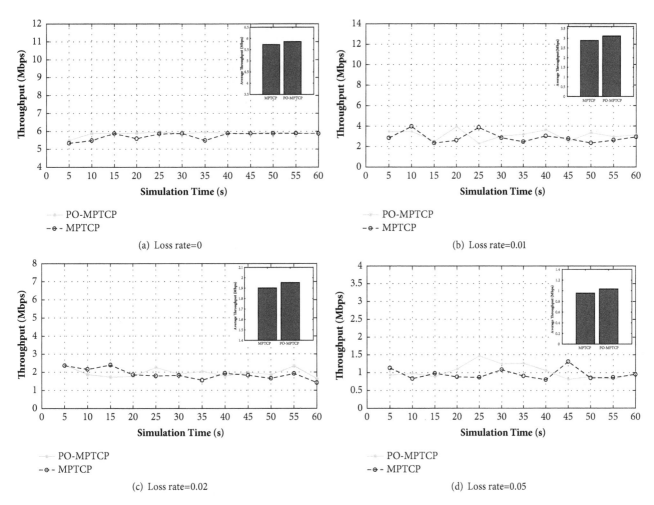

FIGURE 4: Comparison of throughput when (a) loss rate=0, (b) loss rate=0.01, (c) loss rate=0.02, and (d) loss rate=0.05.

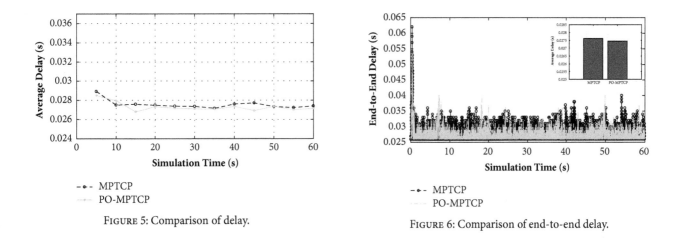

FIGURE 5: Comparison of delay.

FIGURE 6: Comparison of end-to-end delay.

can better meet the transmission quality requirements of streaming media. Our future work will concentrate on deploying PO-MPTCP in actual systems, enabling PO-MPTCP to satisfy high bandwidth requirements for multimedia applications and delay intolerance. In addition, we have studied the practical significance of priority-based queue management, and it provided a theoretical basis for the deployment of MPTCP protocol in future wireless networks.

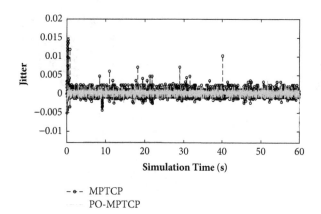

FIGURE 7: Comparison of jitter.

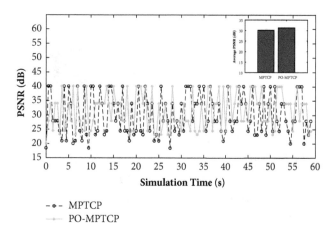

FIGURE 8: Comparison of streaming media PSNR.

Acknowledgments

This work was supported by the National Natural Science Foundation of China (NSFC) under grant no. 61562044; the Natural Science Foundation of Jiangxi Province under grant no. 20171BAB212014; the Project of Soft Science Research Plan of Jiangxi Province under grant no. 20161BBA10010; and the Jiangxi Province Graduate Innovation Project under grant no. YC2017-S144.

References

[1] J. Wu, B. Cheng, C. Yuen, Y. Shang, and J. Chen, "Distortion-aware concurrent multipath transfer for mobile video streaming in heterogeneous wireless networks," *IEEE Transactions on Mobile Computing*, vol. 14, no. 4, pp. 688–701, 2015.

[2] "Facebook," https://www.facebook.com/.

[3] "WeChat," https://www.wechat.com/.

[4] "YouTube," https://www.youtube.com/.

[5] X. Liu, D. Shan, R. Shu, and T. Zhang, "MPTCP tunnel: an architecture for aggregating bandwidth of heterogeneous access networks," *Wireless Communications Mobile Computing*, vol. 2018, Article ID 2045760, 11 pages, 2018.

[6] J. Zeng, Y. Cao, F. Ke, M. Huang, G. Zhang, and W. Lu, "Performance evaluation of secure multipath retransmission mechanism in next generation heterogeneous communication systems," *IET Networks*, vol. 7, no. 2, pp. 61–67, 2018.

[7] Y. Cao, F. Song, G. Luo et al., "(PU)2M2: A potentially underperforming-aware path usage management mechanism for secure MPTCP-based multipathing services," *Concurrency & Computation Practice & Experience*, vol. 30, no. 3, 2017.

[8] J. Wu, B. Cheng, M. Wang, and J. Chen, "Quality-Aware Energy Optimization in Wireless Video Communication with Multipath TCP," *IEEE/ACM Transactions on Networking*, vol. 25, no. 5, pp. 2701–2718, 2017.

[9] R. Matsufuji, D. Cavendish, K. Kumazoe, D. Nobayashi, and T. Ikenaga, "Multipath TCP path schedulers for streaming video," in *Proceedings of the 2017 IEEE Pacific Rim Conference on Communications, Computers and Signal Processing, PACRIM 2017*, pp. 1–6, Victoria, Canada, August 2017.

[10] J. Wu, C. Yuen, B. Cheng, M. Wang, and J. Chen, "Streaming High-Quality Mobile Video with Multipath TCP in Hetero-geneous Wireless Networks," *IEEE Transactions on Mobile Computing*, vol. 15, no. 9, pp. 2345–2361, 2016.

[11] C. Xu, W. Quan, A. V. Vasilakos, H. Zhang, and G.-M. Muntean, "Information-centric cost-efficient optimization for multimedia content delivery in mobile vehicular networks," *Computer Communications*, vol. 99, pp. 93–106, 2017.

[12] Y. Cao, Q. Liu, Y. Zuo, F. Ke, H. Wang, and M. Huang, "Receiver-centric buffer blocking-aware multipath data distribution in MPTCP-based heterogeneous wireless networks," *KSII Transactions on Internet and Information Systems*, vol. 10, no. 10, pp. 4642–4660, 2016.

[13] Y. Morikoshi, H. Abe, and K. Kato, "HayACK: Exploiting characteristically diverse paths to achieve quick ACKing in MPTCP," in *Proceedings of the 9th IEEE International Conference on Cloud Computing Technology and Science, CloudCom 2017*, pp. 383–390, Hong Kong, China, December 2017.

[14] J. Kim, B.-H. Oh, and J. Lee, "Receive Buffer based Path Management for MPTCP in heterogeneous networks," in *Proceedings of the 15th IFIP/IEEE International Symposium on Integrated Network and Service Management, IM 2017*, pp. 648–651, Lisbon, Portugal, May 2017.

[15] C. Jonghwan, D. Han, J. Kim, and C.-K. Kim, "Machine learning based path management for mobile devices over MPTCP," in *Proceedings of the 2017 IEEE International Conference on Big Data and Smart Computing, BigComp 2017*, pp. 206–209, Jeju, Republic of Korea, February 2017.

[16] B. Y. L. Kimura, D. C. S. F. Lima, and A. A. F. Loureiro, "Alternative scheduling decisions for multipath TCP," *IEEE Communications Letters*, vol. 21, no. 11, pp. 2412–2415, 2017.

[17] B. Hayes, Y. Chang, and G. Riley, "Adaptive bitrate video delivery using HTTP/2 over MPTCP architecture," in *Proceedings of the 13th IEEE International Wireless Communications and Mobile Computing Conference, IWCMC 2017*, pp. 68–73, Spain, June 2017.

[18] C. Xu, P. Zhang, S. Jia, M. Wang, and G.-M. Muntean, "Video streaming in content-centric mobile networks: challenges and solutions," *IEEE Wireless Communications Magazine*, vol. 24, no. 5, pp. 157–165, 2017.

[19] Y. Cao, Q. Liu, G. Luo, Y. Yi, and M. Huang, "PR-MPTCP+: Context-aware QoE-oriented multipath TCP partial reliability extension for real-time multimedia applications," in *Proceedings of the 2016 IEEE Visual Communication and Image Processing, VCIP 2016*, pp. 1–4, Chengdu, China, November 2016.

[20] M. A. Jan, P. Nanda, X. He, and R. P. Liu, "PASCCC: priority-based application-specific congestion control clustering protocol," *Computer Networks*, vol. 74, pp. 92–102, 2014.

[21] S. Iniya Shree, M. Karthiga, and C. Mariyammal, "Improving congestion control in WSN by multipath routing with priority based scheduling," in *Proceedings of the 2017 International Conference on Inventive Systems and Control, ICISC 2017*, Coimbatore, India, January 2017.

[22] P. Sabbagh, M. Alaei, and F. Yazdanpanah, "A priority based method for congestion control in Wireless Multimedia Sensor Networks," in *Proceedings of the 8th International Conference on Information and Knowledge Technology, IKT 2016*, pp. 177–182, Hamedan, Iran, September 2016.

[23] A. Skrastins and J. Jelinskis, "Priority-based Session Admission Control method for next generation Internet," in *Proceedings of the 2nd International Conference on Fog and Mobile Edge Computing, FMEC 2017*, pp. 153–158, Valencia, Spain, May 2017.

[24] N. V. Listova, V. V. Fedorenko, V. V. Samoylenko, and I. V. Samoylenko, "Markov's Model of the Different-Priority Traffic Routing Control in a Sensor Node," in *Proceedings of the 2017 IVth International Conference on Engineering and Telecommunication (EnT)*, pp. 155–159, Moscow, Russia, November 2017.

[25] E. Exposito, M. Gineste, L. Dairaine, and C. Chassot, "Building self-optimized communication systems based on applicative cross-layer information," *Computer Standards & Interfaces*, vol. 31, no. 2, pp. 354–361, 2009.

[26] U. C. Berkeley, LBL, USC/ISI and Xerox Parc, NS-2 documentation and software, version 2.35.

[27] Google Code Project, "Multipath-TCP: Implement multipath TCP on NS-2," http://code.google.com/p/multipath-tcp/.

[28] C.-H. Lin, C.-K. Shieh, C.-H. Ke, N. K. Chilamkurti, and S. Zeadally, "An adaptive cross-layer mapping algorithm for MPEG-4 video transmission over IEEE 802.11e WLAN," *Telecommunication Systems*, vol. 42, no. 3-4, pp. 223–234, 2009.

7

A Novel Steganography Technique for SDTV-H.264/AVC Encoded Video

Christian Di Laura, Diego Pajuelo, and Guillermo Kemper

School of Electrical Engineering, Peruvian University of Applied Sciences, Lima 33, Peru

Correspondence should be addressed to Christian Di Laura; christian.dilaura@gmail.com

Academic Editor: Massimiliano Laddomada

Today, eavesdropping is becoming a common issue in the rapidly growing digital network and has foreseen the need for secret communication channels embedded in digital media. In this paper, a novel steganography technique designed for Standard Definition Digital Television (SDTV) H.264/AVC encoded video sequences is presented. The algorithm introduced here makes use of the compression properties of the Context Adaptive Variable Length Coding (CAVLC) entropy encoder to achieve a low complexity and real-time inserting method. The chosen scheme hides the private message directly in the H.264/AVC bit stream by modifying the AC frequency quantized residual luminance coefficients of intrapredicted I-frames. In order to avoid error propagation in adjacent blocks, an interlaced embedding strategy is applied. Likewise, the steganography technique proposed allows self-detection of the hidden message at the target destination. The code source was implemented by mixing MATLAB 2010 b and Java development environments. Finally, experimental results have been assessed through objective and subjective quality measures and reveal that less visible artifacts are produced with the technique proposed by reaching PSNR values above 40.0 dB and an embedding bit rate average per secret communication channel of 425 bits/sec. This exemplifies that steganography is affordable in digital television.

1. Introduction

Over the past decade, digital media have become, without a doubt, part of our daily life. The recent technological achievements in electrical and communications engineering have made feasible the existence of a digital connected world and enormous amounts of data exchange. However, this situation has lately exposed digital media to eavesdropping, counterfeit, and even sabotage, turning it into a major security problem. In pursuit of secure communications, data ciphering techniques have been typically applied and preferred rather than other hiding methods. Notwithstanding, these strategies have failed to protect the reliability of the message itself and have made it completely vulnerable to malicious attacks. In view of this, data concealment techniques, such as steganography, have increased their relevance and catched the attention of researchers. "Steganography," from the Greek *steganos graphos*, means "covered writing" and is considered the art of hiding secret data into a carrier medium so as

to convey the confidential message in such a way that it cannot be noticed or detected [1]. A basic steganography framework consists of an embedder and a detector. The first introduces the secret data using a special algorithm into the cover work, generating the so-called stegoobject, and the latter is responsible for extracting the hidden message using the right algorithm.

As of this writing, there have been plenty of research works on the use of media files, such as audio, images, and video, as cover files for steganography. However, they are not designed and applied to current leading technologies, for example, digital television.

Nowadays, digital terrestrial television broadcasting has been successfully implemented. This technology implies the coding and compression of a high quality audio and video source, using a digital video standard and subsequent digital transmission. In order to reach digital television, several video standards have been proposed: H.261 [2], H.262 [3], H.264/AVC [4], and the latest H.265/High Efficiency Video

Coding (HEVC) [5] (which is still under development for digital television). H.264/AVC, the standard most used in practice, has introduced several improvements on the hybrid video encoding paradigm by adding new coding techniques in the spatial, transform, and residual domain, in search of compression. These changes are mainly seen in the use of new prediction schemes for intra- and interprediction, of variable block size within macroblocks, of a new transform core, of the first entropy coding tools that take into account the importance of the context of the data being coded, and of adaptive strategies to reduce the bit rate. The first television specification using H.264/AVC was the Brazilian Digital Television Standard (SBTVD-T), and it is expected that all digital terrestrial television standards will start using it in the coming years.

Under these circumstances, the lack of steganography techniques and applications designed for digital television becomes a field of much interest. Currently, there are no steganography techniques designed for digital television. Furthermore, similar implementations are limited to the use of audio [6] and images [7, 8] as cover media. The most important related works consist of academic articles on watermaking (similar to steganography with the important difference that the data to be concealed is related to the cover file). Nevertheless, only a few of them are suitable for digital television broadcasting, where a real-time, medium embedding-strength, no bit rate increasing technique is desired.

In [9], for example, an interesting watermarking technique was applied by making use of the coding properties of the CAVLC and inter-prediction. The secret message is embedded in the sign bit of the high frequency coefficients, coded as trailing ones, and in fixed bit codes used in transform blocks of inter-predicted frames. Although the original bit rate is not changed, this technique does not consider the error propagation originated by intra-prediction and leaves the possibility of embedding more data into the video stream.

On the other hand, in [10], a self-detection, random watermarking technique using a key-dependent strategy was proposed. The odd and even characteristics of the quantized residual coefficients are used to hide and identify watermarking bits. As a result, a bit rate increment of less than 1% is achieved using this algorithm. This proposal does not take in account the changes on the local context properties and the final perception of the viewer, as it selects the watermark coefficient randomly, so creating possible visual artifacts.

In [11], the authors suggested the use of a perceptual analysis in order to create a robust watermarking technique for H.264/AVC video. This method uses a human vision model created by Watson [12] that embeds the watermark bits in the quantized residual luminance coefficients of which the quantization step size is at least changed by one. By this procedure, embedding capacity is gained. Even if the human perception is considered, this technique increases the bit rate by more than 5% and demands more computational resources. In addition, the perception model from Watson was initially thought for Joint Pictures Expert Group (JPEG) still images based on the Discrete Cosine Transform (DCT).

H.264/AVC uses another type of transform: the Integer Cosine Transform (ICT), of which the properties tend to be those of the discrete cosine transform but are indeed not completely the same.

Finally, the works cited use only objective quality measures in order to validate their simulation results and the embedding strength of their techniques. However, they do not consider the human real perception of the resultant encoded video sequences. Hence, subjective quality measures must be considered in future works.

This paper aims to present a real-time, low-complexity, self-detection, and reduced-error-propagation-oriented algorithm, which maintains the bit rate of the stegovideo sequences for digital television. For this purpose, secret messages are hidden in the high frequency coefficients of intrapredicted luminance blocks in an interlaced way and making use of the properties of the entropy coder. In addition, simulation results are analyzed with an objective and subjective perception criterion.

The paper is organized as follows: Section 2 briefly presents the extraction and insertion process of video from digital television and discusses details of the embedding, detection, and enhanced features of the steganography proposal. Section 3 shows the experimental results from objective and subjective quality measures. Finally, Section 4 describes the most remarkable conclusions and provides guidelines for future works.

2. Scheme Proposed

In order to apply steganography to H.264/AVC video sequences from digital television, these need to be separated from the raw digital television bit stream. The way the scheme proposed solves this issue is part of the preprocessing stage of the final algorithm. The digital television stream contains video, audio, control, and synchronization information of different television programs, specially packed using the MPEG-2 Systems specification, also known as transport stream (TS) [13, 14]. The TS standard explains how different television programs composed of audio and video packets, both considered Packetized Elementary Stream (PES), control information, and Programs Specific Information (PSI) composed of the Program Association Tables (PAT), Program Map Tables (PMT), and timing information provided by the Program Clock Reference (PCR), are alternately addressed and labeled with a Packet Identifier (PID) and joined into one compliant bit stream. The selected scheme extracts the Elementary Stream (ES) corresponding to the H.264/AVC video of one of the television programs. The insertion mechanism operates in the same way, but in reverse order. A detailed description of both processes, including the embedding of the secret message using steganography and new features of the proposal, is depicted in Figure 1. It is important to emphasize again that there are currently no state-of-the-art steganography techniques designed for digital television.

2.1. H.264/AVC Detection from MPEG-2 TS. A MPEG-2 TS is composed of 188-byte-long transport packets that contain video, audio, data, and control information of the television

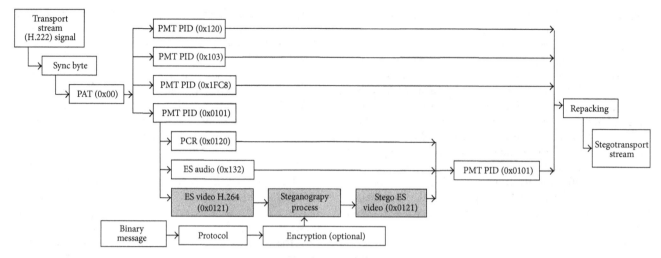

FIGURE 1: Overview of the scheme proposed.

programs. All of these signals are multiplexed in one bit stream. The first step in the entire preembedding process is to extract the video ES of the chosen program from the TS. The procedure works as follows:

(i) *Synchronizing with the transport stream*: The decoder fetches the synchronization byte in the TS, of which the value is always 0x47 base 16 (HEX). Each synchronization byte must be 188 bytes spaced, without considering any additional data introduced for Forward Error Correction (FEC), before its pattern is repeated.

(ii) *Program Specific Information (PSI)*: There are two relevant tables that describe the instantaneous structure of the transport stream and are sent as part of the control information. The first table is the PAT, which is identified when the PID value equals 0x000 HEX as specified in the standard. This table shows the total programs being carried in the TS and their related PID labels. The second table is the PMT. This table allows associating each PID of an ES, such as video, audio, or additional control data, with its corresponding television program.

(iii) *Accessing a program*: After the PIDs of all ES have become known, it is possible to have access to any program carried by the TS and, therefore, to distinguish between different ES. Assuming that the video and audio PID values are 0x121 HEX and 0x132 HEX, respectively, the stream packets of which the PID value equals 0x121 HEX will be assembled into one video ES and supplied to the next decoding phase (the same will happen if the TS is fetched for the audio ES).

After splitting the TS, one video ES is chosen for embedding purposes. Normally, the first video frame to be decoded is called Intraframe (or I-frame), as it is predicted from samples previously decoded belonging to the same frame. In addition, the TS bit stream format allows the detection of I-frames by using a special byte known as *random access indicator*. In some cases, the first frame will have two

partitions or slices: the top is predicted by intraprediction and the bottom by interprediction (also known as P-slice), as is predicted from samples previously coded belonging to other frames or slices.

2.2. Data Hiding Procedure in the H.264/AVC Sequence.

The I-frame, where the secret data will be embedded, is divided into 16×16-pixel regions defined as macroblocks (this way of splitting is done for coding and compression efficiency purposes). Depending on the intraprediction scheme selected during the coding process, they are once more divided into 4×4 or 8×8 block sections. H.264/AVC offers three types of intraprediction modes, mainly intra-16×16, intra-4×4, and intra-8×8 (used in high profiles and some television applications). Generally, intra-16×16 is chosen for frames or slices (part of a frame) with predominant smooth areas and the intra-4×4 for the ones that contain rich amount of details. Intra-8×8 is an especial case and will not be considered in this work. Likewise, since human eyes are more sensitive to changes in flat areas, only intra-4×4 macroblocks have been chosen for data embedding.

Take into account an I-frame, containing a macroblock region that is coded using intra-4×4 prediction mode and divided into block sections of 4×4 dimensions (further known separately as "T" blocks). Now, define "$P(i, j)$" as the pixel values of "T" and "$I(i, j)$" as the corresponding intraprediction block, where "i" and "j" stand for the discrete indexes of the rows and columns of the frame, respectively. Their difference, or residual matrix, is labeled as "$R(i, j)$."

H.264/AVC uses the ICT, based on a 4×4 dimensional and standardized core, for coding luminance and chrominance residual blocks. Thus, "$R(i, j)$" is transformed, scaled, and quantized warranting the orthogonality and orthonormality properties during the process as explained in [15], generating "$C'(u, v)_t$." Consider "$C'(u, v)_t$" as the residual quantized ICT coefficients of block "T," "$S(u, v)_t$" as the steganography data (in binary form) to be embedded, "$C''(u, v)_t$" as the residual quantized ICT coefficients to which steganography has been applied, "Trc" as an

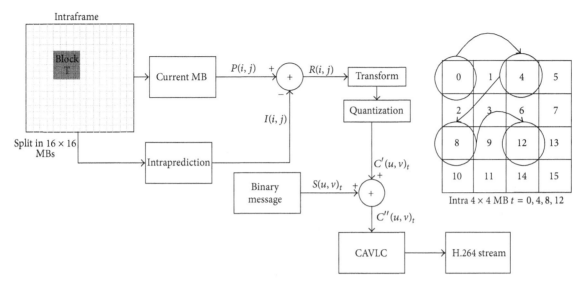

FIGURE 2: Steganography in H.264/AVC.

experimental-achieved threshold, and "u," "v," and "t" as discrete indexes within block "T." The embedding strategy works as follows.

If "$S(u, v)_t = 0 \wedge C'(u, v)_t > \text{Trc.}$" then

$$
C''(u, v)_t = \begin{cases} C'(u, v)_t - 1; & \text{if } C'(u, v)_t \bmod 2 = 1 \\ C'(u, v)_t; & \text{if } C'(u, v)_t \bmod 2 = 0 \end{cases} \quad (1)
$$

$$
u = 0, 1, 2, 4, \quad v = 0, 1, 2, 4, \quad t = 0, 4, 8, 12,
$$

where "$C'(u, v)_t \bmod 2$" returns the remainder after "$C'(u, v)_t$" is divided by "2." The sign of the result is the same as the divisor.

If "$S(u, v)_t = 1 \wedge C'(u, v)_t > \text{Trc.}$" then

$$
C''(u, v)_t = \begin{cases} C'(u, v)_t; & \text{if } C'(u, v)_t \bmod 2 = 1 \\ C'(u, v)_t - 1; & \text{if } C'(u, v)_t \bmod 2 = 0. \end{cases} \quad (2)
$$

According to Figure 2, the steganographic algorithm proposed works at a quantization level because the sending is a lossless operation and information embedded will not change in reception. The embedding algorithm consists in separating the embeddable block from closer neighbors, inside a macroblock, and leaving one macroblock of space between embeddable macroblocks. The separate spaces where the message is to be hidden are used to reduce visible artifacts, so that subjective quality is not degraded.

There is an exceptional case where the self-collusion attack must be avoided. This is accomplished when "$C'(u, v)_t = \text{Trc} + 1 \wedge S(u, v)_t = 0.$" The expected result using (1) would be the same coefficient reduced by one level. However, at the receiver side, the original bit of the hidden message will be lost and the recovering processes will fail. For this reason and only for this special case, the coefficient level is incremented by one. It should be noted that the binary message being embedded could be distributed to make

this singular condition less probable. In addition, the stego TS produced does not differ from the original bit stream structure. This is achieved since the bit stream alienation and Program Clock Reference (PCR) are respected and preserved. The algorithm makes use of CAVLC features for limited control of bit rate. The target is to maintain the same H.264 sequence length or decrease some bytes in order to be able to insert the stego-H.264 sequence in the same amount of TS packets.

Four facts must be considered so as not to increase the bit rate:

(i) Not hiding in zero macroblocks.

(ii) Not choosing Trailing Ones coefficients (T1s), as they have a defined code.

(iii) Not choosing zero coefficients in any nonzero macroblock, as the length will be increased.

(iv) Reducing luminance ICT coefficients in one level that will produce a smaller length than the original.

Finally, the resultant I-frame is repacked into the TS and so ready to be transmitted.

2.3. Hidden Message Extraction. The retrieval of the hidden message is fast and simple. By applying the same process shown in Figure 2 to extract an I-frame, and after entropy decoding the H.264/AVC video, embeddable macroblocks are chosen and ready to extract the hidden message. The way the secret message is recovered, bit by bit, is given in

$$
S(u, v)_t = \begin{cases} 0; & \text{if } C''(u, v)_t \bmod 2 = 0 \\ 1; & \text{if } C''(u, v)_t \bmod 2 = 1. \end{cases} \quad (3)
$$

2.4. Embedding Protocol and Ciphering. With the purpose of enhancing the security of the embedded message and warranting self-detection at the target destination, the proposal ciphers the hidden message prior to the steganography technique using the RC4 algorithm [16] and wraps it into a special designed protocol, which ensures self-detection at the end-peer. RC4, which was chosen due to its programming simplicity and performance [17], encrypts the message by using a private key. Thus, if the steganographic algorithm is broken, the enemy would have to know the secret key and cipher algorithm.

To sum up, in this section a novel and low-complexity steganographic algorithm for digital television was presented. The proposed scheme first decodes the TS from digital television, extracting H.264/AVC video sequences. Afterwards, these are decoded and searched for intrapredicted luma regions, where the secret and previously ciphered messages are hidden into the ICT high frequency residual coefficients using an interlaced embedding strategy and exploiting the properties of the CAVLC entropy encoder, depicted in the steganographic method. Finally, the resultant stegovideo sequences are repacked into the TS stream.

3. Experimental Results

A software simulation of the proposed steganography technique was implemented by mixing MATLAB 2010 b and Java development environments. The most important achievements of the program are the MPEG-2 Systems and H.264/AVC integration, a proprietary code that meets standards. In addition, a novel CAVLC entropy encoder scheme using a lookup-table strategy extracted from [18] is accomplished. This allowed improving the overall encoding and decoding speed for residual luminance coefficients. All experiments are conducted using a transport stream sample from a typical free-to-air television channel, from which three different cover video sequences from the daily program list were extracted. The selected video sequences differed in the changes within the scenes and were addressed as static, moderate, and highly variant.

Static video is characterized by slow and almost null motion in the scene, where the focus of the camera is commonly centered on capturing one object. The moderately variant video is characterized by some scene changes, and highly variant video is distinguished by the fast alternation of uncorrelated scenes. In order to prove the embedding capacity of each video sequence and the amount of distortion introduced, three different randomly selected and different-length secret messages were prepared. Simulation results were compared using two different quality measures. One of them was the objective quality measure known as Peak Signal to Noise Ratio (PSNR) [19] which is a widely adopted method used in engineering to measure the amount of distortion introduced by compression, comparing the original with the stegovideo frames in a pure mathematical way, and the other was the subjective perceptual criterion known as Subjective Difference Grade (SDG), based on ITU-R BS.1116 [20]. The latter was successfully implemented in [21] and is now applied to digital television.

Unlike PSNR, SDG considers the viewer's opinion by taking a survey. The SDG procedure works as follows: There

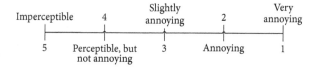

FIGURE 3: Subjective test scores.

are three different digital television sequences labeled as "A," "B," and "C." "A" is always the original sequence, while "B" and "C" are randomly scrambled and one of them contains the original and the other the stegosequence. The viewer is asked to watch "A" and informed that this is the original one and then "B" and "C" without telling them about the content of both sequences. Then, the viewer is requested to punctuate the distortion perceived in "B" in relation to "A" and "C" in relation to "A." The possible marks that can be chosen for this subjective test are detailed in Figure 3, where 5 is assigned when no difference is perceived and 1 when it is very annoying.

After the survey, the SDG value is calculated as a special quality measure function. In this paper, the SDG value is obtained from the difference between the punctuation assigned to the stegofile and the original, as shown in

$$SDG = Score_{Stego} - Score_{Original}. \qquad (4)$$

If the SDG value becomes highly negative, it means that noticeable distortion has been introduced by the steganography technique. If it turns positive or close to zero, however, it can be inferred that perceptual degradation has not been perceived and subjective quality is better.

3.1. Simulation Conditions. The sequences used during the simulations had the following common properties: All are coded in H.264/AVC high profile, use the CAVLC entropy coder and a frame rate of 30 fps, and have a spatial resolution of 720×480 pixels. In addition, the quantization parameter of each macroblock is not fixed and varies adaptively within the different frames, as well as the scan order which could be interlaced or progressive. Furthermore, each test sequence lasts 15 seconds. The opinion survey consists of 27 different questions with a sample of 30 people aged between 20 and 30 years in a well-illuminated environment. These tests consolidate three different message lengths and three different steganography techniques. The steganographic methods are composed of [10], an earlier version of the proposed technique without considering the interlaced strategy explained in Figure 2 and with the main difference that the discrete index "t" had the range $t = 0, 1, \ldots, 15$ and the final proposal. Likewise, the method complexity of [10] and the proposal is depicted in Table 1. The message lengths are estimated as a percentage of the maximum embedding capacity of each video excerpt using the technique in [10].

3.2. Simulation Results. Figure 4 depicts the PSNR of frame 30 for the method proposed in [10], for the steganographic method without interlaced strategy, and for the final proposal, tested with three different messages lengths and three

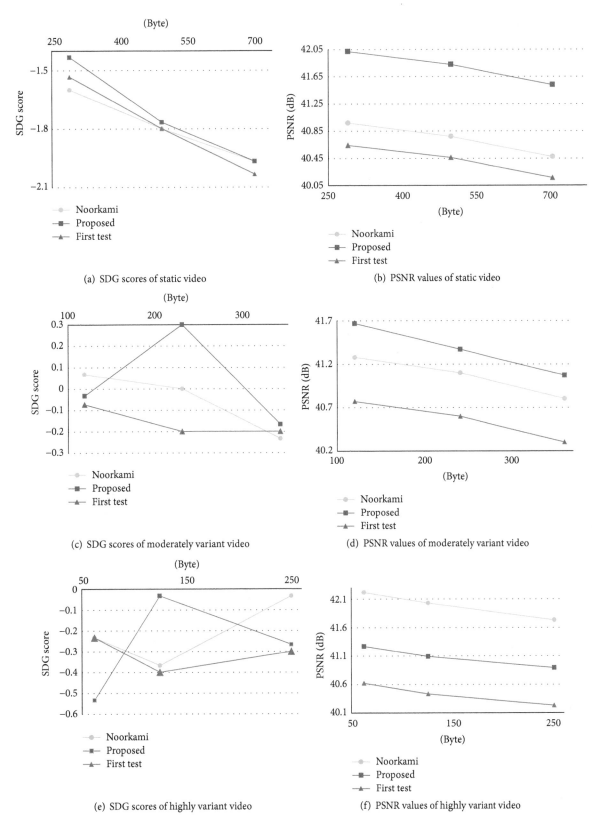

(a) SDG scores of static video

(b) PSNR values of static video

(c) SDG scores of moderately variant video

(d) PSNR values of moderately variant video

(e) SDG scores of highly variant video

(f) PSNR values of highly variant video

FIGURE 4: SDG scores and PSNR values achieved with the first test, proposed algorithm, and [10].

TABLE 1: Comparative table of the technique proposed and [10].

Technique	Hiding component	Applied to	Security	Computational complexity	Maximum embedding bits/Macroblock	Perceptual awareness	Key feature
Reference [10]	CAVLC code word	Intrapredicted I-frames (luminance samples)	Key-dependent strategy based on a public key extracted from the local macroblock features and a private key owned at the target destination	Low	One	No: the algorithm can change low and high frequency residual ICT quantized coefficients	Hidden data randomness due to a key and local macroblock derivatives dependent algorithm
Proposed	CAVLC code word	Intrapredicted I-frames (luminance samples)	The secret message is ciphered using a private key [16] prior to the embedding process and divided into byte units	Lower (security does not rely on the local macroblock features, which demands higher computational resources)	Four	Yes: the algorithm is designed to change only high frequency residual ICT quantized coefficients and in an interlaced way, in order to try to avoid perceptual degradation and error propagation.	Deep understanding of the coding properties of the CAVLC entropy encoder for bit rate control and rapid embedding algorithm purposes

different digital television sequences, respectively. The simulation results show that the PSNR values tend to decrease as the embedded message size increases. However, all the PSNR values are above 40 dB, which is an acceptable range for steganography techniques in the H.264/AVC. In addition, this denotes that the objective quality of the stegosequences is good and that few errors are introduced by the embedding techniques. The results also illustrate that better PSNR values are achieved by the technique proposed for moderately variant and static video, slightly outperforming both [10] and the technique without interlaced strategy. Figure 5 depicts frame 30 of the original video frame, the secret data, and the stegoframe for the different types of video.

Dissimilar results from the PSNR analysis are obtained with respect to the SDG values. These are shown in Figures 4(a), 4(c), and 4(e) and are tested under the same simulation conditions depicted in Figures 4(b), 4(d), and 4(f). First of all, the static sequence clearly shows that as the embedding data length increases, the SDG value rapidly decreases due to high light intensity and fewer camera movements, because the camera is focusing on the center of the scene where the presenter is talking. However, it is a fact that the human eye gets easily used to quasi-invariant scenes and smaller changes are quickly recognized. On the other hand, it is interesting to note that some highly and moderately variant excerpts got positive or near to zero SDG values during the survey. This can be only justified by the movement between the scenes, which becomes an important topic for the analysis,

since changes mask the slight distortions introduced by the steganography technique and increase the complexity of the viewer's choice. For this reason, the PSNR is not sufficient criterion to decide if the designed steganography technique outperforms the other ones. For example, the static video has acceptable PSNR values, but it is the viewer's opinion that it is of bad quality. In this context, it should be pointed out that the steganography technique of the proposal slightly outperforms the rest of hiding methods in the SDG simulations. The technique proposed does not change the ICT coefficient randomly as in [10]. Furthermore, the free spaces left between embeddable macroblocks and the special strategy to select the embeddable blocks manage to reduce visible artifacts and improve the objective and subjective quality of the stegosequences on average. Finally, Table 2 shows the embedded bit rates reached by the proposal and by [10] for several video sequences from digital television, as well as the bit rate increase in percentage related to the original video excerpts.

It should be noted that the technique proposed reached an average embedded bit rate of approximately 425 bits/sec per secret communication channel, without increasing the original video bit rate, but slightly decreasing it instead, and so exemplifying the bit rate control of the proposal over the CAVLC encoder. Table 2 is relevant, as it describes the possible bandwidth limits that applications of steganography in SDTV will face.

(a) Original static video frame

(b) Stegoframe of static video

(c) Original moderately variant video frame

(d) Stegoframe of moderately variant video

(e) Original highly variant video frame

(f) Stegoframe of highly variant video

FIGURE 5: Stegovideo frames excerpts after hiding a secret message (secret data of 80-byte length: *"the two companies are at the forefront of a tantalizing wireless communications concept that has proved hard to produce on a big scale: reduce cellphone costs by relying on strategically placed Wi-Fi routers. And when there are no routers available, fall back on the traditional cellular network"*).

TABLE 2: Embedded bit rate in bits/sec for the technique proposed and that of [10].

Test sequence	Reference [10]		Proposed	
	Embedded bit rate in bits/sec	Bit rate increase in %	Embedded bit rate in bits/sec	Bit rate increase in %
Highly variant	402	0.33	400	−0.16
Moderately variant	544	0.51	464	−0.02
Static	384	0.79	416	>−0.01

4. Conclusion

In this paper, a novel, real-time, affordable, and compressed domain steganography technique for SDBTV digital television sequences is discussed. The secret message is hidden in the high frequency luminance ICT coefficients of intrapredicted 4×4 macroblocks using an interlaced embedding strategy. Furthermore, self-detection at the target destination and enhanced security features are achieved by applying a special embedding protocol and ciphering the secret data prior to the steganographic process.

Simulation results show that the technique proposed maintains a good subjective quality of the stegosequence and that the PSNR analysis is not sufficient criterion to assure that the perceptual quality will not be degraded during the steganographic process. It is very important to take into account the viewer's real perception. This was proved by the different results achieved between the SDG and PSNR measure. Finally, it is worth mentioning that a special care should be provided to static sequences, where slight changes may cause annoying visual artifacts.

A first steganography technique designed for digital television is here presented. In future works, the scheme proposed will be based on intrapredicted 8×8 macroblocks with an adaptive brightness algorithm to reduce the embedding capacity in static sequences and thus preserve subjective quality. In addition, new standardized algorithms for an objective quality measure are under investigation.

Competing Interests

The authors declare that they have no competing interests.

Acknowledgments

The authors would like to thank the Peruvian Institute of Radio and Television (IRTP) for providing the digital television sequences that the work was based on.

References

[1] I. Cox, M. Miller, J. Bloom, J. Fridrich, and T. Kalker, *Digital Watermaking and Steganography*, Morgan Kauffmann, 2008.

[2] ITU-T, "Video codec for audiovisual services at p × 64 kbit/s," Recommendation H.261, ITU-T, 1993.

[3] ISO/IEC 13818-2 and ITU-T Rec. H.262.0, "Information technology—generic coding of moving pictures and associated audio information: video," ISO/IEC JTC 1 and ITU-T, 1995.

[4] ISO/IEC and ITU-T, "Advanced video coding for generic audio-visual services," ISO/IEC 14496-10 and ITU-T Recommendation H.264, ISO/IEC JTC 1, ITU-T, 2010.

[5] G. J. Sullivan, J.-R. Ohm, W.-J. Han, and T. Wiegand, "Overview of the high efficiency video coding (HEVC) standard," *IEEE Transactions on Circuits and Systems for Video Technology*, vol. 22, no. 12, pp. 1649–1668, 2012.

[6] G. Nehru and P. Dhar, "A detailed look of audio steganography techniques using LSB and genetic algorithm approach," *International Journal of Computer Science Issues*, vol. 9, pp. 402–406, 2012.

[7] K.-C. Chang, C.-P. Chang, P. S. Huang, and T.-M. Tu, "A novel image steganographic method using tri-way pixel-value differencing," *Journal of Multimedia*, vol. 3, no. 2, pp. 37–44, 2008.

[8] Y.-F. Sun, D.-M. Niu, G.-M. Tang, and Z.-Z. Gao, "Optimized LSB matching steganography based on Fisher information," *Journal of Multimedia*, vol. 7, no. 4, pp. 295–302, 2012.

[9] B. Mobasseri and Y. N. Raikar, "Authentication of H.264 streams by direct watermarking of CAVLC blocks," in *Security, Steganography, and Watermarking of Multimedia Contents IX*, vol. 6505 of *Proceedings of SPIE*, The International Society for Optical Engineering, San Jose, Calif, USA, January 2007.

[10] M. Noorkami and R. M. Mersereau, "Compressed-domain video watermarking for H. 264," in *Proceedings of the IEEE International Conference on Image Processing (ICIP '05)*, vol. 2, pp. 890–893, Genova, Italy, September 2005.

[11] M. Noorkami and R. M. Mersereau, "A framework for robust watermarking of H.264-encoded video with controllable detection performance," *IEEE Transactions on Information Forensics and Security*, vol. 2, no. 1, pp. 14–23, 2007.

[12] A. B. Watson, "DCT quantization matrices visually optimized for individual images," in *Human Vision, Visual Processing, and Digital Display IV*, vol. 1913 of *Proceedings of SPIE*, pp. 202–216, San Jose, Calif, USA, September 1993.

[13] ISO/IEC and ITU-T, "Information technology—generic coding of moving pictures and associated audio information: systems," ISO/IEC 13818-1 and ITU-T Recommendation H.222.0, ISO/IEC JCT 1, ITU-T, 2006.

[14] J. Arnold, M. Frater, and M. Pickeking, *Digital Television Technology and Standards*, John Wiley & Sons, 2007.

[15] I. E. Richardson, *H.264 and MPEG-4 Video Compression: Video Coding for Next-Generation Multimedia*, John Wiley & Sons, New York, NY, USA, 2003.

[16] W. Stallings, *The RC04 Stream Encryption Algorithm*, 2005, http://cse.spsu.edu/afaruque/it6833/RC4.pdf.

[17] S. O. Sharif and S. P. Mansoor, "Performance analysis of stream and block cipher algorithms," in *Proceedings of the 3rd International Conference on Advanced Computer Theory and Engineering (ICACTE '10)*, pp. V1522–V1525, Chengdu, China, August 2010.

[18] Y. Yi and B. C. Song, "High-speed CAVLC encoder for 1080p 60-Hz H.264 codec," *IEEE Signal Processing Letters*, vol. 15, pp. 891–894, 2008.

[19] S. Winkler and P. Mohandas, "The evolution of video quality measurement: from PSNR to hybrid metrics," *IEEE Transactions on Broadcasting*, vol. 54, no. 3, pp. 660–668, 2008.

[20] ITU-R, "Methods for the subjective assessment of small impairments in audio systems including multichannel sound systems," ITU-R Rec. BS.1116-1, 1997.

[21] G. Kemper and Y. Iano, "An audio compression method based on wavelets subband coding," *IEEE Latin America Transactions*, vol. 9, no. 5, pp. 610–621, 2011.

8

Adaptive Image Compressive Sensing using Texture Contrast

Fang Sun,[1] Dongyue Xiao,[2] Wei He,[1] and Ran Li[1,3]

[1]School of Computer and Information Technology, Xinyang Normal University, Xinyang 464000, China
[2]School of Electrical and Electronic Engineering, Nanyang Institute of Technology, Nanyang 473000, China
[3]School of Computer and Software, Nanjing University of Information Science and Technology, Nanjing 210003, China

Correspondence should be addressed to Ran Li; liran358@163.com

Academic Editor: Jintao Wang

The traditional image Compressive Sensing (CS) conducts block-wise sampling with the same sampling rate. However, some blocking artifacts often occur due to the varying block sparsity, leading to a low rate-distortion performance. To suppress these blocking artifacts, we propose to adaptively sample each block according to texture features in this paper. With the maximum gradient in 8-connected region of each pixel, we measure the texture variation of each pixel and then compute the texture contrast of each block. According to the distribution of texture contrast, we adaptively set the sampling rate of each block and finally build an image reconstruction model using these block texture contrasts. Experimental results show that our adaptive sampling scheme improves the rate-distortion performance of image CS compared with the existing adaptive schemes and the reconstructed images by our method achieve better visual quality.

1. Introduction

The core of traditional image coding (e.g., JPEG) is the image transformation based on Nyquist sampling theorem. It can recover an image without distortion only when the transformation number is greater than or equal to the total pixel number of image. However, limited by computation capability, the wireless sensor cannot tolerate excessive transformations, so traditional image coding is not fit for the wireless sensor with a light load [1, 2]. Besides, owing to the information focus on a few transformation coefficients, the quality of reconstructed image deteriorates greatly once several important coefficients are lost. Recently, the rapid development of Compressive Sensing (CS) [3, 4] introduces a new way to solve these defects in traditional image coding. Breaking the limitation of Nyquist sampling rate, CS accurately recovers signals using partial transformations. The superiority of CS lies in the fact that it can compress image by dimensionality reduction while transforming image, which attracts lots of researchers to develop the CS-based low-complexity coding [5, 6].

Many scholars are devoted to improving rate-distortion performance of image CS. A popular method is adopted to construct a sparse representation model to improve the convergence performance of minimum l_1-norm recovery; for example, Chen et al. [7] predict sparse residual using multihypothesis prediction; Becker et al. [8] exploit the first-order Nesterov's method to perform efficient sparse decomposition; Zhang et al. [9] use both local sparsity and nonlocal self-similarity to represent natural images; Yang et al. [10] use Gaussian mixture model to generate sparser representation. From different perspectives, these sparse representation schemes achieve some improvement of rate-distortion performance. However, their disadvantage is that rapid increase of computational complexity in spatial resolution, for example, the proposed algorithm by Zhang et al. [9], requires about an hour to recover an image of 512 × 512 in size. To avoid the high computational complexity, some works try to improve the quantization performance according to the statistics of CS samples. An efficient quantizer can reduce the amount of bits; for example, Wang et al. [11] exploit the hidden correlations between CS samples to design progressive fixed-rate scalar quantization; Mun and Fowler [12] and Zhang et al. [13] use Differential Pulse-Code Modulation (DPCM) to remove the redundancy between block CS samples. By reducing statistical redundancies, these quantizers obtain some performance improvements with a

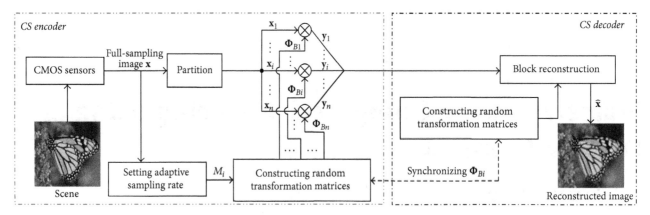

FIGURE 1: Framework of adaptive block CS.

low computational complexity. Despite its less computational burden, the quantization scheme has limited improvement of rate-distortion performance due to the lower redundancies in CS samples [14]. From the above, we can see that there is a tradeoff between computational complexity and quality improvement for image CS. We expect to find a scheme which strikes a balance between the two. Compared with sparse representation and quantization schemes, the feature-based adaptive sampling achieves a satisfying improvement of rate-distortion performance without introducing excessive computations. Its idea is to increase the efficiency of CS sampling by suppressing useless CS samples. The sampling rate of each block is allocated according to various image features; for example, Zhang et al. [15] determine the sampling rate of each block depending on varying block variance; Canh et al. [16] exploit the edge information to adaptively assign the sampling rate for each block. Block variance and edge information mean a low-level vision. They preserve the low-frequency information but neglect the high-frequency texture details attractive to human eyes. Oriented by the two-feature measures, lots of CS samples are invested into those blocks with simple patterns, which results in an undesirable reconstruction quality. To overcome the defect of traditional sampling scheme, useful features should be extracted to express high-level vision. Directed by interesting features, an efficient adaptive scheme can guarantee the recovery of high-frequency details.

Texture as a visual feature is used to reveal similar patterns independent of color and brightness, and it is the mutual inherent property existing in object surfaces; for example, tree, cloud, and fabric have their own texture details. Texture details contain important information on structures of object surfaces, revealing relations between object and its surrounds. Texture details represent high-frequency components which are more attractive to human eyes. In this paper, we propose to set the sampling rate of each block based on texture details. We design texture contrast to measure the varying texture features and assign a high sampling rate to the block with a striking texture contrast. We remove the redundant CS samples of each block with a low-texture contrast. When reconstructing the image, the distribution of texture contrasts is used to weight the global reconstruction model. Experimental results show that the proposed method improves the visual quality of reconstructed image compared with the adaptive schemes based on block variance and edge features.

2. Adaptive Block CS of Image

The framework of adaptive block CS is shown in Figure 1. At CS encoder, the natural scene is first captured by CMOS sensors as a full-sampling image $\mathbf{x}$ with size of $I_r \times I_c$; that is, the total number of pixels N is $I_r \cdot I_c$. Then, divide image $\mathbf{x}$ into small blocks of $B \times B$ in size and let $\mathbf{x}_i$ represent the vectorized signal of the ith ($i = 1, 2, \ldots, n$, $n = N/B^2$) block through raster scanning. Next, the number M_i ($\ll B^2$) of CS samples for each block is set according to image features. We construct a random transformation matrix $\boldsymbol{\Phi}_{Bi}$ of $M_i \times B^2$ in size for each block. Finally, the CS-samples vector $\mathbf{y}_i$ of each block of M_i in length is computed by the following formulation:

$$\mathbf{y}_i = \boldsymbol{\Phi}_{Bi}\mathbf{x}_i, \tag{1}$$

in which the elements of $\boldsymbol{\Phi}_{Bi}$ obey Gaussian distribution. We define sampling rate S_i as follows:

$$S_i = \frac{M_i}{B^2}. \tag{2}$$

The CS-samples vectors of all blocks will be transmitted to the CS decoder. When receiving M_i CS samples of each block, we construct the minimum l_2-l_1 norm reconstruction model as follows:

$$\hat{\mathbf{x}}_i = \arg\min_{\mathbf{x}_i} \left\{ \|\mathbf{y}_i - \boldsymbol{\Phi}_{Bi}\mathbf{x}_i\|_2^2 + \lambda \|\boldsymbol{\Psi}_i\mathbf{x}_i\|_1 \right\}, \tag{3}$$

in which $\|\cdot\|_2$ and $\|\cdot\|_1$ are l_2 and l_1 norms, respectively, $\boldsymbol{\Psi}_i$ is the block transformation matrix, for example, DCT and wavelet matrices, and λ is a fixed regularization factor. Because the objective function of model (3) is convex, it can be solved by using Gradient Projection for Sparse Reconstruction (GPSR) algorithm [17] or Two-step Iterative Shrinkage Thresholding (TwIST) algorithm [18]. CS theory states that the signal can be recovered precisely by using model (3) if

$$M_i \geq c \cdot K_i \ln B^2, \tag{4}$$

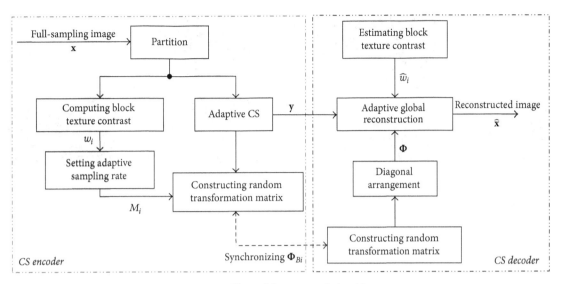

FIGURE 2: Flow of the proposed algorithm.

in which K_i is the sparse degree of the ith block and c is some constant [19]. Due to the nonstationary statistics of nature images, sparse degree of each block distributes nonuniformly. From (4), we can see that blocks with a large sparse degree cannot be accurately reconstructed once the sampling rate is too low; that is, the fixed number of block CS samples is not enough to capture all information on original image. Therefore, the sampling rate of each block should be set adaptively according to its own sparse degree. It is a straightforward method to acquire the block sparse degree that counts those significant transformation coefficients. However, this obviously violates the superiority of CS theory. Once the encoder performs full transformation, image CS has no advantage over the traditional coding. Therefore, it is impractical to directly get block sparse degree using full transformation. To avoid full transformation at encoder, some image features are exploited to indirectly reveal the block sparse degree, for example, block variance, the number of edge pixels. In this indirect way, we can get some improvement of rate-distortion performance; however, these features only reveal the varying of local pixel values, which improves the objective quality of reconstructed image but results in poor visual quality, which is shown especially by the occurrence of many blocking artifacts. In view of the above-mentioned, the proper feature is required to guide the adaptive sampling so as to improve the rate-distortion performance as well as guarantee a better visual quality.

3. Proposed Adaptive Sampling Scheme

Each block in nature image has different texture details. Rich-texture blocks are more attractive to human eyes due to the existence of more high-frequency components while low-texture blocks which have lots of low-frequency components tend to be neglected by human eyes. Therefore, uniform sampling will degrade the quality of reconstructed image. To solve the defect of uniform sampling, we propose to measure varying texture features of each block and then use them to guide the adaptive sampling and reconstruction. The flow of our method is presented in Figure 2. At CS encoder, we firstly generate the texture-feature map $\mathbf{v}_\alpha$ of full-sampling image $\mathbf{x}$. Then, we compute the block texture contrast w_i according to $\mathbf{v}_\alpha$. Afterward, the number M_i of block CS samples is determined adaptively by w_i. Finally, the partial transformation matrix Φ_{Bi} is constructed to perform random sampling. At CS decoder, block texture contrast w_i is estimated again according to M_i. The estimated block texture contrast is used to weight the reconstruction model so as to improve visual quality of high-texture regions.

3.1. Computing Block Texture Contrast. The calculation of texture analysis should not be too much in order to guarantee low encoding complexity. To avoid excessive computations, we use the maximum gradient value in 8-connected region of each pixel to measure the texture variation of each pixel; that is,

$$v(x_{r,c}) = \max \left\{ \left| x_{r,c} - x_{p,q} \right| \right.$$
$$\left. \cdot \left| r - 1 \le p \le r + 1, c - 1 \le q \le c + 1 \right. \right\}, \quad (5)$$

in which $x_{r,c}$ is the luminance value at pixel position (r, c), $x_{p,q}$ is the luminance value at pixel position (p, q) in 8-connected region of $x_{r,c}$, and $|\cdot|$ is the operation to compute absolute value. The texture variation of each pixel in $\mathbf{x}$ can be computed by using (5) and used to construct the matrix $\mathbf{v}$ as follows:

$$\mathbf{v} = \begin{bmatrix} v(x_{1,1}) & \cdots & v(x_{1,I_c}) \\ \vdots & \ddots & \vdots \\ v(x_{1,I_r}) & \cdots & v(x_{I_r,I_c}) \end{bmatrix}. \quad (6)$$

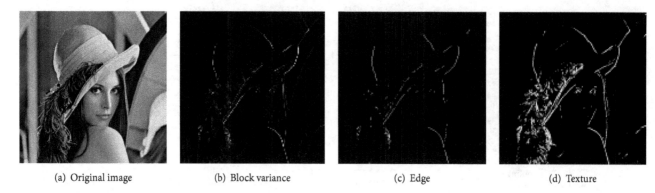

(a) Original image   (b) Block variance   (c) Edge   (d) Texture

FIGURE 3: Comparison of feature maps based on block variance, edge, and texture for 512×512 *Lenna*.

The matrix $\mathbf{v}$ is shrunk by hard-thresholding with threshold α to generate the texture-feature map $\mathbf{v}_\alpha$ as follows:

$$\mathbf{v}_\alpha \left[v \left(x_{r,c} \right) \right] = \begin{cases} v \left(x_{r,c} \right), & v \left(x_{r,c} \right) \geq \alpha \\ 0, & v \left(x_{r,c} \right) < \alpha, \end{cases} \tag{7}$$

in which the value α is set from 0 to 1. In the texture-feature map $\mathbf{v}_\alpha$, value 0 means no difference between current pixel and its neighbors, and value 1 means a big difference between current pixel and its neighbors. The energy of texture features in each block is computed as follows:

$$E_i = \frac{1}{B^2} \sum_{(r,c) \in \Lambda(\mathbf{x}_i)} v_\alpha \left[v \left(x_{r,c} \right) \right], \tag{8}$$

in which $\Lambda(\mathbf{x}_i)$ denotes the pixel position set of $\mathbf{x}_i$. We define the normalized texture-feature energy as the texture contrast, that is,

$$w_i = \frac{E_i}{\sum_{i=1}^n E_i}. \tag{9}$$

Figure 3 shows feature maps based on block variance, edge, and texture, among which the edge feature is extracted by using *Sobel* operator [20]. It can be seen that texture contrasts are highlighted in the region of hair and eye with rich texture details, and the edge features are also presented in the texture-feature map. However, maps of block variance and edge show fewer texture details, making features on block variance and edge not suitable to dominate the adaptive sampling which is meant to intensively capture the information on rich texture details. In view of the above analysis, the proposed texture contrast can guide CS sampling to capture the rich-texture block at a high sampling rate. As the core of traditional image coding, the fast DCT transformation bears computational complexity $O(N \log_2 N)$. For texture extraction, however, that is only $O(N)$, showing a low computational complexity at CS encoder to compute the texture contrast of each block.

3.2. Adaptive Sampling and Reconstruction. Due to nonstationary statistical characteristics of nature image, the block sampling rate varies with the texture contrast, introducing

difficulties in controlling the bit rate. To handle that, we set a total sampling rate S for the whole image and then determine the total number M of CS samples as

$$M = N \cdot S, \tag{10}$$

in which N is the total pixel number. The number of CS samples for each block can be computed by using the block texture contrast w_i as follows:

$$M_i = \text{round} \left[w_i \cdot \left(M - nM_0 \right) + M_0 \right], \tag{11}$$

in which M_0 is the initial sampling number of each block and round$[\cdot]$ is the round operator. After determining the block sampling rate by (11), we assign some high-texture blocks to excessive CS samples, bringing a high-quality recovery of texture region. However, the blocks in non-texture region are assigned to fewer CS samples, leading to a worse reconstruction quality in non-texture region. The big difference of reconstruction quality makes texture region salient to human eyes, and thus degradation of visual quality happens. To solve that, we set the upper bound U of sampling number to be $0.9B^2$ for each block. Once the block sampling number exceeds the upper bound, its sampling number is limited to be U. The redundant CS samples are uniformly assigned to some blocks of which the sampling number is smaller than U. After reallocating the redundant CS samples, if the sampling numbers of some blocks exceed U again, we repeat the above steps until the sampling number of each block is smaller than U. According to the number M_i of block CS samples, we construct random transformation matrix $\mathbf{\Phi}_{Bi}$ and obtain block CS samples vector $\mathbf{y}_i$ by performing (1).

When the block CS samples $\mathbf{y}_i$ are received at CS decoder, (3) is used to reconstruct the image block by block. However, the minimum l_2-l_1 norm reconstruction model has different convergence performances for various block sparse degrees, giving rise to blocking artifacts of reconstructed image. To reduce blocking artifacts, we can perform the adaptive global reconstruction; that is, the image is recovered once by using all block CS samples. First, all block CS samples are arranged in column as follows:

$$\mathbf{y} = \begin{bmatrix} \mathbf{y}_1 \\ \mathbf{y}_2 \\ \vdots \\ \mathbf{y}_n \end{bmatrix} = \begin{bmatrix} \mathbf{\Phi}_{B1} & & & \\ & \mathbf{\Phi}_{B2} & & \\ & & \ddots & \\ & & & \mathbf{\Phi}_{Bn} \end{bmatrix} \begin{bmatrix} \mathbf{x}_1 \\ \mathbf{x}_2 \\ \vdots \\ \mathbf{x}_n \end{bmatrix}. \quad (12)$$

Suppose

$$\mathbf{\Phi} = \begin{bmatrix} \mathbf{\Phi}_{B1} & & & \\ & \mathbf{\Phi}_{B2} & & \\ & & \ddots & \\ & & & \mathbf{\Phi}_{Bn} \end{bmatrix}; \quad (13)$$

then we introduce the elementary matrix $\mathbf{I}$ to rearrange the column vectors block by block to a raster-scanning column vector of image as follows:

$$\begin{bmatrix} \mathbf{x}_1 \\ \mathbf{x}_2 \\ \vdots \\ \mathbf{x}_n \end{bmatrix} = \mathbf{I} \cdot \mathbf{x}. \quad (14)$$

Combining (12), (13), and (14), we get

$$\mathbf{y} = \mathbf{\Phi} \cdot \mathbf{I} \cdot \mathbf{x} = \mathbf{\Theta} \cdot \mathbf{x}. \quad (15)$$

We construct a global reconstruction model as follows:

$$\hat{\mathbf{x}} = \arg\min_{\mathbf{x}} \left\{ \|\mathbf{y} - \mathbf{\Theta}\mathbf{x}\|_2^2 + \lambda \|\mathbf{\Psi}\mathbf{x}\|_1 \right\}, \quad (16)$$

in which $\mathbf{\Psi}$ is the transformation matrix of a whole image $\mathbf{x}$. With block sampling number M_i, which reveals the distribution of block texture contrast, we derive the estimator of block texture contrast from (11) as follows:

$$\widehat{w}_i = \frac{M_i - M_0}{M - nM_0}. \quad (17)$$

Using this estimator of block texture contrast, we weight the first term in (16) as follows:

$$\hat{\mathbf{x}} = \arg\min_{\mathbf{x}} \left\{ \sum_{i=1}^{n} \widehat{w}_i^2 \|\mathbf{y}_i - \mathbf{\Phi}_{Bi}\mathbf{x}_i\|_2^2 + \lambda \|\mathbf{\Psi}\mathbf{x}\|_1 \right\}. \quad (18)$$

By (18), we see that the larger $\widehat{w}_i$ prompts the random projection of block $\mathbf{x}_i$ to be closer to the CS samples vector $\mathbf{y}_i$. According to Johnson-Lindenstrauss (JL) theorem [21], the Euclidean distance between two blocks is similar to that between the corresponding CS-sample vectors [22]; that is, the weighting coefficients can enforce the rich-texture block to approach the original block and relax the requirement for the Euclidean distance between the low-texture block and its original. Therefore, this weighting constraint adaptively adjusts the reconstruction quality of each block according to

the distribution of block texture contrasts. To simplify (18), we construct the diagonal matrix $\mathbf{W}$ as follows:

$$\mathbf{W} = \mathrm{diag}\left(\overbrace{\widehat{w}_1 \cdots \widehat{w}_1}^{M_1}, \ \ldots, \ \overbrace{\widehat{w}_i \cdots \widehat{w}_i}^{M_i}, \ \ldots, \ \overbrace{\widehat{w}_n \cdots \widehat{w}_n}^{M_n} \right), \quad (19)$$

in which $\mathrm{diag}(\cdot)$ is an operator to generate diagonal matrix using the input vector. By using diagonal matrix $\mathbf{W}$, (18) is formed as

$$\hat{\mathbf{x}} = \arg\min_{\mathbf{x}} \left\{ \|\mathbf{W} \cdot (\mathbf{y} - \mathbf{\Theta}\mathbf{x})\|_2^2 + \lambda \|\mathbf{\Psi}\mathbf{x}\|_1 \right\}. \quad (20)$$

Suppose $\tilde{\mathbf{y}} = \mathbf{W}\mathbf{y}$ and $\mathbf{\Omega} = \mathbf{W}\mathbf{\Theta}$; we can get

$$\hat{\mathbf{x}} = \arg\min_{\mathbf{x}} \left\{ \|\tilde{\mathbf{y}} - \mathbf{\Omega}\mathbf{x}\|_2^2 + \lambda \|\mathbf{\Psi}\mathbf{x}\|_1 \right\}. \quad (21)$$

We can see that the weighting reconstruction model is still the minimum l_2-l_1 norm model. Therefore, the traditional CS reconstruction algorithm can still be used to solve (21).

4. Experimental Results

Our method is evaluated on a number of grayscale images of 512 × 512 in size including *Lenna*, *Barbara*, *Peppers*, *Goldhill*, and *Mandrill*. These test images have different smooth, edge and texture details. For the adaptive sampling scheme, the parameters are set as follows: the initial sampling number M_0 of each block is set to be round($0.3M/n$), and the CS samples are quantized by 8-bit scalar quantization. For the adaptive reconstruction scheme, (21) is solved by using GPSR algorithm [17], and the transformation matrix $\mathbf{\Psi}$ uses Daubechies orthogonal wavelet of 4 in length. In all experiments, the block size B is set to be 8, and we set the total sampling rate S to be from 0.1 to 0.5. The Peak Signal to Noise Ratio (PSNR) between the reconstructed image and original image is used in the objective evaluation, but all PSNR values are averaged over 5 trials since the reconstruction quality varies with the randomness of random transformation matrix $\mathbf{\Phi}_{Bi}$. All experiments run under the following computer configuration: Intel(R) Core(TM) i3 @ 3.30 GHz CPU, 8 GB RAM, Microsoft Windows 7 32 bits, and MATLAB Version 7.6.0.324 (R2008a).

4.1. Select Threshold. In our adaptive sampling scheme, α is the only adjustable parameter. Figure 4 shows the impact of different α value on the PSNR value when sample rate S is 0.1, 0.3, and 0.5, respectively. It can be seen that each test image has higher PSNR values with S being 0.3 or 0.5 and α ranging from 0.1 to 0.3, which indicates that our method significantly improves the reconstruction quality at a moderate α value. However, when S is set to be 0.1, higher PSNR value appears with α being near 0.55, and the PSNR value lightly reduces with α increasing from 0.55, which indicates that α should be greater at a low sampling rate. α value is related to the richness of texture details. The greater α is, the more feature points gather in the rich-texture region, while conversely the feature points will spread to the edge and smooth regions. Therefore, when sampling rate S and threshold α are greater, the reconstruction quality of texture

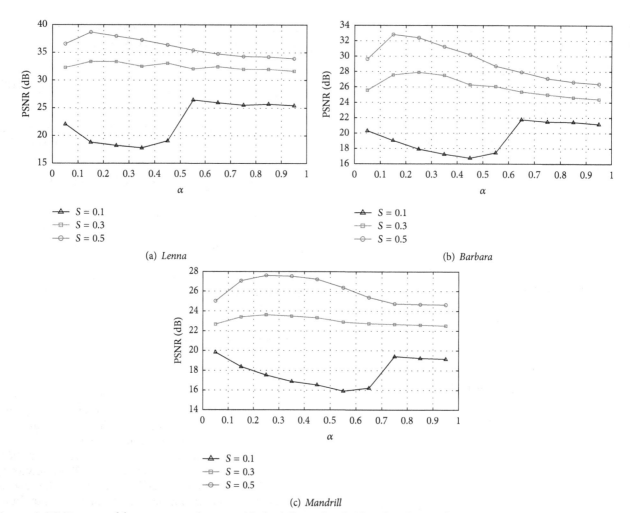

FIGURE 4: PSNR curves of the reconstructed images with the different threshold α when the sampling rate S is 0.1, 0.3, and 0.5, respectively.

region improves effectively, but otherwise for other regions, thus degrading the objective quality of a whole image. On the contrary, a small α could weaken the reconstruction quality of the texture region, which suppresses the improvement of reconstruction quality as well. When the sampling rate S is set to be small, limited by the number of CS samples, fewer CS samples can be assigned to the texture region once α value is low, so the reconstruction quality cannot be improved significantly. Apparently, the better objective quality requires a greater α. Given the above analysis, we set α at 0.15 in our adaptive scheme, in order to guarantee the robust reconstruction quality.

4.2. Performance Evaluation of Adaptive Sampling. Figure 5 shows the reconstructed *Lenna* images using different sampling schemes at CS encoder when S is set at 0.3. For the nonadaptive sampling scheme, some blurs occur in the reconstructed image, but edge and texture details cannot be well preserved. For adaptive sampling schemes, the block-variance based reconstructed image has obvious blocking artifacts. And it is the same with the edge based reconstructed one, though it is more visually pleasant than block-variance based reconstructed one. However, with blocking artifacts being suppressed, our scheme gets better visual quality.

Besides, among the four schemes, our method obtains the highest PSNR value, 1.44 dB and 1.15 dB gains, respectively, compared with the block-variance and edge feature schemes.

4.3. Overall Performance Evaluation. To evaluate the rate-distortion performance of the proposed CS codec including adaptive sampling and reconstruction, we select sparse representation and quantization schemes as benchmarks. For the sparse representation scheme, scalar quantization is used to quantize CS samples; the benchmarks of evaluation are the Multi-Hypotheses Smoothed Projected Landweber (named as MH_SPL) algorithm proposed by [7] and the NESTA algorithm proposed by [8]. For the quantization scheme, the DPCM quantizer proposed by [12] is used as the benchmark of evaluation, and its corresponding reconstruction algorithm is the NESTA algorithm, which is named as DPCM + NESTA. The transformation matrix Ψ remains the same as the proposed algorithm. Figure 6 shows the average rate-distortion performance of different reconstruction algorithms. It can be seen that the proposed method improves the PSNR value as bit rate increases. When bit rate is higher than 1.3 bpp, the PSNR value of our method outperforms other algorithms, and the gap between them gradually increases. Table 1 lists the PSNR values of

(a) Original image

(b) Nonadaptive method (PSNR = 29.61 dB)

(c) Block-variance oriented method (PSNR = 32.12 dB)

(d) Edge oriented method (PSNR = 32.41 dB)

(e) Texture oriented method (PSNR = 33.56 dB)

FIGURE 5: Comparison of visual qualities of 512 × 512 *Lenna* sampled by different methods when the sampling rate S is 0.3.

TABLE 1: Comparison of PSNRs (dB) reconstructed images when using different algorithms.

	Lenna	Barbara	Peppers	Goldhill	Mandrill
S = 0.1					
Sparse representation					
MH-SPL	25.12	21.05	24.41	24.07	19.23
NESTA	21.14	18.90	20.25	21.11	18.04
Quantization					
DPCM + NESTA	21.14	18.90	20.25	21.11	18.04
Proposed	21.04	19.13	20.90	21.14	18.07
S = 0.3					
Sparse representation					
MH-SPL	29.89	24.91	30.08	28.19	21.54
NESTA	27.28	22.99	26.86	26.32	20.46
Quantization					
DPCM + NESTA	27.28	22.99	26.86	26.32	20.46
Proposed	33.32	27.92	32.69	30.51	23.67
S = 0.5					
Sparse representation					
MH-SPL	32.93	27.74	33.21	30.72	23.50
NESTA	30.83	25.52	31.16	29.63	22.77
Quantization					
DPCM + NESTA	30.83	25.52	31.16	29.63	22.77
Proposed	37.79	32.49	36.40	34.61	27.79

TABLE 2: Comparison of execution time(s) to reconstruct an image when using different algorithms.

	Lenna	Barbara	Peppers	Goldhill	Mandrill
S = 0.1					
Sparse representation					
MH-SPL	1.62	1.76	1.53	1.36	1.80
NESTA	198.47	174.76	197.28	115.32	159.45
Quantization					
DPCM + NESTA	224.06	174.07	184.70	191.80	156.42
Proposed	2.57	3.12	1.91	2.27	5.62
S = 0.3					
Sparse representation					
MH-SPL	1.91	3.23	2.12	1.80	2.40
NESTA	134.34	170.11	130.25	130.48	117.25
Quantization					
DPCM + NESTA	152.26	116.98	126.01	125.42	114.77
Proposed	75.71	62.75	37.30	40.00	66.96
S = 0.5					
Sparse representation					
MH-SPL	2.00	3.37	2.12	2.19	2.95
NESTA	120.89	102.80	117.19	110.17	196.12
Quantization					
DPCM + NESTA	120.00	100.81	110.05	107.47	98.36
Proposed	162.54	141.37	155.93	214.95	146.90

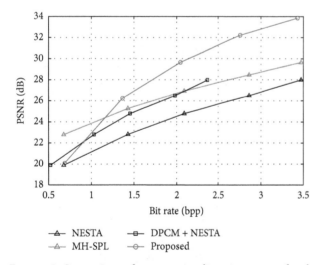

FIGURE 6: Comparison of average rate-distortion curves for the various reconstruction methods.

reconstructed images using different schemes at different sampling rates. It can be seen that the PSNR values of our method are lower than that of MH_SPL algorithm for each test image when the sampling rate *S* is 0.1, but the PSNR values of NESTA and DPCM + NESTA algorithms have little difference from that of our algorithm. However, when the sampling rate *S* is 0.3 or 0.5, our method achieves an obvious PSNR gain compared with other algorithms. Figure 7 shows the visual results of reconstructed *Mandrill* image by different

methods, and it can be observed that the proposed method has better visual quality, especially that the texture details are better preserved when compared with other algorithms.

4.4. Computational Complexity. The proposed adaptive CS scheme involves extraction of texture feature, adaptive sampling, and global reconstruction. Suppose the total pixel number in test image is N, and the total number of CS samples is M. The extraction of texture feature takes $O(N)$ operations, and the computational complexity of adaptive sampling is $O(MN)$. We use GPRS algorithm to solve the global reconstruction model (21), in which transformation matrix Ψ is constructed by Daubechies orthogonal wavelet. According to the analysis of computational complexity in [17], the global reconstruction can be done $O(MN \log_2 N)$. Then we get the total computational complexity $O(N) + O(MN) + O(MN \log_2 N)$.

Table 2 lists the reconstruction times for different schemes at different sample rates. When the total sampling rate S is 0.1, the execution time of our method is close to that of MH_SPL for different test images, but much less than those of NESTA and DPCM + NESTA. As the total sampling rate S increases, the execution time of our method gradually increases as well. When the total sampling rate S is 0.5, our method takes 164.33 s on average to reconstruct an image. Compared with MH_SPL algorithm, our method requires more reconstruction time at a high sampling rate. Therefore, the improvement of PSNR value for our method requires a large amount of computation.

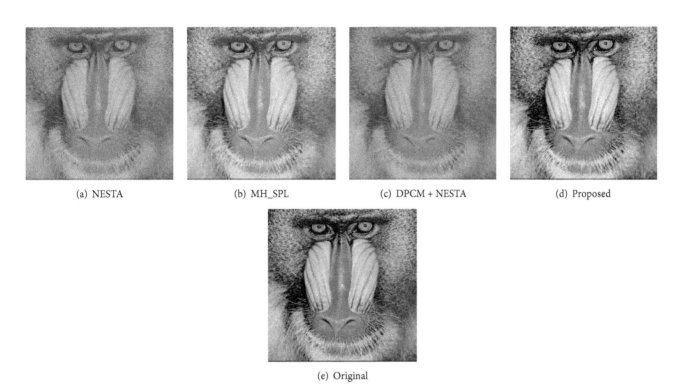

(a) NESTA   (b) MH_SPL   (c) DPCM + NESTA   (d) Proposed

(e) Original

FIGURE 7: Comparison of visual qualities of *Mandrill* reconstructed by different methods when the sampling rate *S* is 0.3.

5. Conclusion

In this paper, we propose to adaptively sample and reconstruct images based on texture contrast. At the CS encoder, we first compute the texture contrast of each block, and then we set the sampling rate of each block adaptively according to the distribution of block texture contrasts. At CS decoder, the texture contrast of each block is used to weight the reconstruction model. Experimental results show that the proposed adaptive sampling and reconstruction algorithm can effectively improve the quality of reconstructed image. Our method has better rate-distortion performance than that of sparse representation and quantization schemes.

Image coding is the application background for our adaptive CS sampling scheme; thus full-sampling image is available at the encoder. However, since the encoder cannot use the full-sampling image for the application of compressive imaging, our method loses its efficacy. Therefore, our further study should be aimed at realizing the adaptive CS sampling in the analog domain for the sake of the application of our method in compressive imaging.

Acknowledgments

This work was supported in part by the National Natural Science Foundation of China, under Grants nos. 61501393 and 61601396, in part by the Key Scientific Research Project of Colleges and Universities in Henan Province of China, under Grant 16A520069, and in part by Youth Sustentation Fund of Xinyang Normal University, under Grant no. 2015-QN-043.

References

[1] S. Xie and Y. Wang, "Construction of tree network with limited delivery latency in homogeneous wireless sensor networks," *Wireless Personal Communications*, vol. 78, no. 1, pp. 231–246, 2014.

[2] P. Guo, J. Wang, X. H. Geng, C. S. Kim, and J.-U. Kim, "A variable threshold-value authentication architecture for wireless mesh networks," *Journal of Internet Technology*, vol. 15, no. 6, pp. 929–935, 2014.

[3] E. J. Candes, J. Romberg, and T. Tao, "Robust uncertainty principles: exact signal reconstruction from highly incomplete frequency information," *IEEE Transactions on Information Theory*, vol. 52, no. 2, pp. 489–509, 2006.

[4] D. L. Donoho, "Compressed sensing," *IEEE Transactions on Information Theory*, vol. 52, no. 4, pp. 1289–1306, 2006.

[5] C. Deng, W. Lin, B.-S. Lee, and C. T. Lau, "Robust image coding based upon compressive sensing," *IEEE Transactions on Multimedia*, vol. 14, no. 2, pp. 278–290, 2012.

[6] Z. Yu, X. Chen, S. Hoyos, B. M. Sadler, J. Gong, and C. Qian, "Mixed-signal parallel compressive spectrum sensing for cognitive radios," *International Journal of Digital Multimedia Broadcasting*, vol. 2010, Article ID 730509, 10 pages, 2010.

[7] C. Chen, E. W. Tramel, and J. E. Fowler, "Compressed-sensing recovery of images and video using multihypothesis predictions," in *Proceedings of the 45th Asilomar Conference on Signals, Systems and Computers (ASILOMAR '11)*, pp. 1193–1198, Pacific Grove, Calif, USA, November 2011.

[8] S. Becker, J. Bobin, and E. J. Candes, "NESTA: a fast and accurate first-order method for sparse recovery," *SIAM Journal on Imaging Sciences*, vol. 4, no. 1, pp. 1–39, 2011.

[9] J. Zhang, D. Zhao, and W. Gao, "Group-based sparse representation for image restoration," *IEEE Transactions on Image Processing*, vol. 23, no. 8, pp. 3336–3351, 2014.

[10] J. Yang, X. Liao, X. Yuan et al., "Compressive sensing by learning a Gaussian mixture model from measurements," *IEEE Transactions on Image Processing*, vol. 24, no. 1, pp. 106–119, 2015.

[11] L. Wang, X. Wu, and G. Shi, "Binned progressive quantization for compressive sensing," *IEEE Transactions on Image Processing*, vol. 21, no. 6, pp. 2980–2990, 2012.

[12] S. Mun and J. E. Fowler, "DPCM for quantized block-based compressed sensing of images," in *Proceedings of the 20th European Signal Processing Conference (EUSIPCO '12)*, pp. 1424–1428, Bucharest, Romania, August 2012.

[13] J. Zhang, D. Zhao, and F. Jiang, "Spatially directional predictive coding for block-based compressive sensing of natural images," in *Proceedings of the 20th IEEE International Conference on Image Processin (ICIP '13)*, pp. 1021–1025, Melbourne, Australia, September 2013.

[14] X. Gao, J. Zhang, W. Che, X. Fan, and D. Zhao, "Block-based compressive sensing coding of natural images by local structural measurement matrix," in *Proceedings of the Data Compression Conference (DCC '15)*, pp. 133–142, Snowbird, Utah, USA, April 2015.

[15] J. Zhang, Q. Xiang, Y. Yin, C. Chen, and X. Luo, "Adaptive compressed sensing for wireless image sensor networks," *Multimedia Tools and Applications*, vol. 76, no. 3, pp. 4227–4242, 2017.

[16] T. N. Canh, K. Q. Dinh, and B. Jeon, "Edge-preserving nonlocal weighting scheme for total variation based compressive sensing recovery," in *Proceedings of the IEEE International Conference on Multimedia and Expo (ICME '14)*, pp. 1–5, Chengdu, China, July 2014.

[17] M. A. T. Figueiredo, R. D. Nowak, and S. J. Wright, "Gradient projection for sparse reconstruction: application to compressed sensing and other inverse problems," *IEEE Journal of Selected Topics in Signal Processing*, vol. 1, no. 4, pp. 586–597, 2007.

[18] J. M. Bioucas-Dias and M. A. T. Figueiredo, "A new TwIST: two-step iterative shrinkage/thresholding algorithms for image restoration," *IEEE Transactions on Image Processing*, vol. 16, no. 12, pp. 2992–3004, 2007.

[19] E. J. Candes and M. B. Wakin, "An introduction to compressive sampling: a sensing/sampling paradigm that goes against the common knowledge in data acquisition," *IEEE Signal Processing Magazine*, vol. 25, no. 2, pp. 21–30, 2008.

[20] W. Gao, X. Zhang, L. Yang et al., "An improved Sobel edge detection," in *Proceedings of the 3rd IEEE International Conference on Computer Science and Information Technology*, pp. 67–71, Chengdu, China, 2010.

[21] S. Dasgupta and A. Gupta, "An elementary proof of a theorem of Johnson and Lindenstrauss," *Random Structures & Algorithms*, vol. 22, no. 1, pp. 60–65, 2003.

[22] K. Zhang, L. Zhang, and M.-H. Yang, "Fast compressive tracking," *IEEE Transactions on Pattern Analysis and Machine Intelligence*, vol. 36, no. 10, pp. 2002–2015, 2014.

9

Video Data Integrity Verification Method based on Full Homomorphic Encryption in Cloud System

Ruoshui Liu ⓘ, Jianghui Liu ⓘ, Jingjie Zhang, and Moli Zhang ⓘ

Information Engineering College, Henan University of Science and Technology, Luoyang 471003, China

Correspondence should be addressed to Jianghui Liu; jihua@haust.edu.cn

Guest Editor: Yuanlong Cao

Cloud computing is a new way of data storage, where users tend to upload video data to cloud servers without redundantly local copies. However, it keeps the data out of users' hands which would conventionally control and manage the data. Therefore, it becomes the key issue on how to ensure the integrity and reliability of the video data stored in the cloud for the provision of video streaming services to end users. This paper details the verification methods for the integrity of video data encrypted using the fully homomorphic crytosystems in the context of cloud computing. Specifically, we apply dynamic operation to video data stored in the cloud with the method of block tags, so that the integrity of the data can be successfully verified. The whole process is based on the analysis of present Remote Data Integrity Checking (RDIC) methods.

1. Introduction

In the current era of rapid development of the Internet and big data technologies [1–5], the emergence of cloud computing becomes inevitable. Cloud computing provides large enterprises with an on-demand solution that enables companies to lease cloud service in the form of infrastructure or software to conduct tasks, e.g., data management, business expansion and service provision [6]. Cloud computing also provides individuals with a variety of cloud services. Typically, cloud provisions of video services have greatly improved the user experience [7]. Video data stored in the cloud share some common characteristics, e.g., large volume, high redundancy, and fast real-time requirement. The compressed video data requires functions such as data location indexing and controllable coding rate. However, cloud computing has been controversial regarding its security since its inception, and users cannot be guaranteed the security of video data in the cloud. In other words, tenants cannot fully trust cloud service providers [8]. Firstly, in multitenant resource sharing environment, tenants normally express concern about their video data which could be leaked, falsified, and unauthorizedly spread by cloud service providers or other tenants. Secondly, there is a risk of illegal access because virtual machines cannot be effectively and

securely isolated. Thirdly, data and processes in cloud computing often exist in a distributed manner; data belonging to multiple parties needs to be shared with assurance of leakage free and verified integrity [9]. These characteristics of video data determine that video data encryption should generally meet the following requirements.

(i) Security. Security is the primary requirement for data encryption. It is generally accepted that when the cost of deciphering the password is greater than that of directly purchasing the video, the cryptosystem is secure. Since the video data can also be regarded as ordinary binary data, conventional passwords can be used in video encryption. In addition, the large amount of video data gives rise to the increased level of difficulty when code-breakers inevitably perform a large number of decoding operations on the encrypted data. Therefore, some typical and fast encryption algorithms can be applied to ensuring security.

(ii) Compression Ratio. Generally speaking, the amount of data before and after encryption and decryption remains unchanged, so the compression ratio keeps unaltered. This feature is called compression rate invariability. Data encryption using the algorithm with the compression rate invariability does not change the physical space in

storage. The transmission rate of encrypted data remains the same.

(iii) Real-Time. As it is required for real-time transmission and access of video data, the use of encryption and decryption algorithms cannot insert too much delay. Therefore, the encryption and decryption algorithms need to be fast.

(iv) Data Format Invariability. The invariability of the data format defined here means that the format of the video data before encryption and after decryption remains unchanged. This feature brings a number of advantages. The important one is to make the time positioning of video data possible. This enables the support of the addition, deletion, cut, and paste operations to the video data.

(v) Data Operability. In some cases, it is required to directly operate on the encrypted data without having to perform the cumbersome process of decrypting and then encrypting. These operations include rate control, image block clipping, addition, and deletion. The algorithms with which some operations become still operable after data is encrypted is said to have data operability.

In the past ten years, there have been many encryption algorithms applied to MPEG video streams [10]. All algorithms can meet different levels of security requirements. Most of the algorithms ensure the real-time nature of video streaming and display processing. Some of them guarantee that the compression ratio is unchanged. In addition, compatibility, operability, abnormality [11], and routing [12, 13] have been also addressed in other algorithms. Based on the difference between the encryption algorithm and the compression coding process, we divide the existing algorithms into the following categories [14]. The first is the direct encryption algorithm in which video data is considered as ordinary data to be directly encrypted. Therefore, the algorithms in this category do not have compatibility. The second is called the selective encryption algorithm in which video data is partially and selectively encrypted, and those algorithms are compatible. The third is called the encryption algorithm with compression function. The algorithms in this categories combine encryption process, the compression and encoding process together, so that they embraces the features of being compressive, compatible, and operable.

This paper proposes a video data integrity checking method based on homomorphic encryption. The user can verify the integrity of the data and support public verification and data dynamics. Using homomorphic tags can greatly reduce the bandwidth requirement for video data integrity checking solution. The proposed method and implemented services are deployed on the cloud system, which reduces the cloud user's communication and computational overhead. It is proved to be feasible through security analysis and performance analysis with experimental results.

2. Related Work

Resource monitoring is an important part for resource management of cloud platform. It provides the basis for resource

allocation, task scheduling and load balancing [15]. Since the cloud computing environment has the characteristics of transparent virtualization and resource flexibility, it is infeasible to apply conventional methods to protect the data security in the cloud platform. Additionally, the collection, transmission, storage, and analysis of a large number of monitored data will bring much cost. Therefore, it is of critical importance to develop new tools suitable for monitoring data in the cloud.

The cryptographic protocol is an essential part of most security modules [16]. In a broad sense, all cryptographic protocols are a special case of secure multiparty computation. They are widely used in many fields, such as financial trading, social networking, real-time monitoring, and information management. Conventional cryptographic protocols often include multiple participants, who may be trusted parties (e.g., the user and authenticated participants) or untrusted parties (unauthenticated participants). Theoretically, all protocols with untrustworthy parties have the potential for the adoption of full homomorphic encryption. Therefore, most applications of all-homomorphic encryption can be considered as a secure multiparty computation. Fully homomorphic encryption allows various operations to be carried out to encrypted data without a private key. This enables computing of sensitive data with encryption to be outsourced, so that data security and privacy problems in the current development of cloud computing can be effectively solved [17]. The general application framework of all-homomorphic encryption is shown in Figure 1.

The homomorphic encryption algorithm is the data obfuscation algorithm in code obfuscation [18]. The data in the program not only contains numbers but also characters. It is insufficient to use homomorphic encryption to numbers only. Moreover, the execution efficiency of the program will be slowed down after the code is obfuscated. The Fourier transform can reduce the amount of calculation and the length of the ciphertext. It can also improve the operational efficiency of the program while ensuring security. The data obfuscation in code obfuscation includes polynomial obfuscation, data conversion obfuscation, etc. Their disadvantage is that the data is easily exposed during encryption and decryption. The relationship between reverse engineering and obfuscation algorithms is shown in Figure 2.

The homomorphic encryption algorithm operates internally, and it can be processed without decryption. As the increase in demand for information security becomes apparent, especially in the applications of cloud computing and e-commerce, research on homomorphic encryption algorithms is constantly deepening [18].

It has been found that not only homomorphic encryption can be applied to cloud computing, a number of computing functions that satisfy multiple additions and few multiplications are also useful for privacy-preserving cloud services. For example, averaging does not require multiplication. Standard deviation requires only one multiplication, and some predictive analysis such as logistic regression requires very few multiplications. In the homomorphic encryption schemes [19], schemes like RSA satisfy the multiplicative homomorphism [20] and others like Pailer satisfy the

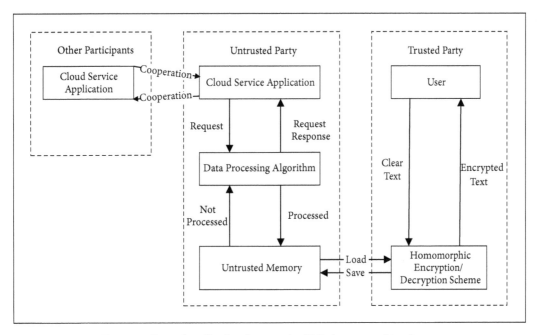

FIGURE 1: General application framework of fully homomorphic scheme.

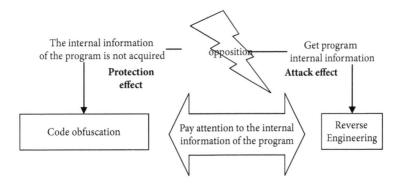

FIGURE 2: The relationship between obfuscation algorithm and reverse engineering.

additive homomorphism [21]. FHE has the property of finite homomorphic operations and is more efficient. In addition, it has a shorter ciphertext size.

When using the protocol based on the homomorphic algorithm to check the integrity of the cloud video files, the network bandwidth resources are consumed much less during the execution process. This is because the servers only need to transfer the integrity evidence to users without returning actual video files. Therefore, it enables users to timely detect whether the video files stored in the cloud are corrupted or lost. It saves users more time for data recovery [20]. However, the data integrity verification protocol based on the homomorphic algorithm usually involves multiple large integer exponentiation operations or multiplication operations on the elliptic curve. This fact gives rise to a larger amount of computation. Specifically, for users with limited computing power [22], it takes a long time for homomorphic tags to be generated for video file blocks before uploading video files to the cloud. The computation of the validity of

the integrity evidence also requires more time. Although the cloud servers have powerful computing capability, they will consume many resources while performing integrity verification for a number of users.

3. Video Data Integrity Verification Scheme

3.1. Security Model. In the process of checking the integrity of cloud video files using a protocol based on a homomorphic algorithm, the cloud storage server sends users the integrity proof without including a subset of video files or video files after calculation. After receiving the integrity proof, users perform verification locally to determine whether the target data block is intact in the cloud. The Diffie-Hellman system [23], RSA system [24], and bilinear pairings [25] are common homomorphic algorithms in this type of protocol. The execution process of these protocols can be mainly divided into the following 7 steps:

Step 1 (initialize parameters). The user and the cloud server negotiate a set of parameters that are shared by both parties.

Step 2 (initialize keys). Keys are usually asymmetric in the algorithm. The public key is disclosed after the user initializes the key, but the private key is kept by the user.

Step 3 (generate homomorphic tags). The user firstly breaks the video file into blocks with the certain size before uploading the video file to the cloud server. Then the user generates a homomorphic tag locally for each video file block. The video file block and the user's private key are taken as input, and the homomorphic tag is the output.

Step 4 (store video files and tags). The user will store and manage the video file and the tag. Then the user uploads the video file to the cloud for online storage. The local copy is deleted to release the local storage space after the transfer is completed. The homomorphic tag can be stored locally, or it cannot be uploaded to the cloud server until it is encrypted using a symmetric encryption algorithm.

Step 5 (the user initiates a verification challenge). The user generates random numbers locally and constructs a challenge message. Then the user transmits the message to the server.

Step 6 (produce evidence of integrity). The server parses the challenge message and reads the corresponding video file block. The algorithm of producing the integrity evidence consists of three inputs, i.e., the video file block, the challenge message, and the parameter obtained in Step 1. The output is the integrity evidence of the video file block. The server returns the resulting integrity evidence to the challenge initiator.

Step 7 (verify the integrity evidence). The user verifies the legitimacy of the integrity evidence after receipt. The algorithm used in this step usually consists of three inputs, i.e., integrity evidence, homomorphic tag and user public key. The output is a Boolean value, representing whether the integrity evidence is valid.

The formal definition and security definition of data integrity verification are based on full homomorphic encryption. The security model used in this article is shown as follows:

Step 1 (initialize). Challenger runs initialization algorithm and enters related security parameters $k, \lambda_p, \lambda_q, m$, and s. He will obtain the homomorphic key K and private key sk, pass the public key to the opponent. The expression is KeyGen$(1^k, l_p, l_q, m, s) \longrightarrow (K, sk)$, where m is the number of message sectors and s is a random seed.

Step 2 (generate). This stage is performed by the data owner to generate the tag for the video file. The user inputs the homomorphic key K, the private key sk, and the video file F to output tag set T, which is the sequential set of tags for each block. The expression is TagGen$(K, sk, F) \longrightarrow T$.

Step 3 (challenge). The data owner executes the algorithm to generate challenge information by blocks as input.

Step 4 (guess). Cloud Storage Service (CSS) executes the algorithm to generate integrity verification by taking inputs of video file, tag set, and challenge.

Step 5 (prove). The data owner executes the algorithm, using the validation p returned by CSS to check the integrity of the video file. The owner takes inputs of the homomorphic key K, the private key sk, challenge *chall*, and verification p. He obtains the output 1 if p is correct, and 0 otherwise. Its expression is Verify$(K, sk, chall, p) \longrightarrow \{1, 0\}$.

3.2. Video Integrity Verification Method Based on Fully Homomorphic Encryption. The video file is stored in blocks, and the data block is used as the minimum unit in the later stages of label generation and evidence verification. In the initialization phase, a series of initialization parameters are generated for the establishment of the hash function. The encryption is performed using the fully homomorphic encryption function. The algorithm KeyGen$(\lambda_p, \lambda_q, m, s) \longrightarrow k$ is applied to obtain the homomorphic key $k = (p, q, \vec{g})$. In the tag generation phase, the client uses a pseudorandom number generator to generate a series of pseudorandom numbers and then multiplies the video file blocks with pseudorandom numbers to obtain the *tag*. The client sends the video file blocks b_i, *tag*, p, and q to the server but saves the generator $\vec{g}$, the hash parameter G, and the *seed* used by the pseudorandom number generator. In the challenge phase, the client uses a pseudorandom number generator to generate n random challenge blocks and then sends it to the server. During the evidence generation phase, the server computes evidences b_c and t_c for the data block and label, respectively; they are later returned to client. In the evidence verification phase, the client uses *seed* to regenerate the corresponding pseudorandom number and verifies that the t_c returned by the server is same as the client-specified t_c. It also verifies whether t_c corresponds to the correct b_c. Finally, it is required to conduct security analysis to this verification scheme. In the challenge phase, the challenger randomly generates k challenge blocks and sends them to A. A generates the integrity verification P of the challenge block. If P passes the verification, then A is considered to have completed a successful deception. Suppose A deletes the challenger's data block and it returns any data block and its corresponding label to the challenger. It can be verified that the returned b_c and t_c are the correct counterparts, but A does not know the random number used to construct tag. What the challenger does is to homomorphically hash the received data block and then generate the pseudorandom number with the same seed as the one used to generate tag. The tag is reconstructed and compared with the tag returned by A. The data blocks and tags returned by A are specified by the challenger.

The video file F is represented as a matrix of $m \times n$, and each cell in the matrix is an element in Z_p. The choice of

```
(1)  Function KeyGen(λ_p, λ_q, m, s).
(2)  do
(3)       q ⟶ q · Gen(λ_q).
(4)       p ⟶ p · Gen(q, λ_p).
(5)  while p = 0 done
(6)  do
(7)       x ⟵ f(p − 1) + 1.
(8)       g_i ⟵ x^{(p−1)/q} mod p.
(9)  while g_i = 1 done
(10) return (p, q, →g)
(11) end
```

ALGORITHM 1: Initialization parameter generation algorithm.

```
(1)  Function q · Gen(λ_q).
(2)  do
(3)       q ⟵ f(2^{λ_q}).
(4)  while q is not prime done
(5)  return q.
(6)  Function p · Gen(q, λ_p)
(7)  for i = 1 to 4λ_p
(8)       x ⟵ f(2^{λ_q}).
(9)       c ⟵ X mod 2q.
(10)      p ⟵ X − c + 1.
(11)      if p is prime then return done
(12)           return p.
(13)      esle
(14)           return 0.
(15) end.
```

ALGORITHM 2: Fully homomorphic tag generation algorithm.

guarantees that each element is less than m and therefore less than $2^{λ_q−1}$. It is shown in

$$F = (b_1 b_2 \cdots b_n) = \begin{bmatrix} b_{11} & \cdots & b_{1n} \\ \vdots & & \vdots \\ b_{m1} & \cdots & b_{mn} \end{bmatrix}. \quad (1)$$

The column j of F is only related to the j-th message block of the video file F and is written as $b_j = (b_{1,j}, \ldots, b_{m,j})$. The addition of the 2 video file blocks is to add the corresponding column vectors directly.

$$b_i + b_j = \left(b_{i,i}, +b_{i,j}, \ldots, b_{m,i} + b_{m,j}\right) \bmod q. \quad (2)$$

Algorithm 1 shows the algorithm of initialization parameter generation, while Algorithm 2 shows the algorithm of fully homomorphic tag generation.

3.3. Security Analysis. In order to verify the security of this scheme, a data-holding game is created. If the opponent A wins the game, A can get all ciphertext data blocks and signature label information correctly. The security of this scheme is based on collision resistance of hash function [26] and the difficulty of Diffie-Hellman problem [27].

Theorem 1. *If the hash function and the homomorphic hash function are nonconflicting, the data integrity checking method in the paper is safe.*

Proof. Given the challenged video file F, the file F is divided into n blocks marked as $F = (F_1, F_2, \ldots, F_n)$. Then F_i is divided into m sectors marked as $F_i = (f_{1i}, f_{2i}, \ldots, f_{mi})$. The game between challenger C and opponent A is described as follows.

Step 1 (generate key). The user executes the algorithm KeyGen to obtain the homomorphic key K and the private key sk, both of them are kept in secret by C.

Step 2 (tag query). At any time, the opponent A can query the label of any block F_i ($1 \leq i \leq n$). C maintains a list of groups with a value of (i, F_i, T_i), named $Tab1$. When A sends a query label (i, F_i), C will check whether the column of $(i, F_i, *)$ exists in $Tab1$. If $(i, F_i, *) \in Tab1$, then C indexes $(i, F_i, *)$ and returns T_i to A. Otherwise, C computes T_i using TagGen algorithm and adds (i, F_i, T_i) to $Tab1$ and returns T_i to A.

Step 3 (proof verification query). At any time, A can start a certification verification query to C. A adaptively select several blocks. The labels of the blocks are queried from C. A certificate is generated for the selected block. A sends the certificate to C and requests C to response. C calls the Verify algorithm to check the proof and returns the verification result to A.

Step 4 (challenge). C randomly selects two values $k_1, k_2 \in Z_q^*$ and challenge block number C. It is required that each pair (l, F_l) should exist in $Tab1$, where $l \in \{\pi k_1, i \mid 1 \leq i \leq c\}$. Then C sends the challenge $chall = \{c, k_1, k_2\}$ to A, and asks A to have proof P of the data of the challenged block.

Step 5 (forgery). A generates a proof $P' = (\overline{F}', \overline{T}')$ based on challenge $chall = \{c, k_1, k_2\}$ and sends it to C, where $\overline{F}' = (\overline{F}'_1, \ldots, \overline{F}'_m)$. A wins if $P' = (\overline{F}', \overline{T}')$ can pass verification. A cannot obtain valid proof if it does not have a challenge block. Then we will prove that if A does not maintain the entire video document, then chances of A winning a data-holding game are negligible.

Step 6 (output). Assuming the opponent A wins, this means that $P' = (\overline{F}', \overline{T}')$ can be proved correct by (3).

If both CSS and the data owner actually perform this scheme, its correctness can be demonstrated as follows:

$$\left(\prod_{i=1}^{c} h_{v_i}^{a_i} \cdot \prod_{t=1}^{m} g_t^{\overline{F}_t}\right)^{sk} \bmod p$$

$$= \left(\prod_{i=1}^{c} h_{v_i}^{a_i} \cdot \prod_{t=1}^{m} g_t^{\sum_{i=1}^{c} a_i f_{tv_i}}\right)^{sk} \bmod p$$

$$= \left(\prod_{i=1}^{c} h_{v_i}^{a_i} \cdot \prod_{i=1}^{c} \prod_{t=1}^{m} g_t^{a_i \cdot f_{tv_i}}\right)^{sk} \bmod p$$

$$= \left(\prod_{i=1}^{c} \left(h_{v_i} \cdot \prod_{t=1}^{m} g_t^{f_{tv_i}} \right)^{a_i} \right)^{sk} \bmod p$$

$$= \prod_{i=1}^{c} \left(\left(h_{v_i} \cdot \prod_{t=1}^{m} g_t^{f_{tv_i}} \right)^{sk} \right)^{a_i} \bmod p$$

$$= \prod_{i=1}^{c} \left(T_{v_i} \right)^{a_i} \bmod p = \overline{T}$$

(3)

$\square$

3.4. Computation Complexity Analysis.

3.4. Computation Complexity Analysis. Four stages contribute to the computation overhead mainly: tag generation, checking request generation, verification information generation, and integrity verification.

(1) In the tag generation phase, tag information is generated for n blocks of data. The computational complexity is $O(n)$. According to Euler's theorem, $\gcd(e, N)$, then $e^{\phi(N)} \bmod N = 1$. Since modulo operations are much more efficient than exponential operations, only the overhead of the exponentiation operation is considered. Therefore, the computation cost of the tag generation stage is $(n + 1)k \times T_{exp}(|N|, N)$, where n is the number of data blocks, $n \times k$ denotes the basic block number, and $T_{exp}(len, num)$ represents the computational time cost of a modulo operation with an exponent of len bits and a module of num for an integer.

(2) In the checking request generation phase, the computational complexity of two random numbers (r, e) is $O(1)$, and the computational overhead is $T_{prng}(|N| + T_{prng}(k))$. $T_{prng}(len)$ indicates the computational overhead time of generating len bits pseudorandom number.

(3) In the verification information generation phase, the computational complexity is $O(n)$. The cloud server first computes $e_r = e^r \bmod N$, which performs a modulo operation with a computing time of $T_{exp}(|N|, N)$. Then it is necessary to generate multiple pseudorandom numbers, where $n \times k$ times large multiplication calculations are required in $\sum_{i=1,j=1}^{i=n,j=k} m_{i,j} h(m_{i,j}) f_i(j) f(i)$. The length of $f_i(j)$ and m_i is d bits, while the length of $h(m_{i,j})$ is h bits. Each $m_{i,j} h(m_{i,j}) f_i(j) f(i)$ and $\sum_{i=1,j=1}^{i=n,j=k} m_{i,j} h(m_{i,j}) f_i(j) f(i)$ are calculated. The total computational overhead of the verification information generation phase is $T_{exp}(|N|, N) + (n \times k + n)T_{prng}(d) + n \times k \times T_{mul}(2d + l + h) + n \times k \times T_{add}(2d + l + h)$, where the computational overhead of $T_{mul}(len)$ represents the multiplication of several len bits, and $T_{add}(len)$ represents the computational overhead of the addition of several len bits.

(4) The computational complexity of the verification integrity phase is $O(n)$. The cloud storage server requires $n + 1$ times of modulo operation and $n - 1$ times of modular multiplication operation. The calculated overhead for the entire phase is $(n + 1)T_{exp}(d, N) + (n - 1)T_{mul}(|N|, N)$, where $sum \times T_{mul}(len, num)$ denotes the time cost of modularization num for num integers of len bits.

TABLE 1: The experimental environment.

parameters	values
CPU	2.4GHz Intel(R) Core i7-4712MQ
Internal Memory Storage	8 GB
Operating System (OS)	Windows 7
Exploitation Environment	VMware WorkStation 10

TABLE 2: File integrity check results.

document names	checking results
A	fail
B	fail
C	success

4. Experimental Results and Analysis

The experiment was run on a PC computer with the configuration shown in Table 1.

This paper uses MIRACL library to implement the prototype of the proposed RDPC scheme in C language, and the implementation is based on Pairing-Based Cryptography (PBC) library and GNU multiarithmetic precision (GMP) library. The homomorphic encryption algorithm is implemented under the framework of VMware WorkStation 10. The scheme in [24] was implemented in simulation for efficiency comparison. Four experiments are performed in the followings according different requirement setup of the proposed scheme.

In order to check the performance of data integrity verification, four metrics are considered, which are security, storage overhead, communication overhead, and computational cost. Security means that each scheme has different security level with different technology. The storage overhead refers to the data block size occupied by metadata in the scheme, and the communication overhead refers to the overhead caused by the communication between the user and the cloud storage server. This mainly exists in the challenging-response link between CSS and TPA. These three conditions determine the computational overhead in data preprocessing stage, integrity proof generation stage, and verification stage.

Experiment 1, three 10MB files (files A, B, and C) are processed, signed, and stored. Then, 10% of the file A is deleted, 10% of the file B is modified, and the file C remains unmodified. Finally, the integrity of the three files is verified. The results are shown in Table 2.

The experimental results show that when the file is deleted or tampered, the integrity of the data cannot be passed by the proposed scheme, but the unmodified file can be verified. It proves the feasibility of this method.

Experiment 2, firstly, a 10MB file is processed and stored in blocks. Then it is tampered with the proportion of 0.1%, 0.2%, 0.4%, 0.6%, 0.8%, 1%, and 1.5%, respectively. Finally, the integrity of the file was verified, and the experiments with each setting were carried out 10, 20, 40, 60, 80, and 100, respectively. The result is shown in Table 3.

The experimental results show that the 10MB file with tampering rate above 0.6% has the success rate of file

TABLE 3: The relationship between the proportion of tampered files and the efficiency of the algorithm.

Number of experiments	Tampering rate (%)						
	0.1	0.2	0.4	0.6	0.8	1.0	1.5
10	8	9	0	10	10	10	10
20	15	17	19	20	20	20	20
40	32	36	37	38	40	40	40
60	55	57	58	60	60	60	60
80	72	73	75	77	79	80	80
100	91	93	94	97	99	100	100

TABLE 4: Relationship between data block and efficiency of algorithm.

Number of experiments	Data blocks						
	50	100	150	200	250	300	400
10	7	8	9	10	10	10	10
20	16	17	19	20	20	20	20
40	33	36	37	38	40	40	40
60	52	54	57	59	60	60	60
80	72	73	76	77	79	80	80
100	93	95	96	97	99	100	100

integrity checking which is 100, and the algorithm checking becomes highly efficient with the increase in the number of experiments runs. This suggests that the integrity of the file can be accurately detected.

Experiment 3, firstly, a 100MB file is processed and stored in chunks. Then data blocks of 50, 100, 150, 200, 250, 300, and 400 for multiple integrity verification are conducted. The experimental results are shown in Table 4.

The experimental results show that the data integrity verification which has the highest data integrity verification has the higher number of successful rate with the increase of in number of data blocks and number of experiment runs. This becomes obvious when the number of data blocks is 200 and above.

Experiment 4, firstly, the time cost of establishing the algorithm is evaluated. This is determined mainly by the parameters p and q. The size of the block is set to 16 kb, the size of the sector is set to 256 bits, $|q| = 257$, and $|p| = 512$. Then we mainly consider the installation time cost of different sizes of p. In order to improve accuracy, we run simulations of different cycles from 1 to 100. The results are shown in Figure 3.

Experimental results show that when $|p| = 512$ and $|p| = 1024$, the installation time costs are relatively stable at 0.16s and 1.28s, respectively. The cost is acceptably low. An experimental evaluation of the computational cost of tag generation is performed. In the experiment, $|p| = 1024$, $|q| = 257$. In both scenarios, each block has the same number of sectors. The result is shown in Figure 4.

Experimental results show that the relationship between the computational cost and number of sectors for two schemes is approximately linear. For example, comparison scheme results in the time cost of about 1.4s to generate a block label with 512 sectors, and the proposed scheme only needs 0.42s. In addition, the computational cost of the label

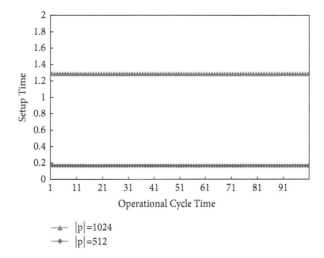

FIGURE 3: The setup time cost.

generation in the comparison program is significantly higher than the proposed program with the increase of number of sectors. Therefore, it can be seen that our proposed scheme is more computational cost effective and feasible.

Finally, the number of sectors per block is set to 512. Since the computational cost of proof generation and verification is mainly determined by the number of challenged blocks, comparison experiments are conducted for different number of challenged blocks. Figures 5 and 6 show the computational cost of proof generation and verification when the parameters are set to $|p| = 1024$, $|q| = 257$.

The experimental results show that the cost of verification and proof generation rises with the increase of the number of challenged blocks. Our proposed scheme has a greater

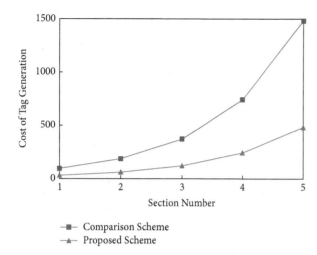

FIGURE 4: Tag generation computational cost.

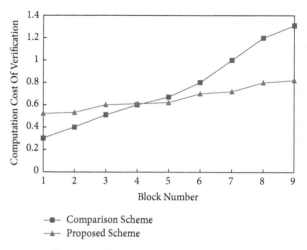

FIGURE 6: Computation cost of verification.

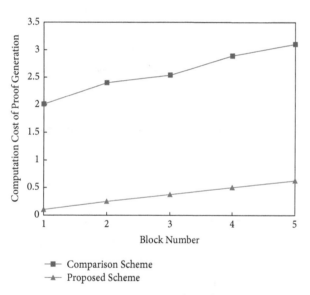

FIGURE 5: Computation cost of proof generation.

5. Conclusion

Cloud services have exploded in the era of cloud computing, and various intrusion activities have put information security at risk. This paper studies the integrity of video data in cloud systems, and we propose a method for verification of video data integrity based on full homomorphic encryption. Firstly, the homomorphic encryption technology is used to initialize the video data, which reduces the time complexity. Secondly, the feasibility of the method was verified through security analysis and performance analysis. The final simulation results show that the proposed scheme is superior to comparison schemes in all aspects, and it suggests that the proposed scheme is serving better for the video data integrity verification purpose in the cloud environment.

Acknowledgments

This work was supported in part by the National Natural Science Foundation of China (NSFC) under Grants no. 61602155 and no. 61370221 and in part by the Industry University Research Project of Henan Province under Grant no. 172107000005.

advantage to the comparison scheme in terms of computation cost, especially with the increase in the number of blocks. When the number of blocks challenged is less than approximately 220, the cost of our scheme is slightly greater than the comparison scheme in Figure 6. However, with the increase of the number of challenge blocks, the overhead of the comparison scheme has grown rapidly, exceeding the proposed scheme. It greatly exceeds the proposed scheme. According to studies, 1% of the errors per 460 blocks occurs for a 1GB video file. This gives rise to a confidence level of 99%. In the comparison scheme, in order to challenge 460 blocks, the proof generation takes 3.1s and the verification takes 1.2s, respectively. In our scheme, they only take 0.52s and 0.8s, respectively. Therefore, our proposed scheme is more feasible.

References

[1] W. Quan, Y. Liu, H. Zhang, and S. Yu, "Enhancing crowd collaborations for software defined vehicular networks," *IEEE Communications Magazine*, vol. 55, no. 8, pp. 80–86, 2017.

[2] B. Feng, H. Zhang, H. Zhou, and S. Yu, "Locator/Identifier Split Networking: A Promising Future Internet Architecture," *IEEE Communications Surveys & Tutorials*, vol. 19, no. 4, pp. 2927–2948, 2017.

[3] H. Zhang, W. Quan, H.-C. Chao, and C. Qiao, "Smart identifier network: A collaborative architecture for the future internet," *IEEE Network*, vol. 30, no. 3, pp. 46–51, 2016.

[4] C. Yuan, Z. Xia, and X. Sun, "Coverless image steganography based on SIFT and BOF," *Journal of Internet Technology*, vol. 18, no. 2, pp. 209–216, 2017.

[5] F. Song, Z. Ai, J. Li et al., "Smart Collaborative Caching for Information-Centric IoT in Fog Computing," *Sensors*, vol. 17, no. 11, p. 2512, 2017.

[6] Q. Wu, M. Zhang, R. Zheng, Y. Lou, and W. Wei, "A QoS-Satisfied Prediction Model for Cloud-Service Composition Based on a Hidden Markov Model," *Mathematical Problems in Engineering*, vol. 2013, Article ID 387083, 7 pages, 2013.

[7] J. Li, W. Yao, Y. Zhang, H. L. Qian, and J. G. Han, "Flexible and fine-grained attribute-based data storage in cloud computing," *IEEE Transactions on Services Computing*, vol. 10, no. 5, pp. 785–796, 2017.

[8] Q. Wu, X. Zhang, M. Zhang, Y. Lou, R. Zheng, and W. Wei, "Reputation Revision Method for Selecting Cloud Services Based on Prior Knowledge and a Market Mechanism," *The Scientific World Journal*, vol. 2014, Article ID 617087, 9 pages, 2014.

[9] Z. Fu, K. Ren, and J. Shu, "Enabling personalized search over encrypted outsourced data with efficiency improvement," *IEEE Transactions on Parallel Distributed Systems*, vol. 27, no. 9, pp. 2546–2559, 2016.

[10] Z. Brakerski and V. Vaikuntanathan, "Efficient fully homomorphic encryption from (standard) LWE," in *Proceedings of the IEEE 52nd Annual Symposium on Foundations of Computer Science (FOCS '11)*, pp. 97–106, Palm Springs, Calif, USA, October 2011.

[11] R. Zheng, J. Chen, M. Zhang, Q. Wu, J. Zhu, and H. Wang, "A collaborative analysis method of user abnormal behavior based on reputation voting in cloud environment," *Future Generation Computer Systems*, vol. 83, pp. 60–74, 2018.

[12] M. Zhang, M. Yang, Q. Wu, R. Zheng, and J. Zhu, "Smart perception and autonomic optimization: A novel bio-inspired hybrid routing protocol for MANETs," *Future Generation Computer Systems*, vol. 81, pp. 505–513, 2018.

[13] M. Zhang, C. Xu, J. Guan, R. Zheng, Q. Wu, and H. Zhang, "A Novel *Physarum*-Inspired Routing Protocol for Wireless Sensor Networks," *International Journal of Distributed Sensor Networks*, vol. 2013, Article ID 483581, 12 pages, 2013.

[14] R. L. Rivest, L. Adleman, and M. L. Dertouzos, *On Data Banks And Privacy Homomorphism Proc of Foundations of Secure Computation*, Academic Press, New York, NY, USA, 1978.

[15] M. Liu and W. An, "Fully Homomorphic Encryption and Its Application," *Journal of Computer Research & Development*, vol. 51, no. 12, pp. 2593–2603, 2014.

[16] H. Yan, G. Chen, and T. Han, "Scope of application of homomorphic encryption algorithm and improvement of efficiency and application," *Computer Engineering and Design*, vol. 38, no. 2, pp. 318–322, 2017.

[17] H. Demin and Y. Xing, "Dynamic cloud storage data integrity verifying method based on homomorphic tags," *Application Research of Computers*, vol. no. 5, pp. 1362–1365, May 2014.

[18] Y. Zhu, H. Wang, Z. HU et al., *Cooperative Provable Data Possession*, Peking University and Arizona University, Beijing, China, 2010.

[19] X. Cao, C. Moore, M. O'Neill, E. O'Sullivan, and N. Hanley, "Optimised multiplication architectures for accelerating fully homomorphic encryption," *Institute of Electrical and Electronics Engineers. Transactions on Computers*, vol. 65, no. 9, pp. 2794–2806, 2016.

[20] J. Chen, H. Ma, and D. Zhao, "Private data aggregation with integrity assurance and fault tolerance for mobile crowd-sensing," *Wireless Networks*, vol. 23, no. 1, pp. 131–144, 2017.

[21] S. Wang, J. Zhou, and J. Liu, "An Efficient File Hierarchy Attribute-Based Encryption Scheme in Cloud Computing," *IEEE Transactions on Information Forensics Security*, vol. 11, no. 6, pp. 1265–1277, 2016.

[22] A. Li, S. Tan, and Y. Jia, "A method for achieving provable data integrity in cloud computing," *The Journal of Supercomputing*, pp. 1–17, 2016.

[23] Y. Yu, M. H. Au, G. Ateniese et al., "Identity-Based Remote Data Integrity Checking with Perfect Data Privacy Preserving for Cloud Storage," *IEEE Transactions on Information Forensics and Security*, vol. 12, no. 4, pp. 767–778, 2017.

[24] Q. Li, J. Ma, R. Li et al., "Secure, efficient and revocable multi-authority access control system in cloud storage," *Computers & Security*, vol. 59, no. C, pp. 45–59, 2016.

[25] L. Ferretti, M. Marchetti, M. Andreolini, and M. Colajanni, "A symmetric cryptographic scheme for data integrity verification in cloud databases," *Information Sciences*, vol. 422, pp. 497–515, 2018.

[26] Z.-H. Zhan, X.-F. Liu, Y.-J. Gong, J. Zhang, H. S.-H. Chung, and Y. Li, "Cloud computing resource scheduling and a survey of its evolutionary approaches," *ACM Computing Surveys*, vol. 47, no. 4, article 63, 2015.

[27] K. Xue, Y. Xue, J. Hong et al., "RAAC: Robust and Auditable Access Control with Multiple Attribute Authorities for Public Cloud Storage," *IEEE Transactions on Information Forensics and Security*, vol. 12, no. 4, pp. 953–967, 2017.

10

Adaptive Geometry Images for Remeshing

Lina Shi,[1] Dehui Kong,[1] Shaofan Wang,[1] and Baocai Yin[2]

[1]Beijing Key Laboratory of Multimedia & Intelligent Software Technology, Faculty of Information Technology,
 Beijing University of Technology, Beijing 100124, China
[2]Faculty of Electronic Information and Electrical Engineering, Dalian University of Technology, Dalian 116024, China

Correspondence should be addressed to Shaofan Wang; wangshaofan@bjut.edu.cn

Academic Editor: Yifeng He

Geometry images are a kind of completely regular remeshing methods for mesh representation. Traditional geometry images have difficulties in achieving optimal reconstruction errors and preserving manually selected geometric details, due to the limitations of parametrization methods. To solve two issues, we propose two adaptive geometry images for remeshing triangular meshes. The first scheme produces geometry images with the minimum Hausdorff error by finding the optimization direction for sampling points based on the Hausdorff distance between the original mesh and the reconstructed mesh. The second scheme produces geometry images with higher reconstruction precision over the manually selected region-of-interest of the input mesh, by increasing the number of sampling points over the region-of-interest. Experimental results show that both schemes give promising results compared with traditional parametrization-based geometry images.

1. Introduction

Triangular meshes are important tools for representing geometric data in computer graphics, due to the ease of generation procedure from point clouds and simple manipulation. However, many applications of meshes such as mesh morphing and mesh compression tend to use triangular meshes with regular structure. Traditional triangular meshes, which have irregular connectivity due to the generation procedure, need to be remeshed. This technique is referred to as *remeshing*. Geometry images are a completely regular remeshing method, which represents a triangular mesh as an image array, where the vertex-set of the mesh is stored as the pixels of the image and where the connectivity of the mesh is intrinsically embedded in the image array. Such a regular structure of meshes is helpful for reducing the representation of geometric data and coworking well with many image-based applications such as image compression and rendering process.

In general, geometry images include three steps: mesh parametrization, resampling, and quantification. The first step maps 3D vertices of the input mesh to regular parametrization domain (square, rectangle, or sphere), the second step imposes sampling over the parametrization domain via interpolation methods, and the third step transforms the coordinates of sampling points to pixel values of an image array. To reconstruct a mesh for geometry images, the vertex-set is obtained from the pixels of the image array, and the edge-set is obtained from the connectivity of the adjacent pixels of the array.

Although fruitful research work was proposed for geometry images, many of them focuses on the mesh parametrization and ignores the importance of the resampling step, which increases the burden of parametrization technique, as the parametrization leads to a complicated and nonconvex optimization which heavily depends on the connectivity of the input mesh (while the resampling scheme depends more on the connectivity of the regular sampling fashion instead of the input mesh). In particular, traditional geometry images have difficulties in achieving optimal reconstruction errors, or in preserving manually selected geometric details. To solve such two issues, we propose two adaptive geometry images. The first scheme produces geometry images with the minimum Hausdorff error, by finding the optimization direction for sampling points based on the Hausdorff distance between the original mesh and the reconstructed mesh.

The second scheme produces geometry images with higher reconstruction precision over the manually selected region-of-interest of the input mesh, by increasing the number of sampling points over the region-of-interest. We compare our schemes with traditional geometry images using state-of-the-art mesh parametrization scheme and adaptive sampling scheme in terms of both reconstruction error and mesh compression. Experimental results on both qualitative comparison and quantitative comparison show that our schemes outperform traditional geometry images.

2. Related Work

2.1. Geometry Images. Gu et al. [1] propose the pioneering work of geometry images, which maps a triangular mesh onto a square domain by using a minimizing-geometric-stretch parametrization and gives a regular sampling for surface geometry. Praun and Hoppe [2] propose spherical parametrization for geometry images, which facilitates the representation of genus-zero closed meshes. Gauthier and Poulin [3] fill nonzero genus meshes and propose spherical parametrization for treating meshes of arbitrary genus. Zhou et al. [4] propose an adaptive sampling scheme for geometry images, which keeps most details of models. Gauthier and Poulin [5] propose another sampling scheme for geometry images to maintain both edge features and sharp features. Meng et al. [6] adopt differential coordinates to correct the vector direction of the reconstruction model, which makes the reconstruction model accurately preserve the detailed features of the original model.

The aforementioned work of geometry images maps models into single-chart geometry images, which tends to produce high geometric stretch and ignore details of models. Alternatively, Tewari et al. [7] propose multichart geometry images by cutting the model into some irregular subslices, but it required a lot of space to store the information of subslices. Carr et al. [8] convert the irregular subslices to quadrilateral subslices. Yao and Lee [9] decompose a mesh into square GIM charts with different resolutions, each of which is adaptively determined by a local reconstruction error. Feng et al. [10] propose geometry images for generating triangular patches based on a curvilinear feature. The feature preserves salient features and supports GPU-based LOD representation of meshes.

2.2. Other Remeshing Methods. Alliez et al. [11] propose an interactive remeshing of irregular geometry, which represents the original mesh as a series of 2D parametrization maps. The algorithm facilitates the real-time interaction and intricate control using a map which controls the sampling density over the surface patch. Alliez et al. [12] propose a polygonal remeshing method using the intrinsic anisotropy of natural or man-made geometry. The authors use curvature directions to drive the remeshing process and determine appropriate edges for the remeshed version in anisotropic regions. The method provides the flexibility to produce meshes ranging from isotropic to anisotropic, from coarse to dense, and from uniform to curvature adapted. Dong et al. [13] propose a new quadrilateral remeshing method for manifolds of

arbitrary genus. The method computes the gradient of smooth harmonic scalar fields defined over the mesh and forms the polygons of the output mesh using two nets of integral lines. Huang et al. [14] propose a quadrangulation method, by extending the spectral surface quadrangulation approach with the coarse quadrangular structure derived from the Morse-Smale complex of an eigenfunction of the Laplacian operator on the input mesh. The quadrilateral mesh is reconstructed from the Morse-Smale complex by computing a globally smooth parametrization. Zhang et al. [15] propose a new method for remeshing a surface into a quadrangle, by constructing a special standing wave on the surface to generate the global quadrilateral structure, which controls the quad size in two directions and precisely aligning the quads with feature lines.

3. Hausdorff Error Driven Geometry Images

We propose Hausdorff error driven geometry images in this section. The key step of our scheme is to find the points, edges, or faces of the original mesh and reconstruction mesh which achieve the maximum Hausdorff distance and then compute the gradient direction of the Hausdorff distance. Our scheme consists of three phases: an initial adaptive sampling, approximate representation of Hausdorff distance, and the adjustment of sampling vertices, which are described in the following three subsections and illustrated in Figure 1. We shall use the calligraphy letter $\mathcal{M}$ for representing a mesh and denote $\mathcal{V}_{\mathcal{M}}$, $\mathcal{F}_{\mathcal{M}}$, $\mathcal{P}_{\mathcal{M}}$ to be the vertex-set, the face-set, and the point-set (i.e., all points within each face) of a mesh $\mathcal{M}$, respectively, and denote $\mathcal{E}_f$, $\mathcal{V}_e$, $\mathcal{V}_f$ to be the edge-set of a face f, the set of two end-vertices of an edge e, and the set of three end-vertices of a face f, respectively.

3.1. Vertex Density Equalization Based Adaptive Sampling. We propose an initial adaptive sampling scheme using a vertex density equalization metric in this subsection. The equalization is adopted along both x-axis direction and y-axis direction direction over the parametrization domain $\Omega := [0, 1]^2$. The algorithm is illustrated as follows:

(1) Employ a $\lfloor n/2 \rfloor \times \lfloor n/2 \rfloor$ uniform partition over Ω, that is, $\Omega = \bigcup_{i,j=1}^{\lfloor n/2 \rfloor} \Omega_{ij}$ with $\Omega_{ij} = [(i-1)/\lfloor n/2 \rfloor, i/\lfloor n/2 \rfloor] \times [(j-1)/\lfloor n/2 \rfloor, j/\lfloor n/2 \rfloor]$, $i, j = 1, \ldots, \lfloor n/2 \rfloor$.

(2) Denote $\Omega_i^x = \bigcup_j \Omega_{ij}$ to be the x-axis partition and find the partition set $\Omega_{i^*}^x$ which contains the greatest number of parametrization vertices.

(3) Divide the partition set $\Omega_{i^*}^x$ into two sets, that is, $\Omega = \bigcup_{i,j=1}^{\lfloor n/2 \rfloor+1, \lfloor n/2 \rfloor} \Omega_{ij}$ with $\Omega_{i^*,j} = [(i^*-1)/\lfloor n/2 \rfloor, (i^*-1/2)/\lfloor n/2 \rfloor] \times [(j-1)/\lfloor n/2 \rfloor, j/\lfloor n/2 \rfloor]$, and $\Omega_{i^*+1,j} = [(i^*-1/2)/\lfloor n/2 \rfloor, i^*/\lfloor n/2 \rfloor] \times [(j-1)/\lfloor n/2 \rfloor, j/\lfloor n/2 \rfloor]$.

(4) Repeat Steps (2) and (3) until the x-axis partition contains $n-1$ partition sets.

(5) Apply Steps (2), (3), and (4) on the y-axis partition in a similar fashion.

The algorithm yields $2(n-1)$ partition sets $\{\Omega_i^x\}_{i=1}^{n-1}$ along x-axis and the other $n-1$ sets $\{\Omega_i^y\}_{i=1}^{n-1}$ along y-axis. The location

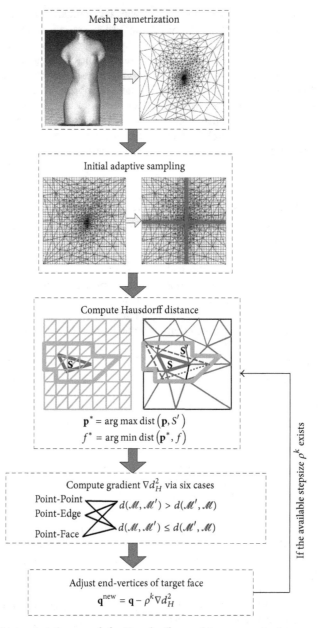

FIGURE 1: A framework for Hausdorff error driven geometry images.

of sampling vertices is then given by the intersections of bounding lines of a partition set along x-axis and a partition set along y-axis, and the sampling rate is $n \times n$. We show the sampling result of venus in Figure 2.

3.2. Representation of Hausdorff Distance between Meshes. Hausdorff distance measures the distance between two 3D meshes (see [16]), which is defined by

$$d_H \left(\mathcal{M}, \mathcal{M}' \right) = \max \left\{ d \left(\mathcal{M}, \mathcal{M}' \right), d \left(\mathcal{M}', \mathcal{M} \right) \right\}, \quad (1)$$

$$d \left(\mathcal{M}, \mathcal{M}' \right) = \max_{\mathbf{p} \in \mathscr{P}_{\mathcal{M}}} \mathrm{dist} \left(\mathbf{p}, \mathcal{M}' \right)$$

$$= \max_{\mathbf{p} \in \mathscr{P}_{\mathcal{M}}} \min_{\mathbf{p}' \in \mathscr{P}_{\mathcal{M}'}} \left\| \mathbf{p} - \mathbf{p}' \right\|. \quad (2)$$

According to the definition, the Hausdorff distance depends only on each face of a mesh together with a small number of faces of the other mesh relatively closed to it. Therefore, in order to speed up the computation of the Hausdorff distance, for each target face of the target mesh, we only choose a few number of faces from the other mesh (i.e., we enlarge the parametrization domain of the target face of the target mesh twice, and the faces are chosen as the faces of the other mesh which share common points with the enlarged target face over the parametrization domain). We illustrate the idea in Figure 3, where $\mathcal{S}$, $\mathcal{S}'$ denote a target face of the target mesh and the selected faces of the sampling mesh, respectively. During the computation of Hausdorff distance from a face $\mathcal{S}$ of original mesh to reconstruction mesh, we need to record three pieces of data: the Hausdorff distance

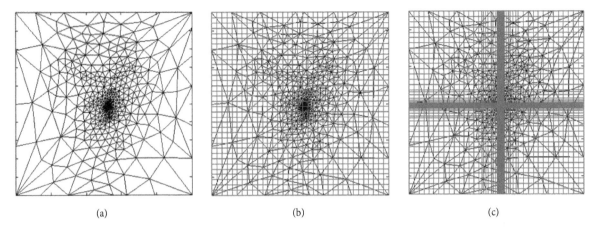

FIGURE 2: The vertex density equalization based adaptive sampling over venus with sampling rate $n \times n$. From (a) to (c): the parametrization mesh, the $[n/2] \times [n/2]$ regular sampling mesh, and the vertex density equalization based adaptive sampling mesh, with $n = 70$.

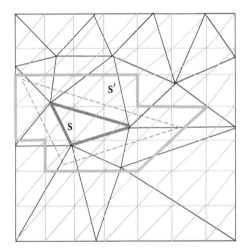

FIGURE 3: Selection of the associated faces with respect to the target face. Black triangles denote the parametrization mesh, green triangles denote the sampling mesh, and red solid triangle denotes a target face $\mathcal{S}$. The red dash triangles denote the enlarged face, and the green bold lines denote the collection $\mathcal{S}'$ of the selected faces of the sampling mesh.

$d(\mathcal{S}, \mathcal{S}')$ from $\mathcal{S}$ to $\mathcal{S}'$, the point $\mathbf{p}^*$ of $\mathcal{S}$ which achieves the Hausdorff distance $\mathbf{p}^* = \arg\max_{\mathbf{p} \in \mathscr{P}_S} \mathrm{dist}\,(\mathbf{p}, \mathcal{S}')$, and the face f^* of $\mathcal{S}'$ which achieves the Hausdorff distance together: $f^* = \arg\min_{f \in \mathscr{F}_{\mathcal{S}'}} \mathrm{dist}\,(\mathbf{p}^*, f)$. Such process is repeated during the computation of Hausdorff distance from a face $\mathcal{S}$ of reconstruction mesh to original mesh.

3.3. Iterative Adjustment of Sampling Vertices. The key step of our scheme is the iterative adjustment of sampling vertices. We first give the distance type judgement between the point and the face which achieve the maximum Hausdorff distance obtained in Section 3.2 and then compute the gradient direction of the Hausdorff distance with respect to the vertex/vertices associated with the maximum Hausdorff distance. The adjustment of the vertices is then applied using

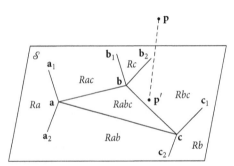

FIGURE 4: Different types of distances between a point $\mathbf{p}$ and a triangle **abc**.

gradient descent method with suitable step length. The whole algorithm stops when no vertices can be adjusted.

(1) Determination of the Distance Type between the Target Point and the Target Face. Similar to [17], the Hausdorff distance between a point and a triangle includes three types: Point-Face, Point-Edge, and Point-Point. We describe the main idea in Figure 4 (see also [17]). We denote $\mathbf{p}'$ to be the projection of $\mathbf{p}$ over the plane containing **abc**. We first judge whether $\mathbf{p}'$ and $\mathbf{a}$ lie in the same side or different sides of line **bc** and judge the relationship of $\mathbf{p}'$ and $\mathbf{b}$ with respect to the line **ca**, as well as the relationship of $\mathbf{p}'$ and $\mathbf{c}$ with respect to the line **ab**. Three judgements give eight cases of results with one of them (i.e., $\mathbf{p}'$ and each of the end-vertices of **abc** lie in different sides of the corresponding edge) always being invalid. Thus the seven cases of results correspond to the seven cases of locations of $\mathbf{p}'$ corresponding to seven types of Hausdorff distance from $\mathbf{p}$ to **abc**. In detail, we denote

$$l_{\mathbf{bc}}\,(x, y) = 0,$$

$$l_{\mathbf{ca}}\,(x, y) = 0, \qquad\qquad (3)$$

$$l_{\mathbf{ab}}\,(x, y) = 0$$

to be the equations of edges **bc**, **ca**, **ab**, respectively. Then we denote

$$\lambda_1 = l_{\mathbf{bc}}(\mathbf{a})\, l_{\mathbf{bc}}\left(\mathbf{p}'\right),$$

$$\lambda_2 = l_{\mathbf{ca}}(\mathbf{b})\, l_{\mathbf{ca}}\left(\mathbf{p}'\right), \qquad (4)$$

$$\lambda_3 = l_{\mathbf{ab}}(\mathbf{c})\, l_{\mathbf{ab}}\left(\mathbf{p}'\right)$$

to be three real numbers for distance type determination. The distance type between the point **p** and the face **abc** is given by

$$
\begin{aligned}
&\text{Point-Face } \mathbf{p}\text{-}\mathbf{abc} &&\text{if } \max\left(\lambda_1, \lambda_2, \lambda_3\right) > 0, \\
&\text{Point-Edge } \mathbf{p}\text{-}\mathbf{bc} &&\text{if } \min\left(\lambda_2, \lambda_3\right) > 0 \geq \lambda_1, \\
&\text{Point-Edge } \mathbf{p}\text{-}\mathbf{ca} &&\text{if } \min\left(\lambda_3, \lambda_1\right) > 0 \geq \lambda_2, \\
&\text{Point-Edge } \mathbf{p}\text{-}\mathbf{ab} &&\text{if } \min\left(\lambda_1, \lambda_2\right) > 0 \geq \lambda_3, \qquad (5) \\
&\text{Point-Point } \mathbf{p}\text{-}\mathbf{a} &&\text{if } \min\left(\lambda_2, \lambda_3\right) \leq 0, \\
&\text{Point-Point } \mathbf{p}\text{-}\mathbf{b} &&\text{if } \min\left(\lambda_3, \lambda_1\right) \leq 0, \\
&\text{Point-Point } \mathbf{p}\text{-}\mathbf{c} &&\text{if } \min\left(\lambda_1, \lambda_2\right) \leq 0.
\end{aligned}
$$

Finally, we obtain the following two distance sets:

$$
\begin{aligned}
\mathscr{D}_1 &= \left\{ d\left(f, \mathscr{M}'\right) : f \in \mathscr{F}_{\mathscr{M}} \right\}, \\
\mathscr{D}_2 &= \left\{ d\left(f', \mathscr{M}\right) : f' \in \mathscr{F}_{\mathscr{M}'} \right\},
\end{aligned} \qquad (6)
$$

where $\mathscr{D}_1$ ($\mathscr{D}_2$, resp.) is the collection of the directed Hausdorff distances from each face of $\mathscr{M}$ ($\mathscr{M}'$, resp.) to the reconstruction mesh $\mathscr{M}'$ (original mesh $\mathscr{M}$, resp.), with the directed Hausdorff distances $d(f, \mathscr{M}')$, $d(f', \mathscr{M})$ defined by (1).

(2) Selection of the Gradient Direction. There are three kinds of objective functions: Point-Face, Point-Edge, and Point-Point and two cases of Hausdorff distance relationship: $\max\mathscr{D}_1 > \max\mathscr{D}_2$ and $\max\mathscr{D}_1 \leq \max\mathscr{D}_2$, which produces six kinds of gradient direction. We introduce them in the following three paragraphs.

Although verbose equations shall be listed, the main idea is simple. The three cases (Point-Point, Point-Edge, and Point-Face) determine the distance equation [(8), (11), and (14)], and the two cases ($\max\mathscr{D}_1 > \max\mathscr{D}_2$ or $\max\mathscr{D}_1 \leq \max\mathscr{D}_2$) determine which point(s) can be moved: when $\max\mathscr{D}_1 > \max\mathscr{D}_2$, we update the location of the target end-vertex (edge, face) on $\mathscr{M}'$ according to the Point-Point (Point-Edge, Point-Face) case; when $\max\mathscr{D}_1 \leq \max\mathscr{D}_2$, we update the locations of the end-vertices of the face containing the

target point (i.e., the point achieving the greatest Hausdorff distance) on $\mathscr{M}'$.

Within the following three paragraphs, we denote $\mathbf{p}^* = (x_{\mathbf{p}^*}, y_{\mathbf{p}^*}, z_{\mathbf{p}^*})$ to be the target point, and denote $f^* = \mathbf{q}_1\mathbf{q}_2\mathbf{q}_3$ to be the target face; that is, f^* is the face of the corresponding mesh of $\mathbf{p}^*$ which achieves the maximum distance from $\mathbf{p}^*$. Note that $\mathbf{p}^*$, f^* belong to different meshes of $\mathscr{M}$, $\mathscr{M}'$. We also denote $\mathbf{p}_1\mathbf{p}_2\mathbf{p}_3$ to be the face containing $\mathbf{p}^*$ and denote α, β, γ to be the barycentric coordinate of $\mathbf{p}^*$ with respect to $\mathbf{p}_1\mathbf{p}_2\mathbf{p}_3$; that is, $\mathbf{p}^* = \alpha\mathbf{p}_1 + \beta\mathbf{p}_2 + \gamma\mathbf{p}_3$. We denote $(x_\square, y_\square, z_\square)$ to be the coordinates of the point $\square$ and denote

$$
\begin{aligned}
x_{ij} &= x_{\mathbf{q}_i} - x_{\mathbf{q}_j}, \\
y_{ij} &= y_{\mathbf{q}_i} - y_{\mathbf{q}_j}, \\
z_{ij} &= z_{\mathbf{q}_i} - z_{\mathbf{q}_j}, \\
&\qquad i, j = 1, 2, 3
\end{aligned} \qquad (7)
$$

to be the differences of coordinates of $\mathbf{q}_1, \mathbf{q}_2, \mathbf{q}_3$.

(a) Point-Point Optimization. The Point-Point distance from $\mathbf{p}^*$ to an end-vertex $\mathbf{q}$ of f^* is given by

$$d_{\mathrm{pp}}^2 = \left(x_{\mathbf{q}} - x_{\mathbf{p}^*}\right)^2 + \left(y_{\mathbf{q}} - y_{\mathbf{p}^*}\right)^2 + \left(z_{\mathbf{q}} - z_{\mathbf{p}^*}\right)^2. \qquad (8)$$

We compute the gradient of d_{pp}^2 in two cases. If $\max\mathscr{D}_1 > \max\mathscr{D}_2$, then $\mathbf{p}^* \in \mathscr{P}_{\mathscr{M}}, \mathbf{q} \in \mathscr{V}_{\mathscr{M}'}$ and we update the location of $\mathbf{q}$ using the gradient of d_{pp}^2 with respect to $\mathbf{q}$, which is given by

$$\nabla_{\mathbf{q}} d_{\mathrm{pp}}^2 = 2\left[x_{\mathbf{q}} - x_{\mathbf{p}^*} \quad y_{\mathbf{q}} - y_{\mathbf{p}^*} \quad z_{\mathbf{q}} - z_{\mathbf{p}^*}\right]^{\top}. \qquad (9)$$

Otherwise, $\max\mathscr{D}_1 \leq \max\mathscr{D}_2$ holds; then we have $\mathbf{p}^* \in \mathscr{P}_{\mathscr{M}'}, \mathbf{q} \in \mathscr{V}_{\mathscr{M}}$ and we shall update the locations of $\mathbf{p}_1, \mathbf{p}_2, \mathbf{p}_3$. Thus we compute the gradient of d_{pp}^2 with respect to $\mathbf{p}_1, \mathbf{p}_2, \mathbf{p}_3$ by

$$\nabla_{[\mathbf{p}_1;\mathbf{p}_2;\mathbf{p}_3]} d_{\mathrm{pp}}^2 = 2 \begin{bmatrix} \alpha\mathbf{M}_1 \\ \beta\mathbf{M}_1 \\ \gamma\mathbf{M}_1 \end{bmatrix} \quad \text{with } \mathbf{M}_1 = \begin{bmatrix} x_{\mathbf{p}^*} - x_{\mathbf{q}} \\ y_{\mathbf{p}^*} - y_{\mathbf{q}} \\ z_{\mathbf{p}^*} - z_{\mathbf{q}} \end{bmatrix}, \qquad (10)$$

where we use the notation $\nabla_{\{\mathbf{q}_1;\dots;\mathbf{q}_m\}} d$ for concatenating the gradient of $d(\mathbf{q}_1, \dots, \mathbf{q}_m)$ with respect to m points $\{\mathbf{q}_1, \dots, \mathbf{q}_m\} \subseteq \mathbb{R}^3$ to form a vector of $\mathbb{R}^{3m}$.

(b) Point-Edge Optimization. Let $\mathbf{q}_1 = (x_1, y_1, z_1)$, $\mathbf{q}_2 = (x_2, y_2, z_2)$ be two end-vertices of the triangle $\mathbf{q}_1\mathbf{q}_2\mathbf{q}_3$. The Point-Edge distance from $\mathbf{p}^*$ to the edge $\mathbf{q}_1\mathbf{q}_2$ is given by

$$d_{\mathrm{pe}}^2$$

$$= \frac{\left\{\left[\left(y_{\mathbf{p}^*} - y_{\mathbf{q}_1}\right) z_{12} - \left(z_{\mathbf{p}^*} - z_{\mathbf{q}_1}\right) y_{12}\right]^2 + \left[\left(z_{\mathbf{p}^*} - z_{\mathbf{q}_1}\right) x_{12} - \left(x_{\mathbf{p}^*} - x_{\mathbf{q}_1}\right) z_{12}\right]^2 + \left[\left(x_{\mathbf{p}^*} - x_{\mathbf{q}_1}\right) y_{12} - \left(y_{\mathbf{p}^*} - y_{\mathbf{q}_1}\right) x_{12}\right]^2\right\}}{x_{12}^2 + y_{12}^2 + z_{12}^2}. \qquad (11)$$

Input. A mesh $\mathscr{M}$ and stepsize threshold $K = 100$
Output. The 3D location of vertices of GIM mesh $\mathscr{M}'$
(1) Apply vertex density equalization on $\mathscr{M}$ (Section 3.1);
(2) Compute $\mathscr{D}_1$, $\mathscr{D}_2$ using (6) (Section 3.2);
(3) If $\max \mathscr{D}_1 > \max \mathscr{D}_2$ then
(4)   Compute the target point $\mathbf{p}^* \leftarrow \arg \max_{\mathbf{p} \in \mathscr{P}_\mathscr{M}} \mathrm{dist}(\mathbf{p}, \mathscr{M}')$;
(5)   Compute the target face $f^* \leftarrow \arg \max_{f \in \mathscr{F}_{\mathscr{M}'}} \mathrm{dist}(\mathbf{p}^*, f)$;
(6)   Judge the distance type between $\mathbf{p}^*$ and f^* using (5);
(7)   Update the position of the end-vertices of f^* using Algorithm 2;
(8) else
(9)   Compute the target point $\mathbf{p}^* \leftarrow \arg \max_{\mathbf{p} \in \mathscr{P}_{\mathscr{M}'}} \mathrm{dist}(\mathbf{p}, \mathscr{M})$;
(10)   Compute the target face $f^* \leftarrow \arg \max_{f \in \mathscr{F}_\mathscr{M}} \mathrm{dist}(\mathbf{p}^*, f)$;
(11)   Judge the distance type between $\mathbf{p}^*$ and f^* using (5);
(12)   Update the position of the end-vertices of f^* using Algorithm 3;
(13) end

ALGORITHM 1: Optimal Hausdorff error driven geometry images.

If $\max \mathscr{D}_1 > \max \mathscr{D}_2$, then $\mathbf{p}^* \in \mathscr{P}_\mathscr{M}$, $\mathbf{q}_1 \mathbf{q}_2 \in \mathscr{E}_{\mathscr{M}'}$ hold, and we shall update the locations $\mathbf{q}_1$, $\mathbf{q}_2$ with the gradient of d_{pe}^2 given by (16). Otherwise, we have $\mathbf{p}^* \in \mathscr{P}_{\mathscr{M}'}$, $\mathbf{q}_1 \mathbf{q}_2 \in \mathscr{E}_\mathscr{M}$, and we update all the end-vertices of the face containing $\mathbf{p}^*$. The gradient of d_{pe}^2 with respect to all the end-vertices of the face is given by

$$\nabla_{[\mathbf{p}_1;\mathbf{p}_2;\mathbf{p}_3]} d_{pe}^2 = \frac{2}{x_{12}^2 + y_{12}^2 + z_{12}^2} \begin{bmatrix} \alpha \mathbf{M}_2 \\ \beta \mathbf{M}_2 \\ \gamma \mathbf{M}_2 \end{bmatrix} \begin{bmatrix} x_{12} \\ y_{12} \\ z_{12} \end{bmatrix} \quad \text{with } \mathbf{M}_2 = \begin{bmatrix} 0 & (x_{\mathbf{p}^*} - x_{\mathbf{q}_1}) y_{12} & (x_{\mathbf{p}^*} - x_{\mathbf{q}_1}) z_{12} \\ (y_{\mathbf{p}^*} - y_{\mathbf{q}_1}) x_{12} & -(y_{\mathbf{p}^*} - y_{\mathbf{q}_1}) x_{12} & -(z_{\mathbf{p}^*} - z_{\mathbf{q}_1}) x_{12} \\ -(x_{\mathbf{p}^*} - x_{\mathbf{q}_1}) y_{12} & 0 & (y_{\mathbf{p}^*} - y_{\mathbf{q}_1}) z_{12} \\ (z_{\mathbf{p}^*} - z_{\mathbf{q}_1}) x_{12} & (z_{\mathbf{p}^*} - z_{\mathbf{q}_1}) y_{12} & -(z_{\mathbf{p}^*} - z_{\mathbf{q}_1}) y_{12} \\ -(x_{\mathbf{p}^*} - x_{\mathbf{q}_1}) z_{12} & -(y_{\mathbf{p}^*} - y_{\mathbf{q}_1}) z_{12} & 0 \end{bmatrix}. \quad (12)$$

(c) Point-Face Optimization. We denote

$$a = y_{\mathbf{q}_1} z_{23} + y_{\mathbf{q}_2} z_{31} + y_{\mathbf{q}_3} z_{12},$$

$$b = z_{\mathbf{q}_1} x_{23} + z_{\mathbf{q}_2} x_{31} + z_{\mathbf{q}_3} x_{12},$$

$$c = x_{\mathbf{q}_1} y_{23} + x_{\mathbf{q}_2} y_{31} + x_{\mathbf{q}_3} y_{12}, \quad (13)$$

$$g = x_{\mathbf{q}_1} \left(y_{\mathbf{q}_3} z_{\mathbf{q}_2} - y_{\mathbf{q}_2} z_{\mathbf{q}_3} \right) + x_{\mathbf{q}_2} \left(y_{\mathbf{q}_1} z_{\mathbf{q}_3} - y_{\mathbf{q}_3} z_{\mathbf{q}_1} \right)$$

$$+ x_{\mathbf{q}_3} \left(y_{\mathbf{q}_2} z_{\mathbf{q}_1} - y_{\mathbf{q}_1} z_{\mathbf{q}_2} \right)$$

to be the coefficients of the equation of the plane where the face $\mathbf{q}_1 \mathbf{q}_2 \mathbf{q}_3$ lies, and the Point-Face distance from $\mathbf{p}^*$ to the face $\mathbf{q}_1 \mathbf{q}_2 \mathbf{q}_3$ is given by

$$d_{pf}^2 = \frac{\left(a x_{\mathbf{p}^*} + b y_{\mathbf{p}^*} + c z_{\mathbf{p}^*} + g \right)^2}{a^2 + b^2 + c^2}. \quad (14)$$

If $\max \mathscr{D}_1 > \max \mathscr{D}_2$, then $\mathbf{p}^* \in \mathscr{P}_\mathscr{M}$, $\mathbf{q}_1 \mathbf{q}_2 \mathbf{q}_3 \in \mathscr{F}_{\mathscr{M}'}$ and we shall update the locations of $\mathbf{q}_1$, $\mathbf{q}_2$, $\mathbf{q}_3$ using the gradient of d_{pf}^2 given by (17). Otherwise, we update the locations of $\mathbf{p}_1$, $\mathbf{p}_2$, $\mathbf{p}_3$ with the gradient of d_{pf}^2 given by

$$\nabla_{[\mathbf{p}_1;\mathbf{p}_2;\mathbf{p}_3]} d_{pf}^2 = \frac{2}{a^2 + b^2 + c^2} \begin{bmatrix} \alpha \mathbf{M}_3 \\ \beta \mathbf{M}_3 \\ \gamma \mathbf{M}_3 \end{bmatrix} \begin{bmatrix} x_{\mathbf{p}^*} \\ y_{\mathbf{p}^*} \\ z_{\mathbf{p}^*} \\ 1 \end{bmatrix} \quad (15)$$

$$\text{with } \mathbf{M}_3 = \begin{bmatrix} a^2 & ab & ac & ag \\ ab & b^2 & bc & bg \\ ac & bc & c^2 & cg \end{bmatrix}.$$

In summary, we show Algorithm 1 for generating the Hausdorff distance geometry images, where we compute the gradient of the directional Hausdorff distance square d^2 in six cases according to the distance type and the quantitative relationship of $\max \mathscr{D}_1$ and $\max \mathscr{D}_2$. Note that when $\max \mathscr{D}_1 > \max \mathscr{D}_2$, we update the end-vertices of the target face f^* on $\mathscr{M}'$ (see Algorithm 2); when $\max \mathscr{D}_1 \leq \max \mathscr{D}_2$, we update the end-vertices of the face $\mathbf{p}_1 \mathbf{p}_2 \mathbf{p}_3$ containing $\mathbf{p}^*$ on $\mathscr{M}'$ (see Algorithm 3). For each of the six cases, we compute the stepsize ρ^k, $k = 0, \ldots, K$ which admits decreasing of the Hausdorff distance; the algorithm terminates provided that no such stepsize can be found.

$$\nabla_{[\mathbf{q}_1;\mathbf{q}_2]}d_{\text{pe}}^2 = \frac{2}{x_{12}^2 + y_{12}^2 + z_{12}^2}\begin{bmatrix} z_{\mathbf{p}^*} - z_{\mathbf{q}_2} & y_{\mathbf{p}^*} - y_{\mathbf{q}_2} & x_{21} \\ x_{\mathbf{p}^*} - x_{\mathbf{q}_2} & z_{\mathbf{p}^*} - z_{\mathbf{q}_2} & y_{21} \\ y_{\mathbf{p}^*} - y_{\mathbf{q}_2} & x_{\mathbf{p}^*} - x_{\mathbf{q}_2} & z_{21} \\ z_{\mathbf{q}_1} - z_{\mathbf{p}^*} & y_{\mathbf{q}_1} - y_{\mathbf{p}^*} & x_{12} \\ x_{\mathbf{q}_1} - x_{\mathbf{p}^*} & z_{\mathbf{q}_1} - z_{\mathbf{p}^*} & y_{12} \\ y_{\mathbf{q}_1} - y_{\mathbf{p}^*} & x_{\mathbf{q}_1} - x_{\mathbf{p}^*} & z_{12} \end{bmatrix}\begin{bmatrix} \left(z_{\mathbf{p}^*} - z_{\mathbf{q}_1}\right)x_{12} - \left(x_{\mathbf{p}^*} - x_{\mathbf{q}_1}\right)z_{12} \\ \left(y_{\mathbf{p}^*} - y_{\mathbf{q}_1}\right)x_{12} - \left(x_{\mathbf{p}^*} - x_{\mathbf{q}_1}\right)y_{12} \\ d_{\text{pe}}^2 \end{bmatrix}. \qquad (16)$$

$$\nabla_{[\mathbf{q}_1;\mathbf{q}_2;\mathbf{q}_3]}d_{\text{pf}}^2 = 2h\begin{bmatrix} 0 & z_{32} & y_{23} & z_{\mathbf{q}_2}y_{\mathbf{q}_3} - y_{\mathbf{q}_2}z_{\mathbf{q}_3} \\ z_{23} & 0 & x_{32} & x_{\mathbf{q}_2}z_{\mathbf{q}_3} - z_{\mathbf{q}_2}x_{\mathbf{q}_3} \\ y_{32} & x_{23} & 0 & y_{\mathbf{q}_2}x_{\mathbf{q}_3} - x_{\mathbf{q}_2}y_{\mathbf{q}_3} \\ 0 & z_{13} & y_{31} & z_{\mathbf{q}_3}y_{\mathbf{q}_1} - y_{\mathbf{q}_3}z_{\mathbf{q}_1} \\ z_{31} & 0 & x_{13} & x_{\mathbf{q}_3}z_{\mathbf{q}_1} - z_{\mathbf{q}_3}x_{\mathbf{q}_1} \\ y_{13} & x_{31} & 0 & y_{\mathbf{q}_3}x_{\mathbf{q}_1} - x_{\mathbf{q}_3}y_{\mathbf{q}_1} \\ 0 & z_{21} & y_{12} & z_{\mathbf{q}_1}y_{\mathbf{q}_2} - y_{\mathbf{q}_1}z_{\mathbf{q}_2} \\ z_{12} & 0 & x_{21} & x_{\mathbf{q}_1}z_{\mathbf{q}_2} - z_{\mathbf{q}_1}x_{\mathbf{q}_2} \\ y_{21} & x_{12} & 0 & y_{\mathbf{q}_1}x_{\mathbf{q}_2} - x_{\mathbf{q}_1}y_{\mathbf{q}_2} \end{bmatrix}\begin{bmatrix} x_{\mathbf{p}^*} \\ y_{\mathbf{p}^*} \\ z_{\mathbf{p}^*} \\ 1 \end{bmatrix} + 2h^2\begin{bmatrix} 0 & z_{23} & y_{32} \\ z_{32} & 0 & x_{23} \\ y_{23} & x_{32} & 0 \\ 0 & z_{31} & y_{13} \\ z_{13} & 0 & x_{31} \\ y_{31} & x_{13} & 0 \\ 0 & z_{12} & y_{21} \\ z_{21} & 0 & x_{12} \\ y_{12} & x_{21} & 0 \end{bmatrix}\begin{bmatrix} a \\ b \\ c \end{bmatrix} \qquad (17)$$

$$\text{with } h = \frac{ax_{\mathbf{p}^*} + by_{\mathbf{p}^*} + cz_{\mathbf{p}^*} + g}{a^2 + b^2 + c^2}$$

4. Enhanced ROI Geometry Images

Region-of-Interest (ROI) is the area that attracts the attention of human visual attention, and the other area is called non-Region-of-Interest (non-ROI). While it is difficult to directly select ROI on the geometry image, the normal vector coordinates from normal images can accurately reflect the original triangular mesh surface's details. Figure 5 shows the geometry image and the normal image of the foot model. When we select the ROI, the normal vector image can be used. The first and second subfigures of Figure 6 illustrate the selection of ROI, where the left subfigure marks the region which contains more information of the model than the region in the middle subfigure.

After the ROI is selected, we transform the ROI of the normal images into the parametrization domain and divide it into five regions according to the right subfigure of Figure 6. We calculate the number of vertices of the parameterized mesh and the number of vertices of the reconstructed mesh within the five regions, respectively. To give a suitable setting of weights of non-ROI vertices, we denote $n_{\text{ideal}} = (n_c/|\mathscr{V}_{\mathscr{M}}|)n^2$ as the ideal number of sampling points in each non-ROI, where n_c is the number of the parameterized mesh vertex and n is the sampling rate. For the four non-ROI, we use the actual number of the reconstructed mesh vertex minus n_{ideal} to obtain four values and arrange them in a descending order. Negative value indicates the insufficient number of sampling points in this area, while positive value indicates the redundant number of sampling points. Finally, the weights are assigned from low to high according to this order. While the weight of ROI is the highest, the weight of each non-ROI region is the same.

Vertex movement must be in its first order domain to ensure that the topology of the final mesh is unchanged. We define $\mathbf{p}_{\text{new}} = (\sum_{i=1}^6 w_i\|\mathbf{p}_0 - \mathbf{p}_i\|\mathbf{p}_i)/\sum_{i=1}^6 w_i\|\mathbf{p}_0 - \mathbf{p}_i\|$ to be the new position of the moving point, where w_i is the weight of the region in which the point locates and $\mathbf{p}_i$ are the 2D coordinates of one-ring neighborhood of $\mathbf{p}_0$ (note that the definition of $\mathbf{p}_{\text{new}}$ tends to move each sampling vertex towards the greater-weight direction within its 1-ring neighborhood). The increasing number of sampling points in the ROI is defined by user. After the increase of the sampling points in the ROI, we use the adaptive sampling scheme of Section 3.3 over ROI, where the optimization function is the directed Hausdorff distance from ROI to the original mesh instead of the symmetric Hausdorff distance, so that the distribution of sampling points of ROI is more suitable.

5. Experimental Results

We show experimental results in this section. The first subsection shows the Hausdorff error driven geometry images while the second subsection shows geometry images with enhanced ROI reconstruction. Both qualitative results and quantitative results are compared. The second subsection also shows results with image compression with JPEG2000 codec.

5.1. Optimal Hausdorff Error Driven Geometry Images. We use two kinds of parametrization method: barycentric parametrization [18] and geometric-stretch parametrization [19] and three sampling methods: regular sampling, [4]'s adaptive sampling, and vertex density equalization adaptive sampling. We do three groups of experiments. Qualitative results are shown in Figure 7, where each column from left to

Input. A target point $\mathbf{p}^*$, a target face f^*, a mesh $\mathcal{M}$ and stepsize threshold $K = 100$, $\rho = 1/2$
Output. New locations of the end-vertices of the face f^*
(1) **switch** *Distance Type* **do**
(2)   **case** *Point-Point*
(3)   Find the closest end-vertex $\mathbf{q}$ of f^* from $\mathbf{p}^*$ by $\mathbf{q} \leftarrow \arg\min_{\mathbf{q} \in \mathcal{V}_{f^*}} \|\mathbf{p}^* - \mathbf{q}\|$;
(4)   Compute the gradient $\nabla_{\mathbf{q}} d_{\mathrm{pp}}^2$ using (9);
(5)   **for** $k = 0, \ldots, K$ **do**
(6)   Update the Hausdorff distance set $\mathscr{D}_1^{\mathrm{pp}}(k)$ using (6) with $\mathbf{q}$ replaced by $\mathbf{q} - \rho^k \nabla_{\mathbf{q}} d_{\mathrm{pp}}^2$;
(7)   **if** $\max \mathscr{D}_1^{\mathrm{pp}}(k) < \max \mathscr{D}_1$ **then**
(8)   Update $\mathbf{q}$ by $\mathbf{q} \leftarrow \mathbf{q} - \rho^k \nabla_{\mathbf{q}} d_{\mathrm{pp}}^2$;
(9)   Break;
(10)   **end**
(11)   **end**
(12)   **if** $\max \mathscr{D}_1^{\mathrm{pp}}(k) \geq \max \mathscr{D}_1, \forall k = 0, \ldots, K$ **then**
            End the algorithm;
(13)   **case** *Point-Edge*
(14)   Find the closest edge of f' from $\mathbf{p}^*$ by $e' \leftarrow \arg\min_{e \in \mathscr{E}_{f^*}} \mathrm{dist}\,(\mathbf{p}^*, e)$;
(15)   Denote $\mathbf{q}_1, \mathbf{q}_2$ to be the end-vertices of e';
(16)   Compute the gradient $\nabla_{[\mathbf{q}_1;\mathbf{q}_2]} d_{\mathrm{pe}}^2$ using (16);
(17)   **for** $k = 0, \ldots, K$ **do**
(18)   Update the Hausdorff distance set $\mathscr{D}_1^{\mathrm{pe}}(k)$ using (6) with $\mathbf{q}_1, \mathbf{q}_2$ replaced by $[\mathbf{q}_1;\mathbf{q}_2] - \rho^k \nabla_{[\mathbf{q}_1;\mathbf{q}_2]} d_{\mathrm{pe}}^2$;
(19)   **if** $\max \mathscr{D}_1^{\mathrm{pe}}(k) < \max \mathscr{D}_1$ **then**
(20)   Update $\mathbf{q}_1, \mathbf{q}_2$ by $[\mathbf{q}_1;\mathbf{q}_2] \leftarrow [\mathbf{q}_1;\mathbf{q}_2] - \rho^k \nabla_{[\mathbf{q}_1;\mathbf{q}_2]} d_{\mathrm{pe}}^2$;
(21)   Break;
(22)   **end**
(23)   **end**
(24)   **if** $\max \mathscr{D}_1^{\mathrm{pe}}(k) \geq \max \mathscr{D}_1, \forall k = 0, \ldots, K$ **then**
            End the algorithm;
(25)   **case** *Point-Face*
(26)   Denote $\mathbf{q}_1, \mathbf{q}_2, \mathbf{q}_3$ to be the end-vertices of f^*;
(27)   Compute the gradient $\nabla_{[\mathbf{q}_1;\mathbf{q}_2;\mathbf{q}_3]} d_{\mathrm{pf}}^2$ using (17);
(28)   **for** $k = 0, \ldots, K$ **do**
(29)   Update the Hausdorff distance set $\mathscr{D}_1^{\mathrm{pf}}(k)$ using (6) with $\mathbf{q}_1, \mathbf{q}_2, \mathbf{q}_3$ replaced by $[\mathbf{q}_1;\mathbf{q}_2;\mathbf{q}_3] - \rho^k \nabla_{[\mathbf{q}_1;\mathbf{q}_2;\mathbf{q}_3]} d_{\mathrm{pf}}^2$;
(30)   **if** $\max \mathscr{D}_1^{\mathrm{pf}}(k) < \max \mathscr{D}_1$ **then**
(31)   Update $\mathbf{q}_1, \mathbf{q}_2, \mathbf{q}_3$ by $[\mathbf{q}_1;\mathbf{q}_2;\mathbf{q}_3] \leftarrow [\mathbf{q}_1;\mathbf{q}_2;\mathbf{q}_3] - \rho^k \nabla_{[\mathbf{q}_1;\mathbf{q}_2;\mathbf{q}_3]} d_{\mathrm{pf}}^2$;
(32)   Break;
(33)   **end**
(34)   **end**
(35)   **if** $\max \mathscr{D}_1^{\mathrm{pf}}(k) \geq \max \mathscr{D}_1, \forall k = 0, \ldots, K$ **then**
            End the algorithm;
(36)   **endsw**
(37) **endsw**

ALGORITHM 2: Update the position of end-vertices of target face f^* when $\max \mathscr{D}_1 > \max \mathscr{D}_2$.

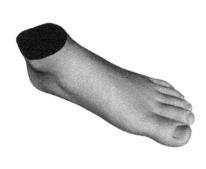
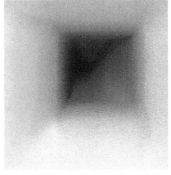

(a)   (b)   (c)

FIGURE 5: Geometry image (b) and normal-map image (c) for foot.

Input. A target point $\mathbf{p}^*$, a target face f^*, a mesh $\mathcal{M}$ and stepsize threshold $K = 100$, $\rho = 1/2$
Output. New locations of the end-vertices of the face $\mathbf{p}_1\mathbf{p}_2\mathbf{p}_3$
(1) **switch** *Distance Type* **do**
(2)   **case** *Point-Point*
(3)   Compute the gradient $\nabla_{[\mathbf{p}_1;\mathbf{p}_2;\mathbf{p}_3]}d_{\mathrm{pp}}^2$ using (10);
(4)   **for** $k = 0,\ldots,K$ **do**
(5)   Update the Hausdorff distance set $\mathscr{D}_2^{\mathrm{pp}}(k)$ using (6) with $\mathbf{p}_1, \mathbf{p}_2, \mathbf{p}_3$ replaced by $[\mathbf{p}_1;\mathbf{p}_2;\mathbf{p}_3] - \rho^k\nabla_{[\mathbf{p}_1;\mathbf{p}_2;\mathbf{p}_3]}d_{\mathrm{pp}}^2$;
(6)   **if** $\max\mathscr{D}_2^{\mathrm{pp}}(k) < \max\mathscr{D}_2$ **then**
(7)   Update $\mathbf{p}_1, \mathbf{p}_2, \mathbf{p}_3$ by $[\mathbf{p}_1;\mathbf{p}_2;\mathbf{p}_3] \leftarrow [\mathbf{p}_1;\mathbf{p}_2;\mathbf{p}_3] - \rho^k\nabla_{[\mathbf{p}_1;\mathbf{p}_2;\mathbf{p}_3]}d_{\mathrm{pp}}^2$;
(8)   Break;
(9)   **end**
(10)   **end**
(11)   **if** $\max\mathscr{D}_2^{\mathrm{pp}}(k) \geq \max\mathscr{D}_2, \forall k = 0,\ldots,K$ **then**
                   End the algorithm;
(12)   **case** *Point-Edge*
(13)   Compute the gradient $\nabla_{[\mathbf{p}_1;\mathbf{p}_2;\mathbf{p}_3]}d_{\mathrm{pe}}^2$ using (12);
(14)   **for** $k = 0,\ldots,K$ **do**
(15)   Update the Hausdorff distance set $\mathscr{D}_2^{\mathrm{pe}}$ using (6) with $\mathbf{p}_1, \mathbf{p}_2, \mathbf{p}_3$ replaced by $[\mathbf{p}_1;\mathbf{p}_2;\mathbf{p}_3] - \rho^k\nabla_{[\mathbf{p}_1;\mathbf{p}_2;\mathbf{p}_3]}d_{\mathrm{pe}}^2$;
(16)   **if** $\max\mathscr{D}_2^{\mathrm{pe}}(k) < \max\mathscr{D}_2$ **then**
(17)   Update $\mathbf{p}_1, \mathbf{p}_2, \mathbf{p}_3$ by $[\mathbf{p}_1;\mathbf{p}_2;\mathbf{p}_3] \leftarrow [\mathbf{p}_1;\mathbf{p}_2;\mathbf{p}_3] - \rho^k\nabla_{[\mathbf{p}_1;\mathbf{p}_2;\mathbf{p}_3]}d_{\mathrm{pe}}^2$;
(18)   Break;
(19)   **end**
(20)   **end**
(21)   **if** $\max\mathscr{D}_2^{\mathrm{pe}}(k) \geq \max\mathscr{D}_2, \forall k = 0,\ldots,K$ **then**
                   End the algorithm;
(22)   **case** *Point-Face*
(23)   Compute the gradient $\nabla_{[\mathbf{p}_1;\mathbf{p}_2;\mathbf{p}_3]}d_{\mathrm{pf}}^2$ using (15);
(24)   **for** $k = 0,\ldots,K$ **do**
(25)   Update the Hausdorff distance set $\mathscr{D}_2^{\mathrm{pf}}$ using (6) with $\mathbf{p}_1, \mathbf{p}_2, \mathbf{p}_3$ replaced by $[\mathbf{p}_1;\mathbf{p}_2;\mathbf{p}_3] - \rho^k\nabla_{[\mathbf{p}_1;\mathbf{p}_2;\mathbf{p}_3]}d_{\mathrm{pf}}^2$;
(26)   **if** $\max\mathscr{D}_2^{\mathrm{pf}}(k) < \max\mathscr{D}_2$ **then**
(27)   Update $\mathbf{p}_1, \mathbf{p}_2, \mathbf{p}_3$ by $[\mathbf{p}_1;\mathbf{p}_2;\mathbf{p}_3] \leftarrow [\mathbf{p}_1;\mathbf{p}_2;\mathbf{p}_3] - \rho^k\nabla_{[\mathbf{p}_1;\mathbf{p}_2;\mathbf{p}_3]}d_{\mathrm{pf}}^2$;
(28)   Break;
(29)   **end**
(30)   **end**
(31)   **if** $\max\mathscr{D}_2^{\mathrm{pf}}(k) \geq \max\mathscr{D}_2, \forall k = 0,\ldots,K$ **then**
                   End the algorithm;
(32)   **endsw**
(33) **endsw**

ALGORITHM 3: Update the position of end-vertices of the face containing $\mathbf{p}^*$ when $\max\mathscr{D}_1 \leq \max\mathscr{D}_2$.

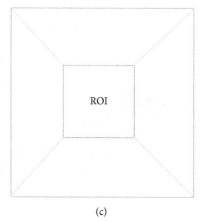

(a)   (b)   (c)

FIGURE 6: ROI selection for foot. From (a) to (c): ROI selection with more details, ROI selection with less details, and the ROI/non-ROI selection scheme.

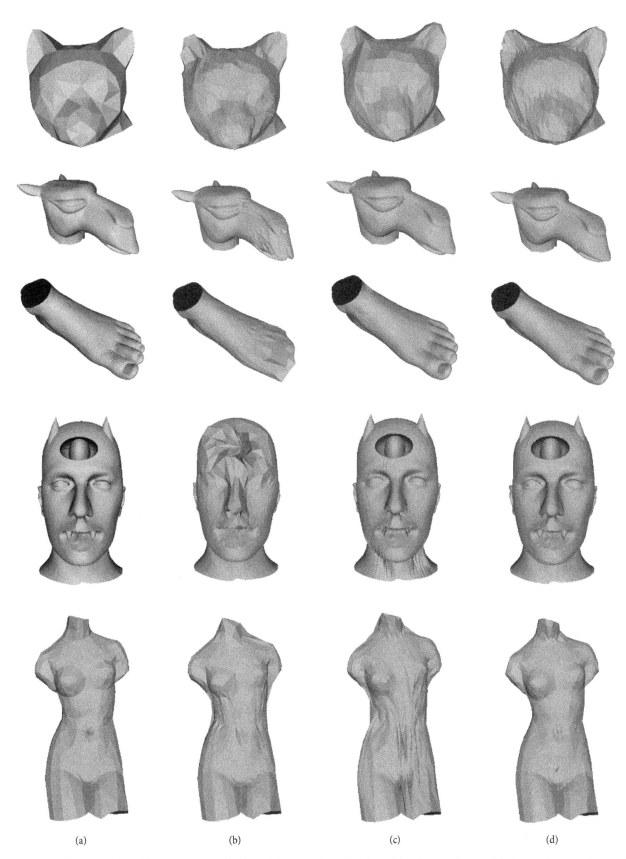

FIGURE 7: Qualitative results with different models. From (a) to (d): the original model, [4]'s sampling model, the regular sampling model, and our sampling model.

TABLE 1: Comparative results of PSNR values of reconstructed models.

Model	Face Num	Vertex Num	Sampling Rate	Regular Sampling	PSNR by Zhou et al. [4]	PSNR by Our model	Hausdorff error Before AS	After AS
Cathead	248	131	45 ∗ 45	47.1377	47.6548	**51.7978**	0.1379	0.0625
Venus	1396	711	70 ∗ 70	50.3154	50.5554	**58.9261**	0.8178	0.0577
Camel	22704	11381	180 ∗ 180	61.4743	56.6976	**71.2418**	0.0102	0.0055
Foot	19974	10010	180 ∗ 180	66.4185	51.8281	**71.3321**	0.0170	0.0129
Mannequin	25888	12977	300 ∗ 300	59.0039	50.2263	**68.4832**	1.6027	0.2300

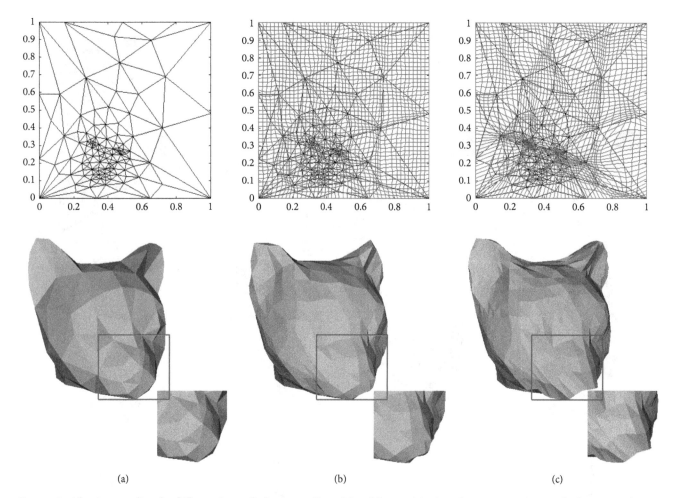

(a)   (b)   (c)

FIGURE 8: Adaptive sampling for different times of adjustment. From (a) to (c) are original mesh, reconstruction mesh after twice adaptive sampling, and reconstruction mesh after 15 times of adaptive sampling.

right is the original model, [4]'s sampling model, the regular sampling model, and our sampling model.

Table 1 shows details of the five models, such as the number of faces and vertices, as well as the reconstruction PSNRs and Hausdorff errors of models before adaptive sampling and after adaptive sampling. Under the specified sampling rate, we can see that our method achieves the greatest PSNR among all methods. By optimizing the reconstructed mesh, the Hausdorff error is reduced. With the same parametrization method, we see from the comparative results that our sampling method is better than [4]'s sampling method. Because

[4]'s method adjusts the sampling points which is based on regular sampling; the effect of the sampling rate is decided by the effect of the sampling rate. Different adjustment times can be obtained for different reconstructed meshes. However, with the increase of adjustment times, the sampling points are distributed within the region of the parametrization domain where more vertices concentrate. In [4], in order to preserve the edge information, detailed regions may not reach the expected reconstruction accuracy. If the detailed regions are up to reconstruction accuracy, the edge information may be lost. Figure 8 shows different reconstructions in terms of

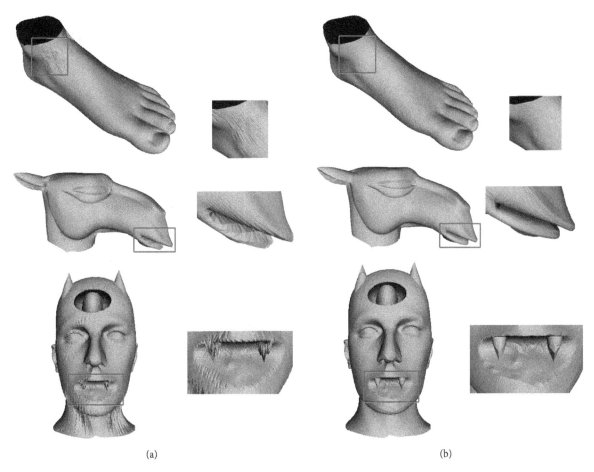

FIGURE 9: Qualitative results of regular sampling method (a) and our method (b).

different times of adjustment, where the first row of black mesh is a parametrization mesh and the red mesh is sampling mesh.

Two methods use different parametrization strategies, and the effect of the barycentric mapping method is worse than the geometric-stretch parametrization method. Figure 9 shows comparative results of the regular sampling and our adaptive sampling, where the reconstruction effect within some detailed regions of ours method is better than the regular sampling method.

5.2. Enhanced ROI Geometry Images. Experiments of enhanced ROI geometry images are given by enhancing the number of ROI sampling points before adaptive sampling and after adaptive sampling. We mainly used the barycentric mapping and regular sampling. The sampling rates are $40 * 40$ (cathead), $80 * 80$ (fist), $150 * 150$ (foot), and $300 * 300$ (davidhead).

Figure 10 shows the qualitative results of ROI reconstructions using different sampling schemes, where the second row is the ROI of original meshes, the third row is the ROI reconstructions using regular sampling, and the fourth row is the ROI reconstructions using enhanced ROI adaptive sampling. We can see from the figure that the sampling

number of ROI can be increased, which improves the quality of the reconstruction of ROI.

Figure 11 shows the qualitative results of ROI reconstructions using JPEG2000 with non-ROI and ROI codecs, where the second row is the ROI reconstructions using non-ROI JPEG2000 codec, and the third row is the ROI reconstructions using ROI JPEG2000 codec, both of which are under the same compression rate. We can see that the reconstruction meshes using ROI codec keep more detailed information than the reconstruction meshes using non-ROI codec.

Table 2 shows quantitative results of enhanced ROI geometry images and traditional geometry images, which indicates that the Hausdorff error is reduced after our adaptive sampling is applied. Moreover, the more sampling points the ROI has, the higher reconstruction precision of ROI we obtain.

6. Conclusions

We propose two kinds of adaptive geometry images for remeshing triangular meshes. The first scheme, referred to as Hausdorff error driven geometry images, achieves minimum Hasdorff distance between original meshes and reconstructed meshes. The second scheme, referred to as enhanced

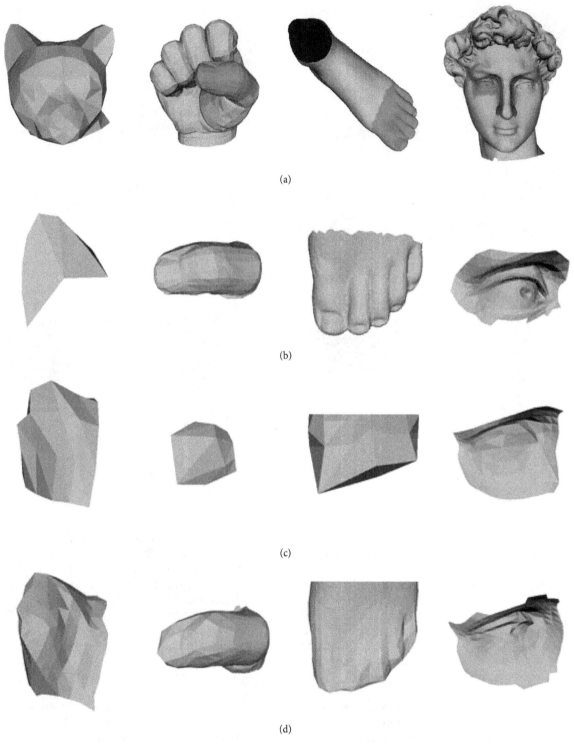

FIGURE 10: Qualitative results of ROI reconstruction. (a) to (d): original meshes, amplified details, reconstructions with traditional sampling rate, and reconstructions with increasing sampling.

ROI geometry images, preserves more details over ROI regions. Experimental results show the effectiveness of our method compared with traditional regular sampling based geometry images. In future work, we shall improve our models by computing Hausdorff distance between meshes using local maximum instead of global one; also we shall consider the parallel implementation of adjusting sample vertices.

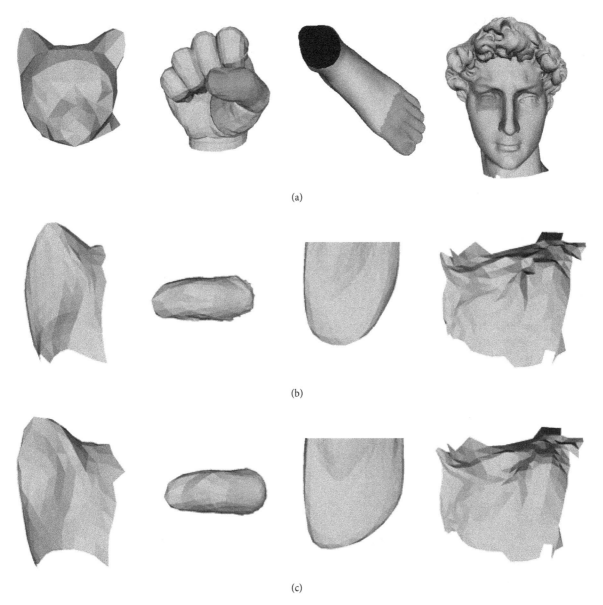

(a)

(b)

(c)

FIGURE 11: Qualitative results of ROI compression with JPEG2000 codec. (a) to (c): original meshes, reconstructions using non-ROI compression, and reconstructions using ROI compression.

TABLE 2: Hausdorff error of different models using ROI sampling scheme.

Model	ROI sampling num		Hausdorff error		Rate	Hausdorff error	
	Before AS	After AS	Before AS	After AS		Non-ROI compress	ROI compress
Cathead	30	147	0.0933	0.0657	1.2	1.1077	0.0931
Fist	16	717	0.0963	0.0129	0.7	0.0381	0.0341
Foot	169	1218	0.1557	0.0367	0.1	0.0767	0.0517
Davidhead	110	360	0.0168	0.0103	0.1	0.0252	0.0251

Acknowledgments

This work was supported by the Natural Science Foundation of China under Grants 61370120, 61632006, and 11601151, the Beijing Natural Science Foundation under Grants 4162009 and 4152009, the Beijing Municipal Science and Technology Project under Grants Z171100000517003 and Z151100002115040, the Beijing Transportation Industry Science and Technology Project, the Funding Project for Academic Human Resources Development in Institutions of Higher Learning Under the Jurisdiction of Beijing Municipality under Grant IDHT20150504, and the Jing-Hua Talents Project of the Beijing University of Technology.

References

[1] X. Gu, S. J. Gortler, and H. Hoppe, "Geometry images," *ACM Transactions on Graphics*, vol. 21, no. 3, pp. 355–361, 2002.

[2] E. Praun and H. Hoppe, "Spherical parametrization and remeshing," *ACM Transactions on Graphics*, vol. 22, no. 3, pp. 340–349, 2003.

[3] M. Gauthier and P. Poulin, "Geometry images of arbitrary genus in the spherical domain," *Computer Graphics Forum*, vol. 28, no. 8, pp. 2201–2215, 2009.

[4] K. Zhou, H. Bao, J. Shi, and Q. Peng, "Geometric signal compression," *Journal of Computer Science and Technology*, vol. 19, no. 5, pp. 596–606, 2004.

[5] M. Gauthier and P. Poulin, "Preserving sharp edges in geometry images," *In Proceedings of Graphics Interface*, pp. 1–6, 2009.

[6] W. Meng, B. Sheng, W. Lv, H. Sun, and E. Wu, "Differential geometry images: remeshing and morphing with local shape preservation," *Visual Computer*, vol. 26, no. 1, pp. 51–62, 2010.

[7] G. Tewari, J. Snyder, P. V. Sander, S. J. Gortler, and H. Hoppe, "Signal-specialized parameterization for piecewise linear reconstruction," in *Proceedings of the the 2004 Eurographics/ACM SIGGRAPH symposium*, p. 55, Nice, France, July 2004.

[8] N. A. Carr, J. Hoberock, K. Crane, and J. Hart, "Rectangular multi-chart geometry images," *Eurographics Symposium on Geometry Processing*, pp. 181–190, 2006.

[9] C. Y. Yao and T. Y. Lee, "Adaptive geometry image," *IEEE Transactions on Visualization and Computer Graphics*, vol. 14, no. 4, pp. 948–960, 2008.

[10] W.-W. Feng, B.-U. Kim, Y. Yu, L. Peng, and J. Hart, "Feature-preserving triangular geometry images for level-of-detail representation of static and skinned meshes," *ACM Transactions on Graphics*, vol. 29, no. 2, article no. 11, 2010.

[11] P. Alliez, M. Meyer, and M. Desbrun, "Interactive geometry remeshing," *ACM Transactions on Graphics*, vol. 21, no. 21, pp. 347–354, 2002.

[12] P. Alliez, D. Cohen-Steiner, O. Devillers, B. Lévy, and M. Desbrun, "Anisotropic polygonal remeshing," *ACM Transactions on Graphics*, vol. 22, no. 3, pp. 485–493, 2003.

[13] S. Dong, S. Kircher, and M. Garland, "Harmonic functions for quadrilateral remeshing of arbitrary manifolds," *Computer Aided Geometric Design*, vol. 22, no. 5, pp. 392–423, 2005.

[14] J. Huang, M. Zhang, J. Ma, X. Liu, L. Kobbelt, and H. Bao, "Spectral quadrangulation with orientation and alignment control," *ACM Transactions on Graphics*, vol. 27, no. 5, article no. 147, 2008.

[15] M. Zhang, J. Huang, X. Liu, and H. Bao, "A wave-based anisotropic quadrangulation method," *ACM Transactions on Graphics*, vol. 29, no. 4, pp. 157–166, 2010.

[16] N. Aspert, D. Santa-Cruz, and T. Ebrahimi, "MESH: Measuring errors between surfaces using the Hausdorff distance," in *Proceedings of the 2002 IEEE International Conference on Multimedia and Expo, ICME 2002*, pp. 705–708, IEEE, Lausanne, Switzerland, August 2002.

[17] M. Bartoň, I. Hanniel, G. Elber, and M. Kim, "Precise Hausdorff distance computation between polygonal meshes," *Computer Aided Geometric Design*, vol. 27, no. 8, pp. 580–591, 2010.

[18] W. T. Tutte, "How to draw a graph," *Proceedings of the London Mathematical Society. Third Series*, vol. 13, pp. 743–767, 1963.

[19] S. Yoshizawa, A. Belyaev, and H. P. Seidel, "A fast and simple stretch-minimizing mesh parameterization," in *Proceedings of the Shape Modeling Applications*, IEEE, Genova, Italy, June 2004.

11

A Novel Preferential Diffusion Recommendation Algorithm based on User's Nearest Neighbors

Fuguo Zhang,[1,2] Yehuan Liu,[1] and Qinqiao Xiong[1]

[1]*School of Information Technology, Jiangxi University of Finance & Economics, Nanchang 330013, China*
[2]*Research Institution for Information Resource Management, Jiangxi University of Finance & Economics, Nanchang 330013, China*

Correspondence should be addressed to Fuguo Zhang; redbird_mail@163.com

Academic Editor: Hyo-Jong Lee

Recommender system is a very efficient way to deal with the problem of information overload for online users. In recent years, network based recommendation algorithms have demonstrated much better performance than the standard collaborative filtering methods. However, most of network based algorithms do not give a high enough weight to the influence of the target user's nearest neighbors in the resource diffusion process, while a user or an object with high degree will obtain larger influence in the standard mass diffusion algorithm. In this paper, we propose a novel preferential diffusion recommendation algorithm considering the significance of the target user's nearest neighbors and evaluate it in the three real-world data sets: MovieLens 100k, MovieLens 1M, and Epinions. Experiments results demonstrate that the novel preferential diffusion recommendation algorithm based on user's nearest neighbors can significantly improve the recommendation accuracy and diversity.

1. Introduction

With the rapid development of Internet in the past years, the amount of online information increases at an exponential speed, which leads to information overload problem. When faced with vast amount of information, we can hardly find the valuable information accurately and quickly. The personalized recommender system is one of the most effective tools to resolve this problem, and it also can help enterprises make the users' potential demand a realistic demand [1, 2].

To date, various recommendation methods have been proposed and developed. One of the most successful recommender system methods is based on the collaborative filtering technique [3–5]. Recently, some physical methods, such as mass diffusion [6–9] and heat conduction [10, 11], have found applications in personalized recommendation. Standard mass diffusion algorithm applied the three-step mass diffusion starting from the target user on a user-object bipartite network, which accurately outperforms the standard collaborative filtering methods [1]. Many different bipartite network based methods [12] are proposed to achieve even better recommendation performance. In [6], Zhou et al. proposed

a hybrid method by combining the mass diffusion and heat conduction to solve the apparent diversity-accuracy dilemma of recommender systems. Motivated by enhancing the preferential diffusion algorithm's ability to find unpopular and niche objects, the preferential diffusion has been designed in [9]. Moreover, Zhang and Zeng proposed a strategy to adding some virtual connections to the networks, which is useful to deal with the cold start problem in recommender system [13].

However, all these methods do not give a high enough weight to the influence of the target user's nearest neighbors in the resource diffusion process. As we all know, birds of a feather flock together. The user's nearest neighbors are the ones who have similar taste with the given user. Therefore we introduce a novel preferential diffusion recommendation algorithm considering the significance of the target user's nearest neighbors in the diffusion process.

2. Methods

A recommender system can be represented by a bipartite network $G(U, O, E)$, where $U = \{u_1, u_2, \ldots, u_m\}$, $O = \{o_1, o_2, \ldots, o_n\}$, and $E = \{e_1, e_2, \ldots, e_q\}$ are the sets of users, objects,

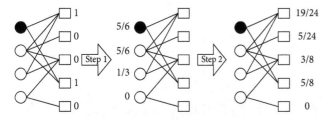

FIGURE 1: Standard mass diffusion algorithm at work on the bipartite user-object network. Users are shown as circles and objects are squares. The target user is indicated by the black circle.

and links, respectively [7]. Denote by $A_{m \times n}$ the adjacency matrix, where the element $a_{ia} = 1$ if the user i has selected the object a and $a_{ia} = 0$ otherwise.

2.1. Standard Mass Diffusion Recommendation Algorithm. As is shown in Figure 1, the standard mass diffusion (SMD) algorithm is equivalent to a three-step random walk process. At first, objects in the bipartite network are assigned an initial resource f, with $f^i = \{f_1^i, f_2^i, \ldots, f_\alpha^i, \ldots, f_n^i\}$ for the target user i. For simplicity, if an object is collected by the user i, its initial resource is assigned to be 1, otherwise it is assigned to be 0. That is to say, the initial resource vector f can be written as

$$f_\alpha^i = a_{i\alpha}. \tag{1}$$

Then, each object's resource is redistributed to the user who has collected the object averagely, and the user's resource is the sum of the resources received from objects. At last, each user's resource was reallocated to the objects which he has collected averagely. The final score of the object's resource can be calculated via the transformation $f' = Wf$, where W is the resource transfer matrix.

$$w_{\alpha\beta} = \frac{1}{k_\beta} \sum_{l=1}^{m} \frac{a_{l\alpha} a_{l\beta}}{k_l}, \tag{2}$$

where k_β is the degree of the object β and k_l is the degree of the user l.

2.2. The Novel Preferential Diffusion Algorithm Based on User's Nearest Neighbors. Following on from previous research [14], the diffusion process of the novel preferential diffusion recommendation algorithm based on user's nearest neighbors (NNMD) is shown in Figure 2. At first, we calculate the Jaccard similarities between the target user i and the other users to get the top N similar neighbors. The formula of Jaccard similarity reads

$$J_{ij} = \frac{\left| N_i \cap N_j \right|}{\left| N_i \cup N_j \right|}, \tag{3}$$

where J_{ij} is the Jaccard similarity between user i and user j and N_i and N_j are the user neighbors set of user i and user j, respectively. Then we can get the objects' initial resource

denoted by the vector f_1, with $f_1^i = \{f_{11}^i, f_{12}^i, \ldots, f_{1\alpha}^i, \ldots, f_{1n}^i\}$ for the target user i. f_1 can be written as

$$f_{1\alpha}^i = a_{i\alpha} + \sum_{k \in U} a_{k\alpha}, \tag{4}$$

where U is the nearest neighbors set of the target user i. In Figure 2, $f_1 = (3, 1, 2, 2, 0)$. But only the objects which the target user i has selected can distribute the resources to users and then redistribute them via the transformation

$$f_2 = W(f_1 f), \tag{5}$$

where W is the same as (2). In Figure 2, $f_2 = (2, 0.5, 1, 1.5, 0)$. Finally, we use the linear combination the resources vectors f_1 and f_2 to get the last objects' resources vector F. That is to say,

$$F = \alpha f_1 + (1 - \alpha) f_2, \tag{6}$$

where α is a variable parameter from 0 to 1.

3. Data and Metrics

3.1. Data. To test the algorithmic performance, we use three benchmark data sets as shown in Table 1. The sparsity of these data sets is shown in the last column of Table 1. They are very sparse, especially Epinions data set. MovieLens 100k and MovieLens 1M data sets [15] were collected by the GroupLens research group. They consist of 100000 ratings from 943 users on 1682 different movies and 1000209 ratings from 6040 users on 3952 different movies, respectively. The ratings are integer numbers in the range of 1 to 5 scales. The Epinions data set [16] consists of 22166 users, 296277 objects, and 922267 ratings. It is noted that Epinions data set is highly sparse. Users only rate a small number of items in the system, and, in order to get better results, we delete those users and objects with degree less than 7. Finally, we get a new data set which consists of 4066 users, 7649 objects, and 154122 ratings. We randomly divide the data sets into two parts: the training set E^T contains 80% of the data and the remaining 20% of data constitutes the probe set E^P.

3.2. Metrics. There has been considerable research in the area of recommender systems evaluation. Accuracy is the most important aspect in evaluating the recommendation algorithmic performance. In this paper, we use ranking score [8] to measure the ability of a recommendation algorithm to generate a ranking list of the target user's uncollected objects that matches the users' preference. For the target user u_i, the recommendation algorithm will return u_i a ranking list of all his unselected objects and, according to E^P, if u_i has selected the object o_j and o_j is at r_{ij}th place in the ranking list, we say the position of o_j is

$$R_{ij} = \frac{r_{ij}}{L}, \tag{7}$$

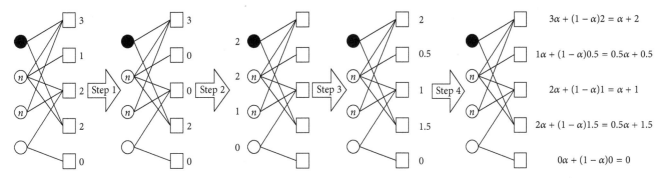

FIGURE 2: A novel preferential diffusion algorithm by user's nearest neighbors at work on the bipartite user-object network. Users are shown as circles and objects are squares. The target user is indicated by the black circle and the nearest neighbors of the target user are the circles which have a letter "n" in them and α is the variable parameter.

TABLE 1: Basic properties of the three data sets and the sparsity is defined as $E/(N_u N_o)$.

Network	E	N_u	N_o	Sparsity
MovieLens 100k	100000	943	1682	0.063
MovieLens 1M	1000209	6040	3952	0.042
Epinions	154122	4066	7649	0.005

TABLE 2: The four cases of the unselected objects of the target user in the recommender system.

User likes	Recommender system recommended	Recommender system did not recommend
Likes	C_{tp}	C_{fn}
Does not like	C_{fp}	C_{tn}

where L is the number of his unselected objects. We obtain the mean value of all the user-object ranking scores in E^P; namely,

$$R = \frac{1}{|E^P|} \sum_{ij \in E^P} R_{ij}. \qquad (8)$$

Clearly, the larger the ranking score, the lower the algorithm's accuracy and vice versa.

In the practical recommender system, we may consider the number of objects that users like in the recommendation list. Therefore, we take another accuracy metric called precision. For a target object o_j and user u_i, there are four cases in the recommender system. The first is that the recommender system recommended the object and user likes it. The second is that recommender system recommended the object but the user does not like it. The third is that the user likes the object but the recommender system did not recommend it. Finally is the case that the user does not like the object and the recommender system did not recommend it. As is shown in Table 2, C_{tp}, C_{fn}, C_{fp}, and C_{tn} denote the number of the objects in the four cases.

For a target user u_i, the precision of recommendation $P_i(L)$ is defined as

$$P_i(L) = \frac{C_{tp}}{L} = \frac{C_{tp}}{C_{tp} + C_{fp}}. \qquad (9)$$

We obtain the mean precision $P(L)$ of all the users in the recommender system. Besides accuracy, diversity is taken into account as another important aspect to evaluate the recommendation algorithm. There are two kinds of diversity. One is called intrauser-diversity [17]; the other is called interuser-diversity [18]. In this paper, we consider the interuser-diversity. It considers the different objects between users in the recommendation list. For two users u_i and u_j, the differences can use be measured by the Hamming distance [18]:

$$H_{ij}(L) = 1 - \frac{S_{ij}(L)}{L}, \qquad (10)$$

where $S_{ij}(L)$ is the number of common objects between u_i and u_j in the recommendation list and L is the length of the recommendation list. Clearly, if u_i and u_j have the same recommendation list, $H_{ij}(L) = 0$, while if the recommendation lists are completely different, $H_{ij}(L) = 1$.

In reality, it has been found that a recommender system which has a high accuracy might not be satisfied by the users [19]. For example, for a film website, recommending the popular films to the users may not always be the best recommendation, because users might have already seen those films in other ways. A good recommender system can find the objects that match the users' preferences and are unlikely to be already known. As a result, the novelty is also often used in evaluating the recommendation algorithmic performance.

The average degree of objects in the recommendation list is widely used to identify the novelty of a recommender system [20], which is defined by

$$N(L) = \frac{1}{ML} \sum_u \sum_{o_\partial \in O_R^i} k_{o_\partial}, \qquad (11)$$

where M is the number of users, O_R^i is the recommendation list for user u_i, and k_{o_∂} is the degree of the object o_∂.

TABLE 3: Algorithmic performance for MovieLens 100k, MovieLens 1M, and Epinions data. The precision, interuser-diversity, and novelty are corresponding to $L = 20$. The parameters for NNMD are $N = 50$ and $\alpha = 0.9$ in MovieLens 100k and MovieLens 1M, while, in Epinions, the parameters are $N = 10$ and $\alpha = 0$. The entries corresponding to the best performance over all methods are emphasized in bold.

Data set	Algorithms	Ranking score	Precision	Interuser-diversity	Novelty
MovieLens 100k	NNMD	**0.059537**	**0.2242**	**0.8401**	**237**
	SMD	0.069011	0.1971	0.6970	279
MovieLens 1M	NNMD	**0.077039**	**0.2726**	**0.8816**	**1340**
	SMD	0.095269	0.1949	0.5865	1828
Epinions	NNMD	**0.180439**	**0.0374**	**0.6787**	**204**
	SMD	0.181141	0.0357	0.6743	205

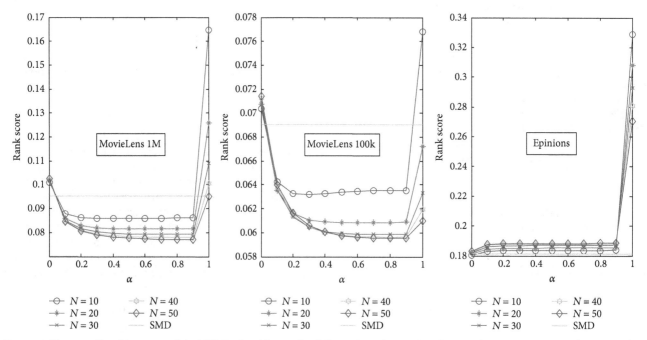

FIGURE 3: The overall ranking score of the NNMD algorithm under different N and α in MovieLens 100k, MovieLens 1M, and Epinions data set and the ranking score of the SMD algorithm in MovieLens 100k, MovieLens 1M, and Epinions.

4. Results and Discussion

In our first set of experiments, we compare the ranking score of the NNMD algorithm under different α and top N (N is the number of the target user's nearest neighbors) with that of the SMD algorithm. The results on MovieLens 100k, MovieLens 1M, and Epinions data are reported in Figure 3. Clearly, we can see that in MovieLens 100k and MovieLens 1M, with the increase of N, the rank score is smaller and smaller; that is to say, the recommendation accuracy is getting better and better. However, when N is more than 30, the change of rank score is very small. Moreover, as long as α is not equal to 0 or 1, the rank score of our method is better than that of the SMD algorithm. It is interesting to note that the optimal parameters of our method are the same in MovieLens 100k and MovieLens 1M, which are $N = 50$ and $\alpha = 0.9$, while, in Epinions, the improvement of the rank score is not significant. When α is greater than 0 or N is greater than 20 the rank score of the NNMD algorithm is a little worse than

that of the SMD algorithm, and, with the change of α and N, the rank scores of the two algorithms are almost the same. But when N is less than 20 and $\alpha = 0$, the rank score of our method is getting better than that of the SMD algorithm. Clearly, we can get the optimal parameters $N = 10$ and $\alpha = 0$ in Epinions.

Then we examined the performance in precision, interuser-diversity, and novelty of our novel algorithm at the optimal parameters N and α. Summaries of the results for all algorithms and metrics on MovieLens 100k, MovieLens 1M, and Epinions data sets are shown in Table 3. The optimal parameters are subject to the lowest ranking score. The other three metrics, namely, precision, interuser-diversity, and novelty, are obtained at the optimal parameters. Clearly, the NNMD algorithm outperforms the SMD algorithm over all four evaluation metrics.

The comparison of precision between NNMD and SMD in three data sets under different length of recommendation list is shown in Figure 4. It clearly indicates that the precision

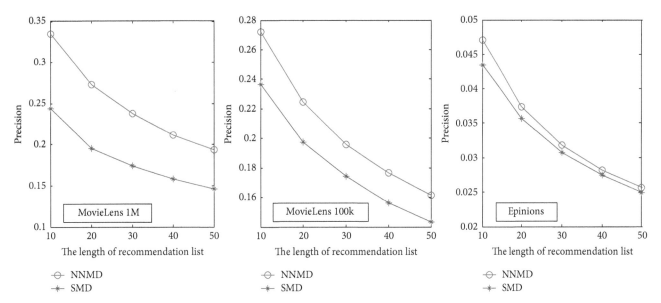

FIGURE 4: The precision of NNMD and SMD algorithm in MovieLens 100k, MovieLens 1M, and Epinions under different length of recommendation list. The parameters for the NNMD algorithm are $N = 50$ and $\alpha = 0.9$ in MovieLens 100k and MovieLens 1M while they are $N = 10$ and $\alpha = 0$ in Epinions.

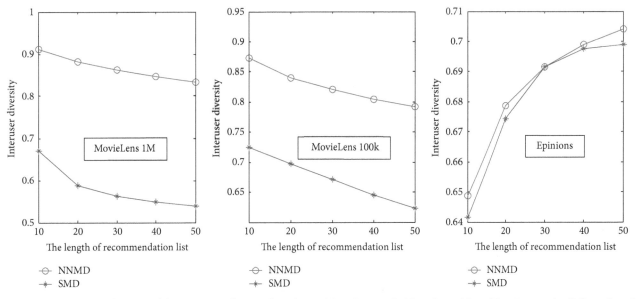

FIGURE 5: The interuser-diversity of the NNMD and SMD algorithm in MovieLens 100k, MovieLens 1M, and Epinions under different length of recommendation list. The parameters for the NNMD algorithm are $N = 50$ and $\alpha = 0.9$ in MovieLens 100k and MovieLens 1M while they are $N = 10$ and $\alpha = 0$ in Epinions.

of the NNMD algorithm is better than that of the NMD algorithm in all the three data sets and it has a very significant improvement in MovieLens 100k and MovieLens 1M. That is to say, our method can recommend objects for users more accurately.

Figure 5 shows the comparison of interuser-diversity between our method NNMD and SMD in three data sets under different length of recommendation list. It clearly shows that interuser-diversity of our NNMD algorithm is better than that of the SMD algorithm in all the three data sets, especially in MovieLens 100k and MovieLens 1M. In

other words, the objects in the recommendation list of our method are more different between users.

Figure 6 shows the comparison of novelty between our method NNMD and SMD in three data sets under different length of recommendation list. It clearly indicates that the novelty of our method is much better than the SMD in Movie-Lens 100k and MovieLens 1M, while, in Epinions, the results of the two algorithms are very similar, but our method also has a little improvement than that of the SMD algorithm.

In summary, the recommendation performance of our method is better than that of the standard mass diffusion. In

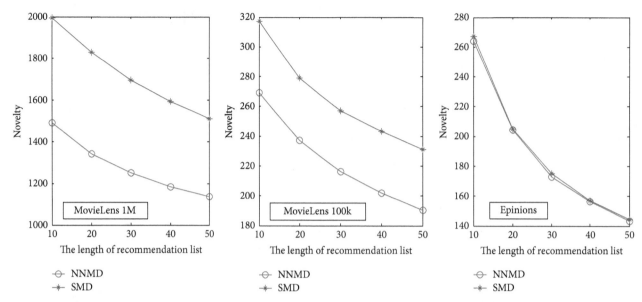

FIGURE 6: The novelty of NNMD and SMD algorithm in MovieLens 100k, MovieLens 1M, and Epinions under different length of recommendation list. The parameters for the NNMD algorithm are $N = 50$ and $\alpha = 0.9$ in MovieLens 100k and MovieLens 1M, while they are $N = 10$ and $\alpha = 0$ in Epinions.

particular, the precision of our method increases an average of 13.27% percent compared to that of the SMD in MovieLens 100k and increases an average of 35.9% percent in MovieLens 1M and increases an average of 4.47% percent in Epinions. Although the improvement of the algorithmic performance in some aspects is not significant in Epinions data set, the reason may be that the data is so sparse that the novel algorithm cannot get the proper user's nearest neighbors and it affects our algorithmic performance.

5. Conclusion and Future Work

Most of network based recommendation algorithms have a tendency to recommend popular objects to the users [1] because the object with high degree has a significant influence in the resource diffusion process. In this paper we propose a novel preferential diffusion recommendation algorithm based on user's nearest neighbors which give a high weight to the influence of the target user's nearest neighbors in the resource diffusion process. Experimental results based on MovieLens 100k, MovieLens 1M, and Epinions data set show that making a suitable adjustment in the parameter α or the size of the user's nearest neighbors set can help recommendation algorithm get a better recommendation performance. It can not only provide more accurate recommendations but also generate more diverse and novel recommendations.

For future work, we intend to consider the level of rating between user and his nearest neighbors. Moreover, we will use the trust data [21, 22] in the network, because it can be used to find the nearest neighbors more accurately in high sparse data set, and it may have a better recommendation performance.

Acknowledgments

This work is partially supported by National Natural Science Foundation of China (Grant nos. 71361012 and 71363022), by National Science Foundation of Jiangxi, China (no. 20161BAB201029), and by the Foundation of Jiangxi Provincial Department of Education (no. GJJ. 150446).

References

[1] T. Zhoua, Z. Kuscsik, J. Liu, M. Medo, J. R. Wakeling, and Y. Zhang, "Solving the apparent diversity-accuracy dilemma of recommender systems," *Proceedings of the National Academy of Sciences of the United States of America*, vol. 107, no. 10, pp. 4511–4515, 2010.

[2] L. Lü, M. Medo, C. H. Yeung, Y. Zhang, Z. Zhang, and T. Zhou, "Recommender systems," *Physics Reports*, vol. 519, no. 1, pp. 1–49, 2012.

[3] J. A. Konstan, B. N. Miller, D. Maltz, J. L. Herlocker, L. R. Gordon, and J. Riedl, "Applying collaborative filtering to usenet news," *Communications of the ACM*, vol. 40, no. 3, pp. 77–87, 1997.

[4] J. S. Breese, D. Heckerman, and C. Kadie, "Empirical analysis of predictive algorithms for collaborative filtering," in *Proceedings of the 14th conference on Uncertainty in Artificial Intelligence*, pp. 43–52, 1998.

[5] G. Adomavicius and A. Tuzhilin, "Toward the next generation of recommender systems: a survey of the state-of-the-art and possible extensions," *IEEE Transactions on Knowledge and Data Engineering*, vol. 17, no. 6, pp. 734–749, 2005.

[6] T. Zhou, J. Ren, M. Medo, and Y. Zhang, "Bipartite network projection and personal recommendation," *Physical Review E*, vol. 76, no. 4, Article ID e046115, 2007.

[7] M. S. Shang, L. Lu, Y. C. Zhang, and T. Zhou, "Empirical analysis of web-based user-object bipartite networks," *Europhysics Letters*, vol. 90, no. 4, Article ID e48006, 2010.

[8] A. Zeng, A. Vidmer, M. Medo, and Y.-C. Zhang, "Information filtering by similarity-preferential diffusion processes," *EPL*, vol. 105, no. 5, Article ID e58002, 2014.

[9] L. Lu and W. Liu, "Information filtering via preferential diffusion," *Physical Review E*, vol. 83, no. 6, Article ID e066119, 2011.

[10] Y. C. Zhang, M. Blattner, and Y. K. Yu, "Heat conduction process On community networks as a recommendation model," *Physical Review Letters*, vol. 99, no. 10, Article ID 154301, 2007.

[11] J. G. Liu, T. Zhou, and Q. Guo, "Information filtering via biased heat conduction," *Physical Review E*, vol. 84, no. 3, Article ID e037101, 2011.

[12] F. Yu, A. Zeng, S. Gillard, and M. Medo, "Network-based recommendation algorithms: a review," *Physica A: Statistical Mechanics and Its Applications*, vol. 452, pp. 192–208, 2016.

[13] F. Zhang and A. Zeng, "Improving information filtering via network manipulation," *Europhysics Letters*, vol. 100, no. 5, Article ID 58005, 2012.

[14] F. G. Zhang, Y. H. Liu, and Q. Q. Xiong, "A novel mass diffusion recommendation algorithm based on user's nearest neighbors," in *Proceedings of the International Symposium on Information Technology Convergence*, 2016.

[15] http://www.grouplens.org/.

[16] http://www.epinions.com/.

[17] T. Zhou, R. Q. Su, R. R. Liu, L. L. Jiang, B. H. Wang, and Y. Zhang, "Accurate and diverse recommendations via eliminating redundant correlations," *New Journal of Physics*, vol. 11, Article ID 123008, 2009.

[18] T. Zhou, L. L. Jiang, R. Q. Su, and Y. C. Zhang, "Effect of initial configuration on network-based recommendation," *Europhysics Letters*, vol. 81, no. 5, pp. 58004–58007, 2008.

[19] M. Ge, C. Delgado-Battenfeld, and D. Jannach, "Beyond accuracy: evaluating recommender systems by coverage and serendipity," in *Proceedings of the 4th ACM Conference on Recommender Systems (RecSys '10)*, pp. 257–260, Barcelona, Spain, September 2010.

[20] Z.-K. Zhang, C. Liu, Y.-C. Zhang, and T. Zhou, "Solving the cold-start problem in recommender systems with social tags," *Europhysics Letters*, vol. 92, no. 2, Article ID 28002, 2010.

[21] C. Martinez-Cruz, C. Porcel, J. Bernabé-Moreno, and E. Herrera-Viedma, "A model to represent users trust in recommender systems using ontologies and fuzzy linguistic modeling," *Information Sciences*, vol. 311, pp. 102–118, 2015.

[22] X. Qian, H. Feng, G. Zhao, and T. Mei, "Personalized recommendation combining user interest and social circle," *IEEE Transactions on Knowledge and Data Engineering*, vol. 26, no. 7, pp. 1763–1777, 2014.

12

A Novel Method of Complexity Metric for Object-Oriented Software

Tong Yi and **Chun Fang**

School of Information Management, Jiangxi University of Finance and Economics, Nanchang 330013, China

Correspondence should be addressed to Tong Yi; 1337742168@qq.com

Guest Editor: Yuanlong Cao

With the rapid development and wide application of multimedia technology, the demand for the actual development of multimedia software in many industries is increasing. How to measure and improve the quality of multimedia software is an important problem to be solved urgently. In order to calculate the complicated situation and fuzziness of software quality, this paper introduced a software quality evaluation model based on the fuzzy matter element by using a method known as the fuzzy matter element analysis, combined with the TOPSIS method and the close degree. Compared with the existing typical software measurement methods, the results are basically consistent with the typical software measurement results. Then, Pearson simple correlation coefficient was used to analyse the correlation between the existing four measurement methods and the metric of practical experience, whose results show that the results of software quality measures based on fuzzy matter element are more in accordance with practical experience. Meanwhile, the results of this method are much more precise than the results of the other measurement methods.

1. Introduction

At present, with the rise and application of multimedia technology, it is a great challenge to provide more reliable technical support and strong technical support for the development of multimedia software. At the same time, object-oriented technology has become the mainstream of current software development, which is suitable for developing multimedia software, for example, using the image processing software Adobe Photoshop developed by C++, using Action Script to develop animation processing software Flash, and using C++ for the Jedi survival and heroic alliance games.

We must point out that multimedia software is a typical complex system; therefore, how to scientifically measure the complexity of multimedia software plays a vital role in developing high-quality multimedia software. Software metrics has become the important and long-term focused research field of software engineering and also became an important and effective method in assessing and predicting software development activities. The purpose of software metrics research is to provide guidance for developing high-quality software [1].

Since the concept of software measurement was first proposed by Rubey R. J. and Hartwick R. D. in 1968[2], the researches, development, and applications have been carried out for more than fifty years. Through literature review, this paper found that previous researches mainly from internal attributes, external attributes, and other aspects of the research of software quality metric. Over these years, many scholars have made a broad and deep research on the software quality metric and prefer to find the key or the important software quality measurement factors from the inner elements of software itself. The factors were measured or counted directly or indirectly to construct the corresponding metric model. Early metrics on structured programs were primarily focused on Lines of Code (LOC) [3], McCabe coloring graph method [4], Function Point Analysis (FPA) [5], etc.

In 1994, Chidamber S. and Kemerer C. proposed a CK metrics set for object-oriented software quality metrics research. The Weighted Methods per Class (WMC), Number of Children (NOC), Depth of Inheritance (DIT), Coupling Between Objects (CBO), Lack of Cohesion (LCOM), and Response for a Class (RFC) are included in set, which are the fundamental of object-oriented software quality metrics.

Padhy N. et al. proposed the three metrics based on CK metrics set and combined WMC, RFC, CBO, DIT. and NOC together [6]. In addition, Misra S. and Adewumi A. et al. proposed a cognitive complexity metrics set for evaluating object-oriented software projects [7], including method complexity, message complexity, attribute complexity, weighted class complexity, and code complexity. According to software measurement experience, Gupta D. L. et al. proposed some possible exist the hypothetical situation in measurement validation and design 14 measurement elements, including WMC, CBO, and RFC. Furthermore, Gupta D. L. et al. took open source software code as the data source and used SPSS software make logistic regression analysis. The results of the study showed that these methods can predict design flaw of class in software quality metric, and software defects prediction methods based on object-oriented metrics are developed [8]. Wang J. and Wang Q. found that dependency relationship is an important reason of software complexity. The dependency relationship can reflect cohesion and coupling between software elements. Meanwhile, cohesion and coupling are recognized as a measure of software quality of the important indicators. Besides, the dependency relationship of software is proved to be an important factor of software defects prediction through the experimental study. It can predict software integration errors and provide help for software quality metric in early stage [9]. The above methods of object-oriented software metrics are all belong to research of software quality metric based on software internal attributes.

However, developers and researchers paid attention to broad software quality characteristics in the process of software quality metric research based on external attributes of software quality. These characteristics include software quality characteristics of ISO/IEC 25010 software quality model in narrow sense and other software quality characteristics associated with software development and application. Gosain A. and Sharma G. defined the dynamic software quality characteristics, including robust, unambiguous, dynamic, discriminating, and machine independent. Then they evaluated cases with Java software and found that the dynamic software quality characteristic has significant positive correlation with maintainability by Pearson correlation analysis and principal component analysis [10]. Similarly, Hu X and Zuo J. et al. choose 6 software quality characteristics from GB/T16260 series of standards. The 6 software quality characteristics include capability, reliability, usability, efficiency, maintainability, and portability. Then the hierarchical model of evaluation is established for research and analysis external attributes of software quality [11].

Class diagram, a very important software model diagram, describes the classes and their relationships among the systems. They can be scientifically constructed whether or not it has a significant impact on the complexity of software. At present, the class complexity measure method is still rare. Marchesi M. [12] uses 7 indicators to measure the complexity of the class diagram from different angles. However, the method only considers the relationship between classes and inheritance, without considering other relationships, such as the association relationship and aggregation relationship.

On the basis of Marchesi M. research, Genero M. [13] uses 14 indicators to further distinguish the relationship between classes and classes, that is, the combination of relative complexity measure and absolute complexity measure. The theories of Dr. Zhang Y. [14], In P. [15], Gosain A. [10], Gupta D. L. [8], and Padhy N. [6] are similar with Genero M's, which use a set of indicators to evaluate the complexity of class diagrams. The advantage of it could analyse the complexity of a class diagram from different perspectives, but its disadvantage is that it is difficult to compare two or two class diagrams. Dr. Zhou Y. transforms UML class diagrams into weighted dependencies. And then he uses the information entropy to define the complexity of UML class diagram [16], which has achieved good measure results. Dr. Yi T. has made improvements on the basis of Dr. Zhou Y. making a comprehensive consideration of interclass relationships, class attributes, and class complexity of the method. He proposed a UML class diagram complexity measurement method based on dependency analysis [17, 18].

In this paper, the research work mentioned above is a part of existing domestic and international research work, but there is no doubt that the results of researches in the UML class diagram model are not enough. One of the important reasons is that UML standard issued by the object management group (OMG) only gives the description of the semantic conceptual level in various modelling elements, which leads to the fact that the researchers often use different weighting indicators for the class diagram model. It means that researchers do not have a uniform standard, resulting in different metrics for the same class diagram. Meanwhile, because of the comprehensiveness, fuzziness, and complexity of the software quality measurement system, the software quality measurement is a process of multiple indicator decision making; the fuzzy matter element theory is introduced in this paper. In order to overcome the limitation of weight precision of the class relationship between two classes in the literature [16–18], this paper proceeds from fuzzy matter element theory, introducing the concept of close degree, and used entropy method to calculate the weight of every indicator; software quality measurement model was established in fuzzy matter element that based on entropy weight and TOPSIS method applied to UML class diagram metric. Firstly, element indicators of UML class diagram constitute the compound fuzzy matrix of matter elements and then fuzzy matrix of matter elements of the optimal subordinate degree obtained with the dimensionless, calculating the weight of each element indicators by entropy method, finally, through TOPSIS method and the concept of Euclid approach degree got comprehensive attribute values of each UML class diagrams. This paper hopes to only use a comprehensive complexity value to evaluate the complexity of UML class diagram and enough really predicts the complexity of software quality.

2. A Novel Method of Complexity Metric for Software Quality

2.1. Building Evaluate Compound Fuzzy Matter Element of Software Quality. Matter element analysis [19] is a new discipline that studies laws and methods for solving incompatible problems. It is an intersecting edge discipline of thinking science, systems science, and mathematics. Matter element analysis itself is not a branch of mathematics. It is a new discipline that develops on the basis of classical mathematics and fuzzy mathematics and is different from them. The new subject, Matter Element Analysis, which was created in 1994 by Chinese scholar Cai Wen, was specifically designed to solve incompatible problems. The fuzzy matter element combines fuzzy set theory and matter element analysis theory, which can not only solve the ambiguity of measurement indicators, but also solve the incompatibility of measurement results. Because of its simple calculation method, reliable evaluation results, and strong practicality, this theory is widely used in logistics science and technology [20], electromechanical [21], architecture [22], and other fields.

The matter element $R = (T, C, X)$ for evaluating the software quality was constructed in this paper, where T denotes the software class diagram to be evaluated, C denotes the evaluation indicator, and X denotes the corresponding magnitude of the evaluation indicator. If X has ambiguity, R is called a fuzzy matter element. If T has n evaluation indicators $C_1, C_2, \ldots, C_n$ whose corresponding magnitudes are $X_1, X_2, \ldots, X_n$, R is said to be n-dimensional fuzzy matter elements[23]. The n-dimensional matter elements of m the software diagrams to be evaluated are combined to form the n-dimensional compound fuzzy matter elements of m the software diagram to be evaluated. R_{mn} is defined as follows:

$$R_{mn} = \begin{pmatrix} & T_1 & T_2 & \cdots & T_m \\ C_1 & X_{11} & X_{21} & \cdots & X_{m1} \\ C_2 & X_{12} & X_{22} & \cdots & X_{m2} \\ \vdots & \vdots & \vdots & & \vdots \\ C_n & X_{1n} & X_{2n} & \cdots & X_{mn} \end{pmatrix} \quad (1)$$

In formula (1), T_i represents the i (i=1,2,... m) software class diagram, C_j is the j (j=1,2,...,n) evaluation indicator of the software class diagram, and X_{ij} represents the corresponding magnitude of the j evaluation indicator of the i software class diagram.

2.2. Dimensionless of Evaluation Indicators. In the evaluation of software class diagrams, there are many evaluation indicators involved. If there are no uniform metrics among the indicators, the evaluation process will be difficult to carry out. In order to compare the different dimension indicators together for comparison, the magnitude of these evaluation indicators must be dimensionless [23]. The dimensionless process is to remove the dimension's influence on the physical value through mathematical methods. There are generally two types of indicators for quantification processing results, some of which are larger and better indicators, that is, positive indicators; others are smaller, better indicators, that is, negative indicators. According to the actual situation, this

paper selects the smaller and better indicators in the software quality evaluation.

$$\max_j = \max \left(X_{1j}, X_{2j}, \ldots, X_{mj} \right) \quad (2)$$

$$\min_j = \min \left(X_{1j}, X_{2j}, \ldots, X_{mj} \right) \quad (3)$$

$$u_{ij} = \frac{\max_j - X_{ij}}{\max_j - \min_j} \quad (4)$$

In formula (4), u_{ij} is the dimensionless result of the j-th evaluation indicator of the i-th software class diagram. $\max_j$ is the maximum value of the j-th evaluation indicator of the software class diagram, and $\min_j$ is the minimum value of the j-th evaluation indicator of the software class diagram.

After the dimensionless treatment of formula (1) through formula (4), formula (5) is obtained, that is, the fuzzy matter element weight matrix of optimal membership degree R'_{mn}.

$$R'_{mn} = \begin{pmatrix} & T_1 & T_2 & \cdots & T_m \\ C_1 & u_{11} & u_{21} & \cdots & u_{m1} \\ C_2 & u_{12} & u_{22} & \cdots & u_{m2} \\ \vdots & \vdots & \vdots & \vdots & \vdots \\ C_n & u_{1n} & u_{2n} & \cdots & u_{mn} \end{pmatrix} \quad (5)$$

2.3. Evaluation Indicator Weight Determining Based on Entropy Method. In the process of software quality evaluation, the weight of an indicator reflects the relative importance of the indicator in the overall evaluation process. Therefore, the determination of weight is very important. Common weight determination methods include entropy method, expert scoring method, and analytic hierarchy process. This paper uses entropy method to calculate weights to achieve the subjective and objective unity of weights. The entropy method is based on the difference in the degree of information contained in each indicator, that is, the utility value of the information to determine the weight of the indicator. It is an objective weighting method.

The formula for calculating the information entropy and weight function in the comprehensive evaluation is as follows: For the software quality evaluation model in question, if there are initial data matrix R_{mn} of the n evaluation indicators of the m software class diagram to be evaluated, each indicator is significantly different in the dimension, order of magnitude, and merits of indicators. Therefore, the initial data must be standardized:

$$y_{ij} = \frac{X_{ij}}{\sum_{i=1}^m X_{ij}}, \quad i = 1, 2, \ldots, m; \quad j = 1, 2, \ldots, n \quad (6)$$

Get information entropy of the j-th evaluation indicator according to formula (7):

$$e_j = -k \sum_{i=1}^m y_{ij} \ln y_{ij}, \quad j = 1, 2, \ldots, n \quad (7)$$

The constant k in formula (7) is related to the number of samples, m, and $k = 1/\ln m$ is often taken. Because of information entropy e_j can be used to measure the information utility value of the j-th evaluation indicator. When the sample is completely disordered, $e_j = 1$; meanwhile, the information value of e_j is zero for the utility value of the comprehensive evaluation. Therefore, the information utility value of an evaluation indicator is determined by the difference between 1 and the information entropy e_j of the evaluation indicator; that is,

$$h_j = 1 - e_j, \quad j = 1, 2, \ldots, n \tag{8}$$

The entropy method is used to estimate the weight of the evaluation indicator. Its essence is to use the information utility value of the evaluation indicator to measure. When the difference h_j is higher, the importance of the evaluation is bigger, so the weight of the j-th evaluation indicator is

$$w_j = \frac{h_j}{\sum_{j=1}^{n} h_j}, \quad j = 1, 2, \ldots, n \tag{9}$$

Fuzzy matter element weight matrix of optimal membership degree is

$$R_w = \begin{pmatrix} C_1 & C_2 & \cdots & C_n \\ w_j & w_1 & w_2 & \cdots & w_n \end{pmatrix} \tag{10}$$

2.4. Fuzzy Compound Matter Element for Evaluating the Quality Characteristics. R_s is a weighted fuzzy compound matter element for evaluating the quality characteristics, and then there are

R_s

$$= \begin{pmatrix} & T_1 & T_2 & \cdots & T_m \\ C_1 & C_{11} = w_1 u_{11} & C_{21} = w_1 u_{21} & C_{m1} = w_1 u_{m1} \\ C_2 & C_{12} = w_2 u_{12} & C_{22} = w_2 u_{22} & C_{m1} = w_2 u_{m2} \\ \vdots & & & \\ C_n & C_{1n} = w_n u_{1n} & C_{2n} = w_n u_{2n} & C_{mn} = w_n u_{mn} \end{pmatrix} \tag{11}$$

In formula (11), $C_{ij} (i = 1, 2, \ldots, m; j = 1, 2, \ldots, n)$ the calculation value of the j-th evaluation indicator of the i-th software class diagram is represented.

2.5. Calculating Comprehensive Evaluation of Software Quality. TOPSIS (Technique for Order Preference by Similarity to Ideal Solution) [24] is a multiobjective decision-making method. The basic idea is to define the ideal solution and negative ideal solution of the decision problem. It is assumed that the ideal solution is the optimal program and the negative ideal solution is the worst program. If there is an evaluation plan in the feasible evaluation plan, the evaluation plan is the closest to the ideal, while far away from the negative ideal solution, we call this program the optimal program.

Further determine the ideal solution vector C^+ and negative ideal solution vector C^- of matrix R_s:

$$C^+ = (C_1^+, C_2^+, \ldots, C_n^+),$$
$$C_j^+ = \max \{C_{1j}, C_{2j}, \ldots, C_{mj}\}, \quad j = 1, 2, \ldots, n \tag{12}$$
$$C^- = (C_1^-, C_2^-, \ldots, C_n^-),$$
$$C_j^- = \min \{C_{1j}, C_{2j}, \ldots, C_{mj}\}, \quad j = 1, 2, \ldots, n \tag{13}$$

There are several ways to calculate the distance between ideal solutions and negative ideal solutions, such as Euclidean distance, Manhattan distance, Chebyshev distance, and so on. Among them, Euclidean distance is an easy-to-understand distance calculation method, which is derived from the distance formula between two points in Euclidean geometry. In this paper, the Euclidean distance is used, and its calculation formula is as follows [23]:

$$S_i^+ = \|C^+ - C_i\| = \sqrt{\sum_{j=1}^{n} (C^+ - C_{ij})^2}, \quad i = 1, 2, \ldots, m \tag{14}$$

$$S_i^- = \|C_i - C^-\| = \sqrt{\sum_{j=1}^{n} (C_{ij} - C^-)^2}, \quad i = 1, 2, \ldots, m \tag{15}$$

In formula (14) and formula (15), $C_i = (C_{i1}, C_{i2}, \cdots, C_{in})^T$; C_i is the i-th column vector of matrix R_s.

In this paper, the comprehensive evaluation of software quality adopts entropy method for consideration. The source has S_i^+ and S_i^-. The binary entropy function can be used to calculate the weights of the Euclidean distance between each class diagram to be evaluated and the ideal solution.

$$H^+ = H(S_i^+) = -S_i^+ \log_2 S_i^+ - (1 - S_i^+) \log_2 (1 - S_i^+),$$
$$i = 1, 2, \ldots, m \tag{16}$$

Similarly, the binary entropy function is used to calculate the weights of the Euclidean distances of each class diagram to be evaluated and the negative ideal solution; namely,

$$H^- = H(S_i^-) = -S_i^- \log_2 S_i^- - (1 - S_i^-) \log_2 (1 - S_i^-),$$
$$i = 1, 2, \ldots, m \tag{17}$$

According to the concept of close degree [23], combined with the uncertainty of the ideal solution and the negative ideal solution, the fuzzy matter element software quality metric measures the software quality by the following uncertainty-weighted fusion method. The calculation formula is as follows:

$$Z_i = \frac{H^+ S_i^+}{H^+ S_i^+ + H^- S_i^-}, \quad i = 1, 2, \ldots, m \tag{18}$$

In formula (18), the value is between 0 and 1. The closer the value is to 0, the evaluation object complexity is smaller and the closer to the optimal ideal level.

3. Case Analysis

3.1. Data Sources. In order to validate the measurement method proposed in this paper, we will do an experiment to estimate the metric values. With the permission of Genero M., we selected twenty-six UML class diagrams [13] related to the bank information systems as the object of the experiment. For better representation, NDep represents dependency, NAssoc represents normal association, NAgg represents aggregation, NGen represents generalization, NM represents class method, NA represents class attribute, and NC represents the number of classes. For specific indicators and data for details, see Table 1.

3.2. Model Establishment. According to the above theory and evaluation indicator system, the steps for establishing a fuzzy matter element evaluation model are as follows.

Step 1. Construct the composite fuzzy matrix of matter elements according to Table 1.

Step 2. Calculate the degree of optimal membership. According to the compound fuzzy matter element matrix determined in the first step, the degree of optimal membership is calculated using formula (4), and the fuzzy matter element matrix of optimal membership degree is obtained.

$$
R'_{26\times7} =
\begin{pmatrix}
 & T_1 & T_2 & T_3 & T_4 & \cdots & T_{25} & T_{26} \\
NDep & 1 & 1 & 1 & 1 & \cdots & 0 & 1 \\
NAssoc & 0.928571 & 0.928571 & 0.928571 & 0.785714 & \cdots & 0 & 0.642857 \\
NAgg & 1 & 0.888889 & 0.777778 & 1 & \cdots & 0.555556 & 0 \\
NGen & 1 & 1 & 1 & 1 & \cdots & 0.333333 & 0.708333 \\
NM & 1 & 0.955556 & 0.922222 & 0.955556 & \cdots & 0.155556 & 0.233333 \\
NA & 1 & 0.961538 & 0.903846 & 0.942308 & \cdots & 0.269231 & 0.423077 \\
NC & 1 & 0.967742 & 0.935484 & 0.967742 & \cdots & 0.354839 & 0.612903
\end{pmatrix}
\tag{19}
$$

Step 3. Based on the fuzzy matter element matrix of optimal membership degree $R'_{27\times7}$, according to formula (6), formula (7), formula (8), formula (9), formula (10), and formula (11) by entropy method to obtain each indicator weights that composes the fuzzy matter element weight matrix of optimal membership degree R_w,

$$
R_w =
\begin{pmatrix}
 & c_1 & c_2 & c_3 & c_4 & c_5 & c_6 & c_7 \\
w_j & 0.17124 & 0.143127 & 0.150199 & 0.124097 & 0.189334 & 0.191128 & 0.184991
\end{pmatrix}
\tag{20}
$$

Step 4. Get R_s by formula (11).

$$
R_s =
\begin{pmatrix}
 & T_1 & T_2 & T_3 & T_4 & \cdots & T_{25} & T_{26} \\
NDep & 0.017124 & 0.017124 & 0.017124 & 0.017124 & \cdots & 0 & 0.017124 \\
NAssoc & 0.132904 & 0.132904 & 0.132904 & 0.112457 & \cdots & 0 & 0.09201 \\
NAgg & 0.150199 & 0.13351 & 0.116821 & 0.150199 & \cdots & 0.083444 & 0 \\
NGen & 0.124097 & 0.124097 & 0.124097 & 0.124097 & \cdots & 0.041366 & 0.087902 \\
NM & 0.189334 & 0.18092 & 0.174608 & 0.18092 & \cdots & 0.029452 & 0.044178 \\
NA & 0.191128 & 0.183777 & 0.17275 & 0.180101 & \cdots & 0.051458 & 0.080862 \\
NC & 0.184991 & 0.179024 & 0.173056 & 0.179024 & \cdots & 0.065642 & 0.113382
\end{pmatrix}
\tag{21}
$$

TABLE 1: Twenty-six UML class diagrams evaluation indicators.

Class diagrams	NDep	NAssoc	NAgg	NGen	NM	NA	NC
1	0	1	0	0	8	4	2
2	0	1	1	0	12	6	3
3	0	1	2	0	15	9	4
4	0	3	0	0	12	7	3
5	0	1	3	0	21	14	5
6	0	2	0	0	12	6	3
7	1	3	0	0	13	8	4
8	0	2	2	2	14	10	6
9	1	1	0	0	12	9	3
10	0	2	3	2	22	14	7
11	0	2	3	4	30	18	9
12	0	3	3	2	39	19	7
13	1	3	2	2	35	22	8
14	0	0	0	4	30	11	5
15	0	0	0	10	30	12	8
16	0	0	0	18	38	17	11
17	2	11	6	10	76	42	20
18	1	11	6	16	88	41	23
19	1	7	6	20	94	45	21
20	3	13	7	24	98	56	33
21	0	1	5	2	47	28	9
22	0	3	5	20	65	31	18
23	0	11	6	21	79	44	26
24	0	1	5	19	69	32	17
25	4	14	4	16	84	42	22
26	0	5	9	7	77	34	14

Note: Genero metric values from Genero M.'s experiment in Table 1.

Step 5. Software quality measurement values of fuzzy matter element in this paper are calculated by formula (12), formula (13), formula (14), formula (15), formula (16), formula (17), and formula (18).

$$
\begin{aligned}
Z_i = (&0.02089, 0.101997, 0.339518, 0.205419, \\
&0.856791, 0.106658, 0.251853, 0.510079, \\
&0.105591, 1.075057, 1.733703, 2.00285, \\
&1.906329, 0.606743, 1.143489, 2.588069, \\
&8.394743, 9.021374, 8.872664, 9.91465, \\
&3.522168, 6.674977, 9.271023, 6.446144, \\
&8.760155, 7.146074)
\end{aligned} \tag{22}
$$

3.3. Data Analysis

3.3.1. Comparing the Experiment Results of Four Metrics. To verify the effectiveness and practicability of the proposed measurement method, this paper plans to compare with the method proposed by Dr. Zhou Y. [16] and the method

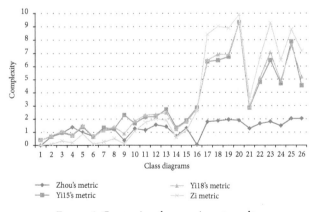

FIGURE 1: Comparing the experiment results.

proposed by Dr. Yi T. [17, 18] in the three aspects, understandability, analysability, and maintainability. For convenient discussion, the method of Dr. Zhou Y. and the method of Dr. Yi T. are called Zhou metric [16], Yi15 metric [17], and Yi18 metric [18]; the measurement method proposed in this paper is called Z_i metric, as shown in Table 2.

Comparing the experimental results of the above four software quality measurement models, as shown in Figure 1,

TABLE 2: Comparing the experiment results of measurement methods.

Class diagrams	Zhou metric	Yi15 metric	Yi18 metric	Z_i metric	Understandability	Analysability	Maintainability
1	0	0.42	0.41176	0.02089	1	1	1
2	0.673012	0.67	0.73657	0.101997	2	2	2
3	0.940493	0.97	1.07097	0.339518	2	2	2
4	1.386294	0.76	0.7987	0.205419	2	2	2
5	0.989909	1.41	1.50423	0.856791	2	2	2
6	0.693147	0.65	0.66949	0.106658	2	2	2
7	1.14688	1.33	1.13783	0.251853	2	3	3
8	1.206376	1.26	1.40369	0.510079	3	3	3
9	0.381909	2.3	0.9008	0.105591	2	2	2
10	1.271002	1.67	1.8433	1.075057	3	3	3
11	1.16503	2.16	2.29233	1.733703	3	3	3
12	1.553338	2.18	2.34555	2.00285	3	3	3
13	1.414547	2.72	2.48526	1.906329	3	3	3
14	0.693147	1.34	1.237	0.606743	2	2	2
15	1.303487	1.88	1.80312	1.143489	2	3	3
16	0.04308	2.85	2.7398	2.588069	4	4	4
17	1.787461	6.35	6.45495	8.394743	6	6	6
18	1.8612	6.45	6.90285	9.021374	6	6	6
19	1.949444	6.72	6.88925	8.872664	6	5	6
20	1.883662	9.31	9.29632	9.91465	6	6	7
21	1.277816	2.85	2.91541	3.522168	3	3	3
22	1.649751	4.79	5.10804	6.674977	5	5	5
23	1.794866	6.45	7.04766	9.271023	6	6	6
24	1.480208	4.68	4.88021	6.446144	5	5	5
25	2.020782	7.86	7.5702	8.760155	6	5	6
26	2.030221	4.53	5.19316	7.146074	4	5	5

and comparing them with the understandability, analysability, and maintainability of the class diagrams obtained by the practical experience, it is found that the four metric results are similar. But also some interesting results are found.

(1) For the class diagram 4, the Zhou metric has higher values for the computational class diagram 4 complexity, the Yi15 metric and the Yi18 metric have lower values for the complexity of the class diagram 4, and the complexity of the class diagram 4 that the practical experience has obtained has lower values. The complexity of class diagram 4 calculated using the fuzzy matter element model in this paper is low, which is consistent with the actual experience.

(2) For the class diagram 9, the Zhou metric and the Yi18 metric have lower values for the computational class diagram 9 complexity, the Yi15 metric has higher values for the complexity of the class diagram 9, and the complexity of the class diagram 9 that the practical experience has obtained has lower values. The complexity of class diagram 9 calculated using the fuzzy matter element model in this paper is low, which is consistent with the actual experience.

(3) For the class diagram 16, the Zhou metric has lower values for the computational class diagram 16 complexity,

the Yi15 metric and the Yi18 metric have higher values for the complexity of the class diagram 16, and the complexity of the class diagram 16 that the practical experience has obtained has higher values. The complexity of class diagram 16 calculated using the fuzzy matter element model in this paper is high, which is consistent with the actual experience.

(4) For the class diagram 19, the Yi18 metric for the complexity of the class diagram 19 has lower values than the class diagram 18, the Zhou metric and the Yi15 metric have higher values for the computational class diagram 19 complexity, and the complexity of the class diagram 19 that the practical experience obtained has lower values than the class diagram 18. The complexity of class diagram 19 calculated using the fuzzy matter element model in this paper is consistent with actual experience.

(5) For the class diagram 25 and the class diagram 26, the Zhou metric shows that the 26th class diagram complexity is higher than the 25th class diagram complexity and the Yi15 metric and Yi18 metric methods show the 26th class diagram complexity lower than it. The complexity of the class diagrams 25 and 26 obtained by the practical experience is opposite with the Zhou metric, which is in consistent with

TABLE 3: Correlation coefficient and correlation intensity.

Correlation coefficient absolute value	Correlation intensity
$\|r\| = 0$	Zero correlation
$0 < \|r\| \leq 0.3$	Weak correlation
$0.3 < \|r\| \leq 0.5$	Low correlation
$0.5 < \|r\| \leq 0.8$	Significant correlation
$0.8 < \|r\| \leq 1$	High correlation
$\|r\| = 1$	Completely correlation

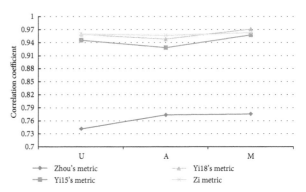

FIGURE 2: Pearson simple correlation analysis.

the complexity of the class diagram calculated by using the fuzzy matter element model in this paper.

3.3.2. Pearson Simple Correlation Coefficient Test. In order to further discuss the existing correlation between the results of complexity metric and the value of understandability, the value of analysability, and the value of maintainability, we propose the Pearson simple correlation coefficient to test whether or not the complexity measure method is consistent with the practical experience. Pearson simple correlation coefficient is calculated as follows:

$$r_{xy} = \frac{\sum_{i=1}^{n}\left(X_i - \overline{X}\right)\left(Y_i - \overline{Y}\right)}{\sqrt{\sum\left(X_i - \overline{X}\right)^2}\sqrt{\sum\left(Y_i - \overline{Y}\right)^2}} \quad (23)$$

The correlation intensity between the two variables refers to Table 3.

Using the well-known statistical software SPSS for correlation analysis and the results of the correlation analysis are shown in Table 4.

Through the comparison and data analysis in Table 4, we can find that this paper's UML class diagram metric is consistent with practical experience in the understandability, analysability, and maintainability. The value of the UML class diagrams complexity measure Z_i is calculated by fuzzy matter element model, which is compared with practical experience. The Pearson simple correlation coefficient between Z_i and the value of the understandability of practical experience is 0.959. The Pearson simple correlation coefficient between Z_i and the value of the analysability of practical experience is 0.956. The Pearson simple correlation coefficient between Z_i and the value of the maintainability of practical experience is 0.962. Zhou metric is significantly correlated with the class diagram of practical experience. But the fuzzy matter element model metrics, Yi15 metric, and Yi18 metric are highly correlated with the class diagram of practical experience. Therefore, the complexity measure method of this paper is consistent with the practical experience from the view of average.

3.3.3. The Analysis of the Visualization of Measurement Results. In order to compare the abovementioned four metrics methods more intuitive, the classification results of this

paper are shown in Figure 2. For better representation, U represents the understandability, A represents the analysability, and M represents the maintainability.

From Figure 2, we can find that this paper's results are closer to 1. It suggests that the class diagram complexity calculated by the fuzzy matter element model is consistent with the value of practical experience by comparing with other metrics. This method can quickly calculate the comprehensive attribute value of the software class diagrams. Meanwhile, the results of this study can be more accurately to reflect the software complexity. So the measurement model proposed in this paper is relatively better.

4. Conclusions

This paper uses the basic theory and method of matter element analysis, combined with fuzzy set theory and TOPSIS method to establish a fuzzy matter element model based on entropy weight and TOPSIS method. It is applied to the evaluation of software class diagram, and at the same time the difference between the entropy values as a weight, making full use of the information in the original data, to a certain extent reduces the subjectivity of weight determination; the evaluation results are in good agreement with the actual situation, indicating that the method is reasonable and feasible.

Acknowledgments

This research has been supported by the Science and Technology Foundation of Jiangxi Provincial Department of Education (Project Name: Research on Software Complexity Measurement Based on Multiple Attribute Decision Making).

TABLE 4: The correlation analysis of the complexity measurement results.

Metric methods	Understandability	Analysability	Maintainability	Average
Zhou metric	0.741∗∗	0.773∗∗	0.775∗∗	0.763
Yi15 metric	0.945∗∗	0.928∗∗	0.957∗∗	0.949667
Yi18 metric	0.959∗∗	0.948∗∗	0.971∗∗	0.959333
Z_i metric	0.959∗∗	0.956∗∗	0.962∗∗	0.959

Note: ∗∗ indicates significant correlations at the 0.01 level in bilateral test.

References

[1] X. Zhou, X.-K. Chen, J.-S. Sun, and F.-Q. Yang, "Software measurement based reusable component extraction in object-oriented system," *Acta Electronica Sinica*, vol. 31, no. 5, pp. 649–653, 2003.

[2] R. J. Rubey and R. D. Hartwick, "Quantitative measurement of program quality," *ACM National Computer Conference*, vol. 23, pp. 671–677, 1968.

[3] B. Hardekopf and C. Lin, "The ant and the grasshopper: Fast and accurate pointer analysis for millions of lines of code," *ACM SIGPLAN Notices*, vol. 42, no. 6, pp. 290–299, 2007.

[4] T. J. McCabe, "A complexity measure," *IEEE Transactions on Software Engineering*, vol. SE-2, no. 4, pp. 308–320, 1976.

[5] N. Choursiya and R. Yadav, "An enhanced function point analysis (FPA) method for software size estimation," *International Journal of Computer Science and Information Technologies*, vol. 6, no. 3, pp. 2797–2799, 2015.

[6] N. Padhy, S. Satapathy, and R. P. Singh, "Utility of an object oriented reusability metrics and estimation complexity," *Indian Journal of Science and Technology*, vol. 10, no. 3, pp. 1–9, 2017.

[7] S. Misra, A. Adewumi, L. Fernandez-Sanz, and R. Damasevicius, "A suite of object oriented cognitive complexity metrics," *IEEE Access*, vol. 6, pp. 8782–8796, 2018.

[8] D. L. Gupta and K. Saxena, "Software bug prediction using object-oriented metrics," *Sādhanā*, vol. 42, no. 5, pp. 655–669, 2017.

[9] J. Wang and Q. Wang, "Analyzing and predicting software integration bugs using network analysis on requirements dependency network," *Requirements Engineering*, vol. 21, no. 2, pp. 161–184, 2016.

[10] A. Gosain and G. Sharma, "A dynamic size measure for object oriented software," *International Journal of Systems Assurance Engineering and Management*, vol. 8, pp. 1209–1221, 2017.

[11] X. Hu, J. Zuo, and K. Wang, "Study on AHP-based quantification of software quality," *Computer Application and Software*, vol. 30, no. 11, pp. 138–141, 2013.

[12] M. Marchesi, "OOA metrics for the Unified Modeling Language," in *Proceedings of the 2nd Euromicro Conference on Software Maintenance and Reengineering, CSMR 1998*, pp. 67–73, Italy, March 1998.

[13] M. Genero, M. Piattini, and M. Chaudron, "Quality of UML models," *Information and Software Technology*, vol. 51, no. 12, pp. 1629-1630, 2009.

[14] Y. Zhang, J. Tao, and L. Qian, "A metrics suite for class complexity based-on UML," *Computer Science*, vol. 29, no. 10, pp. 128–132, 2002.

[15] P. In, S. Kim, and M. Barry, "UML-based object-oriented metrics for architecture complexity analysis," in *Proceedings of the Ground System Architectures Workshop the Aerospace Corporation*, March 2003.

[16] H. Lu, Y. Zhou, B. Xu, H. Leung, and L. Chen, "The ability of object-oriented metrics to predict change-proneness: A meta-analysis," *Empirical Software Engineering*, vol. 17, no. 3, pp. 200–242, 2012.

[17] T. Yi, "On the application of information entropy-based multi-attribute decision in UML class diagram metrics," *International JoUrnal of u- and e-Service, Science and Technology*, vol. 8, no. 6, pp. 105–116, 2015.

[18] T. Yi and C. Fang, "A complexity metric for object-oriented software," *International Journal of Computers and Applications*, pp. 1–6, 2018.

[19] F. Geng and X. Ruan, "Campus network information security risk assessment based on FAHP and matter element model," in *Intelligent Computing Methodologies*, vol. 10363, pp. 298–306, 2017.

[20] Y. Hu, "Comprehensive evaluation of multi index panel data based on fuzzy matter element analysis," *Statistics & Decision*, no. 14, pp. 32–35, 2016.

[21] H. Jiang, Q. Zhang, and J. Peng, "An improved cloud matter element model based wind farm power quality evaluation," *Power System Technology*, vol. 38, no. 1, pp. 205–210, 2014.

[22] W. J. You, Z. S. Xu, and D. L. Liu, "On the fire risk assessment for the ancient buildings based on the matter element analysis," *Journal of Safety & Environment*, vol. 17, no. 3, pp. 873–878, 2017.

[23] Q. Pang, H. Wang, and Z. Xu, "Probabilistic linguistic term sets in multi-attribute group decision making," *Information Sciences*, vol. 369, pp. 128–143, 2016.

[24] R. N. Sun, B. Zhang, and T. T. Liu, "Service ranking method based on improved entropy TOPSIS," *Journal of Chinese Computer Systems*, vol. 38, no. 6, pp. 1221–1226, 2017.

13

Model Aspects of Open Access to Multimedia Broadcast Services in the Evolved Packet System

Ivaylo Atanasov and Evelina Pencheva

Technical University of Sofia, 8 Kliment Ohridski Boulevard, 1000 Sofia, Bulgaria

Correspondence should be addressed to Evelina Pencheva; enp@tu-sofia.bg

Academic Editor: Hwang JN

Multimedia broadcast is the most efficient method to distribute identical content to multiple users in the Evolved Packet System (EPS). EPS enables efficient usage of network resources and provisioning of quality of service for every user. Third-party control allows applications in an enterprise domain to invoke network functions like multimedia broadcast. In this paper, an approach to modeling the behavior of Service Capability Server (SCS) for multimedia broadcast in EPS is presented. Third-party applications can access multimedia broadcasting capabilities by using Parlay X Web Service interfaces. The SCS for multimedia broadcast exposes Parlay X interfaces toward 3rd-party applications and control protocols toward the network. The SCS functional behavior has to be synchronized with the application view on message broadcast and the state of the network resources intended for the broadcast session. Models of multicast session, IP connectivity session, and bearers' and charging session are proposed and formally described using the notation of Label Transition Systems. The concept of weak bisimilarity is used to prove that models expose equivalent behavior; that is, they are synchronized.

1. Introduction

The Evolved Packet System (EPS) is standardized to provide ubiquitous access to multimedia services from any end user device. It encompasses both access network and core network. The multimedia packet core network plays an important role in providing superior user experience from services and applications. It is in charge of provisioning quality of service (QoS) for multimedia bearer services and charging mechanisms.

Multimedia broadcast/multicast service (MBMS) allows data to be transmitted to multiple endpoints. It allows optimizing network resources using a distribution mechanism. The broadcast mode is a unidirectional point-to-multipoint transmission of multimedia data (e.g., text, audio, picture, and video) from a single source entity to all users in a broadcast service area. A broadcast service received by the end user device involves one or more successive broadcast sessions. A broadcast service might, for example, consist of a single ongoing session (e.g., a media stream) or may involve several intermittent sessions over an extended period of time [1, 2]. Examples of content appropriate to a distribution scheme are broadcasting TV channels and distribution of area-based multimedia messaging service including commonly interested traffic, weather, or emergency information. The content provider (broadcast/multicast source) may provide discrete and continuous media, as well as service descriptions and control data. The multimedia content may be provided by a 3rd-party content provider.

The broadcast mode is intended to efficiently use EPS resources. Current research on MBMS covers different aspects related to optimisation of radio technology used for data transmission. Relatively low attention is paid on MBMS third-party control, which allows third-party providers from an IT domain to create applications that use network connections, streaming, messaging, and multimedia.

In this paper, we discuss some model aspects of deployment open access on multimedia message broadcast service in EPS. The open service access allows third-party applications to use broadcast function in the network. The Parlay X

Web Services (WS) model provides a high level of abstraction of communication network functions and it facilitates the development of value added applications.

The paper is organized as follows. In Section 2, the related work is presented and the novelty of the proposed approach is highlighted. In Section 3, the broadcast service architecture in EPS is discussed where the Broadcast Multicast Service Centre (BMSC) mediates between third-party applications and the network infrastructure. Next, the Parlay X Message Broadcast WS functionality is analyzed in Section 4. The behavior of BMSC is modeled by formal descriptions of MBMS session state and message broadcast status in Section 5. In Section 6, it is proved that models considering QoS and charging aspects of MBMS are synchronized. The conclusion summarizes the contribution.

2. Related Work

Research community has studied different architectural aspects of MBMS deployment in next generation networks. In [3], the authors propose service architecture for efficient content delivery based on enhanced MBMS in LTE (Long-Term Evolution), which reduces backhaul traffic. A context-aware architecture for social networking multimedia distribution, which enhances the evolved MBMS systems by adding users' situation knowledge on their assessments and allows personalized services delivery over optimized networks, is proposed in [4]. In [5], the authors describe the design and implementation of an open-source virtualized platform that supports both LTE broadcast services and video streaming services and analyze service performance.

The performance of enhanced MBMS in LTE has been thoroughly examined in previous research works. A comparison of multicast/broadcast services support in LTE-advanced and WiMAX IEEE 802.16m is provided in [6]. Challenges in supporting multicast services over LTE with particular attention to resource management, considered as key aspects for efficient provisioning of MBMS services over cellular networks, are analyzed in [7]. In [8], the authors discuss the relationship between LTE evolved MBMS and next generation broadcast television and propose some recommendations aimed at improving efficiency of the respective systems. In [9], the authors present a compact, convenient model for broadcasting in LTE, as well as a set of efficient algorithms to define broadcasting areas and to actually perform content scheduling. A joint multicast/unicast scheduling strategy for MBMS delivery, which improves QoS performance, is proposed in [10]. In [11], the authors propose a method for forming broadcasting area and assignment of content to them so that radio resources are efficiently exploited and user requests satisfied. In [12], a distributed resource allocation scheme is proposed, which includes device-to-device communication broadcasting groups and minimizes interference relationships. In [13], MBMS with inherently low requirement for network resources as a candidate solution for using such resources in a more efficient manner is proposed. High level considerations related to implementation of a session controller, supporting application programming interfaces for message broadcasting/multicasting, can be found in [14].

The proposed solutions have to be implemented by the telecom network operator. We study another multimedia broadcasting issue that has been scarcely addressed so far, namely, third-party control which allows external applications outside the network to control service provisioning. Our research is focused on two standardized technologies whose synergy has not been studied to date. The Parlay X WS is technology aimed at providing a horizontal service architecture which may be shared by different applications. It defines highly abstracted technology neutral application programming interfaces (APIs). Integration of MBMS and Parlay X requires translation of high level interfaces into telecommunication control protocols. The innovative approach to efficient MBMS provisioning requires considering also other advanced network functions such as policy-based quality of service control and flexible charging. We examine how three different functions in EPS, related to multimedia broadcasting, policy and charging control, and third-party control can collaborate and take the advantage of network convergence in provisioning of value added services.

3. Broadcast Service Architecture in EPS

Different broadcast business cases may be considered and the relevance of each used case is up to network operators and their relationship with the content owners, agencies, and broadcasters. Used case examples include mobile TV, digital radio, video on demand, electronic magazines and newspapers, and configuration and management of intelligent objects with internet connectivity.

As to 3GPP TS 23.246, the components of the 3GPP solution of MBMS are MBMS bearer service and MBMS user service. The MBMS bearer service enables efficient distribution of content to multiple users while MBMS user service is used by user devices when specific end user applications are activated. The architecture of MBMS for EPS with the proposed third-party control is depicted in Figure 1.

The multimedia content that has to be broadcasted is provided by an Application Sever (AS). The MBMS AS may be deployed by network operator or third-party application provider. The Broadcast Multicast Service Centre (BMSC) stores multimedia content to be transmitted, controls the multimedia broadcast service, and interacts with media sources and the end users' devices via Packet Data Network Gateway (PDN GW). It provides interfaces for both signaling and data transfer to the MBMS GW. The MBMS Gateway (GW) distributes the data received from the BMSC to the relevant base stations in the access network. The Mobility Management Entity (MME) communicates with the access network in the concerned area, relaying session control information received by MBMS GW [15].

The end users discover the available MBMS services by service announcement, which provides information about services. Service announcement is used to distribute to users information about MBMS, service activation parameters like IP multicast address, and service start time. Service announcement mechanisms may include short message broadcasting, MBMS broadcasting or multicasting mode,

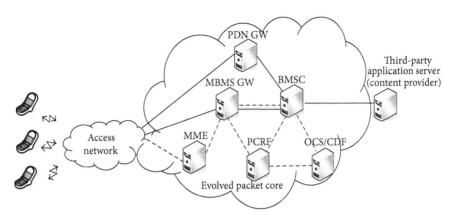

FIGURE 1: Reference architecture of MBMS for EPS.

and a push mechanism. Service announcement details may be found in [16].

An MBMS service may contain multiple distinct multimedia streams and it is provided by session setup and termination. Each session is bundled with bearer establishment and release. Signaling procedures related to MBMS session initiation, update, and termination are specified in [15].

In EPS, the network controls QoS parameters for session broadcast MBMS bearer services. QoS Class Identifier, Allocation and Retention Priority, Maximum Bit Rate (MBR), and Guaranteed Bit Rate (GBR) are applicable to MBMS bearer service, where the MBR is set to be equal to the GBR. The QoS management in EPS is provided by means of policy and charging control (PCC) which allows network operator to authorize and control the usage of resources intended for multimedia traffic [17]. PCC ensures that multimedia services are provided with appropriate transport and charging. The Policy and Charging Rule Function (PCRF) encompasses policy control decision and flow based charging control functions. It receives MBMS session information from BMSC as well as information from the access network and makes policy-based decisions about bearer service session, which are then provided to the MBMS GW. The PCC decisions determine the QoS treatment of the bearer traffic.

Both MBMS content provider and MBMS user may be charged for multimedia broadcasting sessions. EPS provides offline and online charging mechanisms [18]. The BMSC contains triggers that generate events for online and offline charging. The Online Charging System (OCS) performs real-time credit control and its functionality includes transaction handlings, online correlation, and management of user account balances. The Charging Data Function (CDF) receives offline charging information from BMSC and creates call detail records.

4. Parlay X Message Broadcast Web Service

The Parlay X Message Broadcast WS (MBWS) allows third-party applications to send messages to end user devices in a specific geographical area [19]. It provides APIs for sending a broadcast message to the network, for monitoring the delivery status of a sent broadcast message, and for notifications about the message delivery status.

The *sendBroadcastMessage* operation is used to send a broadcast message into the designated area(s).

The *getBroadcastStatus* operation is used by the 3rd-party application to retrieve the status of sent broadcast message. The broadcast status values are as follows:

(i) *MessageWaiting*. The message is still queued and not delivered to the network yet.

(ii) *Broadcasting*. The message is being broadcasted as many as requested in the send operation.

(iii) *Broadcasted*. The message is successfully delivered to network as many as requested.

(iv) *BroadcastImpossible*. This indicates a final state that delivery of broadcast message is impossible due to specific reasons.

(v) *BroadcastUnknown*. The message delivery state is unknown.

Figure 2 illustrates the MBMS time line and the message status as seen by 3rd-party application. The *cancelBroadcastMessage* operation may be used by the third-party application to cancel message broadcasting. The operation affects the subsequent broadcast message delivery.

The *notifyBroadcastDeliveryReceipt* operation is used to notify the third-party application about the delivery status of the message. In order to receive notification the third-party application needs to start notifications using *startDeliveryReceiptNotification* operation. The application may end the receipt of notifications using the *stopDeliveryReceiptNotification* operation.

We propose a modified model compared to that presented in [19], which is shown in Figure 3. In *Null* state, there is no message to be broadcasted. As far as the *BroadcastUnknown* state is of temporary kind it is absorbed by the *BroadcastImpossible* and *Broadcasting* states.

5. Model Aspects of Broadcast Multicast Service Centre

5.1. Modeling Views on Message Broadcast. BMSC needs to communicate with the third-party application using the

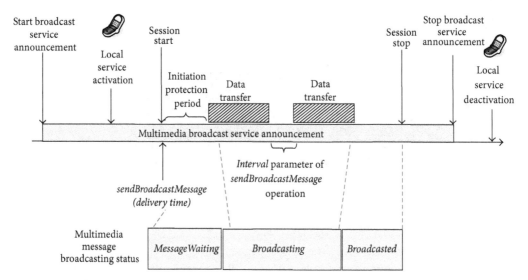

FIGURE 2: Multimedia broadcast service time line and the parameters of *sendBroadcastMessage* operation.

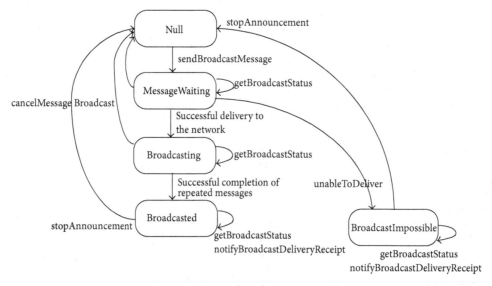

FIGURE 3: Message broadcast state model.

Parlay X MBWS. Toward the network, BMSC has to communicate with MBMS GW to maintain the MBMS session; PCRF to provide information about the MBMS session and to receive notifications about bearers authorized for the session; and CDF to send charging data. Therefore, the BMSC behavior has to be synchronized with the behavior of MBMS GW, PCRF, and CDF, and its view on the MBMS session has to be synchronized with the application view on the state of message broadcast. MBMS GW is in charge of establishment of IP-CAN resources for the MBMS session where IP-CAN stands for Internet Protocol Connectivity Access Network. PCRF controls the QoS that has to be assured for the MBMS session and CDF gathers charging data.

Figure 4 shows the respective state models that have to be synchronized with the BMSC behavior. The BMSC has to transform the MBWS operations and to control

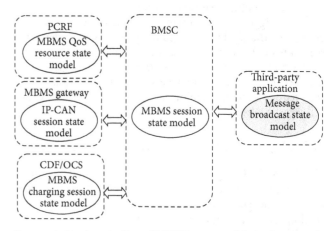

FIGURE 4: Synchronization of MBMS state models in the network and the 3rd-party application view on the message broadcast state.

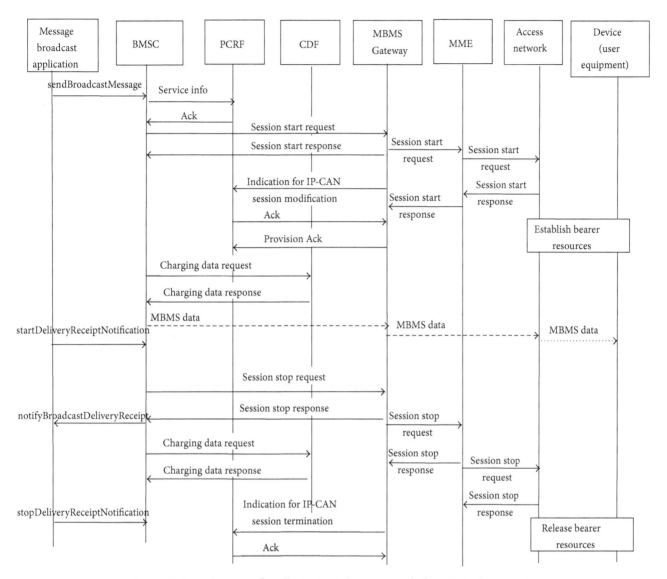

FIGURE 5: Typical message flow illustrating 3rd-party control of MBMS in the network.

the MBMS session appropriately. In practice, the state models of BMSC, MBMS GW, PCRF, and CDF should expose direct correspondence between the transitions and the information they provide; that is, they have to expose equivalent behavior.

The MBMS session state model describes the states of the MBMS session and it is maintained by MBMS GW. The MBMS QoS provisioning requires an MBMS QoS state model reflecting the state of bearer resources allocated by PCRF for the broadcast session. The control protocol used for PCC is Diameter. Similar considerations are applied to the MBMS charging model which holds the states of the MBMS charging session. The control protocol used for charging is also Diameter.

Typical information flows related to multimedia message broadcasting with MBMS session establishment, QoS resource authorization, notification about message broadcast status, and reporting offline charging data are shown in Figure 5.

The MB WS can be used for remote management of intelligent devices like smart meters, which are uniquely identified, gather information from their environment, and communicate that information with network applications. Remote entity management provides means for managing device life cycle including software and firmware upgrade and configuration management. With the increasing number of connected devices, the device management becomes cumbersome and costly for the device operator. So, an EPS operator can sell the MBMS to the device operator to keep the fleet updated. The MBMS can deliver all the software and firmware updates as well as configurations needed to manage the devices up to date.

It is a general assumption that IP connectivity is provided to all devices, which means that for each device there is an established default bearer. Let us assume that the device operator makes use of a message broadcast application. By using the application, the device operator sets the target area, where the devices are deployed, and writes a message with configuration data. Then the message broadcast application invokes the MB WS which in turn sends a message delivery operation to the BMSC. Subsequently EPS functional entities supporting MBMS deliver the configuration data to all devices in the target area.

When the message broadcast application invokes *sendBroadcastMessage* operation the BMSC opens a Diameter session with the PCRF for the multimedia broadcast session and provides the required session information. The BMSC can subscribe to QoS events related to MBMS bearer resources. The BMSC performs the MBMS session start procedure. The MBMS GW in turn indicates to the PCRF that an IP-CAN session modification is required and waits for PCC rules. Based on session information, the PCRF performs session authorization and sends an acknowledgement with the PCC decisions to the MBMS Gateway. The MBMS starts resources reservation in the access network. When the IP-CAN session modification is completed the MBMS GW sends acknowledgement to the PCRF. The BMSC waits for resource authorization and reservation during the initial protection period and the message broadcast status is *MessageWaiting*. Before starting the MBMS data transfer, the BMSC contacts with the CDF in order to provide charging information. The MBMS content is sent by the BMSC to the MBMS gateway, and then to the respective part of access network. During the MBMS data transfer the message broadcast status is *Broadcasting*. The broadcasted content is received and decoded by the devices (user equipment) that are authorized to join the MBMS service. Using the message broadcast application and the interfaces of the MBWS, the device operator can subscribe for notifications about message delivery (*startDeliveryReceiptNotification* operation) and be notified of a broadcast delivery status of a specific area. Once the MBMS data (configuration data) are broadcasted, the BMSC starts the procedure for session termination, which is followed by release of bearer resources authorized for the MBMS session. The BMSC contacts with the CDF to write the charging data. The message broadcast status becomes *Broadcasted*. The *stopDeliveryReceiptNotification* operation is used to end delivery receipt notification. The content provider is charged for the broadcasted content. The PCRF enables also QoS-based charging. The PCC mechanism supports traffic plane event reporting (e.g., bearer lost) which may reflect in charging. In case of active subscription, the PCRF may notify the BMSC about any QoS events occurring during message broadcasting.

In the course of service provisioning, the BMSC needs to maintain in a synchronized manner three state machines describing the MBMS session, QoS resources authorized for the session, and charging session. These state machines have to be synchronized with the application view on the states of the message broadcast.

On receiving an indication about IP-CAN session modification, the PCRF may reject the requested modification (due to overloading in the respective access network or spending credit limits of the content provider in case of online charging). In this case, the PCRF rejects the IP-CAN session modification requested by the MBMS GW and notifies the

BMSC about the event during the initial protection period. The message broadcast status becomes *BroadcastImpossible*. During message waiting or broadcasting, the device operator may decide to cancel message broadcast. In this case, the third-party application invokes the *cancelBroadcastMessage* operation to request cancelation of the previous *sendBroadcastMessage*. The BMSC in turn initiates session termination toward the MBMS GW and PCRF, which results in IP-CAN session termination and release of QoS resources.

In the next subsection, we provide formal description of the models representing the view on message broadcast of third-party application, BMSC, MBMS GW, PCRF, and CDF, respectively. This will be used to prove formally that the models are synchronized.

5.2. Formal Description of Models Representing Message Broadcast Status. Let us present the state machines as labeled transition systems (LTS).

Definition 1. A *labeled transition system* (LTS) is a quadruple $(S, Act, \rightarrow, s_0)$, where S is countable set of states, Act is a countable set of elementary actions, $\rightarrow \subseteq S \times Act \times S$ is a set of transitions, and $s_0 \in S$ is the set of initial states.

5.2.1. Application View on Message Broadcast Status. The message broadcast status from application point of view may be *Null*, *MessageWaiting*, *Broadcasting*, or *Broadcasted*. The status is *Null* when there is no message to be broadcasted. The status is *MessageWaiting* if the message is waiting to be delivered to the network. The status is *Broadcasting* or *Broadcasted* if the MBMS data transfer is ongoing or terminated, respectively.

By $T_{App} = (S_{App}, Act_{App}, \rightarrow_{App}, s_0{}^{App})$ an LTS representing the 3rd-party view on the message broadcast status is denoted where

(i) S_{App} = {Null, MessageWaiting, Broadcasting, Broadcasted, BroadcastImpossible};

(ii) Act_{App} = {sendMessage, getBroadcastStatus, notifyBroadcastDeliveryReceipt, cancelMessage, successfulDelivery, unsuccessfulDelivery, stopAnnouncement, unableToDeliver, successfulMessageCompletion};

(iii) $\rightarrow_{App}$ = {Null sendMessage MessageWaiting, MessageWaiting getBroadcastStatus MessageWaiting, MessageWaiting unsuccessfulDelivery Null, MessageWaiting successfulDelivery Broadcasting, MessageWaiting cancelMessage Null, MessageWaiting unableToDeliver BroadcastImpossible, Broadcasting successfulMessageCompletion Broadcasted, Broadcasting cancelMessage Null, Broadcasting getBroadcastStatus Broadcasting, Broadcasted stopAnnouncement Null, Broadcasted getBroadcastStatus Broadcasted, Broadcasted notifyBroadcastDeliveryReceipt Broadcasted, BroadcastImpossible getBroadcastStatus BroadcastImpossible, BroadcastImpossible notifyBroadcastDeliveryReceipt BroadcastImpossible, BroadcastImpossible stopAnnouncement Null};

(iv) $s_0{}^{App}$ = {Null}.

The *getBroadcastStatus* and *notifyBroadcastDeliveryReceipt* operations do not change the session state or message broadcast status.

5.2.2. BMSC Model of MBMS Session. The simplified BMSC view on the MBMS session states includes the following states. In *MBMSIdle* state, there is no MBMS session. When the application invokes the *sendBroadcastMessage* operation, the BMSC sends session information to the PCRF, a session start request to the MBMS GW, and it moves to *InitialWaiting* state. While being in *InitialWaiting* state, the BMSC waits for resource authorization and QoS resource reservation. The time delay between a session start indication and actual data should be long enough for the required network actions. When the network is ready to send MBMS data, the BMSC sends charging data and moves to *DataTransfer* state. In *DataTransfer* state, MBMS data are transferred to any user equipment which is present. When the MBMS user service determines that there are no more data to send, the BMSC initiates session termination, sends charging data, and moves to *MBMSIdle* state. In *InitialWaiting* or *DataTransfer* state, the BMSC may be notified about any problems related to MBMS bearers and the MBMS session is terminated. It is also possible for third-party application to invoke the *cancelBroadcastMessage* operation while the BMSC is in *InitialWaiting* or *DataTransfer* state, which cancels the MBMS session.

By $T_{\text{BMSC}} = (S_{\text{BMSC}}, Act_{\text{BMSC}}, \rightarrow_{\text{BMSC}}, s_0^{\text{BMSC}})$ an LTS representing the BMSC view on the message broadcast status is denoted where

(i) $S_{\text{BMSC}} = \{$MBMSIdle, InitialWaiting, DataTransfer$\}$;

(ii) $Act_{\text{BMSC}} = \{$sendBroadcastMessage, initialPeriod, dataTransferStop, resourceFailed, resourceLost, cancelBroadcastMessage$\}$;

(iii) $\rightarrow_{\text{BMSC}} = \{$MBMSIdle sendBroadcastMessage InitialWaiting, InitialWaiting initialPeriod DataTransfer, InitialWaiting resourceFailed MBMSIdle, InitialWaiting cancelBroadcastMessage MBMSIdle, DataTransfer dataTransferStop MBMSIdle, DataTransfer resourceLost MBMSIdle$\}$; DataTransfer cancelBroadcastMessage MBMSIdle$\}$;

(iv) $s_0^{\text{BMSC}} = \{$MBMSIdle$\}$.

Figure 6 illustrates the MBMS session state machine.

5.2.3. MBMS GW Model of IP-CAN Session. The MBMS GW view on the IP-CAN session states for the MBMS user service includes the following states. In *IPCANIdle* state, there is no dedicated IP-CAN session. On receiving session start instructions, the MBMS GW indicates an IP-CAN session modification to the PCRF and moves to *WaitForPCCRules* state. In *WaitForPCCRules* state, the MBMS waits for authorization of IP-CAN session modification. Upon receiving the PCC rules, the MBMS GW initiates IP-CAN session establishment in the access network and moves to *ResourceReservation* state. The MBMS GW moves to *SessionActive* state after it receives an acknowledgement that the resources in the access

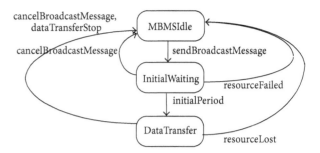

FIGURE 6: MBMS session state machine.

network are reserved. The transition to *ResourceRelease* state occurs when a session stop request is received by the BMSC. In *ResourceRelease* state, the MBMS waits for the release of IP-CAN bearers. In *WaitForTermAck* state, the MBMS GW waits for acknowledgement for session termination from PCRF and then moves to the initial *IPCANIdle* state. In *ResourceReservation* or *SessionActive* state, network, the MBMS GW may receive indications from the PCRF that the bearer modification fails or that the bearers are lost. These cause the transition to *IPCANIdle* state.

By $T_{\text{MBMS}} = (S_{\text{MBMS}}, Act_{\text{MBMS}}, \rightarrow_{\text{MBMS}}, s_0^{\text{MBMS}})$ an LTS representing the MBMS GW view on the MBMS IP-CAN session state is denoted where

(i) $S_{\text{MBMS}} = \{$IPCANIdle, WaitForPCCRules, ResourceReservation, SessionActive, ResourceRelease, WaitForTermAck$\}$;

(ii) $Act_{\text{MBMS}} = \{$sessionStart, pccRules, ipCanBearerEstablishment, sessionStop, sessionCancel, ipCanBearerRelease, ipCanSessionTermAck, ipCanBearerFailed, ipCanBearerLost$\}$;

(iii) $\rightarrow_{\text{MBMS}} = \{$IPCANIdle sessionStart WaitForPCCRules, WaitForPCCRules pccRules ResourceReservation, WaitForPCCRules sessionCancel IPCANIdle, ResourceReservation ipCanBearerEstablishment SessionActive, ResourceReservation sessionCancel IPCANIdle, ResourceReservation ipCanBearerFailed IPCANIdle, SessionActive sessionCancel ResourceRelease, SessionActive sessionStop ResourceRelease, SessionActive ipCanBearerLost IPCANIdle, ResourceRelease ipCanBearerRelease WaitForTermAck, WaitForTermAck ipCanSessionTermAck IPCANIdle$\}$;

(iv) $s_0^{\text{MBMS}} = \{$IPCANIdle$\}$.

The IP-CAN session state machine is depicted in Figure 7.

5.2.4. PCRF Model of MBMS QoS Resources. The PCRF view on the state of QoS resource intended for MBMS session is as follows. In *ResourceNull* state, no QoS resources are authorized for the MBMS session. When the BMSC sends session information, the PCRF performs session binding which takes into account the IP-CAN parameters and moves to *IPCanSession* state storing this information. In *IPCanSession* state, the PCRF may receive an indication about IP-CAN session

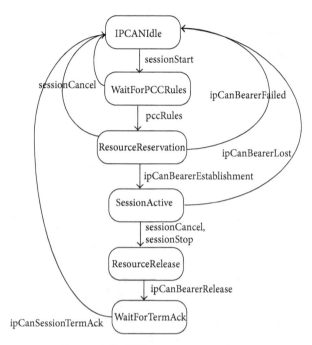

FIGURE 7: IP-CAN session state machine.

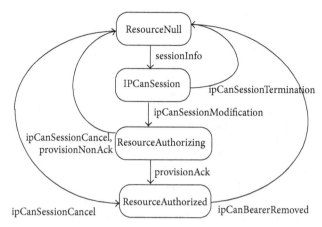

FIGURE 8: QoS resource state machine.

modification and correlates appropriate service information with IP-CAN session. In *ResourceAuthorizing* state, the PCRF makes policy decisions and sends them as PCC rules to the MBMS GW. On receiving provision acknowledgement the PCRF moves to *ResourceAuthorized* state. The QoS resources for the MBMS session are authorized and reserved, and the MBMS data transfer can start. When the MBMS GW detects that the IP-CAN session termination is required, it sends an indication to the PCRF. In case of subscription, the PCRF may find the PCC rules that require the BMSC to be notified and sends a notification. The QoS resources authorized for the MBMS session are released which causes the transition to *ResourceNull* state. In *ResourceAuthorizing* state, the PCRF may decide to reject the IP-CAN session modification. Also, during MBMS data transfer any QoS problems may be reported by the MBMS GW to the PCRF, thus affecting the online charging. In case the MBMS GW reports that all bearer resources authorized for the MBMS session are lost, the PCRF moves to *ResourceNull* state.

By $T_{PCRF} = (S_{PCRF}, Act_{PCRF}, \rightarrow_{PCRF}, s_0^{PCRF})$ an LTS representing the PCRF GW view on the QoS resource state is denoted where

(i) S_{PCRF} = {ResourceNull, IPCanSession, ResourceAuthorizing, ResourceAuthorized};

(ii) Act_{PCRF} = {sessionInfo, ipCanSessionModification, provisionAck, provisionNonAck, ipCanSessionTermination, ipCanBearerRemoved, ipCanSessionCancel};

(iii) $\rightarrow_{PCRF}$ = {ResourceNull sessionInfo IPCanSession, IPCanSession ipCanSessionModification ResourceAuthorizing, IPCanSession ipCanSessionTermination ResourceNull, ResourceAuthorizing provisionAck ResourceAuthorized, ResourceAuthorizing

ipCanSessionCancel ResourceNull, **ResourceAuthor**izing provisionNonAck ResourceNull, ResourceAuthorized ipCanSessionCancel ResourceNull, ResourceAuthorized ipCanBearerRemoved ResourceNull};

(iv) s_0^{PCRF} = {ResourceNull}.

Figure 8 illustrates the QoS resource state machine.

5.2.5. MBMS Charging Session Model. Both offline and online charging are possible. By applying policy and charging control on MBMS sessions, online charging can reflect the QoS experience during message broadcasting. The BMSC collects charging data such as identification of the content source, type of user service, type of bearer resources used to deliver the content broadcast, and identification of users receiving the service. The BMSC collects also charging data such as session duration, data transfer time, and data volume for mobile users receiving the service through MBMS and/or content providers delivery of the MBMS content. The triggers for charging data are bearer service initiation and termination. In *ChargingIdle* state, no charging data are gathered. Charging data are provided by the BMSC upon MBMS session initiation, IP-CAN bearer resource establishment/failure, and MBMS session termination. The charging data are sent to the CDF (in case of offline charging) or to the Online Charging System. On receiving charging data related to session start, the charging session moves to $Active_{initial}$ state. In $Active_{initial}$ state, when charging data for IP-CAN session establishment are received, the charging session moves to $Active_{transfer}$ state. The charging data stop instructions may be received due to normal completion of message broadcast, due to some problems in the network, or due to message broadcast cancelation by the third-party application. On receiving charging data stop instructions the charging session moves to *ChargingIdle* state.

By $T_{CS} = (S_{CS}, Act_{CS}, \rightarrow_{CS}, s_0^{CS})$ an LTS representing the charging session states is denoted where

(i) S_{CS} = {ChargingIdle, $Active_{initial}$, $Active_{transfer}$};

(ii) Act_{CS} = {chargingDataStart$_{init}$, chargingData-Start$_{interim}$, chargingDataStop$_{normal}$, chargingDataStop$_{canceled}$, chargingDataStop$_{failed}$};

(iii) $\rightarrow_{CS}$ = {ChargingIdle chargingDataStart$_{init}$ Active$_{initial}$, Active$_{initial}$ chargingDataStart$_{interim}$ Active$_{transfer}$, Active$_{transfer}$ chargingDataStop$_{normal}$ ChargingIdle, Active$_{initial}$ chargingDataStop$_{failed}$ ChargingIdle, Active$_{initial}$ chargingDataStop$_{canceled}$ ChargingIdle, Active$_{transfer}$ chargingDataStop$_{canceled}$ ChargingIdle Active$_{transfer}$ chargingDataStop$_{failed}$ ChargingIdle};

(iv) $s_0{}^{CS}$ = {ChargingIdle}.

The charging session state machine is depicted in Figure 9.

Having formal description of the models representing message broadcast status as seen by both the third-party application and the network, we can prove that these models are synchronized; that is, they expose equivalent behavior.

6. Formal Verification of Models

6.1. Bisimilarity Concept. Intuitively, in terms of observed behavior, two state machines are equivalent if one state machine displays a final result and the other state machine displays the same result. The idea of equivalence is formalized by the concept of bisimilarity [20]. Strong bisimilarity requires existence of homomorphism between transitions in both state machines. In practice, strong bisimilarity puts strong conditions for equivalence which are not always necessary. For example, internal transitions can present actions, which are intrinsic to the system (i.e., not observable). In weak bisimilarity, internal transitions can be ignored.

The concept of weak bisimilarity is used to study some model aspects of BMSC.

We will use the following notations:

(i) $s \xrightarrow{a} s'$ stands for the transition (s, a, s');

(ii) $s \xrightarrow{a}$ means that $\exists s' : s \xrightarrow{a} s'$;

(iii) $s \xRightarrow{\mu} s_n$, where $\mu = a_1, a_2, \ldots, a_n : \exists s_1, s_2, \ldots, s_n$, such that $s \xrightarrow{a_1} s_1 \cdots \xrightarrow{a_n} s_n$;

(iv) $s \xRightarrow{\mu}$ means that $\exists s'$, such as $s \xRightarrow{\mu} s'$;

(v) $\xRightarrow{\widehat{\mu}}$ means $\Rightarrow$ if $\mu \equiv \tau$ or $\xRightarrow{\mu}$, otherwise,

where τ is one or more internal (invisible) actions.

Definition 2. Two labeled transition systems $T = (S, A, \rightarrow, s_0)$ and $T' = (S', A, \rightarrow', s_0')$ are *weakly bisimilar* $(T \sim T')$ if there is a binary relation $U \subseteq S \times S'$ such that if $s_1 U t_1 : s_1 \subseteq S$ and $t_1 \subseteq S'$, then $\forall a \in Act$:

(i) $s_1 \xRightarrow{a} s_2$ implies $\exists t_2 : t_1 \xRightarrow{\widehat{a}}' t_2$ and $s_2 U t_2$;

(ii) $t_1 \xRightarrow{a}' t_2$ implies $\exists s_2 : s_1 \xRightarrow{a} s_2$ and $s_2 U t_2$.

So in order to prove that considered LTS expose equivalent behavior, it is necessary to identify a relation between their states that satisfies the above conditions.

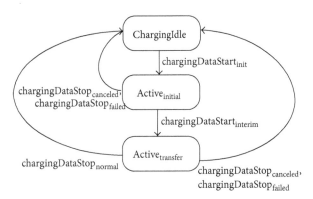

FIGURE 9: Charging session state machine.

6.2. Equivalence of Models Representing Message Broadcast Status

6.2.1. Behavioral Equivalence between Models of IP-CAN Session and QoS Resources. It can be shown that the MBMS GW model of MBMS session and PCRF model of MBMS QoS resources provide the lower level of abstraction, so we will start with considering the synchronization aspects of these models.

Proposition 3. *The labeled transition systems T_{MBMS} and T_{PCRF} are weakly bisimilar.*

Proof. To prove the bisimilarity between two labeled transition systems, it has to be proved that there exists a bisimilar relation between their states. By U_{MP} a relation between the states of T_{MBMS} and T_{PCRF} is denoted where

$$U_{MP} = \{(\text{IpCANIdle, ResourceNull}), (\text{WaitForPCCRules, IpCanSession}), (\text{ResourceReservation, ResourceAuthorizing}), (\text{SessionActive, ResourceAuthorized})\}.$$

The following homomorphism based on functional mapping may be defined between transitions of T_{MBMS} and T_{PCRF}:

$$h_{MP}(\text{sessionStart}) = h_{MP}(\text{sessionInfo});$$

$$h_{MP}(\text{pccRule}) = h_{MP}(\text{ipCanSessionModification});$$

$$h_{MP}(\text{ipCanBearerEstablishment}) = h_{MP}(\text{provisionAck});$$

$$h_{MP}(\text{sessionStop}) = h_{MP}(\text{ipCanSessionTermination});$$

$$h_{MP}(\text{sessionCancel}) = h_{MP}(\text{ipCanSessionCancel});$$

$$h_{MP}(\text{ipCanBearerFailed}) = h_{MP}(\text{provisionNonAck});$$

$$h_{MP}(\text{ipCanBearerLost}) = h_{MP}(\text{ipCanBearerRemoved}).$$

The homomorphism between the T_{MBMS} and T_{PCRF} messages shows the action's similarity.

Table 1 represents the functional mapping between the transitions in the IP-CAN session state machine and transitions in the QoS resources state machine.

Based on the established relation between the states of T_{MBMS} and T_{PCRF}, and on the homomorphism h_{MP} between

TABLE 1: Functional mapping between transitions of T_{MBMS} and T_{PCRF}.

Transitions in T_{MBMS}	Transitions in T_{PCRF}	Event
IPCANIdle sessionStart WaitForPCCRules	ResourceNull sessionInfo IPCanSession	MBMS session initiation
WaitForPCCRules pccRules ResourceReservation	IPCanSession ipCanSessionModification ResourceAuthorizing	IP-CAN session modification request
ResourceReservation ipCanBearerEstablishment SessionActive	ResourceAuthorizing provisionAck ResourceAuthorized	IP-CAN session modification authorization
SessionActive sessionStop ResourceRelease, ResourceRelease ipCanBearerRelease WaitForTermAck, WaitForTermAck ipCanSessionTermAck IPCANIdle	ResourceAuthorized ipCanSessionTermination ResourceNull	MBMS session stop
ResourceReservation ipCanBearerFailed IPCANIdle	ResourceAuthorizing provisionNonAck ResourceNull	IP-CAN session modification authorization fails
SessionActive ipCanBearerLost IPCANIdle	ResourceAuthorized ipCanBearerRemoved ResourceNull	All bearers are lost during data transfer
ResourceReservation sessionCancel IPCANIdle	ResourceAuthorized ipCanSessionCancel ResourceNull	The application cancels the MBMS user service during resource reservation
WaitForPCCRules sessionCancel IPCANIdle	IPCANSession ipCanSessionCancel ResourceNull	The application cancels the MBMS user service during resource authorization
SessionActive sessionCancel ResourceRelease, ResourceRelease ipCanBearerRelease WaitForTermAck, WaitForTermAck ipCanSessionTermAck IPCANIdle	ResourceAuthorized ipCanSessionCancel ResourceNull	The application cancels the MBMS user service during data transfer

their transitions, it is proved that $T_{\text{MBMS}} \sim T_{\text{PCRF}}$; that is, they are weakly bisimilar and expose equivalent behavior. □

6.2.2. Equivalence of Models of MBMS Session, IP-CAN Session, and QoS Resources. A higher level of abstraction on the network resource state for MBMS is provided by the state of MBMS session.

Proposition 4. *The labeled transition systems T_{BMSC}, T_{MBMS}, and T_{PCRF} are weakly bisimilar.*

Proof. The weak bisimilarity has the property transitivity; that is, as a relation it is transitive. Then, having proved that $T_{\text{MBMS}} \sim T_{\text{PCRF}}$, it has to be proved that $T_{\text{BMSC}} \sim T_{\text{MBMS}}$.

By U_{BMP} a relation between the states of T_{BMSC}, T_{MBMS}, and T_{PCRF} is denoted where

U_{BMP} = {(MBMSIdle, IpCANIdle), (InitialWaiting, WaitForPCCRules), (DataTransfer, SessionActive)}.

The following homomorphism based on functional mapping may be defined between transitions of T_{BMSC}, T_{MBMS}, and T_{PCRF}:

$h_{\text{BMP}}(\text{sendBroadcastMessage}) = h_{\text{BMP}}(\text{sessionzStart}) = h_{\text{BMP}}(\text{sessionInfo})$;

$h_{\text{BMP}}(\text{initialPeriod}) = h_{\text{BMP}}(\text{pccRule}) = h_{\text{BMP}}(\text{ipCanSessionModification})$;

$h_{\text{BMP}}(\text{dataTransferStop}) = h_{\text{BMP}}(\text{sessionStop}) = h_{\text{BMP}}(\text{ipCanSessionTermination})$;

$h_{\text{BMP}}(\text{cancel}) = h_{\text{BMP}}(\text{sessionCancel}) = h_{\text{BMP}}(\text{ipCanSessionCancel})$;

$h_{\text{BMP}}(\text{resourcesFailed}) = h_{\text{BMP}}(\text{ipCanBearerFailed}) = h_{\text{BMP}}(\text{provisionNonAck})$;

$h_{\text{BMP}}(\text{resourcesLost}) = h_{\text{BMP}}(\text{ipCanBearerLost}) = h_{\text{BMP}}(\text{ipCanBearerRemoved})$.

TABLE 2: Functional mapping between transitions of T_{BMSC} and T_{MBMS}.

Transitions in T_{BMSC}	Transitions in T_{MBMS}	Event
MBMSIdle sendBroadcastMessage InitialWaiting	IPCANIdle sessionStart WaitForPCCRules	MBMS session initiation
InitialWaiting initialPeriod DataTransfer	WaitForPCCRules pccRules ResourceReservation, ResourceReservation ipCanBearerEstablishment SessionActive	IP-CAN session modification request IP-CAN session modification authorization
DataTransfer dataTransferStop MBMSIdle	SessionActive sessionStop ResourceRelease, ResourceRelease ipCanBearerRelease WaitForTermAck, WaitForTermAck ipCanSessionTermAck IPCANIdle	MBMS session stop
InitialWaiting resourceFailed MBMSIdle	ResourceReservation ipCanBearerFailed IPCANIdle	IP-CAN session modification authorization fails
DataTransfer resourceLost MBMSIdle	SessionActive ipCanBearerLost IPCANIdle	All bearers are lost during data transfer
InitialWaiting cancelBroadcastMessage MBMSIdle	WaitForPCCRules sessionCancel IPCANIdle ResourceReservation sessionCancel IPCANIdle	The application cancels the MBMS user service during resource reservation
DataTransfer cancelBroadcastMessage MBMSIdle	SessionActive sessionCancel ResourceRelease, ResourceRelease ipCanBearerRelease WaitForTermAck, WaitForTermAck ipCanSessionTermAck IPCANIdle	The application cancels the MBMS user service during resource authorization

The functional mapping between the transitions in the MBMS session and IP-CAN state machines represented in Table 2 shows that U_{BMP} is a bisimilar relation.

From the homomorphism h_{BMP} and bisimilar property of U_{BMP} it follows that $T_{\text{BMSC}} \sim T_{\text{MBMS}}$.

From the bisimulation transitivity it follows that $T_{\text{BMSC}} \sim T_{\text{MBMS}} \sim T_{\text{PCRF}}$.

This means that MBMS session state machine, IP-CAN state machine, and the QoS resources state machine are weakly bisimilar. □

6.2.3. Equivalence of Application and Network Models. The highest level of abstraction on message broadcast status is provided by 3rd-party application. Its view has to be synchronized also with the network resource state and charging session state.

Proposition 5. *The labeled transition systems T_{App}, T_{BMSC}, T_{MBMS}, T_{PCRF}, and T_{CS} are weakly bisimilar.*

Proof. By U_{ABMPC} a relation between the states of T_{App}, T_{BMSC}, T_{MBMS}, T_{PCRF}, and T_{CS} is denoted where

U_{ABMPC} = {(Null, MBMSIdle, IpCANIdle, ResourceNull, ChargingIdle), (MessageWaiting, InitialWaiting, WaitForPCCRules, IpCanSession, Active$_{\text{initial}}$), (Broadcasting, DataTransfer, SessionActive, ResourceAuthorized, Active$_{\text{transfer}}$)}.

The following homomorphism based on functional mapping may be defined between transitions of T_{App}, T_{BMSC}, T_{MBMS}, T_{PCRF}, and T_{CS}:

$h_{\text{ABMPC}}(\text{sendMessage})$ = $h_{\text{ABMPC}}(\text{sendBroadcastMessage})$ = $h_{\text{ABMPC}}(\text{sessionStart})$ = $h_{\text{ABMPC}}(\text{sessionInfo})$ = $h_{\text{ABMPC}}(\text{sendBroadcastMessage})$ = $h_{\text{ABMPC}}(\text{chargingDataStart}_{\text{init}})$;

$h_{\text{ABMPC}}(\text{successfulDelivery})$ = $h_{\text{ABMPCC}}(\text{initialPeriod})$ = $h_{\text{ABMPC}}(\text{pccRule})$ = $h_{\text{ABMPC}}(\text{ipCanSessionModification})$ = $h_{\text{ABMPCC}}(\text{chargingDataStart}_{\text{interim}})$;

h_{ABMPC}(successfulMessageCompletion) = h_{ABMPC}(dataTransferStop) = h_{ABMPC}(sessionStop) = h_{ABMPC}(ipCanSessionTermination) = h_{ABMPC}(chargingDataStop$_{normal}$);

h_{ABMPC}(cancelMessage) = h_{ABMPC}(cancel) = h_{ABMPC}(sessionCancel) = h_{ABMPC}(ipCanSessionCancel) = h_{ABMPC}(chargingDataStop$_{canceled}$);

h_{ABMPC}(unsuccessfulDelivery) = h_{ABMPC}(resourcesFailed) = h_{ABMPC}(ipCanBearerFailed) = h_{ABMPC}(provisionNonAck) = h_{ABMPC}(chargingDataStop$_{failed}$).

In order to define a weak bisimilar relation between the states of T_{App}, T_{BMSC}, T_{MBMS}, T_{PCRF}, and T_{CS} we establish the valid sequences of ordered transitions from - $\rightarrow_{App}$, - $\rightarrow_{BMSC}$, - $\rightarrow_{MBMS}$, - $\rightarrow_{PCRF}$, and - $\rightarrow_{CS}$ that correspond to U_{ABMPC}.

Let $\tau_i^{App} \subset \rightarrow_{App}$, where $i \in \{1, \ldots, 6\}$, be the following transition sequences:

τ_1^{App} = (Null sendMessage MessageWaiting);

τ_2^{App} = (MessageWaiting getBroadcastStatus MessageWaiting, MessageWaiting successfulDelivery Broadcasting);

τ_3^{App} = (Broadcasting getBroadcastStatus Broadcasting, Broadcasting successfulMessageCompletion Broadcasted, Broadcasted getBroadcastStatus Broadcasted, Broadcasted notifyBroadcastDeliveryReceipt Broadcasted, Broadcasted stopAnnouncement Null);

τ_4^{App} = (MessageWaiting unableToDeliver BroadcastImpossible, BroadcastImpossible getBroadcastStatus BroadcastImpossible, BroadcastImpossible notifyBroadcastDeliveryReceipt BroadcastImpossible, BroadcastImpossible stopAnnouncement Null);

τ_5^{App} = (MessageWaiting cancelMessage Null);

τ_6^{App} = (Broadcasting cancelMessage Null).

Let $\tau_i^{BMSC} \subset \rightarrow_{BMSC}$, where $i \in \{1, \ldots, 6\}$, be following transition sequences:

τ_1^{BMSC} = (MBMSIdle sendBroadcastMessage InitialWaiting);

τ_2^{BMSC} = (InitialWaiting initialPeriod DataTransfer);

τ_3^{BMSC} = (DataTransfer dataTransferStop MBMSIdle);

τ_4^{BMSC} = (InitialWaiting resourceFailed MBMSIdle);

τ_5^{BMSC} = (InitialWaiting cancelBroadcastMessage MBMSIdle);

τ_6^{BMSC} = (DataTransfer resourceLost MBMSIdle).

Let $\tau_i^{MBMS} \subset \rightarrow_{MBMS}$, where $i \in \{1, \ldots, 6\}$, be the following:

τ_1^{MBMS} = (IPCANIdle sessionStart WaitForPCCRules);

τ_2^{MBMS} = (WaitForPCCRules pccRules ResourceReservation, ResourceReservation ipCanBearerEstablishment SessionActive);

τ_3^{MBMS} = (SessionActive sessionStop ResourceRelease, ResourceRelease ipCanBearerRelease WaitForTermAck, WaitForTermAck ipCanSessionTermAck IPCANIdle);

τ_4^{MBMS} = (ResourceReservation ipCanBearerFailed IPCANIdle);

τ_5^{MBMC} = (WaitForPCCRules sessionCancel IPCANIdle, ResourceReservation sessionCancel IPCANIdle);

τ_6^{MBMS} = (SessionActive ipCanBearerLost IPCANIdle).

Let $\tau_i^{PCRF} \subset \rightarrow_{PCRF}$, where $i \in \{1, \ldots, 6\}$, be the following:

τ_1^{PCRF} = (ResourceNull sessionInfo IPCanSession);

τ_2^{PCRF} = (IPCANSession ipCanSessionModification ResourceAuthorizing, ResourceAuthorizing provisionAck ResourceAuthorized);

τ_3^{PCRF} = (ResourceAuthorized ipCanSessionTermination ResourceNull);

τ_4^{PCRF} = (ResourceAuthorizing provisionNonAck ResourceNull);

τ_5^{PCRF} = (IPCANSession ipCanSessionCancel ResourceNull, ResourceAuthorized ipCanSessionCancel ResourceNull);

τ_6^{PCRF} = (ResourceAuthorized ipCanBearerRemoved ResourceNull).

Let $\tau_i^{CS} \subset \rightarrow_{CS}$, where $i \in \{1, \ldots, 6\}$, be following transition sequences:

τ_1^{CS} = (ChargingIdle chargingDataStart$_{init}$ Active$_{initial}$);

τ_2^{CS} = (Active$_{initial}$ chargingDataStart$_{interim}$ Active$_{transfer}$);

τ_3^{CS} = (Active$_{transfer}$ chargingDataStop$_{normal}$ ChargingIdle);

τ_4^{CS} = (Active$_{initial}$ chargingDataStop$_{failed}$ ChargingIdle);

τ_5^{CS} = (Active$_{initial}$ chargingDataStop$_{canceled}$ ChargingIdle);

τ_6^{CS} = (Active$_{transfer}$ chargingDataStop$_{canceled}$ ChargingIdle).

Then, based on the defined homomorphism h_{ABMPC} between the actions of T_{App}, T_{BMSC}, T_{MBMS}, T_{PCRF}, and T_{CS}, it follows that for U_{ABMPC} the sequences (τ_i^{App}, τ_i^{BMSC}, τ_i^{MBMS}, τ_i^{PCRF}, τ_i^{CS}) for $i \in \{1, \ldots, 6\}$ agree with Definition 2 for weak bisimilarity.

Hence, the state machines that represent the 3rd-party application view on message broadcast, MBMS session, IP-CAN session, QoS resources, and charging session are bisimilar; that is, these state machines expose equivalent behavior. □

7. Conclusion

In EPS there are specific features, nodes, and interfaces defined to support broadcasting of content to multiple users simultaneously. Parlay X Message Broadcast WS allows third-party applications to send messages to all mobile terminals in a specific geographical area. The deployment of 3rd-party control on multimedia broadcasting implies more research on synergy between WS APIs and respective communication control protocols.

The paper presents a study on modeling aspects of a network node that mediates between 3rd-party application servers and the evolved packet core of a mobile network. It explores the way the network agnostic WS interfaces collaborate with specific control functionality in order to provide value added multimedia broadcasting services.

The results regard model aspects of the behavior of a Service Capability Server, namely, BMSC, which exposes Parlay X WS interfaces toward applications and "talks" network protocols toward the network. The focus is on collaboration of different functionalities, namely, service control, session management, QoS control, and charging control. In the context of message broadcast, we modeled the states of MBMS session, IP-CAN session, QoS resources, and charging session and showed that these models are synchronized with the 3rd-party application view on message broadcast. The proof is based on functional mapping between the transitions in state machines and the identification of a homomorphism between actions. The concept of weak bisimilarity is used to prove that the state machines expose equivalent behavior. Thus, the novelty of contribution might be summarized as model definitions and proof for bisimilarity.

The utilization of standardized Message Broadcast APIs provides a unified approach for 3rd-party application management and provisioning. It allows development of converged multimedia broadcast applications in a way which is independent of the underlying access technologies.

References

[1] D. Lecompte and F. Gabin, "Evolved multimedia broadcast/multicast service (eMBMS) in LTE-advanced: overview and Rel-11 enhancements," *IEEE Communications Magazine*, vol. 50, no. 11, pp. 68–74, 2012.

[2] J. Calabuig, J. F. Monserrat, D. Gozálvez, and O. Klemp, "Safety on the roads: LTE alternatives for sending ITS messages," *IEEE Vehicular Technology Magazine*, vol. 9, no. 4, pp. 61–70, 2014.

[3] I. Stephanasik, I. Chochliouros, G. Lymperopoulos, and K. Berberidis, "Optimal video delivery in mobile networks using a cache-accelerated multi area eMBMS architecture," in *Artificial Intelligence Applications and Innovations*, vol. 437 of *IFIP Advances in Information and Communication Technology*, pp. 13–23, Springer, Berlin, Germany, 2014.

[4] F. C. Pinto, N. Carapeto, A. Videira, T. Frazão, and M. Homem, "Context-aware multimedia distribution to mobile social communities," *International Journal of Handheld Computing Research*, vol. 4, no. 3, pp. 63–92, 2013.

[5] C. M. Lentisco, M. Aguayo, L. Bellido, E. Pastor, D. De-Antonio-Monte, and A. G. Bolivar, "A virtualized platform for analyzing LTE broadcast services," in *Proceedings of the European Conference on Networks and Communications (EuCNC '15)*, pp. 512–516, Paris, France, June 2015.

[6] J. Calabuig, J. Monserrat, D. Martin-Sacristan, and J. Olmos, "Comparison of multicast/broadcast services in Long Term Evolution Advanced and IEEE 802.16 m networks," *Wireless Communications and Mobile Computing*, vol. 14, no. 7, pp. 717–728, 2014.

[7] G. Araniti, M. Condoluci, and A. Molinaro, "Resource management of multicast services over LTE," in *Convergence of Broadband, Broadcast, and Cellular Network Technologies*, pp. 77–93, IGI Global, 2014.

[8] G. K. Walker, J. Wang, C. Lo, X. G. Zhang, and G. Bao, "Relationship between LTE broadcast/eMBMS and next generation broadcast television," *IEEE Transactions on Broadcasting*, vol. 60, no. 2, pp. 185–192, 2014.

[9] F. Malandrino, C. Casetti, C. F. Chiasserini, and S. Zhou, "Real-time scheduling for content broadcasting in LTE," in *Proceedings of the IEEE International Symposium on Modelling, Analysis & Simulation of Computer and Telecommunication Systems*, pp. 126–131, Paris, France, September 2014.

[10] A. de la Fuente, A. G. Armada, and R. P. Leal, "Joint multicast/unicast scheduling with dynamic optimization for LTE multicast service," in *Proceedings of the 20th European Wireless Conference (EW '14)*, pp. 462–467, Barcelona, Spain, May 2014.

[11] C. Borgiattino, C. Casetti, C. F. Chiasserini, and F. Malandrino, "Efficient area formation for LTE broadcasting," in *Proceedings of the 12th Annual IEEE International Conference on Sensing, Communication, and Networking (SECON '15)*, pp. 202–210, IEEE, Seattle, Wash, USA, June 2015.

[12] C. W. Yeh, M. J. Shih, G. Y. Lin, and H. Y. Wei, "LTE-D broadcast with distributed interference-aware D2D resource allocation," in *Proceedings of the 7th International Conference on Ubiquitous and Future Networks (ICUFN '15)*, pp. 165–170, Sapporo, Japan, July 2015.

[13] Y.-H. Xu, C.-O. Chow, M.-L. Tham, and H. Ishii, "An enhanced framework for providing multimedia broadcast/multicast service over heterogeneous networks," *Journal of Zhejiang University Science*, vol. 15, no. 1, pp. 63–80, 2014.

[14] J. H. Kim, S. K. Kim, and B. S. Lee, "Message service method and message service system," US Patent 8478313 B2, 2013.

[15] 3GPP, "Multimedia Broadcast/Multicast Service (MBMS); architecture and functional description," 3GPP TS 23.246, 2015, Release 13.

[16] 3GPP, "Multimedia Broadcast/Multicast Service (MBMS); protocols and codecs," 3GPP TS 26.346, 2015, Release 13.

[17] 3GPP TS 23.203, "Policy and Charging control architecture," Release 13, v13.5.0, 2015.

[18] 3GPP, "Telecommunication management; charging management; charging architecture and principles," 3GPP TS 32.240, 2015, Release 13, v13.0.0.

[19] 3GPP, "Open Service Access (OSA); parlay X web services; part 15: message broadcast," 3GPP TS 29.199-15, 2009, Release 9.

[20] L. Fuchun, Z. Qiansheng, and C. Xuesong, "Bisimilarity control of decentralized nondeterministic discrete-event systems," in *Proceedings of the 33rd Chinese Control Conference (CCC '14)*, pp. 3898–3903, IEEE, Nanjing, China, July 2014.

14

A Survey of Standardized Approaches towards the Quality of Experience Evaluation for Video Services: An ITU Perspective

Debajyoti Pal⬙ and Tuul Triyason

IP Communications Laboratory, School of Information Technology, King Mongkut's University of Technology Thonburi, Bangkok 10140, Thailand

Correspondence should be addressed to Debajyoti Pal; debajyoti.pal@gmail.com

Academic Editor: Homero Toral Cruz

Over the past few years there has been an exponential increase in the amount of multimedia data being streamed over the Internet. At the same time, we are also witnessing a change in the way quality of any particular service is interpreted, with more emphasis being given to the end-users. Thus, silently there has been a paradigm shift from the traditional Quality of Service approach (QoS) towards a Quality of Experience (QoE) model while evaluating the service quality. A lot of work that tries to evaluate the quality of audio, video, and multimedia services over the Internet has been done. At the same time, research is also going on trying to map the two different domains of quality metrics, i.e., the QoS and QoE domain. Apart from the work done by individual researchers, the International Telecommunications Union (ITU) has been quite active in this area of quality assessment. This is obvious from the large number of ITU standards that are available for different application types. The sheer variety of techniques being employed by ITU as well as other researchers sometimes tends to be too complex and diversified. Although there are survey papers that try to present the current state of the art methodologies for video quality evaluation, none has focused on the ITU perspective. In this work, we try to fill up this void by presenting up-to-date information on the different measurement methods that are currently being employed by ITU for a video streaming scenario. We highlight the outline of each method with sufficient detail and try to analyze the challenges being faced along with the direction of future research.

1. Introduction

There has been a rapid advance in various video services and its applications, like video telephony, High-Definition (HD) and Ultrahigh-Definition (UHD) television, Internet protocol television (IPTV), and mobile multimedia streaming in recent years. Thus, quality assessment of videos that are being streamed and watched online has become an area of active research. As per a report published in [1–3], video streaming over the Internet is becoming increasingly popular and accounts for more than 55% of the overall traffic. A lot of work has been done by several researchers towards the quality assessment of streaming multimedia services [4–8]. At the same time, organizations like the International Telecommunication Union (ITU) also have in place different models and standardization efforts towards the perceived video quality evaluation under a variety of application scenarios. The main

objective of this paper is to provide an up-to-date review of this research field from a standard ITU perspective.

Figure 1 shows a typical video streaming scenario over the Internet. Broadly, three distinct regions are identified as the production network (head-end), the distribution network (carrier), and the consumer network (tail end). Relevant contents are created, edited, encoded, and stored in suitable multimedia databases ready to be transported to the end-users (consumer network) over the Internet with the help of streaming servers. This multimedia traffic has to pass through the unreliable Internet (distribution network) where they are fragmented into various IP segments and ultimately delivered to the consumer end where they are displayed on a variety of devices like television, computers, or mobile phones. The inherent unreliable service provided by the Internet necessitates the use of perceptual quality evaluation schemes for such video traffic.

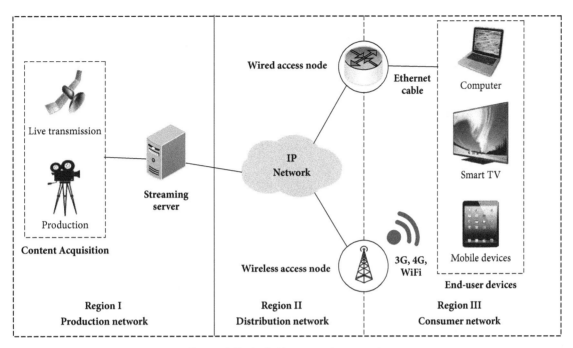

FIGURE 1: Typical video streaming scenario.

We segregate the multimedia streaming scenario presented in Figure 1 to two different types based upon the ownership use case of the Internet as the Internet protocol television (IPTV) service and over-the-top (OTT) streaming service. YouTube, Netflix, Hulu, etc. are prime examples of the OTT service. IPTV runs on a private, fully controlled network and hence has the advantage of tight control and guaranteed (overprovisioned) bandwidth [9]. IPTV typically uses the User Datagram Protocol (UDP) at the transport layer, and hence in case of any packet loss retransmission does not happen. Still, the reliability of IPTV service is generally high because the video traffic is being carried over a fully controlled network (usually private). On the contrary, in case of OTT services, the contents are streamed over the open and unmanaged public Internet. Thus, IPTV services utilize a network that guarantees a Quality of Service (QoS), which differentiates them from the other OTT services. Quality of Experience (QoE) provisioning for OTT services is a far more challenging job as compared to IPTV services. Hence, for this work we focus only on those ITU standards that do not include IPTV services. More specifically, we focus on video streaming over the public Internet only.

The main goal of this article is to summarize the current and other emerging approaches of video quality evaluation of a streaming service within the scope of ITU. Often due to the sheer variety of the different ITU standards, it becomes difficult for a new researcher to select a suitable method. This work aims to bridge the aforementioned gap by carefully analyzing the relevant ITU standards in detail and giving suitable recommendations as to which standard to choose for a specific context.

We begin by presenting the concepts related to QoS and QoE in Section 2 along with the interrelationship between them. Sections 3 and 4 present the review of subjective and objective methods, respectively. In Section 5, we discuss the current challenges in video quality measurement and the future trends. Finally, Section 6 provides the conclusion.

2. QoS and QoE

We begin the survey process by explaining the key concepts of QoS and QoE explicitly highlighting their differences.

2.1. QoS Concepts

2.1.1. QoS Definition. QoS has been defined by ITU-T as *"totality of characteristics of a telecommunications service that bear on its ability to satisfy stated and implied needs of the user of the service"* [15]. This definition of QoS is extremely generic in nature and needs to be reapplied in a specific application context. Figure 2 shows the concept of end-to-end QoS that is commonly prevalent in almost all scenarios. Terminal equipment refers to the devices that are used either by the service provider or by the consumer in order to provide/avail a particular service. Access network is a combination of the access medium and technology used for a particular service (e.g., wireless, cable, ADSL). Access network generally belongs to a specific service provider. Core network refers to the IP backbone network, which is usually controlled by different stakeholders. The QoS contribution of the core network is governed by the technology used (digital multiplexing, IP, etc.) and transmission media (air, cable, optical, etc.) along with other factors. While specifying the end-to-end QoS, it is necessary to state the specified operating conditions in which a service is supported over a connection (connectionless or connection-oriented) scheme. QoS is also affected by factors like traffic and routing [16]. Each of the elements presented in Figure 2 affects the QoS in

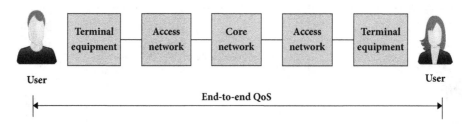

FIGURE 2: The concept of end-to-end QoS.

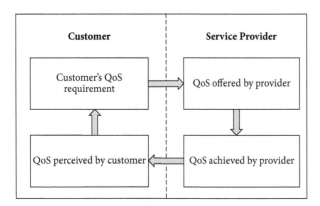

FIGURE 3: Four Viewpoints of QoS [10].

its own way. In addition, it is evident that QoS comprises both network performance (NP) and non-network-related factors. Bit-error rate, latency, and jitter are some of the NP related factors, while tariff levels, service-repair time, etc. are the non-network parameters. Four different angles from which QoS can be viewed are discussed next.

2.1.2. Viewpoints of QoS and Their Interrelationship. We can classify the different perspectives of QoS into four different types as shown in Figure 3.

(i) *Customer's QoS requirement* refers to the quality level of any application that is expected by the end-users and expressed in nontechnical terms. The customer is not bothered about how a service is offered or about the internals of the network/application design; rather the focus is on the overall end-to-end quality.

(ii) *QoS offered by the provider* refers to the level of service quality that the provider is expected to provide to the customers. The level of quality is expressed by values assigned to QoS parameters. Primarily this is used for planning purpose and framing of Service Level Agreements (SLA) between the provider and the customer.

(iii) *QoS achieved by the provider* refers to the quality level of the service that the provider actually delivers to the customer, which ideally should be the same as the QoS offered by the provider. In reality, the values are different and the performance is compared across the two groups over a certain period.

(iv) *QoS perceived by the customer* refers to the satisfaction level that the customer "*believes*" to have experienced. This is usually assessed from data gathered through customer surveys or individual assessment by a customer for the service.

The four viewpoints are interconnected as shown in Figure 3. Logically, the process starts at the customer's QoS requirement stage. These requirements act as input suggestions to the service provider who plans to offer the desired level of quality. Most of the time, the planned level of service quality is not met due to several factors. As discussed before, these factors are primarily NP related ones like packet loss, jitter, latency, and throughput. A tradeoff between the cost incurred to deliver the ideal quality and the viability of the overall business model has to be done, which affects the service quality in general. The service is ultimately delivered to the customers who perceive the real quality that is achieved by the provider.

From the above discussion, it is clear that the customer viewpoint is the most important one for any service to be successful. This is exactly the reason why ITU has a separate recommendation in [11] that defines a model for multimedia QoS categories from an end-user viewpoint. Next, a brief overview of this recommendation is provided.

2.1.3. QoS Requirements of Different Application Types. Different types of applications are identified like voice, video, and web browsing, with each having different performance requirements for achieving a good perceived quality. Figure 4 shows a classification based upon the overall requirements of the applications in terms of two important QoS parameters, namely, packet loss and one-way delay.

The applications have been classified into eight distinct groups. Some applications such as conversational voice and video are sensitive to delay, but can tolerate a certain extent of packet loss. On the other hand, applications like Fax are sensitive to packet loss, but can withstand delay to a certain extent. Other interactive applications like online gaming are extremely sensitive to both packet loss and delay. These facts are presented in a more clear fashion in Figure 5. The figure shows four distinct delay types depending upon the extent of user interaction involved.

The recommended range of QoS values for some important applications have been provided in Table 1 [11]. The target values of certain applications like audio streaming, videophone, and video streaming are outdated as of 2018. For example, in case of video streaming the typical data rates

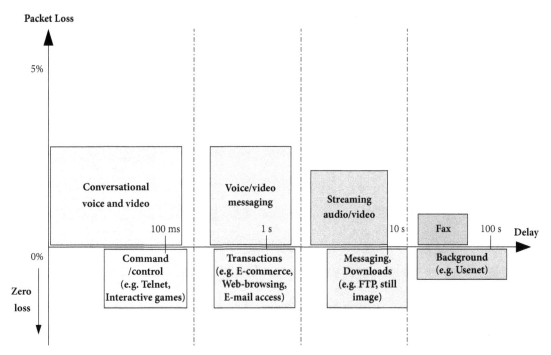

FIGURE 4: QoS requirements for different applications.

	Conversational voice and video	Voice/video messaging	Streaming audio and video	Fax
Error tolerant	Conversational voice and video	Voice/video messaging	Streaming audio and video	Fax
Error intolerant	Command/ Control	Transactions	Messaging, Downloads	Background (e.g. Usenet)
	Interactive (delay << 1 s)	**Responsive** (delay ~2 s)	**Timely** (delay ~10 s)	**Non-critical** (delay >> 10 s)

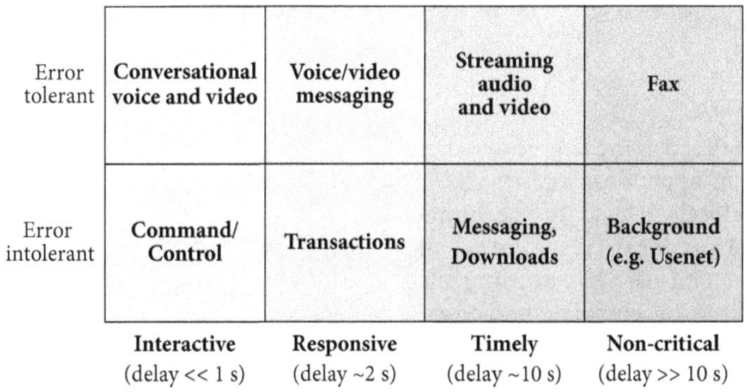

FIGURE 5: QoS requirements for different applications [11].

TABLE 1: Performance target for different applications.

Application	Typical Data Rates	Performance Parameters and Target Values		
		One-way Delay	Jitter	Packet Loss
Conversational Voice	4–64 kbps	<150 ms (preferred) <400 ms (limit)	<1 ms	<3%
Voice Messaging	4–32 kbps	<1 s (playback) <2 s (record)	<1 ms	<3%
Audio Streaming	16–128 kbps	<10 s	<1 ms	<1%
Videophone	16–384 kbps	<150 ms (preferred) <400 ms (limit)	-	<1%
Video Streaming	16–384 kbps	<10 s	-	<1%
Web Browsing and HTML	NA	<2 s	NA	Zero
E-commerce Services	NA	<2 s	NA	Zero
Interactive Games	NA	<200 ms	NA	Zero

NA: not applicable.

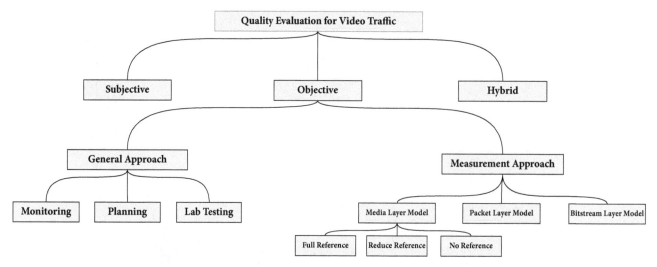

FIGURE 6: Categorization of different quality assessment methodologies by ITU for video applications.

can easily shoot up to the order of tens of Mbps instead of 384 kbps due to an increase in the network throughput as well as the video resolutions [17]. Similarly, with the advent of modern techniques like dynamic adaptive streaming over HTTP (DASH based streaming), the upper and lower bounds of the other QoS parameters like jitter, one-way delay, and packet loss also need to be updated.

2.2. QoE Concepts

2.2.1. QoE Definition. QoE is defined as the degree of delight or annoyance of the user of an application or service [18, 19]. The concept of QoE is closely related to the human auditory and visual system (HAS and HVS, respectively) and the overall satisfaction that the end-user has in using such a service. Thus, QoE also refers to a complete end-to-end experience that has been shown previously in Figure 2. It is obvious that for any service to succeed, it must provide a good experience to the end-users. A lot of work is being done by ITU towards the quality assessment of various application types. For this article, however, we concentrate only on the video streaming applications. Next, a general overview of the different QoE assessment methodologies being employed by ITU has been provided.

2.2.2. QoE Assessment Methodologies. Confining the scope of this work to video streaming only, Figure 6 shows an overview of the different QoE assessment methodologies being currently used by ITU. Irrespective of the methodology used, the QoE assessment technique must be valid and reliable. The concept of validity versus reliability has been shown in Figure 7. Validity describes how well a method measures what it is intended to measure, while reliability refers to the accuracy of a method in terms of scattering of results (for example, when a test assessment is repeated) [20].

The end-user experience can be measured using two broad techniques: subjective and objective tests [12]. Subjective tests that involve human subjects are considered the most accurate means of quality estimation. Objective tests on the

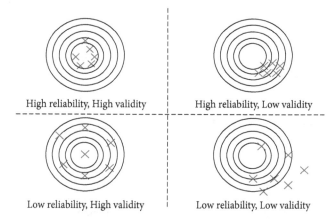

FIGURE 7: Concept of validity versus reliability [12].

other hand use some mathematical formulae or algorithms to predict the quality. Despite the accuracy of the objective methods being lesser than the subjective ones, they are preferred in many situations as they are automatic, i.e., easy and faster to be carried out and much cheaper than the subjective tests.

One way to categorize the objective methods is by a general approach, which lists down the different application scenarios in which a particular objective model can be used. There are three specific use-cases as mentioned below:

(i) *Monitoring*: in which a particular objective model is used for live quality assessment of a video application. This is a real time usage scenario that assesses the video quality, e.g., ITU-T P.1202.

(ii) *Planning*: in which an objective model can be used for network planning before an actual service startup. Mainly these models are used as network planning tools in which they help in selecting IP-network transmission settings such as the video format, video codec, and video bitrates with the assumption that the

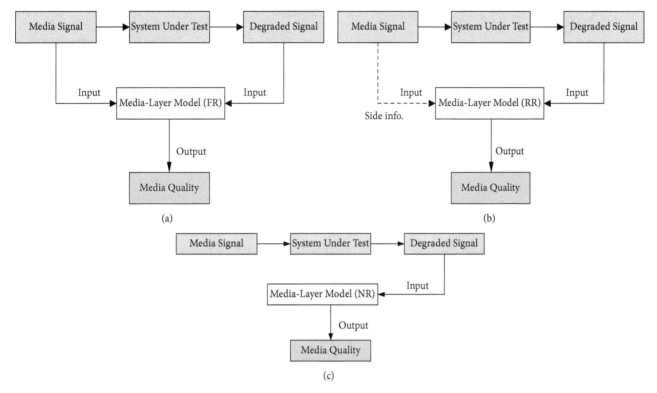

FIGURE 8: Conceptual view of media layer model: (a) FR methods, (b) RR methods, (c) NR methods.

underlying network is subjected to packet loss, e.g., ITU-T G.1071.

(iii) *Lab testing*: in which quality assessment is done in a typical laboratory setup. This type of approach is used when commercially it is not feasible to assess the quality or in certain situations that require the presence of the original source signal for the purpose of quality measurement or during the development and testing of particular equipment, e.g., ITU-T J.341.

In the second approach, the objective methods are classified based upon the type of measurement used as follows:

(i) *Media layer model*: this uses actual audio/video signals as their input. They also take into account codec compression and the channel characteristics. These types of models can further be subdivided into three different types depending upon the extent of the original reference signal that they have for quality assessment:

  (1) *Full reference (FR) methods* in which a reference video is compared frame-by-frame with a distorted video sequence in order to obtain the quality. The comparison can be from many aspects like color processing, spatial and temporal features, contrast features, etc. These methods are generally used in lab-testing environments, e.g., ITU-T J.247.

  (2) *Reduced reference (RR) methods* in which certain characteristics/features of the reference

signal are extracted out and used for the quality evaluation of the distorted signal. Hence, instead of the entire reference signal, only subsets of its features are used for quality assessment, e.g., ITU-T J.246.

  (3) *No reference (NR) methods* are those that do not require the reference video to be present while assessing the quality of the distorted video sequences. These methods are generally used for real time quality assessment of videos, e.g., ITU-T P.1201. Both the RR and NR methods can be applied to either the mid-points or the end-points of the network.

Figures 8(a), 8(b), and 8(c) show the conceptual view of the FR, RR, and NR type media layer models just discussed.

(ii) *Packet layer model*: this utilizes only the packet header information for the purpose of QoE prediction. These models do not have the ability to check the payload information. Therefore, they are not suitable for situations that require the presence of media contents. Generally, such model types are used as network-probes at the mid-points or end-points of the network. Figure 9 shows the conceptual view of a packet layer model, e.g., ITU-T P.1201.

(iii) *Bitstream layer model*: this type takes into account not only the encoded bitstream information, but also the packet header information while assessing the video quality. They are actually a combination of the media

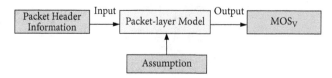

FIGURE 9: Conceptual view of packet layer model.

FIGURE 10: Conceptual view of bitstream layer model.

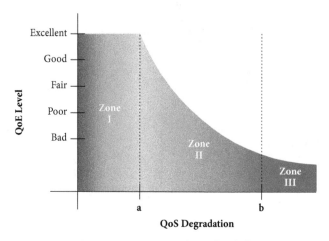

FIGURE 11: QoS-QoE relationship [13].

layer and packet layer models. Figure 10 shows the conceptual view of a bitstream layer model. These are ideal for live quality monitoring purpose, e.g., ITU-T P.1202.

A third approach to QoE assessment known as the hybrid method uses a combination of the subjective and objective techniques [21, 22]. In this method, typically at the beginning a subjective test is carried out to gather the opinion from the people regarding the quality of the test video sequences under consideration. These test-videos are impaired by one or more QoS factors (NP or non-NP related) depending upon the experimental scenario and requirements. Thereafter, mathematical techniques like linear or nonlinear regression, different types of neural networks, or other machine learning algorithms are used for creating a quality prediction model based upon the subjective scores. This approach tries to take into account the advantages of both the subjective and objective techniques [23], e.g., ITU-T G.1070.

2.3. The Relationship between QoS and QoE. After an elaborate explanation of QoS and QoE from an ITU perspective, now we present the interdependence between them. A possible relationship between the two has been shown in Figure 11. The QoS-QoE relationship has been separated into three distinct zones. Zone I (marked in green) shows the ideal region where the perceived video QoE should be.

The users experience an excellent viewing quality. A certain QoS level needs to be maintained (corresponding to point "*a*" on the graph) in order to achieve this QoE. This point "*a*" represents the ideal threshold QoS level (in terms of packet loss, jitter, network throughput, or other factors) that should be maintained theoretically by all the concerned stakeholders. Zone II shows a diminishing QoE region where further deterioration in the QoS values results in a sharp drop in QoE. The point "*b*" on the graph represents the actual threshold value below which the user will probably stop using the service. There is no exact relationship that models this region of diminishing QoE [24, 25]. However, a number of ITU recommendations like ITU-T G.1070, ITU-T G.1071, and ITU-T P.1201 attempt to model this scenario. Zone 3 (marked in red) shows the region where the QoE is extremely poor and should be avoided under all circumstances.

The taxonomy of all the ITU recommendations related to video streaming that have been covered in this survey is shown in Figure 12.

3. Subjective Methodologies

In this section, we present the relevant subjective methods that are used for video streaming applications.

3.1. ITU-T Recommendation P.910. Noninteractive subjective assessment methods for evaluating the one-way overall video quality of multimedia applications such as videoconferencing, storage, and retrieval applications have been covered in ITU Recommendation P.910 [26]. The number of subjects in the tests varies from 4 to 40.

3.1.1. Overall Experiment Design. The test is usually carried out in a recording environment that has sufficient lighting. The lighting conditions should be representative of a typical office scenario rather than studio lighting. Specifically, the ambient lighting of the room should be between 100 lux and 10,000 lux.

The reference video sequences that are used for showing to the human subjects are extremely important. Perceived video quality depends largely on the type of video content [27–30]. Hence, while selecting the reference sequences, spatial information (SI) and temporal information (TI) are two critical factors that must be taken into account. SI gives an indication to the amount of spatial details that each frame

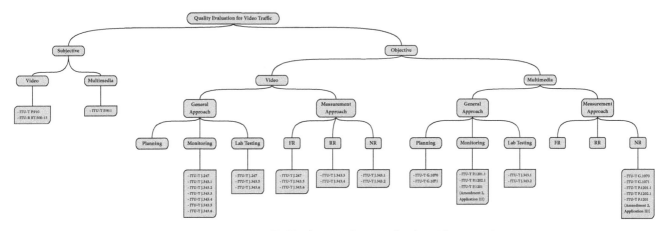

FIGURE 12: Taxonomy of ITU recommendations related to video streaming.

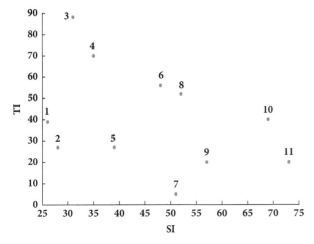

FIGURE 13: SI/TI values of some commonly used video sequences by ITU [14].

has and it has a higher value for more spatially complex scenes. The SI value for every video frame is calculated by filtering each one of them using the Sobel filter followed by computing the standard deviation. The maximum value in the frame represents the SI content of the scene. Similarly, TI values give an indication of the amount of temporal changes in a particular video sequence and it has a higher value for sequences having greater amount of motion. Equations (1) and (2) show the calculation of the SI and TI values, respectively:

$$SI = \max_{time} \left\{ std_{space} \left[Sobel \left(F_n \right) \right] \right\} \qquad (1)$$

$$TI = \max_{time} \left\{ std_{space} \left[F_n \left(i, j \right) - F_{n-1} \left(i, j \right) \right] \right\}, \qquad (2)$$

where F_n is the video frame at time n, std_{space} the standard deviation across all the pixels for each filtered frame, and max_{time} the corresponding maximum value in the considered time interval.

Figure 13 shows the SI and TI values of some commonly used video sequences [14]. The publicly available video

database of VQEG is used most frequently while selecting the reference videos [31]. The relevant video details are given in Table 2. Table 3 summarizes the viewing conditions that must be satisfied. Normally, at-least 4 different types of video sequences should be used in a particular test.

Next, we present a brief overview of the different methods that are used by this recommendation.

3.1.2. Different Test Methods. Four different types of methods are used in this recommendation and they are classified as Absolute Category Rating (ACR), Absolute Category Rating with Hidden Reference (ACR-HR), Degradation Category Rating (DCR), and Pair Comparison (PC) method. Each of these techniques is discussed next.

(i) *ACR method*: here the distorted test sequences are presented one at a time and the users give opinion scores (typically on a scale of 1 to 5), which are averaged into a Mean Opinion Score (MOS) [32]. Table 4 shows the MOS scale. The timing diagram of the stimulus presentation has been shown in Figure 14(a). The users are shown video sequences, which typically last for 10 seconds followed by a voting time interval of 10 seconds approximately, wherein the subjects need to enter their opinion in the form of MOS scores. The video presentation time can be increased or decreased depending on the test sequences.

(ii) *ACR-HR method*: it is similar to the ACR method, with an exception that the reference version of each presented distorted test sequence is also shown to the subjects. This is referred to as the hidden reference condition. The subjects give their opinion in the form of MOS scores. However, for final quality assessment a differential quality score (DMOS) is computed for each distorted sequence and its corresponding reference one as per the following equation:

$$DMOS = MOS_S - MOS_R + 5, \qquad (3)$$

where MOS_S represents the MOS of a particular distorted video sequence and MOS_R represents the

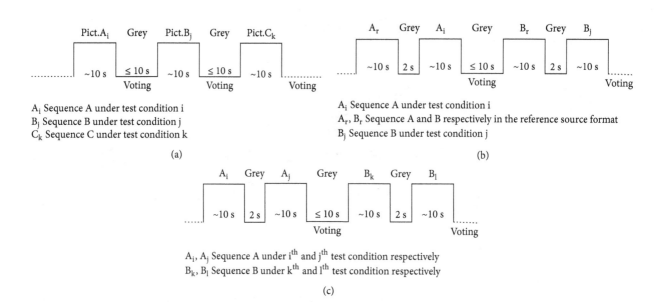

FIGURE 14: Timing diagram for stimulus presentation: (a) ACR/ACR-HR, (b) DCR, (c) PC.

TABLE 2: Relevant video details.

Seq No.	Seq Name	Frame Rate	Chroma Format	Content Complexity
1	Harbor	60 fps	4.2.0	1014
2	Ice	60 fps	4.2.0	756
3	DucksTakeOff	50 fps	4.2.0	2728
4	ParkJoy	50 fps	4.2.0	2450
5	Crew	60 fps	4.2.0	1053
6	CrowdRun	50 fps	4.2.0	2688
7	Akiyo	30 fps	4.2.0	255
8	Soccer	60 fps	4.2.0	2704
9	Foreman	30 fps	4.2.0	1140
10	Football	30 fps	4.2.0	2760
11	News	30 fps	4.2.0	1470

TABLE 3: Summary of viewing conditions.

Parameter	Settings
Viewing distance	1–8 times picture height
Peak luminance of screen	100–200 cd/m
Ratio of luminance of inactive screen to peak luminance	≤0.05
Ratio of luminance of screen, when displaying only black level in a complete dark room to a peak white	≤0.1
Background room illumination	≤20 lux

TABLE 4: MOS scale.

Rating	Meaning
5	Excellent
4	Good
3	Fair
2	Poor
1	Bad

MOS of its corresponding reference sequence. DMOS is also measured on a scale of 1 to 5 identical to MOS. If the distorted video sequence has a better quality than its corresponding reference one, the DMOS value will be greater than 5, which is valid and indicative of an excellent quality (better than the reference one).

Similarly, when the values of MOS_S and MOS_R are the same, the DMOS value is maximum, i.e., 5, indicating no perceptual difference in quality between the distorted and the reference video sequences. The timing diagram is the same as the ACR method.

(iii) *DCR method*: in this type, the test sequences are presented in pairs. In a pair, the reference sequence is always shown first followed by the distorted sequence. The timing diagram for this type of method has been shown in Figure 14(b). The two sequences should be perfectly synchronized; i.e., both of them must start

TABLE 5: DCR 5 level opinion scale.

Rating	Meaning
5	Imperceptible
4	Perceptible but not annoying
3	Slightly annoying
2	Annoying
1	Very annoying

TABLE 6: Continuous quality scale.

Rating	Meaning
80–100	Excellent
60–80	Good
40–60	Fair
20–40	Poor
0–20	Bad

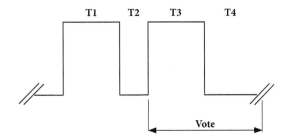

FIGURE 15: Timing diagram for stimulus presentation (variant 1).

and stop at the same frame. In this case, the subjects are asked to rate the distorted sequences with respect to the reference on a 5-point scale. Table 5 presents the 5-level opinion scale.

(iv) *PC method*: in this method, the test sequences are presented in pairs like DCR. However, none of the sequences in the pair is a reference sequence. Instead, all the distorted sequences are combined in all possible combinations and then presented in pairs to the subjects. After each presentation, a judgment is made by the subject on which is the preferred sequence in the pair. The timing diagram has been shown in Figure 14(c).

3.1.3. Comparison of the Test Methods. The most crucial decision is to choose the right technique for a particular application. Normally, the choice is between applications that require or do not require the presence of the reference sequences. The DCR method should be chosen when testing the fidelity of transmission with respect to the reference signal. ACR is easy, fast to implement, and hence commonly used. The basic advantage of ACR-HR over ACR is that the memory effect of the reference sequences can be removed from the subjective scores. PC method should be used when a high discriminatory power is required on the subjective scores.

3.2. ITU-R Recommendation BT.500-13. This recommendation gives different methodologies for assessing the picture and video quality for any generic application scenario, not only restricting to a video streaming case [33]. Considering the popularity of the methods that have been outlined in this recommendation, we chose to include them as a part of this survey. The subjects can be experts or nonexperts depending upon the objectives of the assessment. Minimum 15 observers must be present with no limits on the upper bound. Next, the different test methodologies that are enumerated in this recommendation are presented.

Different Test Methods. Five different types of test procedures are described. They are the Single Stimulus Continuous Quality Evaluation (SSCQE) method, Double Stimulus Continuous Quality Scale (DSCQS) method, Double Stimulus Impairment Scale (DSIS) method, Simultaneous Double Stimulus for Continuous Evaluation (SDSCE) method, and the Stimulus Comparison Adjectival Categorical Judgment (SCACJ) method. The first one is an example of a single stimulus technique, while all the remaining four are examples

of double stimulus methods, wherein both the reference and distorted video sequences must be presented simultaneously.

(i) *SSCQE method*: this is a single stimulus method that enables a continuous evaluation of the distorted video sequences on a scale that has been shown in Table 6. The items are normalized in a range of 0 to 100. Generally, each video sequence lasts for at-least 5 minutes.

(ii) *DSIS method*: this is a type of cyclic method in the sense that the subject is at first presented with the original sequence and then with the same impaired sequence. Each sequence is generally reproduced either one (variant 1) or two times (variant 2), after which the subject evaluates the distorted video sequence using an opinion scale that has been shown in Table 5. Interpretations for both the DCR and DSIS methods are the same. The timing diagrams for variants 1 and 2 are shown in Figures 15 and 16, respectively. For both the variants, the subjects need to watch the video sequence during the time slots T_1 and T_3 and voting is permitted only in T_4. Time slots T_1 and T_3 are approximately of 10 seconds duration each, with T_2 being around 3-second pause/gap period and T_4 lasting for 5–11 seconds. T_1 time slot shows the reference sequence, followed by the distorted sequence in T_3.

(iii) *DSCQS method*: this is also a type of cyclic method in which the subject is asked to view a pair of video sequences consecutively, with both of them being from the same source, but one being the original reference sequence and the other one the distorted version of the same source. The subjects assess the quality of both the sequences on a continuous scale that has been shown in Table 6. In this case, the subjects do not know that whether a particular sequence is a reference one or the distorted version. The

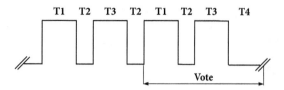

FIGURE 16: Timing diagram for stimulus presentation (variant 2).

TABLE 7: SCACJ quality scale.

Rating	Meaning
−3	Much worse
−2	Worse
−1	Slightly worse
0	The same
+1	Slightly better
+2	Better
+3	Much better

general timing diagram of the stimulus presentation for DSCQS method is the same as the second variant of the DSIS method (shown in Figure 16). However, the interpretations of the time slots T_1, T_2, T_3, and T_4 are different. In time slots T_1 and T_3 the test sequences are presented (in no particular order and generally changed across different sequences in a pseudorandom fashion) while in slot T_4 the voting is done. T_2 represents a short gap period between T_1 and T_3. Recommended values for the four time slots are the same as those in the case of the DSIS method.

(iv) *SDSCE method*: in this procedure, the subjects are allowed to watch two video sequences simultaneously, where one sequence is the reference and the other one its distorted counterpart. Generally, both the sequences are shown side by side and the subjects know which is the reference sequence and which is its distorted version. This method is generally used for judging the fidelity of the video information. It is recommended when the video sequences are of longer duration (at-least 5 minutes) and uses the same scale that has been presented in Table 6.

(v) *SCACJ method*: this is an example of a stimulus comparison method and similar to the double stimulus methods discussed above. However, the only difference is that the reference sequences are not shown in this case and only the distorted sequences are presented to the subjects. The subject has to rate the quality of the second video in comparison to the first one based upon the scale which has been shown in Table 7.

3.3. ITU-T Recommendation P.911. This recommendation presents the different subjective quality assessment methods for multimedia applications [34]. The number of subjects varies from 6 to 40. It uses four different techniques, namely, ACR, DCR, PC, and SSCQE. All these techniques have

already been discussed in the previous sections. The only difference is in the stimulus type that is shown to the users. In this case video sequences are shown which have an audio counterpart. Therefore, the subjects evaluate the overall multimedia quality. However, in case of the previous recommendations, the videos normally do not have any audio portion. Next, a brief summary of the subjective methods discussed above and their shortcomings is presented.

3.4. Summary of Subjective Methods. Subjective methods are more accurate in gauging the user opinion when compared to the objective ones. A variety of techniques is available and a proper one should be chosen based upon the time available and application requirement. If time is not a constraint, then any of the methods discussed above can be used. For time critical conditions, generally ACR or ACR-HR method is preferred. Similarly, presence or absence of reference content also affects the choice of a particular technique. Sometimes, the duration of the video sequence that needs to be evaluated also plays a judgmental role in deciding which technique is to be chosen. For longer video sequences, normally SSCQE or SDSCE is used. Requirements related to certain specific quality aspects can also sometimes dictate a specific choice.

Reliability of subjects is one of the crucial factors that affect the quality of the results obtained from these subjective techniques. Human perception is often influence by factors like ambient room conditions, emotional and mental state of the subjects, personal profile (age, gender, etc.) that can affect the results obtained [35, 36].

It is obvious from the above discussion that a number of different subjective techniques are available. Hence, for a new researcher it becomes rather confusing which method to select out of the numerous alternatives. In Table 8 we try to provide a guideline to the best subjective technique that should be considered depending upon certain requirements like video duration, presence/absence of reference videos, and need for video repetition.

4. Objective Methodologies

In this section, we provide an overview of the objective models that are used for video streaming and listed in Figure 12. For each model, the overall methodology is discussed along with the mathematical relationships and algorithms wherever necessary.

4.1. ITU-T Recommendation G.1070. This recommendation proposes an algorithm that estimates the videophone quality and is specifically useful for the QoS/QoE planners [37]. This multimedia model takes input from the network and application layers of the TCP/IP protocol stack.

4.1.1. Overall Model Framework. The overall framework of the model has been shown in Figure 17. Certain video and speech quality parameters are given as inputs to the model and there are three main outputs: $V_q(S_q)$, $S_q(V_q)$, and MM_q. $V_q(S_q)$ refers to the video quality influenced by the speech quality, $S_q(V_q)$ refers to the speech quality influenced by the

TABLE 8: Guidelines to choose a proper subjective approach.

Parameter	Technique								
	ACR	ACR-HR	DCR	PC	SSCQE	DSIS	DSCQS	SDSCE	SCACJ
Stimulus type	Single	Single	Double	Comparison	Single	Double	Double	Double	Comparison
Video duration	10 s	10 s	10 s	-	5 m	10 s	10 s	5 m	-
Explicit video reference	No	No	Yes	No	No	Yes	No	Yes	No
Hidden video reference	No	Yes	No	No	No	No	Yes	No	No
Video repetition	Yes	Yes	Yes	Yes	No	Yes	Yes	No	Yes
Quality evaluation scale	Table 4	Table 4	Table 5	-	Table 6	Table 5	Table 6	Table 6	Table 7

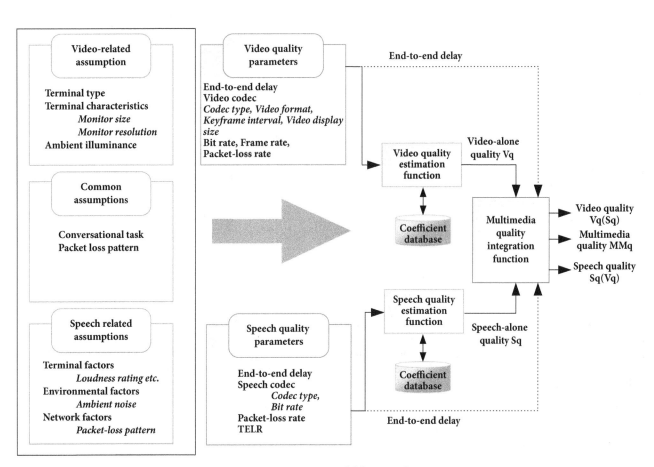

FIGURE 17: G.1070 model framework.

video quality, and MM_q refers to the overall multimedia quality outputted by the model. In this survey for every recommendation, which produces a multimedia quality as output, we concentrate only on the video quality evaluation part. Therefore, our discussion will focus only on the video quality V_q. Packet loss rate and jitter are the factors considered from the network layer, while bitrate, frame rate, codec type, and video format are the application layer factors.

4.1.2. General Model Equations. The overall video quality predicted by the model is given by

$$V_q = 1 + I_{\text{Coding}} \exp\left(-\frac{P_{pl_V}}{D_{Ppl_V}}\right), \quad (4)$$

where I_{Coding} represents the basic video quality affected by the coding distortion, D_{Ppl_V} expresses the degree of video quality robustness due to packet loss, and P_{pl_V} denotes the packet loss percentage. I_{Coding} is further expressed as

$$I_{\text{Coding}} = I_{O_{fr}} \exp\left\{-\frac{\left(\ln\left(F_{rV}\right) - \ln\left(O_{fr}\right)\right)^2}{2 D_{FrV}{}^2}\right\}, \quad (5)$$

where O_{fr} is an optimal frame rate that maximizes the video quality at each video bitrate B_{rV} and is expressed as

$$O_{fr} = \nu_1 + \nu_2 B_{rV},$$

$$1 \leq O_{fr} \leq 30, \ \nu_1 \text{ and } \nu_2 \text{ constants}, \quad (6)$$

where $F_{rV} = O_{fr}$, $I_{Coding} = I_{Ofr}$, I_{Ofr} represents maximum video quality at each video bitrate B_{rV} and is expressed as

$$I_{Ofr} = v_3 - \frac{v_3}{1 + (B_{rV}/v_4)^{v_5}}, \tag{7}$$

$$0 \leq I_{Ofr} \leq 4, \ v_3, v_4 \text{ and } v_5 \text{constants}.$$

D_{FrV} represents the degree of video quality robustness due to frame rate F_{rV} and is expressed as

$$D_{FrV} = v_6 + v_7 B_{rV}, \quad 0 < D_{FrV}, \ v_6 \text{ and } v_7 \text{ constants}. \tag{8}$$

The packet loss robustness factor D_{Ppl_V} introduced in (4) is expressed as

$$D_{Ppl_V} = v_{10} + v_{11} \exp\left(-\frac{F_{rV}}{v_8}\right) + v_{12} \exp\left(-\frac{B_{rV}}{v_9}\right), \tag{9}$$

$$0 < D_{Ppl_V}.$$

All the coefficients v_1 to v_{12} are dependent on the codec type, the video format, and the video display size and need to be found out by carrying suitable subjective tests.

Equation (4) highlights the fact that ITU-T G.1070 takes into account factors from the network as well as the application layer when evaluating the video quality. Therefore, this method is suitable when any new codec is to be tested for judging their performance. All the equations from (4) to (9) are generic in nature and show how this technique can be ported to a specific context (like evaluating the performance of a new codec along with the network QoS factors) by evaluating the coefficients v_1 to v_{12}. ITU has validated this model only for a limited number of codecs (MPEG-2 and MPEG-4) across VGA, QVGA, and QQVGA resolutions [38, 39]. However, following the procedure that has been outlined through (4)–(9), this model has been extended to other recent codecs like H.265/HEVC and VP9 also [40, 41].

4.2. ITU-T Recommendation G.1071. This recommendation provides an opinion model for network planning of video and audio streaming applications [42]. Two application areas are addressed by this objective technique: a high-resolution area including IPTV and a low-resolution area including services like mobile TV. For reasons that we discussed previously, this survey presents only the mobile streaming application that is an IP based service. This algorithmic model tries to estimate the impact of typical IP layer impairments on the end-user QoE over transport formats such as Real Time Transport Protocol (RTP) over User Datagram Protocol (UDP), Motion Picture Experts Group-2 Transport Stream (MPEG2-TS) over UDP or RTP/UDP, and 3rd Generation Partnership Project Packet-Switched Steaming Service (3GPP-PSS) over RTP. Dynamic adaptive streaming over HTTP or DASH streaming that is currently being used by commercial services like YouTube and Netflix is not taken into account by this model.

4.2.1. Overall Model Framework. The overall model framework has been shown in Figure 18. The general way by which this model works is similar to [43] with an exception in

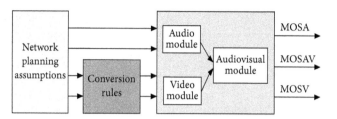

FIGURE 18: Overall G.1071 model framework.

the input that it takes. While as input this model takes into account different network planning parameters like the video bitrate, video codec type, video resolution, and the packet loss rate, the one described in [43] uses the IP packet header information to extract relevant parameters for predicting the video quality. Since the primary video quality estimation block is the same for both models, a conversion rule is applied for those planning parameters that are not taken into account by [43] in order to make it compatible. As output, this model provides three parameters:

(i) *audiovisual Quality (MOS_{AV})* on a scale of 1–5,

(ii) *video only MOS (MOS_V)* on a scale of 1–5 (without audio stream),

(iii) *audio only MOS (MOS_A)* on scale of 1–5 (without video stream).

Here we discuss only MOS_V. When compared against similar subjective tests, this model attains a Root Mean Square Error (RMSE) value of 0.60 and a Pearson Correlation Coefficient (PCC) value of 0.78 across 1430 different sample video types.

4.2.2. General Model Algorithm. The overall video quality MOS_V can be classified into three different types, MOS_{VC}, MOS_{VP}, and MOS_{VR}, where

MOS_{VC} is video MOS in case of no packet loss and no rebuffering *(video quality due to compression)*,

MOS_{VP} is video MOS in case of packet loss but no rebuffering *(video quality due to packet loss)*,

MOS_{VR} is video MOS in case of no packet loss but only rebuffering *(video quality due to rebuffering)*.

An elaborate methodology to calculate the three different types of MOS_V has been provided in [42]. However, in order to highlight the factors that this model takes into consideration and motivate the readers to port this for codecs that have not been tested by ITU yet, we present a snapshot of the calculation process by introducing three different algorithms. The same procedure can be applied to any other codec for evaluating the video quality. This ITU model is primarily used for planning purposes only. Since it does not take into account any reference video, it is an example of a NR scheme.

MOS_{VC} is calculated as per Algorithm 1. For this algorithm, V_{CCF} represents the video content complexity factor, i.e., the spatiotemporal complexity of the video sequence and

(1) set $MOS_{MAX} = 5$
(2) set $MOS_{MIN} = 1$
(3) set $V_{DC} = 0$
(4) **if** $(videoFrameRate \geq 24)$

(5)   compute $V_{DC} = \dfrac{MOS_{MAX} - MOS_{MIN}}{1 + (V_{NBR}/v_3 \times V_{CCF} + v_4)^{(v_5 \times V_{CCF} + v_6)}}$

(6)   compute $MOS_{VC} = MOS_{MAX} - V_{DC}$

(7) **else**

(8)   compute $V_{DC} = \dfrac{MOS_{MAX} - MOS_{MIN}}{1 + (V_{NBR}/v_3 \times V_{CCF} + v_4)^{(v_5 \times V_{CCF} + v_6)}}$

(9)   compute $MOS_{VC} = (MOS_{MAX} - V_{DC}) \times \left(1 + v_1 \times V_{CCF} - v_2 \times V_{CCF} \times \log\left(\dfrac{1000}{videoFrameRate}\right)\right)$

(10) **end if**

ALGORITHM 1: Calculation of MOS_{VC}.

(1) set $MOS_{MIN} = 1$
(2) set $V_{DP} = 0$
(3) denote $scene = (slicing\ OR\ freezing)$
(4) **if** $(scene = slicing)$

(5)   compute $V_{DP} = (MOS_{VC} - MOS_{MIN}) \times \dfrac{\left(V_{AIRF \times V_{IR}}/\left(v_7 \times V_{CCF} + v_8\right)\right)^{v_9} \times \left(V_{PLEF}/\left(v_{10} \times V_{CCF} + v_{11}\right)\right)^{v_{12}}}{1 + \left(V_{AIRF \times V_{IR}}/\left(v_7 \times V_{CCF} + v_8\right)\right)^{v_9} \times \left(V_{PLEF}/\left(v_{10} \times V_{CCF} + v_{11}\right)\right)^{v_{12}}}$

(6) **else**

(7)   compute $V_{DP} = (MOS_{VC} - MOS_{MIN}) \times \dfrac{\left(V_{IR}/\left(v_7 \times V_{CCF} + v_8\right)\right)^{v_9} \times \left(V_{PLEF}/\left(v_{10} \times V_{CCF} + v_{11}\right)\right)^{v_{12}}}{1 + \left(V_{IR}/\left(v_7 \times V_{CCF} + v_8\right)\right)^{v_9} \times \left(V_{PLEF}/\left(v_{10} \times V_{CCF} + v_{11}\right)\right)^{v_{12}}}$

(8) **end if**
(9) compute $MOS_{VP} = MOS_{VC} - V_{DP}$

ALGORITHM 2: Calculation of MOS_{VP}.

it can vary from an initial default value of 0.5 to a maximum value of 1. It has to be calculated for every sequence used. V_{NBR} represents the normalized video bitrate in kbps and depends upon the video frame rate. The coefficients v_1 to v_6 are provided by ITU for H.264 and MPEG4 encoded video sequences at QCIF, QVGA, and HVGA resolutions only.

The procedure for calculating MOS_{VP} is given in Algorithm 2. V_{DP} represents the video quality distortion due to packet loss, which can lead to either a slicing or video freezing scenario. Depending upon the scenario V_{DP} is calculated appropriately. V_{AIRF} represents the average impairment rate of the video frames whereas V_{IR} represents the impairment rate of the entire video stream itself. Both of these values lie between 0 and 1, with 0 depicting the best and 1 the worst case. V_{PLEF} represents the video packet loss event frequency, which is incremented by 1 each time a slicing or freezing event occurs. v_7 to v_{12} are the coefficients provided by ITU for the same set of conditions as discussed before.

Algorithm 3 summarizes the procedure for calculation of MOS_{VR}. NRE represents the number of rebuffering events, ARL represents the average rebuffering length, and MREEF represents the multiple rebuffering events effect factor. The coefficients v_{13} to v_{18} are obtained in the same fashion as discussed before for the other coefficients.

4.3. ITU-T Recommendation P.1201/P.1201.1. This recommendation provides a parametric nonintrusive assessment of audiovisual media streaming quality [43]. This is a nonintrusive model based upon the packet header information, which provides certain algorithms for evaluating the audiovisual quality of IP based video services. The packet header information is fed to the algorithm in a Packet Capture Format (PCAP).

This model has 2 subparts: ITU-T P.1201.1 and ITU-T P.1201.2 [44, 45]. While the first one is intended for low-resolution application areas like mobile TV, the second one targets a high-resolution IPTV service. As output, the algorithm estimates the audio, video, and combined audiovisual quality in terms of the 5-point MOS scale.

Primarily, these models are used for in-service monitoring of perceived transmission quality or for maintenance purpose. As such they can be deployed either at the endpoints of the transmission system, i.e., the service provider or customers premises, or in the middle of the network as monitoring points. This model works only for a UDP based streaming service. An alternative version has been proposed in [46] that uses TCP for a nonadaptive and progressive download type media streaming. Table 9 summarizes the

(1) set $MOS_{MIN} = 1$
(2) set $V_{DR} = 0$
(3) set $Video_{Quality} = 0$
(4) denote $scene = (rebuff\ AND\ packet\ loss)\ OR\ rebuff$
(5) **if** $(scene = rebuff\ AND\ packet\ loss)$
(6)   set $Video_{Quality} = MOS_{VP}$
(7) **else**
(8)   set $Video_{Quality} = MOS_{VC}$
(9) **end if**
(10) compute $V_{DR} = (Video_{Quality} - MOS_{MIN}) \times \dfrac{(NRE/v_{13})^{v_{14}} \times (ARL/v_{15})^{v_{16}} \times (MREEF/v_{17})^{v_{18}}}{1 + (NRE/v_{13})^{v_{14}} \times (ARL/v_{15})^{v_{16}} \times (MREEF/v_{17})^{v_{18}}}$
(11) compute $MOS_{VR} = Video_{Quality} - V_{DR}$

ALGORITHM 3: Calculation of MOS_{VR}.

TABLE 9: Application areas, test factors, and technology used by the ITU-T P.1201.1 model.

Type	Description
Application intended	In-service monitoring of audio, video and audio-visual streaming quality
Transport protocol	UDP
Model input (primary)	Packet header information (PCAP files)
Model input (out-of-band)	Codec related factors like bit-rate, frame rate, GOP structure, resolution, etc.
Input video bit-rate range	40–6000 kbps
Input packet loss type	Random and bursty
Input packet loss range	0–10% (random loss) 0–10% (4-state Markov model-bursty loss)
Input frame rate	5–30 fps
Input video resolution	HVGA, QVGA and QCIF
Video codecs	MPEG4 Part 2, H.264 (MPEG4 Part 10)

main input types and scope of this model. For any other specific factor or technology used that has not been mentioned in Table 9, the model needs to be retrained and revalidated. An overview of the model inputs and outputs has been shown in Figure 19.

The packet header information is obtained dynamically from the transport layer in a PCAP file format (interface I.2). Since this model is used for monitoring the video quality in real time, the transport layer input information (in the form of transport header) is dynamic by nature. Relevant information from this PCAP file is filtered out by interface I.3 and fed to the core MOS estimation module. Additional information about the media stream and the decoder behavior is taken out of band in a static manner with certain predefined values. This is the function of the interface I.1. Interface I.4 provides information about the rebuffering information that is extracted and measured at the end-points and provided as an input to the core MOS estimation module.

Three model outputs are provided: MOS_A, MOS_V, and MOS_{AV} referring to the audio only, video only, and combined audiovisual quality all in a MOS scale of 1–5. The overall block diagram of the ITU-T P.1201.1 model has been shown in Figure 20.

The parameter extraction modules for audio, video, and audiovisual scenarios are labeled as PEA, PEV, and PER,

respectively. The procedure for calculating the overall video quality MOS_V is the same that has been presented previously in Algorithms 1, 2, and 3. For video, only MOS_V of the model attains a RMSE value of 0.535 (based on 1430 samples) and PCC value of 0.830.

4.4. ITU-T Recommendation P.1202/P.1202.1. This recommendation is similar to the ITU-T P.1201 discussed above. However, in order to evaluate the perceived quality, this algorithm takes into account the bitstream information also, as well as the packet header information that has been used in the previous case [47]. Similar to the previous algorithm, in this case also the model can be subdivided into two parts: ITU-T P.1202.1, which is targeted towards low-resolution areas like mobile video streaming, and ITU-T P.1202.2, which is targeted towards high-resolution IPTV application [48, 49]. Since this model parses information from both the IP header and the payload, it is more accurate when compared to the previous algorithm but requires more computational effort. Also for this model to work, the payload data must be in an unencrypted form. There is another striking difference between this model and ITU-T P.1201 with reference to the number of outputs. P.1202 provides only 1 video MOS as the output, whereas P.1201 provides 3 outputs (audio only, video only, and audiovisual MOS). A summary of the application

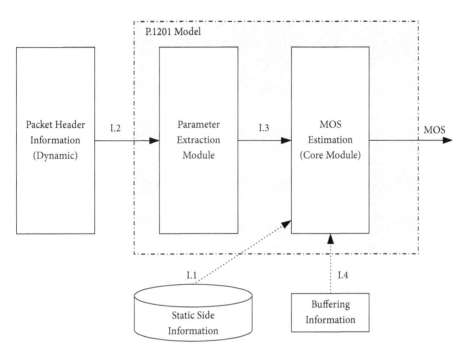

FIGURE 19: Overview of model inputs and output.

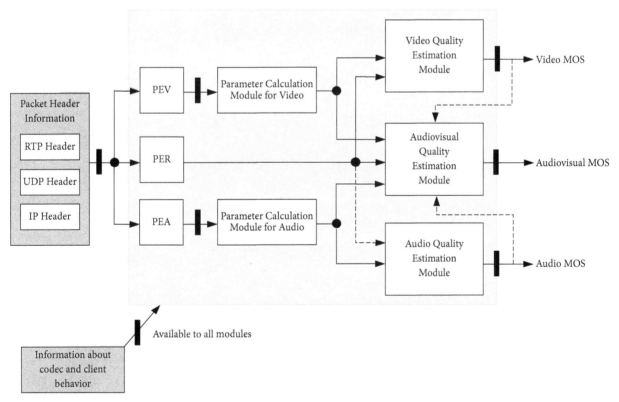

FIGURE 20: Overall block diagram of ITU-T P.1201.1 model.

areas, test factors, and technology used by this model has been presented in Table 10. An overview of the model interfaces is shown in Figure 21. Interface I.1 provides the static information about the media stream and the decoder. These have certain predefined values and obtained from packet information or player application program interface (API). Interface I.2 provides the detailed packet layer header and payload data information in the form of a PCAP file. Relevant parameters are extracted from the PCAP file by the interface I.3. The model outputs a video only MOS.

TABLE 10: Application areas, test factors, and technology used by the ITU-T P.1202.1 model.

Type	Description
Application intended	In service monitoring of video streaming quality and quality assessment of live networks including transmission and encoding related errors
Transport protocol	UDP
Model input	Packet header and payload information (unencrypted)
Input video bit-rate range	50–6000 kbps
Input packet loss type	Random and bursty
Input packet loss range	0–6% (random loss) 0–6% (4-state Markov model-bursty loss)
Input frame rate	12.5–30 fps
Input video resolution	HVGA, QVGA and QCIF
Video codecs	H.264/AVC (baseline profile)

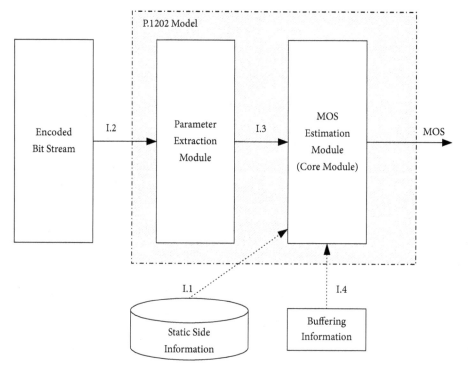

FIGURE 21: Overview of ITU-P.1202 model interfaces.

The model description in a block diagram format has been shown in Figure 22. H.264 encoded video bitstream, along with other side information (error concealment type, rebuffering, etc.), is taken as input; relevant parameters are extracted out and then aggregated, which are then used to predict the video QoE.

Compression, slicing, freezing, and rebuffering are the four different types of artifacts considered by this model and included in the final video MOS. Each of them is calculated separately and they are finally aligned together to the same level (MOS) by using suitable mapping functions. This model attains a RMSE value of 0.357 (across 982 sequences) and a PCC value of 0.918.

4.5. ITU-T Recommendation J.247. This recommendation provides guidelines on the selection of an appropriate video

quality measurement method when a full reference is available [50]. Presently this model has 4 different flavors: Video Quality Expert Group (VQEG) Proponent A (NTT, Japan), VQEG Proponent B (OPTICOM, Germany), VQEG Proponent C (Psytechnics, UK), and VQEG Proponent D (Yonsei University, South Korea). All these 4 models have been tested across video sequences having resolution of VGA, CIF, and QCIF only. All of them take the same inputs and provide the same output in terms of the video MOS (outperforming the commonly used Peak Signal to Noise Ratio (PSNR) model) [51]. Depending upon the operational requirement, these models can predict the quality of videos that have been impaired by codec related factors only, network transmission related factors, or a combination of both. Table 11 lists down the factors for which this model has been evaluated.

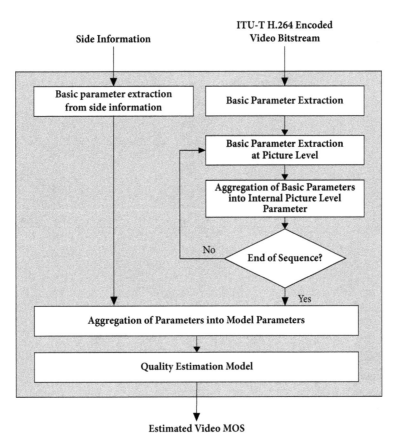

FIGURE 22: Block diagram of ITU-P.1202.1 model.

TABLE 11: Application areas, test factors, and technology used by the ITU-T J.247 model.

Type	Description
Application intended	Real time in-service quality monitoring at source and at remote destination (when copy of the source is available) and lab testing
Model input	Reference video and impaired video (transmission errors with packet loss and temporal errors of pausing with skipping)
Input video bit-rate range	16 kbps–4 mbps
Input packet loss type	Random
Input frame rate	5–30 fps
Input video resolution	QCIF, CIF and VGA
Video codecs	H.264/AVC, VC-1, Windows Media 9, Real Video (RV 10), MPEG-4 (Part 2), DivX, Cinepak, H.261, H.263, H.263+, Sorenson and Theora

The performance overview for the 4 different models across the 3 different resolutions has been shown in Table 12. The PCC values are obtained by comparing the objective scores across the three different resolutions against the subjective data from 984 end-users. Figure 23 shows the comparison of the model performances (in terms of PCC values only). The outlier ratio is obtained by using the standard error of the mean as per the formulae given in

$$\text{outlier ratio (OR)} = \frac{\text{(total no of outliers)}}{N}, \quad (10)$$

where an outlier is a point for which

$$\left| \left(\text{MOS}_{\text{Subjective}} - \text{MOS}_{\text{Objective}} \right) \right|$$

$$> C_1 \times \frac{\sigma \left(\text{DMOS}(i) \right)}{\sqrt{N_{\text{Subjects}}}}. \quad (11)$$

In (11), C_1 is a constant that depends on the nature of the score distribution (Gaussian, exponential, etc.), $\sigma(\text{DMOS}(i))$ represents the standard deviation of the individual scores associated with the ith video clip, and N_{Subjects} is the number of viewers per video clip i.

TABLE 12: Model performance overview.

Model	Resolution	PCC	RMSE	Outlier Ratio
NTT		0.786	0.621	0.523
OPTICOM		0.825	0.571	0.502
Psytechnics	VGA	0.822	0.566	0.524
Yonsei		0.805	0.593	0.542
PSNR		0.713	0.714	0.615
NTT		0.777	0.604	0.538
OPTICOM		0.808	0.562	0.513
Psytechnics	CIF	0.836	0.526	0.507
Yonsei		0.785	0.594	0.522
PSNR		0.656	0.720	0.632
NTT		0.819	0.551	0.497
OPTICOM		0.841	0.516	0.461
Psytechnics	QCIF	0.830	0.517	0.458
Yonsei		0.756	0.617	0.523
PSNR		0.662	0.721	0.596

TABLE 13: Model input across different variants.

Model Type	Model Name	Required Inputs
Hybrid NR (encrypted)	RST-V model	Processed video sequence (PVS) and encrypted bitstream
	YHyNRe model	PVS and encrypted bitstream
Hybrid NR	YHyNR model	PVS and non-encrypted bitstream
Hybrid RR (encrypted)	YHyRRe model	PVS, extracted features from source reference channel (SRC) and encrypted bitstream
Hybrid RR	YHyRR model	PVS, features extracted from SRC and non-encrypted bitstream
Hybrid FR (encrypted)	PEVQ-S (e)	PVS, SRC and encrypted bitstream
	YHyFRe model	PVS, SRC and encrypted bitstream
Hybrid FR	PEVQ-S	PVS, SRC and non-encrypted bitstream
	YHyFR model	PVS, SRC and non-encrypted bitstream

4.6. ITU-T Recommendation J.343. This recommendation specifies objective methods that use bitstream data in addition to the processed video sequences [52]. As this is a bitstream model, it has additional information about the payload data like codec type, bitrate, frame rate, spatial, and temporal shifts apart from the transmission errors like delay and packet loss. Six different application areas are addressed by it through [53–58]. This model can work in FR, RR, and NR modes for both encrypted and unencrypted video payload data. Table 13 shows a summary of the inputs that this model can take across its different variants.

Figures 24–26 show the hybrid NR, RR, and FR models (for both encrypted and nonencrypted video data). While the NR models have access to the bitstream and the PVS data, the RR models have access to the bitstream data and the source video sequences having some reduced set of features, and the FR models have full access to the bitstream data along with the entire source video sequences. For all the versions, the encrypted model does not have access to the video payload data and operates without parsing the packet payload.

Table 14 enlists the various parameters for which the models have been tested. The model performance summary has been shown in Table 15. PCC and RMSE values have been used for calculating the model performance statistics. For

each of the models, relevant subjective tests are carried out, the results of which are fitted using a third order monotonic polynomial function. In case of the NR models, MOS values are used (obtained from the ACR subjective technique), while for the RR and FR models DMOS values are used (obtained from the ACR-HR subjective technique) for evaluating the model accuracy.

From the above discussion it is clear that a variety of objective techniques that can be used in a number of different scenarios are available. For evaluating the video quality, while some models take in account the presence of reference video signals (FR and RR methods), others do not have this requirement. Similarly, each of the models has been tested for specific codecs only corresponding to specific resolutions. In order to generalize them for different codecs and other factors like resolution and content complexity, we have provided a snapshot of the relevant methodologies. The video sequences that are used for testing the models also vary in terms of the video duration, content complexity, etc. Some of the ITU models are best suited for network monitoring (ITU-T P.1201 series), whereas some are used for network or QoS/QoE planning (ITU-T G.1070, ITU-T G.1071), while the others are used for laboratory testing purpose (ITU-T J.247). Due to this wide variety of objective ITU techniques, it becomes

TABLE 14: Application areas, test factors, and technology used by the ITU-T J.343 model series.

Type	Description
Application intended	Monitoring the quality of deployed networks and lab testing purpose
Input video bit-rate range	1–30 mbps (HD) and 100 kbps–3 mbps (VGA/WVGA)
Input frame rate	25 and 29.97 fps (FHD)/25 and 30 fps (VGA/WVGA)
Input video resolution	FHD, VGA and WVGA
Video codecs	MPEG-4 Part 10
Length of test sequences	10 s and 15 s (in case of buffering)

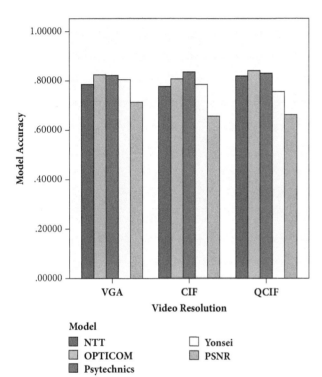

FIGURE 23: Comparison of model performances.

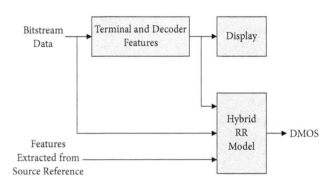

FIGURE 25: Block diagram of hybrid RR models.

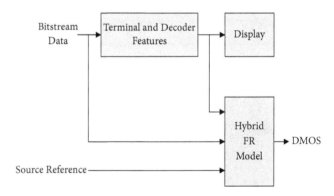

FIGURE 26: Block diagram of hybrid FR models.

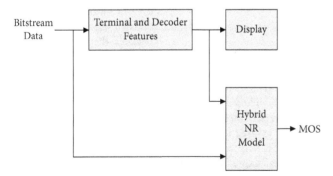

FIGURE 24: Block diagram of hybrid NR models.

can be made depending upon the research context. Table 16 highlights the network and application parameters that each of the models takes into account along with their intended purpose. Therefore, based upon the parameters of interest for quality prediction and the application scenario, it will be easy to choose a particular reference model.

5. Current Limitations and Challenges

A lot of work is going on within ITU to assess the quality of video streaming services. However, a number of shortcomings exist especially for the quality evaluation of videos that are streamed to mobile devices. We enlist here the challenges that are being faced and should be addressed.

The primary dilemma is in the existence of numerous models, the basic aim of which is to measure the video QoE and the varied type of inputs that they take in predicting the quality. Each model takes a different input based upon either

confusing for a researcher to select an appropriate method depending upon the requirements. Therefore, in order to make the model selection process easier, we list down certain factors in Table 16 that can serve as the baseline for selecting the most appropriate model under a specific circumstance. Once a particular model is selected, the necessary changes

TABLE 15: Model performance summary.

Model	Resolution	PCC	RMSE
Hybrid NR YHyNR model	VGA	0.78	0.59
	WVGA	0.81	0.56
	FHD	0.85	0.52
Hybrid NR (encrypted) RST-V model	VGA	0.76	0.61
	WVGA	0.79	0.59
	FHD	0.77	0.64
Hybrid NR (encrypted) YHyNRe model	VGA	0.72	0.66
	WVGA	0.77	0.62
	FHD	0.78	0.61
Hybrid RR YHyRR model	VGA	0.80	0.57
	WVGA	0.84	0.52
	FHD	0.86	0.52
Hybrid RR (encrypted) YHyRRe model	VGA	0.79	0.58
	WVGA	0.84	0.53
	FHD	0.84	0.55
Hybrid FR PEVQ-S	VGA	0.81	0.57
	WVGA	0.83	0.55
	FHD	0.88	0.48
Hybrid FR YHyFR model	VGA	0.80	0.66
	WVGA	0.84	0.61
	FHD	0.86	0.52
Hybrid FR (encrypted) PEVQ-S (e)	VGA	0.81	0.57
	WVGA	0.83	0.55
	FHD	0.88	0.48
Hybrid FR YHyFRe model	VGA	0.72	0.58
	WVGA	0.79	0.52
	FHD	0.84	0.55

network parameters (packet loss, delay, jitter, etc.) or video characteristics (bitrate, frame rate, resolution, content type, etc.) or a combination of both. There can be variations among the network parameters itself. For example, the packet loss pattern may be random or bursty by nature. Similar situations can arise in case of delay also.

The assessment methodologies are also different in terms of the subjective, objective, and hybrid methods. To make the situation even more complex, the different QoS factors (network or application level) as outlined in this survey are not sufficient in predicting the QoE accurately. QoE is strongly influenced by external factors like the type of device used in viewing, the surrounding environmental conditions, and other factors. For majority of the models, the video sequences that are selected from the VQEG database are very short in duration (roughly 10 s only) and hence their ability to portray a real life-streaming scenario is questionable. In addition, the effect of using videos lesser or greater than 10 seconds on the subjective quality assessment has not been accounted for [59, 60].

When streaming is done on mobile devices, the characteristics of the device itself should be taken into account because the viewing experience is quite different on small form factor mobile screens and conventional televisions [61, 62]. There are several limitations to the mobile devices in terms of the variety of screen sizes, display resolution, limited battery backup, limited storage, and other connectivity problems [63]. Currently, none of the existing ITU models considers the peculiarities that are unique to a mobile streaming environment. Despite the fact that more than 55% of the overall Internet traffic is generated by some form of multimedia streaming over a mobile device, lack of a model that particularly addresses this scenario leaves a great void and a lot of scope for further research into this aspect [3].

In a mobile video streaming environment, the inherent unreliable nature of the wireless networks should also be kept in mind. A detailed analysis of the video QoE over a WiFi network and other mobile networks like 2G, 3G, and 4G should be carried out with sufficient detail. Often the low speeds that are associated with mobile networks result in a poor video QoE, which has prompted companies like Google to release a new version of the most popular YouTube application named as YouTube Go that is supposed to work in low speed networks [64]. Thus, ITU should have in place

TABLE 16: Objective model selection criterion.

Model	Network Factors	Application Factors	Video Sequence Duration	Video Codec	Video Resolution	Packet Loss Type	Model Type	Service Category	Intended Purpose
ITU-T G.1070	PL, J	BR, FR, CT, VR	10 seconds	MPEG-2, MPEG-4	VGA, QVGA and QQVGA	Random	NR	Video Telephony	QoS/QoE Planning
ITU-T G.1071	PL, J	BR, FR, CT, VR	8–24 seconds	MPEG-4, ITU-T H.264	QCIF, QVGA, HVGA	Uniform, Bursty	NR	Video Streaming	Network Planning
ITU-T P.1201 Series	PL, J, T	×	8–24 seconds	MPEG-4, ITU-T H.264	QCIF, QVGA, HVGA	Random, Bursty	NR	Video Streaming	Network Monitoring
ITU-T P.1202 Series	PL, J, T	BR, FR, CT, VR	10–16 seconds	ITU-T H.264	QCIF, QVGA, HVGA	Random, Bursty	NR	Video Streaming	Network Monitoring
ITU-T J.247 Series	PL	BR, FR, CT	×	H.264/AVC, RV 10, WM 9, MPEG-4 (Part 2)	QCIF, CIF, VGA	×	FR	Video Telephony, Video Streaming	Laboratory Testing, Network Monitoring
ITU-T J.343 Series	PL, J, T	BR, FR, CT, VR	×	H.264/AVC	VGA, WVGA, HD	Random, Bursty	NR, RR, FR	Video Streaming	Network Monitoring

PL: packet loss, J: jitter; T: throughput, BR: bitrate; FR: frame rate, CT: video content type; VR: video resolution.

models that simulate these wireless environments in detail and are targeted towards mobile devices considering the recent trend of watching videos online.

Most of the ITU models use videos having low resolutions of VGA, HVGA, CIF, and QCIF only. Practically, only the J.343 series take into account HD resolution. This is in sharp contrast to the current trend where 4K is gaining in popularity. In fact streaming services like YouTube and Netflix have contents that can be streamed in 4K. However, ITU does not provide any model that is dedicated towards such high-resolution videos. Recent advances in virtual reality (VR) and augmented reality (AR) platforms coupled with the availability of mobile devices that can support these have carved out a new way in which videos are being watched by the users. These recent trends and changing viewing habits should be incorporated into future ITU models.

6. Conclusion

Video streaming has become extremely popular these days, which allows the users to watch videos anytime and anywhere. However, for the success of such a service, the quality provided to the end-users must be excellent. There are a number of challenges being faced particularly in a mobile streaming environment. The QoE should be calculated keeping in mind not only the network QoS factors like packet loss, jitter, delay, and throughput and application QoS factors like bitrate, frame rate, and content complexity, but also the nature and characteristics of the mobile devices being used together with the surrounding environment.

In this article, we have presented an in-depth review of the standardized approaches being followed by ITU towards the video quality evaluation. Proper definitions of QoS and QoE have been provided along with the interrelationship between the two. Taxonomy of all the ITU models has been provided based on a general approach and the measurement methodology used. The basic overview and working of all the objective models are provided with suitable diagrams and algorithms/mathematical formulae. Finally, the current drawbacks are discussed along with the scope of future work.

Acknowledgments

The authors would like to thank Dr. Borworn Papasratorn from the School of Information Technology, KMUTT, for sharing his long expertise in telecommunications research and providing the guidelines for writing an effective review paper.

References

[1] "2013 Video Index-TV is no longer a single screen in your Living Room," Ooyala Corp, USA, 2013.

[2] G. O. Young, "Synthetic structure of industrial," in *Plastics*, J. Peters, Ed., vol. 3, pp. 15–64, McGraw-Hill, New York, NY, USA, 2nd edition, 1964.

[3] *Cisco Global Mobile Data Traffic Forecast Update Report 2014-2019*, Cisco Corp, USA, 2016.

[4] Z. Cheng, L. Ding, W. Huang, F. Yang, and L. Qian, "A unified QoE prediction framework for HEVC encoded video streaming over wireless networks," in *Proceedings of the 12th IEEE International Symposium on Broadband Multimedia Systems and Broadcasting, BMSB 2017*, Cagliari, Italy, June 2017.

[5] S. Mori and M. Bandai, "QoE-aware quality selection method for adaptive video streaming with scalable video coding," in *Proceedings of the 2018 IEEE International Conference on Consumer Electronics (ICCE)*, pp. 1–4, Las Vegas, NV, USA, January 2018.

[6] L. Yu, T. Tillo, and J. Xiao, "QoE-Driven dynamic adaptive video streaming strategy with future information," *IEEE Transactions on Broadcasting*, vol. 63, no. 3, pp. 523–534, 2017.

[7] M. García-Pineda, J. Segura-García, and S. Felici-Castell, "A holistic modeling for QoE estimation in live video streaming applications over LTE Advanced technologies with Full and Non Reference approaches," *Computer Communications*, vol. 117, pp. 13–23, 2018.

[8] J. Nightingale, Q. Wang, C. Grecos, and S. Goma, "The impact of network impairment on quality of experience (QoE) in H.265/HEVC video streaming," *IEEE Transactions on Consumer Electronics*, vol. 60, no. 2, pp. 242–250, 2014.

[9] H. J. Kim and S. G. Choi, "A study on a QoS/QoE correlation model for QoE evaluation on IPTV service," in *Proceedings of the 12th International Conference on Advanced Communication Technology: ICT for Green Growth and Sustainable Development, ICACT 2010*, pp. 1377–1382, Phoenix Park, Korea, February 2010.

[10] "Communication Quality of Service: A Framework and Definition," ITU-T Recommendation G.1000, November 2001.

[11] "End-user Multimedia QoS Categories," ITU-T Recommendation G.1010, November 2001.

[12] "Reference Guide to Quality of Experience Assessment Methodologies," ITU-T Recommendation G.1011, July 2016.

[13] M. Fiedler, T. Hossfeld, and P. Tran-Gia, "A generic quantitative relationship between quality of experience and quality of service," *IEEE Network*, vol. 24, no. 2, pp. 36–41, 2010.

[14] D. Pal and V. Vanijja, "A no-reference modular video quality prediction model for H.265/HEVC and VP9 codecs on a mobile device," *Advances in Multimedia*, vol. 2017, Article ID 8317590, pp. 1–19, 2017.

[15] "Definitions of terms related to Quality of Service," ITU-T Recommendation E.800, September 2008.

[16] C. Xu, P. Zhang, S. Jia, M. Wang, and G.-M. Muntean, "Video streaming in content-centric mobile networks: challenges and solutions," *IEEE Wireless Communications Magazine*, vol. 24, no. 5, pp. 157–165, 2017.

[17] C. Ge, N. Wang, G. Foster, and M. Wilson, "Toward QoE-Assured 4K Video-on-Demand Delivery Through Mobile Edge Virtualization with Adaptive Prefetching," *IEEE Transactions on Multimedia*, vol. 19, no. 10, pp. 2222–2237, 2017.

[18] "Amendment 5: New Definitions for inclusion in Recommendation ITU-T P.10/G.100," ITU-T Recommendation P.10/G.100 Amendment 5, July 2016.

[19] *Definitions on Quality of Experience*, Qualinet White Paper from the 5th Qualinet Meeting, March 2013.

[20] W. Robitza, A. Ahmad, P. A. Kara et al., "Challenges of future multimedia QoE monitoring for internet service providers," *Multimedia Tools and Applications*, vol. 76, no. 21, pp. 22243–22266, 2017.

[21] S. Winkler and P. Mohandas, "The evolution of video quality measurement: from PSNR to hybrid metrics," *IEEE Transactions on Broadcasting*, vol. 54, no. 3, pp. 660–668, 2008.

[22] O. B. Maia, H. C. Yehia, and L. de Errico, "A concise review of the quality of experience assessment for video streaming," *Computer Communications*, vol. 57, pp. 1–12, 2015.

[23] M. Ghareeb and C. Viho, "Hybrid QoE assessment is well-suited for Multiple Description Coding video streaming in overlay networks," in *Proceedings of the 8th Annual Conference on Communication Networks and Services Research, CNSR 2010*, pp. 327–333, Montreal, Canada, May 2010.

[24] H. Rifaï, S. Mohammed, and A. Mellouk, "A brief synthesis of QoS-QoE methodologies," in *Proceedings of the 10th International Symposium on Programming and Systems, ISPS' 2011*, pp. 32–38, Algiers, Algeria, April 2011.

[25] H. J. Kim and S. G. Choi, "QoE assessment model for multimedia streaming services using QoS parameters," *Multimedia Tools and Applications*, pp. 1–13, 2013.

[26] "Subjective Video Quality Assessment Methods for Multimedia Applications," ITU-T Recommendation P.910, April 2008.

[27] K. Gu, J. Zhou, J.-F. Qiao, G. Zhai, W. Lin, and A. C. Bovik, "No-reference quality assessment of screen content pictures," *IEEE Transactions on Image Processing*, vol. 26, no. 8, pp. 4005–4018, 2017.

[28] A. Khan, L. Sun, and E. Ifeachor, "Content clustering based video quality prediction model for MPEG4 video streaming over wireless networks," in *Proceedings of the 2009 IEEE International Conference on Communications, ICC 2009*, Germany, June 2009.

[29] H. Malekmohamadi, W. A. C. Fernando, and A. M. Kondoz, "Content-based subjective quality prediction in stereoscopic videos with machine learning," *IEEE Electronics Letters*, vol. 48, no. 21, pp. 1344–1346, 2012.

[30] T. Ghalut, H. Larijani, and A. Shahrabi, "Content-Based Video Quality Prediction Using Random Neural Networks for Video Streaming over LTE Networks," in *Procceedings of the IEEE International Conference on Computer and Information Technology; Ubiquitous Computing and Communications; Dependable*, pp. 1626–1631, Liverpool, England, 2015.

[31] "VQEG Standard Database," https://www.its.bldrdoc.gov/vqeg/downloads.aspx.

[32] "Methods for Objective and Subjective Assessment of Speech and Video Quality," ITU-T Recommendation P.800.1, July 2016.

[33] "Methodology for the Subjective Assessment of the Quality of Television Pictures," ITU-R Recommendation BT.500-13, January 2012.

[34] "Subjective Audiovisual Quality Assessment Methods for Multimedia Applications," ITU-T Recommendation P.911, December 1998.

[35] R. Stankiewicz and A. Jajszczyk, "A survey of QoE assurance in converged networks," *Computer Networks*, vol. 55, no. 7, pp. 1459–1473, 2011.

[36] K. Seshadrinathan, R. Soundararajan, A. C. Bovik, and L. K. Cormack, "Study of subjective and objective quality assessment of video," *IEEE Transactions on Image Processing*, vol. 19, no. 6, pp. 1427–1441, 2010.

[37] "Opinion Model for Video-telephony Applications," ITU-T Recommendation G.1070, July 2012.

[38] N. D. Narvekar, T. Liu, D. Zou, and J. A. Bloom, "Extending G.1070 for video quality monitoring," in *Proceedings of the 2011 12th IEEE International Conference on Multimedia and Expo, ICME 2011*, pp. 1–4, Barcelona, Spain, July 2011.

[39] B. Belmudez and S. Möller, "Extension of the G.1070 video quality function for the MPEG2 video codec," in *Proceedings of the 2010 2nd International Workshop on Quality of Multimedia Experience, QoMEX 2010*, pp. 7–10, IEEE, Trondheim, Norway, June 2010.

[40] D. Pal, T. Triyason, and V. Vanijja, "Extending the ITU-T G.1070 opinion model to support current generation H.265/HEVC video codec," in *Proceedings of the International Conference on Computational Science and Its Applications*, vol. 9787, pp. 106–116, Beijing, China, 2016.

[41] D. Pal and V. Vanijja, "G.1070 model extension at full HD resolution for VP9/HEVC codec," *Journal of Telecommunication, Electronic and Computer Engineering*, vol. 8, no. 9, pp. 139–147, 2016.

[42] "Opinion Model for Network Planning of Video and Audio Streaming Applications," ITU-T Recommendation G.1071, November 2016.

[43] "Parametric Non-Intrusive Assessment of Audiovisual Media Streaming Quality," ITU-T Recommendation P.1201, October 2012.

[44] "Parametric non-intrusive Assessment of Audiovisual Media Streaming Quality: Lower Resolution Application Area," ITU-T Recommendation P.1201.1, October 2012.

[45] "Parametric non-intrusive Assessment of Audiovisual Media Streaming Quality: Higher Resolution Application Area," ITU-T Recommendation P.1201.2, October 2012.

[46] "Use of ITU-T P.1201 for Non-adaptive, Progressive Download type Media Streaming," ITU-T Recommendation P.1201 Amendment 2:New Appendix III, December 2013.

[47] "Parametric non-intrusive Bitstream Assessment of Video Media Streaming Quality," ITU-T Recommendation P.1202, October 2012.

[48] "Parametric non-intrusive Bitstream Assessment of Video Media Streaming Quality-Lower Resolution Application Area," ITU-T Recommendation P.1202.1, October 2012.

[49] "Parametric non-intrusive Bitstream Assessment of Video Media Streaming Quality-Higher Resolution Application Area," ITU-T Recommendation P.1202.2, May 2013.

[50] "Objective Perceptual Multimedia Video Quality Measurement in the Presence of a Full Reference," ITU-T Recommendation J.247, August 2008.

[51] "Perceptual Visual Quality Measurement Techniques for Multimedia Services over Digital Cable Television Networks in the Presence of a Reduced Bandwidth Reference," ITU-T J.246, August 2008.

[52] "Hybrid Perceptual Bitstream Models for Objective Video Quality Measurements," ITU-T Recommendation J.343, November 2014.

[53] "Hybrid-NRe Objective Perceptual Video Quality Measurement for HDTV and Multimedia IP-based Video Services in the Presence of Encrypted Bitstream Data," ITU-T Recommendation J.343.1, November 2014.

[54] "Hybrid-NR Objective Perceptual Video Quality Measurement for HDTV and Multimedia IP-based Video Services in the Presence of Non-encrypted Bitstream Data," ITU-T Recommendation J.343.2, November 2014.

[55] "Hybrid-RRe Objective Perceptual Video Quality Measurement for HDTV and Multimedia IP-based Video Services in the Presence of a Reduced Reference Signal and Encrypted Bitstream Data," ITU-T Recommendation J.343.3, November 2014.

[56] "Hybrid-RR Objective Perceptual Video Quality Measurement for HDTV and Multimedia IP-based Video Services in the Presence of a Reduced Reference Signal and Non-encrypted Bitstream Data," ITU-T Recommendation J.343.4, November 2014.

[57] "Hybrid-FRe Objective Perceptual Video Quality Measurement for HDTV and Multimedia IP-based Video Services in the Presence of a Full Reference Signal and Encrypted Bitstream Data," ITU-T Recommendation J.343.5, November 2014.

[58] "Hybrid-FR Objective Perceptual Video Quality Measurement for HDTV and Multimedia IP-based Video Services in the Presence of a Full Reference Signal and Non-encrypted Bitstream Data," ITU-T Recommendation J.343.6, November 2014.

[59] F. M. Moss, K. Wang, F. Zhang, R. Baddeley, and D. R. Bull, "On the optimal presentation duration for subjective video quality assessment," *IEEE Transactions on Circuits and Systems for Video Technology*, vol. 26, no. 11, pp. 1977–1987, 2016.

[60] C. G. Bampis, Z. Li, A. K. Moorthy, and I. Katsavounidis, "Study of temporal effects on subjective video quality of experience," *IEEE Transactions on Image Processing*, vol. 26, no. 11, pp. 5217–5231, 2017.

[61] W. Song, D. Tjondronegoro, and M. Docherty, "Exploration and optimization of user experience in viewing videos on a mobile phone," *International Journal of Software Engineering and Knowledge Engineering*, vol. 20, no. 8, pp. 1045–1075, 2010.

[62] H. Knoche, J. D. McCarthy, and M. A. Sasse, "Can small be beautiful? assessing image resolution requirements for mobile TV," in *Proceedings of the 13th ACM International Conference on Multimedia, MM 2005*, pp. 829–838, Singapore, November 2005.

[63] S. Park and S.-H. Jeong, "Mobile IPTV: Approaches, challenges, standards, and QoS support," *IEEE Internet Computing*, vol. 13, no. 3, pp. 23–31, 2009.

[64] "YouTube Go application," Available at https://play.google.com/store/apps/details?id=com.google.android.apps.youtube.mango&hl=en, Last accessed 14th September, 2017.

15

Rate-Distortion and Rate-Energy-Distortion Evaluations of Compressive-Sensing Video Coding

Bingyu Ji, Ran Li, and Changan Wu

School of Computer and Information Technology, Xinyang Normal University, Xinyang 464000, China

Correspondence should be addressed to Ran Li; liran358@163.com

Academic Editor: Jintao Wang

Compressive-Sensing Video Coding (CSVC) is a new video coding framework based on compressive-sensing (CS) theory. This paper presents the evaluations on rate-distortion performance and rate-energy-distortion performance of CSVC by comparing it with the popular hybrid video coding standard H.264 and distributed video coding (DVC) system DISCOVER. Experimental results show that CSVC achieves a poor rate-distortion performance when compared with H.264 and DISCOVER, but its rate-energy-distortion performance has a distinct advantage; moreover, its energy consumption of coding is approximately invariant regardless of reconstruction quality. It can be concluded that, with a limited energy budget, CSVC outperforms H.264 and DISCOVER, but its rate-distortion performance still needs improvement.

1. Introduction

Video communication is an important type of data communication. Compression coding must be done before high-dimensional video signal is transmitted in channels with limited bandwidth. Therefore, video compression coding has become a hot research topic in digital video communication. The international video coding standard H.264 [1], jointly developed by ISO/IEC and the ITU-T, has been widely used in various video technologies, and H.264 has achieved great commercial success. H.264 standard uses motion estimation and discrete cosine transform to eliminate temporal and spatial redundancy of video sequences, and its coding complexity is much greater than decoding complexity. For instance, when the test sequence *Foreman* with CIF format is processed by H.264 codec, the encoding time is about 50 to 90 times as long as the decoding time in different quantization steps, which means that H.264 has strong applicability for the situation of one coding and multiple decoding, such as video broadcasting and video on demand. For the wireless communication equipment, long-time encoding means reduced economics and practicality; therefore, video coding method with low coding complexity is needed as an alternative. In this case, DVC [2], which was first proposed by Wyner

and Ziv in information coding theory [3], has received widespread attention. In the initial stage of DVC research, the main codec algorithms include Wyner-Ziv video coding [4], PRISM video coding [5], hierarchical Wyner-Ziv video coding [6], and DVC scheme based on wavelet coding [7]. With an aim of improving coding performance, European Union scientific research institutions put forward special research plan, and, based on the existing research, develop a DVC standard program called DISCOVER (DIStributed COding for Video sERvices) [8]. DISCOVER makes the low-complexity video coding performance further enhanced. But the feedback channel [9] and the virtual channel [10] in DISCOVER scheme are highly controversial, which is an important engineering problem hindering its popularization and application. CS theory [11–13] combined with video coding has led to the emergence of a new low-complexity video coding scheme called CSVC [14]. The scheme still retains the distributed characteristics and does not depend on feedback channel or virtual channel and has great engineering application potential, which has attracted many scholars' attention [15–17].

At present, there is still a lack of discussion on the comparison of rate-distortion performance between CSVC,

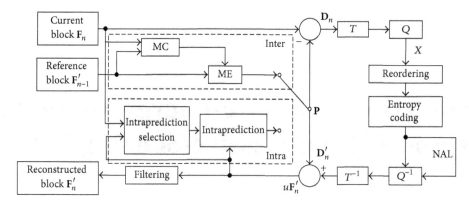

FIGURE 1: H.264 codec architecture.

H.264, and DISCOVER. It will help to clarify the upper limit of performance improvement of CSVC by obtaining the result of the performance difference between the three video coding schemes. The rate-distortion performance cannot show the relationship between coding energy consumption and video reconstruction quality. Therefore, rate-energy-distortion performance [18] also needs an objective evaluation of CSVC, H.264, and DISCOVER. This paper first summarizes the basic framework and technical details of H.264 and DISCOVER. Next, a typical algorithm of CSVC will be described in detail. Finally, on the basis of the theories exposition, rate-distortion performance and rate-energy-distortion performance of the three video coding schemes are evaluated, and the performance difference between the three video coding schemes is then fully discussed. The experimental results show that, under the test of CIF videos, respectively, named *Bus, Football, Foreman, and Mobile*, in terms of the rate-distortion performance, H.264 is optimal and DISCOVER follows while CSVC is the worst and has a large performance difference from the other two; but, in terms of rate-energy-distortion performance, CSVC is optimal, DISCOVER follows, and H.264 is the worst. The results also reveal a fact that the energy consumption of CSVC is approximately the same regardless of reconstruction quality, while, for H.264 and DISCOVER, there is a close correlation between recovery quality and the energy consumption of coding. As a result, it can be concluded that when low energy consumption is demanded, CSVC program can give full play to its advantages, but its rate-distortion performance still needs improvement.

2. Typical Video Coding Schemes

2.1. H.264. H.264 system is divided into two levels in function: Video Coding Layer (VCL) and Network Abstraction Layer (NAL). Its codec framework is shown in Figure 1. In the coding process, there are two options to predict the current image block F_n: interprediction and intraframe prediction. When interprediction is adopted, the motion vector of current block F_n is obtained by the motion estimation according to the reference block, and then the predicted frame P could be obtained by the motion compensation method;

when intraprediction is used, the predicted block in the current frame is the weighted average of the selected adjacent decoded blocks of the current block. After the predictive frame is determined, the main steps of codec process are as follows.

Step 1. Calculate the residual D_n between the current block F_n and the predicted value P.

Step 2. Obtain the quantized coefficient X by transforming and quantizing D_n.

Step 3. Form the bit stream by reordering and entropy coding of quantized coefficient X.

Step 4. Transmit the bit stream to the decoder side through NAL; at the same time, use part of the bit stream, which could be decoded on the encoder side, as reference frame.

The core technology of H.264 is mainly reflected on its improvement in the interframe and intraframe predictive coding, for example, using 4×4 integer discrete cosine transform technology instead of the former 8×8 discrete cosine transform technology to avoid mismatches in inverse transformation.

2.2. DISCOVER. The codec framework of DISCOVER system is shown in Figure 2. The encoder side carries on video processing in Group of Pictures (GOP) whose length is determined by the specific situation. The length of GOP will be increased to reduce time redundancy when the image contains a small amount of motion; on the other hand, the length can be shortened accordingly if there is a large amount of motion. For each group, video frames are divided into WZ frames and key frames. H.264 is used for intracoding and decoding of key frame; meanwhile, WZ frame is encoded by Wyner-Ziv encoder, and the core steps of decoding process are given as follows because of its complexity.

Step 1. Extract side information from key frames.

Step 2. Simulate the extracted side information by virtual channel to generate the correlated noise.

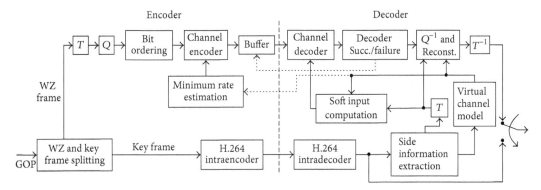

FIGURE 2: DISCOVER codec architecture.

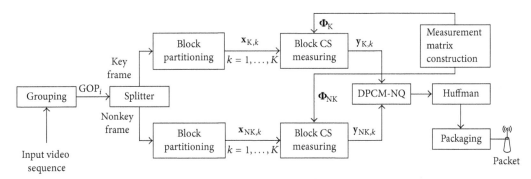

FIGURE 3: CSVC encoder architecture.

Step 3. Perform the soft input calculation on the correlated noise and the transformed side information.

Step 4. Verify the soft input calculation result by the information transmitted from encoder side to judge whether the decoding is successful or not.

In the channel coding process, DISCOVER uses Low Density Parity Check Accumulation (LDPCA) code, which is rate-compatible and is closer to the capacity of all types of channels when compared with Turbo code. The complexity of overall system will be increased because of the request of cumulative syndrome sent from decoder side to encoder side. Therefore, the minimum quantity of syndrome that each bit plane can transmit is set based on the Wyner-Ziv rate-distortion constraint in DISCOVER decoder side to reduce the number of requests and hence obtain higher compression efficiency.

3. Compressive-Sensing Video Coding

CSVC system follows WZ video coding system which is proposed by Wyner-Ziv et al. [4] in the way that it also divides video stream into key frames and nonkey frames, and two different methods are used to implement encoding and decoding of the two types of frames. For key frames, traditional video intraframe coding framework is adopted, or high-rate CS codec is introduced to ensure the high quality of reconstructed key frames. For nonkey frames, low-rate CS measurement is adopted. Side information is first extracted

from high-quality key frames and then is combined with the measurement vectors for joint reconstruction of nonkey frames. In the early research of Distributed Compressed Sensing (DCS) video, DCS theory was first proposed in [19], which also demonstrated the possibility of the combination of distributed coding and CS. Since then, domestic and foreign scholars have devoted much attention to the research of DCS video. Typical examples are DIStributed video Coding Using Compressed Sampling (DISCUCS), proposed by Prades-Nebot et al. [20], DIStributed video COmpression Sensing (DISCOS), proposed by Do et al. [21], and improved DISCOS, proposed by Tramel and Fowler [22]. On the basis of the above research, we propose the CSVC system with superior performance in [14]. In this paper, we will evaluate H.264, DISCOVER, and CSVC system in terms of rate-distortion performance and rate-energy-distortion performance. The codec process of CSVC system is described in detail below.

3.1. Encoder Framework. The encoder framework of CSVC system is shown in Figure 3. First, the input video sequence is divided into several GOPs, and key frames and nonkey frames are separated in the group. Then, the key frames and the nonkey frames are divided into K nonoverlapping subblocks of size $B \times B$ pixels, and each block is arranged in raster order as column vector of length B^2 ($B^2 = N$). Finally, the measurement matrix is constructed to calculate the measurement vector of each block as follows:

$$\mathbf{y}_{K,k} = \mathbf{\Phi}_K \cdot \mathbf{x}_{K,k} \quad k = 1, \ldots, K,$$
$$\mathbf{y}_{NK,k} = \mathbf{\Phi}_{NK} \cdot \mathbf{x}_{NK,k} \quad k = 1, \ldots, K, \tag{1}$$

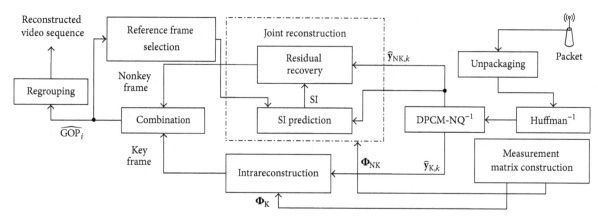

FIGURE 4: CSVC decoder architecture.

where $\mathbf{x}_{K,k}$ and $\mathbf{x}_{NK,k}$ denote the kth subblock of the key frame and the nonkey frame, respectively, and $\mathbf{\Phi}_{K,k}$ and $\mathbf{\Phi}_{NK,k}$ are the measurement matrix constructed by the random Hadamard matrix. For the key frames, the size of the measurement matrix $\mathbf{\Phi}_{K,k}$ is $M_K \times N$, so the measurement rate is $S_K = M_K/N$. For nonkey frames, the size of measurement matrix $\mathbf{\Phi}_{NK,k}$ is $M_{NK} \times N$, so the measurement rate is $S_{NK} = M_{NK}/N$.

Then the measurement vectors $\mathbf{y}_K$ and $\mathbf{y}_{NK}$ of blocks will be transmitted to the quantizer to form bit stream. CSVC system uses the nonuniform quantizer based on Differential Pulse-Code Modulation (DPCM), DPCM-NQ for short, which first computes the residual of measurement value between adjacent subblocks to reduce coding redundancy and then quantifies the residual. In consideration of the high frequency of small residual value, the nonuniform quantization is used to process the residual of each subblock in order to reduce the quantization error. Supposing that the mth measurement residual of the kth subblock is $d_k(m)$, it can be compressed according to μ law as follows:

$$\begin{aligned} d_{comp} &= f\left[d_k(m)\right] \\ &= \operatorname{sgn}\left[d_k(m)\right] \cdot \frac{\log\left(1 + \mu \left|d_k(m)/D\right|\right)}{\log\left(1 + \mu\right)}, \end{aligned} \quad (2)$$

where D is the maximum measurement residual of the current frame, $\operatorname{sgn}[\cdot]$ represents the symbolic function, and μ is 10. In the inverse quantization, the estimated value of $d_k(m)$ is calculated using the following decompression formula:

$$\begin{aligned} \widehat{d}_k(m) &= f^{-1}\left(d_{comp}\right) \\ &= \frac{\operatorname{sgn}\left[d_{comp}\right] \cdot D}{\mu} \cdot \left[\left(1 + \mu\right)^{d_{comp}} - 1\right]. \end{aligned} \quad (3)$$

After the residual of each block is quantized, the quantized data of all the blocks are subjected to Huffman coding and are encapsulated into data packets to be sent to the decoder side.

3.2. Decoder Framework. The decoder framework of CSVC system is shown in Figure 4. After the data packets are

received on the decoder side, the measurement vectors $\widehat{\mathbf{y}}_{K,k}$ of key frames and $\widehat{\mathbf{y}}_{NK,k}$ of nonkey frames can be obtained by Huffman decoding and inverse quantization. For key frames, the intraframe reconstruction model is used as follows:

$$\widehat{\mathbf{x}}_K = \arg\min_{\mathbf{x}} \left\{ \left\|\widehat{\mathbf{y}}_K - \mathbf{\Theta}_K \mathbf{E} \cdot \mathbf{x}\right\|_2 + \lambda \left\|\mathbf{\Psi} \cdot \mathbf{x}\right\|_1 \right\}, \quad (4)$$

where

$$\widehat{\mathbf{y}}_K = \begin{bmatrix} \widehat{\mathbf{y}}_{K,1} \\ \widehat{\mathbf{y}}_{K,2} \\ \vdots \\ \widehat{\mathbf{y}}_{K,K} \end{bmatrix},$$

$$\mathbf{\Theta}_K = \begin{bmatrix} \mathbf{\Phi}_K & & & 0 \\ & \mathbf{\Phi}_K & & \\ & & \mathbf{\Phi}_K & \\ 0 & & & \mathbf{\Phi}_K \end{bmatrix}, \quad (5)$$

$$\mathbf{E} \cdot \mathbf{x} = \begin{bmatrix} \mathbf{x}_{K,1} \\ \mathbf{x}_{K,2} \\ \vdots \\ \mathbf{x}_{K,K} \end{bmatrix},$$

$\mathbf{\Psi}$ is the sparse transform matrix of the video frame $\mathbf{x}$, and λ represents the regularization factor. The reconstructed model (4) can be solved by a variety of still image CS reconstruction algorithms. To ensure high-quality recovery of key frames, CSVC system uses multihypothesis smoothing Landweber iterative algorithm used in [22] to solve model (4).

For the nonkey frame, we firstly obtain the side information $\mathbf{x}_{SI}$ of the current nonkey frame by carrying out the side information prediction of the adjacent reconstructed key frame and then calculate the residual measurement vector between the measurement vector of each block and its side information as follows:

$$
\hat{\mathbf{y}}_R =
\begin{bmatrix}
\hat{\mathbf{y}}_{R,1} \\
\hat{\mathbf{y}}_{R,2} \\
\vdots \\
\hat{\mathbf{y}}_{R,K}
\end{bmatrix}
=
\begin{bmatrix}
\hat{\mathbf{y}}_{NK,1} - \boldsymbol{\Phi}_{NK}\mathbf{x}_{SI,1} \\
\hat{\mathbf{y}}_{NK,2} - \boldsymbol{\Phi}_{NK}\mathbf{x}_{SI,2} \\
\vdots \\
\hat{\mathbf{y}}_{NK,K} - \boldsymbol{\Phi}_{NK}\mathbf{x}_{SI,K}
\end{bmatrix}
$$

$$
=
\begin{bmatrix}
\boldsymbol{\Phi}_{NK} \cdot (\mathbf{x}_{NK,1} - \mathbf{x}_{SI,1}) \\
\boldsymbol{\Phi}_{NK} \cdot (\mathbf{x}_{NK,2} - \mathbf{x}_{SI,2}) \\
\vdots \\
\boldsymbol{\Phi}_{NK} \cdot (\mathbf{x}_{NK,K} - \mathbf{x}_{SI,K})
\end{bmatrix},
\tag{6}
$$

where

$$
\boldsymbol{\Theta}_{NK} =
\begin{bmatrix}
\boldsymbol{\Phi}_{NK} & & & 0 \\
& \boldsymbol{\Phi}_{NK} & & \\
& & \ddots & \\
0 & & & \boldsymbol{\Phi}_{NK}
\end{bmatrix}
\tag{7}
$$

$$
\mathbf{r}_{NK,i} = \mathbf{x}_{NK,i} - \mathbf{x}_{SI,i}.
$$

So (6) can be transformed into

$$
\hat{\mathbf{y}}_R = \boldsymbol{\Theta}_{NK}\mathbf{E} \cdot \mathbf{r}_{NK},
\tag{8}
$$

where $\mathbf{r}_{NK}$ is the residual between nonkey frame $\mathbf{x}_{NK}$ and side information $\mathbf{x}_{SI}$. According to (8), the residual reconstruction model of nonkey frame can be established as follows:

$$
\hat{\mathbf{r}}_{NK} = \arg\min_{\mathbf{r}} \left\{ \|\hat{\mathbf{y}}_R - \boldsymbol{\Theta}_{NK}\mathbf{E} \cdot \mathbf{r}\|_2 + \eta \|\mathbf{P} \cdot \mathbf{r}\|_1 \right\},
\tag{9}
$$

where $\mathbf{P}$ is the sparse transform matrix of the residual $\mathbf{r}_{NK}$ and η denotes the regularization factor. The residual reconstruction model (9) is still solved using Landweber iterative algorithm. Finally, the reconstruction of nonkey frame can be calculated as follows:

$$
\hat{\mathbf{x}}_{NK} = \mathbf{x}_{SI} + \hat{\mathbf{r}}_{NK}.
\tag{10}
$$

The features of CSVC system constructed according to the above codec process are as follows: (1) compared to DISCOVER, CSVC system eliminates virtual channel and feedback channel, and thus the difficulty of engineering is reduced; (2) since there is no correlation between the CS measurement and image content, the code rate is determined only by the measurement rate, which makes it easier for CSVC system to control the code rate; (3) each measurement value contains all the image information; therefore, it is easy to implement scalable coding; (4) the data security can be enhanced by the random generation of the measurement matrix. The above features endow CSVC system with more engineering value and make it become a potential new DVC scheme. We are more concerned about the comparison of coding energy consumption between CSVC system and H.264 and DISCOVER, so, in the experiment part, the coding energy consumption of the three systems will be evaluated in detail.

4. Experimental Results and Analysis

The performances of H.264, DISCOVER, and CSVC are evaluated, respectively, using four standard video sequences named *Foreman*, *Bus*, *Mobile*, and *Football* in CIF format. H.264 adopts the standard coding configuration of JM19.0 model and implements intramode; DISCOVER uses the default encoding configuration; and CSVC adopts the experimental parameter configuration in [14]. The rate-distortion and rate-energy-distortion performances of the three encoders are compared, where rate-distortion reflects the relationship between the code rate and the Peak Signal-Noise Ratio (PSNR) while rate-energy-distortion reflects the relationship between the coding time and PSNR. Using the same experimental platform, the coding time is proportional to the energy consumption; therefore, it can represent the level of coding energy consumption. The experimental platform is MATALB R2012b; the computer system is 64-bit Windows 7 operating system with an installation memory of 8.00 GB and Intel Core i7-4900 processor whose frequency is 3.60 GHz.

4.1. Evaluation on Rate-Distortion Performance. Figure 5 shows the rate-distortion curves for H.264, DISCOVER, and CSVC encoders under different test video sequences. It can be seen from Figure 5 that the PSNR values of the whole reconstructed video processed by different encoder always grow in a positive trend when the code rates increase. On the whole, the encoding effects of H.264 and DISCOVER are always better than CSVC encoder. For the test videos *Bus* and *Football*, at the same code rate, the video reconstruction effect of H.264 is the best; for *Foreman* and *Mobile*, at the same code rate and in the specific code rate range, the coding effect of DISCOVER is even better than H.264. It can be seen that the rate-distortion performance of H.264 is optimal, DISCOVER follows, and CSVC is the worst and has a big performance difference from the other two. For CSVC, the measurement rate determines the bitrate. When the measurement rate is 0.05, the bitrate is about 6000 kbits/s. If we further decrease the measurement rate, the bitrate will be lower than 6000 kbits/s. The average PSNR of reconstructed video gradually decreases with the measurement rate linearly decreasing. The variation of PSNR curve is smooth, and the PSNR value cannot suddenly reduce when the bitrate drops to below 6000 kbits/s.

4.2. Evaluation on Rate-Energy-Distortion Performance. Figure 6 shows the rate-energy-distortion curves for H.264, DISCOVER, and CSVC encoders under different test video sequences. It can be seen from Figure 6 that, for any video, under the same PSNR value, the encoding time of CSVC is the shortest, DISCOVER follows, and H.264 is the longest. In particular, the average encoding time of CSVC is only about 3 seconds, which means that the energy consumption of CSVC is much lower than DISCOVER and H.264 on the same recovery level. With the PSNR value of reconstructed video increasing, the encoder time of H.264 and DISCOVER gradually increases. But the change of encoder time under DISCOVER framework is steeper and H.264 framework

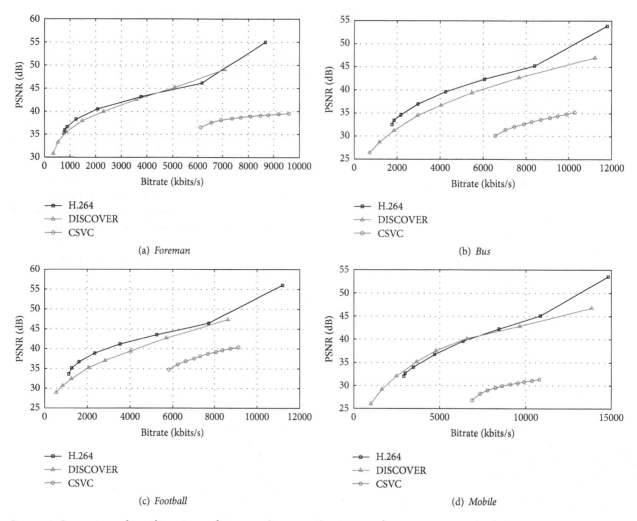

FIGURE 5: Comparison of rate-distortion performance of H.264, DISCOVER, and CSVC encoder under different test video sequences.

more gentle, which shows that H.264 has a high dependency on energy consumption with its promotion of performance, and DISCOVER also needs a certain amount of energy input. The computational complexity of CS measuring determines the energy consumption at encoder. Suppose M denotes the number of CS measurements for a video frame and L denotes the total number of pixels in a video frame. The computational complexity of CS measuring is $O(ML)$. Because M is far below L, the variation of energy consumption is very small when changing M. However, M is an important factor for the reconstruction quality of video frame. The reconstruction quality can be improved effectively with small increments of M. Therefore, the slope of the rate-energy-distortion curve is almost vertical, indicating that the small investment of energy consumption can get the significant improvement of reconstruction quality. It can be seen that the rate-energy-distortion performance of CSVC is optimal, DISCOVER follows, H.264 is the worst. Among the three, the energy consumption of CSVC is approximately invariant regardless of reconstruction quality, while the reconstruction quality of H.264 and DISCOVER has a great correlation with the energy consumption of coding.

5. Conclusions

This paper has conducted an experiment-driven analysis of rate-distortion and rate-energy-distortion performances of CSVC algorithm and compares them with that of H.264 and DISCOVER. The rate-distortion and rate-energy-distortion performances of the three systems are evaluated under the same experimental environment. Experiment results show that the rate-distortion performance of CSVC has a large performance difference from H.264 and DISCOVER, but its rate-energy-distortion performance has a greater advantage; that is, the rapid improvement of its reconstruction quality does not depend on coding energy input. Therefore, on the premise that communication bandwidth is effectively improved, CSVC can be used as a candidate for future wireless video communication because of its characteristics, which provides wireless video terminals limited by energy consumption and computing power with more possibilities.

At present, the rate-distortion performance of CSVC is still not ideal, and there is still some way to go before we put CSVC into practical use. Efforts should be made in the

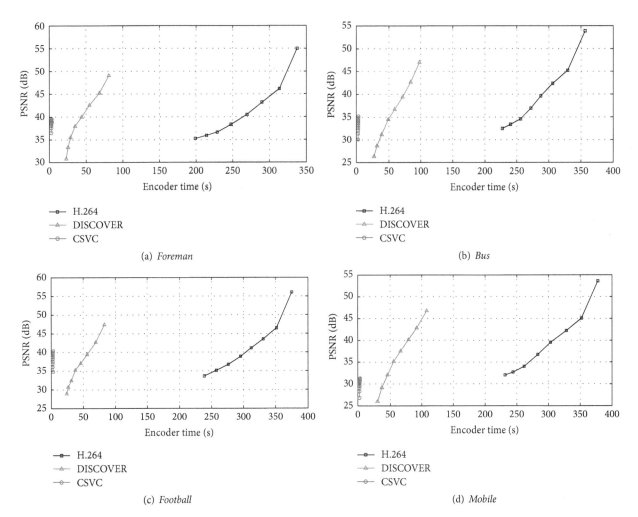

FIGURE 6: Comparison of rate-energy-distortion performance of H.264, DISCOVER, and CSVC encoder under different test video sequences.

following areas to improve the rate-distortion performance of CSVC.

(1) Side Information Estimation. Rate-distortion performance of CSVC is greatly related to the accuracy of side information estimation, which means that high-quality side information immensely reduces the required supply of bit load from encoder side. Therefore, finding the appropriate motion estimation algorithm to obtain more accurate side information and realizing the optimal reconstruction of decoding will become the key to improving the rate-distortion performance of CSVC.

(2) A Priori Structural Feature Modeling of Video Frames. Images of the same type often have similar structural information. Therefore, the reconstructed model can be constructed by evaluating the structural information of the decoded video frames and extracting the prior knowledge, which can reduce code rate and improve the reconstruction quality. For example, the statistical correlation structure can be used in the image transformation coefficient and a tree structure can be adopted for the wavelet coefficient. However, due to the complexity and uncertainty of natural

images, further study should be made on how to use a priori knowledge to construct a suitable model.

(3) Quantization Measurement. Uniform quantization is the major method adopted to quantify the CS measurement currently. But the traditional entropy coding method is not ideal for compressing the uniform quantization values because of the statistical independence between the uniform quantization values. Then, how to express the CS value with the least number of bits with the constraint of information-theoretic rate-distortion coding theorem is one of the key topics of the following research. Therefore, it is necessary to propose a new nonuniform quantization method to establish statistical correlation between quantization values and hereby to design a new entropy coding method matching the statistical correlation.

The above-mentioned further researches are employed at decoder to improve the rate-distortion performance of CSVC, but the CS measuring at encoder guarantees the advantage of CSVC in rate-energy-distortion performance. Therefore, the rate-energy-distortion performance cannot be affected while improving the rate-distortion performance of CSVC.

Acknowledgments

This work was supported in part by the National Natural Science Foundation of China, under Grant no. 61501393, in part by the Key Scientific Research Project of Colleges and Universities in Henan Province of China, under Grant 16A520069, in part by Youth Sustentation Fund of Xinyang Normal University, under Grant no. 2015-QN-043, and in part by Scientific Research Foundation of Graduate School of Xinyang Normal University, under Grant no. 2016KYJJ10.

References

[1] J. Ostermann, J. Bormans, P. List et al., "Video coding with H.264/AVC: tools, performance, and complexity," *IEEE Circuits and Systems Magazine*, vol. 4, no. 1, pp. 7–28, 2004.

[2] B. Girod, A. M. Aaron, S. Rane, and D. Rebollo-Monedero, "Distributed video coding," *Proceedings of the IEEE*, vol. 93, no. 1, pp. 71–83, 2005.

[3] A. D. Wyner and J. Ziv, "The rate-distortion function for source coding with side information at the decoder," *IEEE Transactions on Information Theory*, vol. 22, no. 1, pp. 1–10, 1976.

[4] A. Aaron, S. Rane, R. Zhang, and B. Girod, "Wyner-Ziv coding for video: applications to compression and error resilience," in *Proceedings of the Data Compression Conference (DCC '03)*, pp. 93–102, Snowbird, Utah, USA, March 2003.

[5] R. Puri, A. Majumdar, and K. Ramchandran, "PRISM: a video coding paradigm with motion estimation at the decoder," *IEEE Transactions on Image Processing*, vol. 16, no. 10, pp. 2436–2448, 2007.

[6] Q. Xu and Z. Xiong, "Layered Wyner-Ziv video coding," in *Proceedings of the Visual Communications and Image Processing 2004*, pp. 83–91, IEEE, San Jose, Calif, USA, January 2004.

[7] W. Liu, L. Dong, and W. Zeng, "Motion refinement based progressive side-information estimation for Wyner-Ziv video coding," *IEEE Transactions on Circuits & Systems for Video Technology*, vol. 20, no. 12, pp. 1863–1875, 2010.

[8] X. Artigas, J. Ascenso, M. Dalai, S. Klomp, D. Kubasov, and M. Ouaret, "The discover codec: architecture, techniques and evaluation," in *Proceedings of the 26th Picture Coding Symposium (PCS '07)*, pp. 1103–1120, Lisbon, Portugal, November 2007.

[9] J. Slowack, J. Škorupa, N. Deligiannis, P. Lambert, A. Munteanu, and R. van de Walle, "Distributed video coding with feedback channel constraints," *IEEE Transactions on Circuits & Systems for Video Technology*, vol. 22, no. 7, pp. 1014–1026, 2012.

[10] C. Brites and F. Pereira, "Correlation noise modeling for efficient pixel and transform domain Wyner-Ziv video coding," *IEEE Transactions on Circuits and Systems for Video Technology*, vol. 18, no. 9, pp. 1177–1190, 2008.

[11] E. J. Candes, J. Romberg, and T. Tao, "Robust uncertainty principles: exact signal reconstruction from highly incomplete frequency information," *IEEE Transactions on Information Theory*, vol. 52, no. 2, pp. 489–509, 2006.

[12] D. L. Donoho, "Compressed sensing," *IEEE Transactions on Information Theory*, vol. 52, no. 4, pp. 1289–1306, 2006.

[13] E. J. Candes and M. B. Wakin, "An introduction to compressive sampling: a sensing/sampling paradigm that goes against the common knowledge in data acquisition," *IEEE Signal Processing Magazine*, vol. 25, no. 2, pp. 21–30, 2008.

[14] R. Li, H. Liu, R. Xue, and Y. Li, "Compressive-sensing-based video codec by autoregressive prediction and adaptive residual recovery," *International Journal of Distributed Sensor Networks*, vol. 2015, Article ID 562840, 19 pages, 2015.

[15] Y. Liu, X. Zhu, L. Zhang, and S. H. Cho, "Distributed compressed video sensing in camera sensor networks," *International Journal of Distributed Sensor Networks*, vol. 2012, Article ID 352167, 10 pages, 2012.

[16] C. Di Laura, D. Pajuelo, and G. Kemper, "A novel steganography technique for SDTV-H.264/AVC encoded video," *International Journal of Digital Multimedia Broadcasting*, vol. 2016, Article ID 6950592, 9 pages, 2016.

[17] Y. Lahbabi, E. H. Ibn Elhaj, and A. Hammouch, "Adaptive streaming of scalable videos over P2PTV," *International Journal of Digital Multimedia Broadcasting*, vol. 2015, Article ID 283097, 10 pages, 2015.

[18] S. Pudlewski and T. Melodia, "Compressive video streaming: design and rate-energy-distortion analysis," *IEEE Transactions on Multimedia*, vol. 15, no. 8, pp. 2072–2086, 2013.

[19] D. Baron, M. B. Wakin, M. F. Duarte, S. Sarvotham, and R. G. Baraniuk, "Distributed compressive sensing," http://arxiv.org/abs/0901.3403.

[20] J. Prades-Nebot, Y. Ma, and T. Huang, "Distributed video coding using compressive sampling," in *Proceedings of the Picture Coding Symposium (PCS '09)*, pp. 1–4, Chicago, Ill, USA, May 2009.

[21] T. T. Do, Y. Chen, D. T. Nguyen, N. Nguyen, L. Gan, and T. D. Tran, "Distributed compressed video sensing," in *Proceedings of the 16th IEEE International Conference on Image Processing (ICIP '09)*, pp. 1393–1396, IEEE, Cairo, Egypt, November 2009.

[22] E. W. Tramel and J. E. Fowler, "Video compressed sensing with multihypothesis," in *Proceedings of the Data Compression Conference (DCC '11)*, pp. 193–202, Snowbird, Utah, USA, March 2011.

16

A Novel Approach to Reduce the Unicast Bandwidth of an IPTV System in a High-Speed Access Network

El Hassane Khabbiza, Rachid El Alami, and Hassan Qjidaa

LESSI Laboratory, Department of Physics, Faculty of Sciences Dhar El Mahraz, Sidi Mohammed Ben Abdellah University, Fez, Morocco

Correspondence should be addressed to El Hassane Khabbiza; elhassane.khabbiza@usmba.ac.ma

Academic Editor: Jintao Wang

Channel change time is a critical quality of experience (QOE) metric for IP-based video delivery systems such as Internet Protocol Television (IPTV). An interesting channel change acceleration scheme based on peer-assisted delivery was recently proposed, which consists of deploying one FCC server (Fast Channel Change Server) in the IP backbone in order to send the unicast stream to the STB (Set-Top Box) before sending the normal multicast stream after each channel change. However, deploying such a solution will cause high bandwidth usage in the network because of the huge unicast traffic sent by the FCC server to the STBs. In this paper, we propose a new solution to reduce the bandwidth occupancy of the unicast traffic, by deploying the FCC server capabilities on the user STB. This means that, after each channel change request, the STB will receive the unicast traffic from another STB instead of the central server. By using this method, the unicast traffic will not pass through the IP network; it will be a peer-to-peer communication via the Access Network only. Extensive simulation results are presented to demonstrate the robustness of our new solution.

1. Introduction

Recently, the IPTV (Internet Protocol Television) solution has become widely used since it provides various services such as multicast TV, Video on Demand (VOD), and Pause Live TV (PLTV), taking advantage of the IP network expansion and the increase of Internet users.

Instead of traditional TV, which provides large bandwidth and no single video delivery to each user, IPTV distribution requires a strict requirement on both performance and reliability needs, lower latency, tighter control of jitter, and small packet loss in order to guarantee the expected video quality.

Figure 1 illustrates the basic topology of an IPTV system. When a user switches to a specific channel (or when the user turns on his/her STB), the STB sends a request to join the corresponding multicast group using IGMP (Internet Group Management Protocol) [1]. Then, if successful, the IPTV platform delivers the video stream encapsulated in RTP (Real-Time Transport Protocol) packet to the user through the AGR (Aggregated Router), AN (Access Node), and HG (Home Gateway).

During each channel change, the STB sends the IGMP multicasting message to join the new channel; during this change, the STB must wait more for the arrival of the decodable frame, which is called the I-frame. In order to solve this problem, many techniques have been proposed to reduce this waiting time; one of the most famous techniques is the unicast peer-assisted solution, which consists in sending the I-frame faster to allow the STB to decode the multicast stream instead of waiting for the arrival of the original I-frame.

The objective of this paper is to propose a novel method to reduce the bandwidth occupancy of the unicast traffic consumed during channel changes by enabling communication between STBs. Using this method, the STB will join the stream, decode it, and display it on the user screen. In addition, at the same time, STB can buffer this stream for several seconds to deliver it to another STB (which belongs to the same AN) in case it is required by that STB.

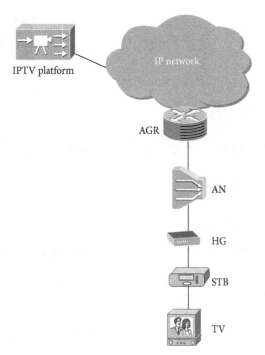

FIGURE 1: Architecture of the IPTV system.

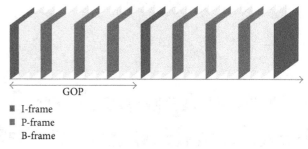

FIGURE 2: Typical frame structure.

This paper is organized as follows. Section 2 reviews the methods used for reducing the channel change time. The proposed method is detailed in Section 3. In Section 4, we evaluate our method followed by a conclusion in Section 5.

2. Related Work

The video stream is composed of a series of frames (or pictures) taken at regular intervals (typically every 33.3 or 40 milliseconds); the bitrate of this stream will be significantly high and can reach up to 200 Mb/s for SDTV (Standard Definition Television) and up to 1 GB/s for HDTV (High Definition Television) [2].

Since network bandwidth is a scarce resource, many compression techniques have been recently used to save network bandwidth and storage. Efficient media stream schemes have therefore been developed, such as MPEG-2 and MPEG-4, taking advantage of the temporal correlation between frames. This correlation can significantly increase the compression efficiency.

The video stream in this scheme is compressed into a series of frames grouped in a group of pictures (GOP) as illustrated in Figure 2. Each GOP is composed of three frames: I-frame, P-frame, and B-frame. The I-frame is the reference frame, which exploits the spatial correlation of pixels within the frame, and it is very independent of the other frames. The P- and B-frames are predicted frames and depend always on other frames to be decoded; they cannot be decoded alone.

To decode the video stream, the decoder needs an I-frame, which is the reference frame, as it is the basic information for decoding all GOP. To increase the playout

time and reduce delay, it is highly recommended to transmit the I-frame frequently. However, transmitting the I-frame more frequently will increase the bitrate of the video stream because those frames are relatively larger than P- and B-frames.

The choice of the GOP size should be well suited to have an average between GOP size and decoding delay. Generally, there is a tradeoff between the playout performance on the one hand and the compression efficiency on the other hand; in practice, the GOP duration is usually chosen to be between 1 and 3 seconds.

2.1. Channel Change Delay. In the traditional TV systems, the channel change time (CCT) was almost simultaneous (around 200 milliseconds), as the user just needs to change the carrier frequency, demodulate the content, and display it on the TV screen.

With the digitalization and compression of the video stream, the channel change time (CCT) has increased significantly; generally, in IPTV systems, this has three underlying components [3]:

(i) Decoding delay: the time between the user entry of a channel change and receipt of decodable multicast data.

(ii) IGMP delay: the time needed to process the IGMP leave and join messages.

(iii) Buffering delay: the time needed to buffer the content before displaying it on the user TV.

In the last few years, many techniques [4] have been proposed as a solution to mitigate the CCT of IPTV systems. Most of those techniques focused on reducing the decoding delay based on an auxiliary stream, which starts with an I-frame. This auxiliary stream is sent to the STB when the user changes the channel in order to allow the STB to catch the I-frame earlier and start decoding and displaying it on the screen without being obliged to wait until the arrival of the original I-frame, which will help to minimize the CCT.

There have been three basic techniques to exploit the auxiliary stream.

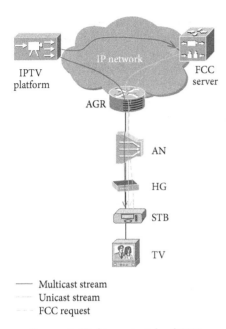

FIGURE 3: Working principle of FCC.

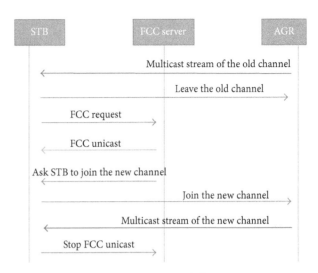

FIGURE 4: FCC work flow.

Technique 1. Prejoin the most likely next channel based on user behavior or the adjacent channel in parallel with the current channel [5–7]. This way, the STB will decode the stream of the new channels very quickly since it has already received the I-frame before switching the channel.

Technique 2. Encode a low-quality auxiliary stream with frequent I-frames into the regular stream for each channel [8, 9].

Technique 3. This technique is FCC unicast-based, which consists in deploying one Fast Channel Change (FCC) server in the network in order to buffer the media stream and deliver it to the STB with a higher speed after each channel change request [10–12].

2.2. FCC Unicast-Based. FCC based on unicast is the most popular channel change solution deployed by operators over the world because of its simplicity and reliability, and it does not require any modification in the other network elements to implement it. Figure 3 shows one simple topology of an IPTV system based on FCC unicast solution, and Figure 4 illustrates the working mechanism of this technique.

This solution consists of installing one FCC server inside the IP backbone in order to cover the maximum number of ANs; this server is connected to the multicast source to catch the last few seconds of the content stream for each channel. Once the IPTV user presses the button on the remote control to change the channel, the STB will immediately send one FCC request to the FCC server to request the unicast in parallel with an IGMP leave message in order to leave the previous multicast group corresponding to the previous channel. The FCC server sends to the STB a short stream of

video from the new channel for immediate playback, starting at some entry point in the past.

The FCC server sends the data to the STB at a data rate faster than the channel's data rate and after a few seconds catches up with the multicast stream for that channel, and then the FCC server instructs the STB to join the new channel.

After joining the new channel and receiving the first multicast packet, the STB informs the FCC to stop the unicast stream [13].

2.3. FCC Unicast Bandwidth Evaluation. FCC based unicast does not take into consideration the transmission bandwidth limitation, because the unicast stream is used in parallel with the multicast stream to deliver the IPTV service to the end user. Bandwidth limitations become more and more serious when the users switch the channels in a frequent or simultaneous manner due to their own behavior (searching for interesting programs) or to avoid commercial breaks (advertisements).

This bandwidth will be added to the multicast bandwidth and bandwidth of other services (especially when the AN is offering other services to the end users), such as HSI (High-Speed Internet), VoIP (Voice over IP), and POTS (Plain Old Telephone Service), which can cause many congestion problems between the AN and the AGR and between the AGR and the IP backbone.

The total unicast bandwidth ($\mathbf{b}_t$) consumed during the channel change for one AN is the sum of all the unicast traffic ($\mathbf{b}_i$) sent to each STB during each channel change (as shown in Figure 5) and can be expressed by the following function:

$$\mathbf{b}_t = \sum_{i=1}^{\substack{\text{Number of online IPTV users}}} \mathbf{b}_i. \tag{1}$$

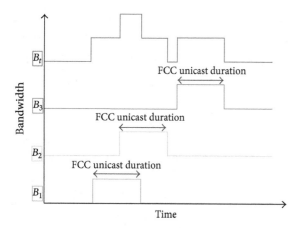

FIGURE 5: FCC unicast bandwidth.

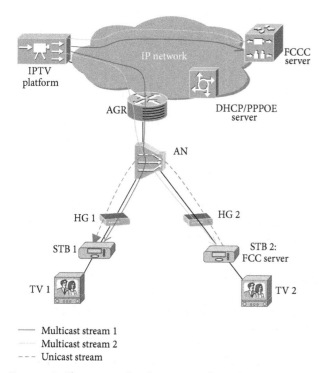

— Multicast stream 1
····· Multicast stream 2
- - - Unicast stream

FIGURE 6: The proposed solution to reduce the FCC unicast bandwidth.

3. The New FCC Unicast-Based Solution

To reduce the unicast bandwidth consumed during the channel changes of all IPTV users connected to one AN, we proposed a new solution as shown in Figure 6, which consists of the implementation of the FCC server capabilities on each user STB in parallel with the central FCC server, which will act as an FCC controller (FCCC) and at the same time as a traditional FCC server. Once the STB receives the channel stream, it will decode and display it on the user screen and at the same time can buffer this stream for several seconds to deliver it to another STB (which belongs to the same AN) in case it is required by that STB.

Our proposition is mainly addressed to high-speed Access Network technologies such as VDSL (Very High Bit

Rate Digital Subscriber Line) [14], GPON (Gigabit Passive Optical Network) [15], and Ethernet which provide a large uplink bandwidth.

To determine the user's physical location, we will exploit dynamic access protocols such as DHCP [16] (Dynamic Host Configuration Protocol) and PPPOE [17] (Point-to-Point Protocol over Ethernet) since they are the most popular protocols used for IPTV authentication.

We propose to enable the DHCP option 82 [18] or PPPOE option 82 [19] (depending on the access protocol DHCP or PPPOE) on the AN. This way, the AN information will be sent to the access server through the DHCP discovery or PPPOE Active Discovery Initiation (PADI) messages. Once the access server gets this information, it will forward it (with STB IP address) to the FCC server to build the FCC database (Figure 7).

3.1. Possible Scenarios. During each channel change, five scenarios could happen.

Scenario 1 (STB keeps joining the same channel during the FCC period). Figure 8 shows the workflow and main steps during this scenario. When the user wants to switch the channel to a new one, the STB1 sends one FCC request to the FCCC server; the FCCC server will first update the information related to STB1 in the FCC database including the time of the channel change, the STB IP address, and the ID of the new channel.

The time at which the channel has been changed will be added to that database in order to facilitate the verification of the buffer fulfillment and to decide whether this STB can act as an FCC for other STBs or not.

When the FCCC server finds out that one STB is already connected to the same AN and is joining the new channel with a full buffer, the FCCC server will request this STB (STB2) to send the stream to STB1.

At some point, the STB2 instructs the STB1 to join the new channel. After joining the new channel and receiving the first multicast packet, the STB1 informs the STB2 to stop the unicast stream.

Scenario 2 (STB changes the channel during the FCC period). If the STB changes the channel during the FCC period, the STB (receiver) will request the FCCC to resume the stream delivery by reporting the last RTP sequence number to the FCCC [20].

Scenario 3 (STB switched off during the FCC period). If the STB is switched off during the FCC period, the STB (receiver) will request the FCCC to resume the stream delivery by reporting the last RTP sequence number to the FCCC.

Scenario 4 (in case there is some packet loss during the delivery of the stream). In case there is some packet loss during the stream delivery, the STB (receiver) can demand the missing RTP packet from the FCCC server by reporting the sequence number of this packet.

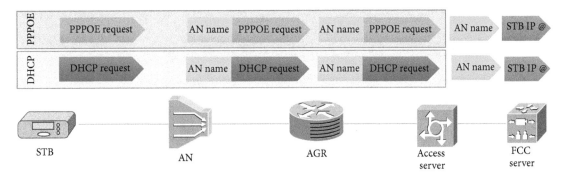

FIGURE 7: Collecting the STB location information.

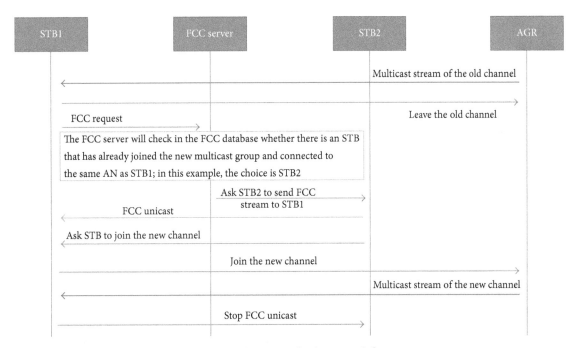

FIGURE 8: The proposed solution work flow.

Scenario 5 (there is no STB that can satisfy the requirement). If the FCCC server does not find any STB fulfilling the requirements of the FCC server, it will deliver the unicast stream by itself as described previously in the section titled FCC Unicast-Based.

The datagram in Figure 9 resumes the main steps of the new solution.

3.2. FCCC Algorithm. The novelty in this contribution is that the new FCC controller server (the FCCC) has two functions: the first one is the normal FCC server and the second function is the FCC control server, which will control and select the suitable STB to act as a local FCC server.

The FCCC builds the FCC database based on the information received from the access server and channel change requests. The database is composed of multiple databases; each Access Node has its own database in the FCCC, and we

consider the FCCC database as a matrix (Figure 10) where the number of columns is the number of online STBs and the number of rows is the buffer time divided by the time sampling interval.

Once the FCCC server receives one FCC request, it will update the entry of the STB in the database. To save memory, the FCC server will record only the information about some few seconds. For example, in Figure 10, the STB4 is changing from channel 3 to channel 1, and after receiving the channel change request from the STB, the FCCC server will update row number 4 corresponding to the STB4 at time t from channel 3 to channel 1.

The FCCC server will then analyze all matrix rows to check whether one STB has a full buffer for channel 1. After verification, the result will be STB2 since this STB is receiving the traffic of this channel over a long period higher than buffer duration, which means STB2 has a full buffer and therefore can be used as an FCC server.

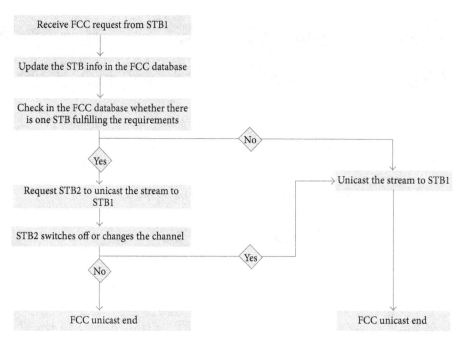

FIGURE 9: The proposed FCC solution main steps.

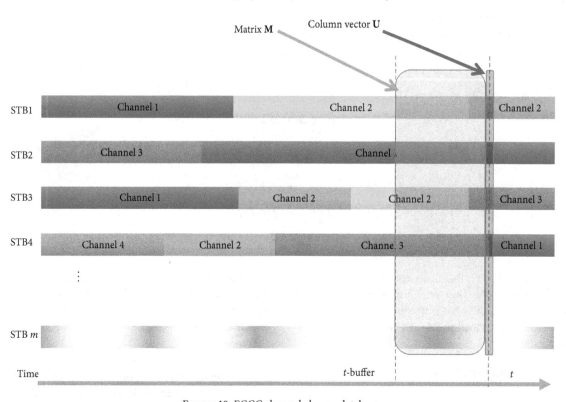

FIGURE 10: FCCC channel change database.

To avoid the congestion of uplink traffic and load problems, the FCCC will not select the STB more than once during the FCC period. After each FCC selection, the FCCC will start a countdown timer (the timer duration is equal to the FCC duration) and bind it to the selected STB; this way, the FCCC will not select this STB because the timer has not yet expired; once the timer expires, the STB can be selected again as an FCC server.

Generally, the FCCC server calculates the STB ID, which can act as an FCC server for the user k at the instant t based on the following function:

$$\max \left\{ \left[I_n - \left((C + I_n)^{-1} \right)^{\alpha} \right] \times \left[\left((S - I_n)^{-1} \right)^2 + I_n \right]^{\alpha} \times \left[\left((P - I_n)^{-1} \right)^2 + I_n \right]^{\alpha} \times V \right\}, \tag{2}$$

where

(i) $\mathbf{I}_n$ is a unit matrix;

(ii) $\mathbf{C}$ is a square matrix, of size m, with elements of vector $\mathbf{U}$ on the main diagonal and zero elsewhere:

$$\mathbf{C} = \begin{pmatrix} \mathbf{U}(1) & \cdots & 0 \\ \vdots & \ddots & \vdots \\ 0 & \cdots & \mathbf{U}(m) \end{pmatrix}; \qquad (3)$$

(iii) $\mathbf{U}$ is a column vector of size m, which contains the information about each STB at the instant t; this vector will be used to exclude the STB, which is switched off at the instant t; even its buffer is full as per the FCCC database;

(iv) α is an infinity integer, to neglect the values lower than one by applying the factor;

(v) $\mathbf{S}$ is a square matrix, of size m, which consists of diagonal values, each equal to the sum of rows, elements of matrix $\mathbf{M}$, and zero elsewhere:

$$\mathbf{S} = \frac{1}{n * \mathbf{U}(k)} \times \begin{pmatrix} \sum_{i=1}^{n} \mathbf{M}(1,i) & \cdots & 0 \\ \vdots & \ddots & \vdots \\ 0 & \cdots & \sum_{i=1}^{n} \mathbf{M}(m,i) \end{pmatrix}; \quad (4)$$

(vi) $\mathbf{P}$ is a square matrix, of size m, which consists of diagonal values each equal to the multiplication of rows, elements of matrix $\mathbf{M}$, and zero elsewhere:

$$\mathbf{P} = \frac{1}{\mathbf{U}(k)^n} \times \begin{pmatrix} \prod_{i=1}^{n} \mathbf{M}(1,i) & \cdots & 0 \\ \vdots & \ddots & \vdots \\ 0 & \cdots & \prod_{i=1}^{n} \mathbf{M}(m,i) \end{pmatrix}; \quad (5)$$

(vii) $\mathbf{M}$ is the channel change matrix, which contains the latest channel changes information for each user; it is composed of n column and m rows;

(viii) n = Buffer Duration/Δt;

(ix) Δt is the sampling interval, the distance between points at which information is taken;

(x) buffer duration is the duration of the FCC buffer;

(xi) m is the number of online STBs;

(xii) $\mathbf{V}$ is a column vector of size m, with numbers increasing by increments of 1.

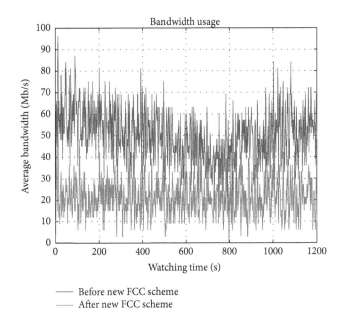

FIGURE 11: FCC bandwidth usage before and after using the new FCC scheme.

Note

(i) In the main function, the matrices $\mathbf{P}$, $\mathbf{S}$, and $\mathbf{C}$ have been modified in order to eliminate the non-one elements by applying the functions $[((x-1)^{-1})^2 + 1]^{\alpha}$ and $[1 - ((1+x)^{-1})^{\alpha}]$.

(ii) If the result of the function above is zero, this means no STB with the described requirements; in this case, the FCCC should take charge of the delivery of the unicast stream to the STB k.

4. Performance Evaluation

To confirm the performance and efficiency of the proposed scheme, we created a simulation of the unicast bandwidth between AN and AGR using MATLAB.

We have considered in this example (Figure 11) that we have 120 users that can change up to 60 SD channels (the speed of each channel is 3 Mb/s) in total, frequently for a period of 1200 seconds. The FCC buffer has a capacity of 3 seconds.

The new solution reduced the unicast bandwidth sent by the FCCC to the STBs during the channels change; local FCC servers (STBs) replace the central FCCC server to forward the unicast traffic needed during the channel change.

Figure 12 shows the bandwidth behavior in terms of the number of channels; the number of users is fixed at 60 users and they can perform up to 40 channel changes during a period of 400 seconds. We remark in this example that when the number of channels is smaller to the users number, the efficiency of our scheme is very important because the probability of finding more users watching the same channel is high. This means that when a user switches to a new channel, we have a higher chance of finding another user

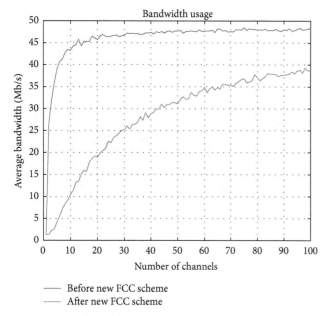

FIGURE 12: Bandwidth behavior in terms of the number of channels.

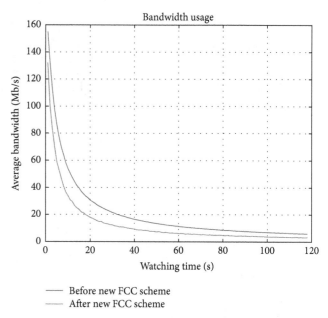

FIGURE 14: Bandwidth behavior in terms of watching time.

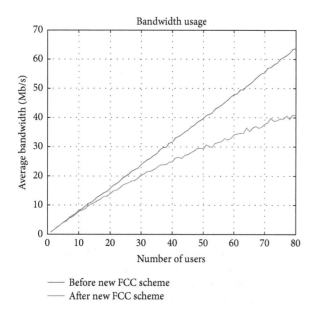

FIGURE 13: Bandwidth behavior in terms of the number of users.

watching the same channel, which can support sending the unicast stream instead of the central FCC server.

Increasing the number of channels means that users have more choices during channel surfing, so when a user switches to a new channel, it is harder to find more people watching the same channel.

In the old scheme, the unicast bandwidth consumed by all users during channels change is proportional to the number of users, but in the new scheme this bandwidth decreases once the number of users becomes higher than the number of channels. This means that we have good optimization once we have more users watching the same channel as illustrated in Figure 13.

Figure 14 shows the bandwidth behavior in terms of watching duration; the old and new schemes behave in a similar way when the watching duration is long, but when the users switch the channels frequently, the new scheme becomes more optimal regarding saving bandwidth.

In summary, the simulation of the proposed scheme shows very good management of the bandwidth of the AN uplink port especially when there are a significantly high number of channel change requests and the number of users is higher than the number of channels available.

5. Conclusion and Future Work

We presented in this paper a new solution to efficiently manage bandwidth resources of unicast traffic on IP networks during IPTV channel change by implementing the unicast peer-assisted solution on the user STB. This means that if there is one STB already joining one channel and this channel is requested by another STB, which is connected to the same Access Node, this STB can deliver the FCC unicast traffic to its neighbor instead of the central FCC server (FCCC). In cases where there is no STB joining this channel, the FCCC will deliver the unicast traffic to STB by itself as per the old FCC unicast-based method.

The full process is controlled by the central FCC server based on the information collected from channel change requests received from the STBs and STBs' locations received from the access server.

Our solution does not need any additional resource or new hardware integration in the other network elements; it requires only some software upgrade on both the FCC server and the user STB. For future development, we will expand this new solution to optimize the unicast bandwidth of the PLTV (Pause Live TV) by taking benefit from the communication between the user STBs.

References

[1] S. Shoaf and M. Bernstein, "Introduction to IGMP for IPTV Networks," 2006.

[2] F. M. V. Ramos, "Mitigating IPTV zapping delay," *IEEE Communications Magazine*, vol. 51, no. 8, pp. 128–133, 2013.

[3] V. Joseph and S. Mulugu, Deploying next generation multicast-enabled applications: label switched multicast for MPLS VPNs, VPLS, and wholesale Ethernet. Morgan Kaufmann, 2011.

[4] X. Tian, Y. Cheng, and X. Shen, "Fast channel zapping with destination-oriented multicast for IP video delivery," *IEEE Transactions on Parallel and Distributed Systems*, vol. 24, no. 2, pp. 327–341, 2013.

[5] C. Cho, I. Han, Y. Jun, and H. Lee, "Improvement of channel zapping time in IPTV services using the adjacent groups join-leave method," in *Proceedings of the 6th International Conference on Advanced Communication Technology: Broadband Convergence Network Infrastructure*, pp. 971–975, kor, February 2004.

[6] J. O. Farmer and S. Thomas, "Minimizing Channel Change Time for Ip Video," 2006.

[7] C. Y. Lee, C. K. Hong, and K. Y. Lee, "Reducing channel zapping time in IPTV based on user's channel selection behaviors," *IEEE Transactions on Broadcasting*, vol. 56, no. 3, pp. 321–330, 2010.

[8] J. M. Boyce and A. M. Tourapis, "Method and Apparatus Enabling Fast Channel Change for Dsl System," WO/2005/112465, 2005".

[9] J. Boyce and A. Tourapis, "Fast efficient channel change [set-top box applications]," in *Proceedings of the 2005 Digest of Technical Papers. International Conference on Consumer Electronics, 2005. ICCE.*, pp. 1-2, Las Vegas, NV, USA, January 2005.

[10] N. Degrande, K. Laevens, D. De Vleeschauwer, A.-L. Bell, and R. Sharpe, "Increasing the User Perceived Quality for IPTV Services," *IEEE Communications Magazine*, vol. 46, no. 2, pp. 94–100, 2008.

[11] H. A. Goosen and E. J. Rak, Video streaming system including a fast channel change mechanism, 2011.

[12] N. Cohen, "Fast channel switching for digital TV," US 2006/0143669 A1, 2006.

[13] R. Haimi-Cohen and J. P. Hearn, "Fast channel change handling of late multicast join," US 8,161,515 B2, 2012.

[14] I. T. U. Recommendation, G. 993.2 (02/2006) Very high speed Digital subscriber lines," Telecommun. Stand. Sect. ITU.

[15] G. ITU, 984.1: Gigabit-capable Passive Optical Networks (GPON): General characteristics , ITU-T, March, 2008.

[16] R. Droms, "Dynamic Host Configuration Protocol," RFC Editor RFC2131, 1997.

[17] L. Mamakos, K. Lidl, J. Evarts, D. Carrel, D. Simone, and R. Wheeler, "A Method for Transmitting PPP Over Ethernet (PPPoE)," RFC Editor RFC2516, 1999.

[18] M. Patrick, "DHCP Relay Agent Information Option," RFC Editor RFC3046, 2001.

[19] V. Mammoliti, G. Zorn, P. Arberg, and R. Rennison, "DSL Forum Vendor-Specific RADIUS Attributes," RFC Editor RFC4679, 2006.

[20] B. Ver, A. Begen, T. Van, and Z. Vax, "Unicast-Based Rapid Acquisition of Multicast RTP Sessions," RFC Editor RFC6285, 2011.

17

A Prediction Method of Mobile User Preference based on the Influence between Users

Yancui Shi ⓘ, Jianhua Cao ⓘ, Congcong Xiong, and Xiankun Zhang

Institute of Computer Science and Information Engineering, Tianjin University of Science & Technology, Tianjin, China

Correspondence should be addressed to Yancui Shi; syc@tust.edu.cn

Academic Editor: Yifeng He

User preference will be impacted by other users. To accurately predict mobile user preference, the influence between users is introduced into the prediction model of user preference. First, the mobile social network is constructed according to the interaction behavior of the mobile user, and the influence of the user is calculated according to the topology of the constructed mobile social network and mobile user behavior. Second, the influence between users is calculated according to the user's influence, the interaction behavior between users, and the similarity of user preferences. When calculating the influence based on the interaction behavior, the context information is considered; the context information and the order of user preferences are considered when calculating the influence based on the similarity of user preferences. The improved collaborative filtering method is then employed to predict mobile user preferences based on the obtained influence between users. Finally, the experiment is executed on the real data set and the integrated data set, and the results show that the proposed method can obtain more accurate mobile user preferences than those of existing methods.

1. Introduction

The popularity of the mobile terminal (e.g., smart phone, tablet) and the improvement of the wireless network (e.g., 3G, 4G, 5G) means mobile users can access information or services anytime and anywhere [1, 2]. Hence, the mobile user wants to obtain personalized information timely and accurately from the "information ocean". In the mobile network, due to the extensive growth of mobile network services, it is time-consuming and frustrating for mobile users to find the information or services that meet their needs. As a filtering tool of information, the personalized recommender system can solve the above problem well; this system has also been applied in e-commerce (e.g., Amazon, eBay, Netflix), information retrieval (e.g., Google, Baidu), e-tourism, and Internet advertising [3]. The key of the personalized recommender system is how to accurately predict the user preference.

In the recommender system, the common prediction method of the user's preference is collaborative filtering (CF), which predicts the target user's preference according to the preferences of the nearest neighbors who have similar preferences to those of the target user. However, user preference is not only impacted by the nearest neighbors but by family, friends, colleagues, and other users. Hence, knowing how to find the most influential users to the target user is vital. Currently, the research about the influence measurement methods mainly focuses on the micro-blog application [4–6], while the research about the mobile social network is relatively small.

The mobile network has unique characteristics. The mobile terminal not only provides the tool for users to telecommute and access information but provides the ability to access the contextual information due to the improvement of the hardware. For example, not only can it obtain the explicit contextual information directly, such as time, location, and weather, but it can obtain the implicit contextual information using statistical analysis and reasoning, such as through user interest and social relations [7]. According to the mobile user behavior recorded by the mobile terminal, it can obtain more realistic social relationships and more accurate user influence, thus improving the accuracy of the predicted mobile user preference.

To summarize, the contributions of the paper are as follows: (1) A new calculation method of the influence of the users is proposed, which considers the topology of the mobile social network and the behavior that the mobile user has when using mobile network services. The mobile social network is constructed by analyzing the communication behavior between users. (2) A new calculation method of the influence between users is proposed, which considers the influence of users, the similarity of mobile user preferences, and the interaction behavior between users under context. When calculating the similarity of mobile user preferences, the context information and the order of user preferences are considered. (3) An improved prediction method of mobile user preference is proposed, which considers the obtained influence between users.

2. Related Work

In the mobile network, users can access information or services anytime and anywhere by smart phone, such as WeChat, QQ, micro-blog, Youku, and meituan.com. Take meituan.com, for example; there are a massive number of items, and knowing how to accurately find the items that the user is interested in is very important.

In the recommender system, the common prediction method of the user's preference is CF. To improve the accuracy of the predicted user preferences using CF, the researchers employ the matrix factorization [8], introduce the user's trust [9], or rely on context information [10]. Although the matrix factorization can solve the sparsity problem, it cannot find the accurate nearest neighbors due to not considering the social information of the users. The methods that introduce context information can more exactly locate user preferences, but they further aggravate the sparsity problem. Hence, the accuracy of the whole user preference is lower.

In addition, the user's preference is also impacted by family, friends, classmates, or followed celebrities. For example, the choices of users will be impacted by family or friends who use meituan.com, while the user will be impacted by followed celebrities on Youku. Hence, it is feasible to introduce the influence of users on the prediction method of user preferences. To find the accurate nearest neighbors, some researchers introduced the user's trust in the prediction model [11, 12]. However, in the above methods, the authors only considered the interaction of voice calls and SMSs (short message or messaging service), so the obtained relationship is not all encompassing and accurate. With reference to the method, in the paper, the influence between users is considered in the prediction model of mobile user preferences.

Currently, the measurement methods of the user influence are divided into three categories: the method based on network topology, the method based on user behavior, and the method based on interaction behavior [13, 14]. The method based on network topology measures the influence according to the nodes (the centrality, closeness centrality, etc.) or the edges (edge betweenness, common neighbors, etc.) [15, 16]. Muruganatham et al. considered that every calculation method of centrality had its advantage and disadvantage, so a variety of calculation methods of centrality were employed to measure user influence [17]. However,

the method did not evaluate the obtained influence, and it only gave the user's rank according to the influence obtained by different methods. Brown et al. employed the improved k-shell decomposition method to measure the influence of a Twitter user by analyzing the network topology [4]. According to information from the user's Twitter account, Cossu used the traditional user characteristics and the unique characteristics of the Twitter user to measure the user's influence [5]. These characteristics included the local topology, the whole topology, and other features associated with the network structure. The method employed an F-score and mean average precision in the evaluation. Whether the methods were based on nodes or on edges, they did not consider the information of the user behavior and simply calculated the influence according to the network topology, so the accuracy of the obtained user influence was not ideal.

To improve the accuracy of the obtained user influence, some researchers measured the user influence by analyzing the user behaviors, which included the login behavior and the information generated by users (e.g., comments, forwarding) [18]. For example, by analyzing the user's behavior related to economics, Bakshy et al. calculated user influence in social advertising according to the social information [19]. Mao et al. considered the network topology and user behavior to measure the influence of the micro-blog user accurately and employed the Spearman rank correlation coefficient as the evaluation [20]. Similarly, Verenich et al. measured user influence according to the number of users that used some product latter than the target user and employed the mean decrease accuracy and the area under the cumulative gains score as the evaluation [21]. Rabiger et al. extracted some user features (community structure, activity, the quality of releasing information, the user centrality) and employed the supervised method to learn about the user's influence [6]. Tommasel et al. proposed a new formula to measure the user's influence according to the network topology and user behavior information [22]. However, the calculation methods based on network topology and based on user behavior both only consider the influence that user has in the social network without considering the specific influence between users.

The calculation method of the influence based on the interaction information considers the interaction behavior between users, such as forwarding and commenting. Anger et al. considered the content of communication between users and mutual information in the constructed model of influence [23]. Cataldi et al. proposed a calculation method of user influence based on domain by analyzing the mutual information between users [24]. Guo et al. employed the maximum likelihood estimation to calculate the influence between users by analyzing the history logs of user behavior [25]. Liu et al. proposed the time-based influence graph (TIG) model and algorithm based on the network topology and time dimension according to the characteristics of the mobile data [1]. The algorithm considered the dynamics of the mobile data, the user behavior, and user mutual behavior incomplete, without considering the impact of the context and the similarity of the user's preferences. In the algorithm, accuracy is employed to measure the obtained influence.

3. The Proposed Method

In the paper, the used variables are defined as follows: U represents the set of mobile users; $N_U = |U|$ represents the number of mobile users, $u_i \in U$ and $i = 1,2,...N_U$; W represents the set of interaction ways that the mobile user used; $N_W = |W|$ represents the number of interaction ways, $w_l \in W$ and $l = 1,2,...N_W$; S represents the set of the mobile network services; $N_S = |S|$ represents the types of mobile network services, $s_k \in S$ and $k = 1,2,...N_S$; C represents the set of the context instances; $N_C = |C|$ represents the number of the context instances, $C_r \in C$ and $r = 1,2,...N_C$; and P_{u_i,s_k,C_r} represents the preference of u_i toward s_k under C_r, which is set in the integer in [0, 5]. Currently, the value of influence is set in the interval [0, 1] in the most research; therefore, the setting is adopted in the paper.

Definition 1 (the influence of the user, I_{u_i}). The u_i generates influence toward the other users due to his behavior in the social network. The influence of the user is used to measure influence macroscopically.

Definition 2 (the influence between users, I_{u_i,u_j}). The u_i generates influence toward the u_j due to his behavior, the interaction behavior with u_j, the common preference with u_j, and the other factors, $u_j \in U$, $j \neq i$. The influence between users is used to measure influence microscopically.

In addition, an important problem that needs to be solved is how to integrate the obtained multiple kinds of influence. The method in [22] calculated the influence based on network topology and user behavior, respectively, and set the same weight value when integrating the influence. The method in [23] extracted many user features, calculated the influence of each feature, and set the same weight value for each obtained influence. In the paper, multiple factors are considered. Considering the importance of each factor toward influence is different; hence, the weight of each factor is set to the optimal value, according to experimental results.

3.1. The Influence of the User. The steps of calculating the influence of the user are as follows.

(1) The Quantification of Interaction Behavior between Users. The interaction between users is not only achieved by the basic means of communication (voice, SMS, etc.) but it is achieved by the instant message software installed in the mobile terminal (WeChat, QQ, etc.). The different interaction methods have different measurements. For example, the SMS uses the number of messages for measurement, while the voice call uses the duration for measurement. In addition, the times of interaction also impact the relationships between users. Suppose the duration for which u_1 communicates with u_2 is 100 minutes and the time of communication is 1, while the duration for which u_1 communicates with u_3 is also 100 minutes and the time of communication is 10. Obviously, the relationship between u_1 and u_3 is better than that between u_1 and u_2. Hence, in the paper, the interaction volume employs

the duration (or the number of messages) and the times for measurement.

The voice call is continuous, so the times of communication are computed easily. To avoid introducing harassing phone, only when the communication duration is longer than 10 seconds or the times of communication are more than one, the communication is regarded as effective. When using SMS or instant message software, a communication is not a message, but the whole process of interacting, which consists of many messages. Take the SMS, for example; in a communication, the two parties usually use multiple messages to interact. In the paper, we adopted the following rules to determine a communication using SMS or instant message software: (1) all messages cannot come from a party, and (2) the interval between messages is less than 5 minutes. The quantification formula of the interaction behavior between users is as follows:

$$V_{u_i,u_j} = \sum_{w_l \in W} \left(a_1 * \frac{L_{u_i,u_j,w_l}}{\overline{L_{w_l}}} + a_2 * \frac{T_{u_i,u_j,w_l}}{\overline{T_{w_l}}} \right) \quad (1)$$

where V_{u_i,u_j} represents the quantification value of the interaction behavior between u_i and u_j, $u_i, u_j \in U$, $j \neq i$; L_{u_i,u_j,w_l} represents the duration for which u_i interacts with u_j using w_l; $\overline{L_{w_l}}$ represents the means of the duration for which all users interact using w_l; T_{u_i,u_j,w_l} represents the times at which u_i interacts with u_j using w_l; $\overline{T_{w_l}}$ represents the means of the times at which all users interact using w_l; and a_1 and a_2 represent the weight of the duration and times of the interaction, respectively, and $a_1 + a_2 = 1$. In addition, the formula shows that the quantification value of interaction behavior is symmetrical; that is, $V_{u_i,u_j} = V_{u_j,u_i}$.

(2) The Construction of the Mobile Social Network. In the paper, the undirected graph $G(V,E)$ is employed to represent the mobile social network; V represents the set of the nodes in the social network, which is the set of mobile users; and E represents the set of edges in the social network. When $V_{u_i,u_j} > V_{\text{threshold}}$, $e(u_i,u_j) = 1$, it represents the existing social relationship between u_i and u_j, or else $e(u_i,u_j) = 0$ represents the fact that there is no social relationship between u_i and u_j. Here, $e(u_i,u_j) \in E$, and $V_{\text{threshold}}$ represents the threshold used to judge whether there is social relationship between users.

(3) The Calculation of the Influence of the User. When calculating the influence of the user, the network topology and user behavior are considered. The centrality is employed to reflect the impact of the network topology; the mean amount of the interaction between the target user and other users and the usage of the mobile network services (video, game, music, news, etc.) by the target user are employed to reflect the impact of user behavior.

The centrality measures the user's influence on the social network according to the number of the target users' neighbors. The more the neighbors are, the greater the influence is [14]. In Internet, a social network consists of the users in the virtual world. While in the mobile network, a social network is gradually transitioning to that which consists of the users in the physical world, and the trust between users also increases. On a mobile social network, the user generally interacts with acquaintances, such as family, friends, colleagues, and classmates, by voice or SMS. However, the contacts of WeChat or QQ could be acquaintances or could be strangers. When employing the centrality to measure the influence of the user, there will be some deviation regarding the obtained influence when only considering the number of the target user's neighbors. Suppose in the mobile social network that the numbers of neighbors of u_1 and u_2 are both 100 and that 98 neighbors of u_1 are acquaintances, while 2 neighbors of u_2 are acquaintances. Obviously, when only considering the number of neighbors, the influence of u_1 is equal to that of u_2. Actually, however, the influence of u_1 is greater than that of u_2.

The current instant messaging software can synchronize with the telephone book. Therefore, it can confirm whether the contact is an acquaintance through judging whether the contact is in the telephone book. If the contact is in the telephone book, it is regarded as an acquaintance; otherwise, it is regarded as a stranger. The formula of the centrality is as follows [13]:

$$C_{u_i} = \frac{\sum_{u_j \in U_i} n_{u_j}}{N_U - 1} \qquad (2)$$

where $u_i \in U$, U_i represents the set of the u_i's neighbors; the formula that is used to calculate n_{u_j} is as follows:

$$n_{u_j} = \begin{cases} 1 & u_j \in U'_i \\ \theta & u_j \notin U'_i \end{cases} \qquad (3)$$

where U'_i represents the set of contacts that u_i's telephone book includes; the value of θ is set to (0,1).

The greater the amount of interaction between the target user and the other users, the larger the implied contribution that the target user provides and, thus, the greater the user's influence. In the paper, the mean amount of the interaction between users is employed to measure the influence of the user; the formula is as follows:

$$\overline{V}_{u_i} = \frac{\sum_{u_j \in U_i} n_{u_j} * V_{u_i,u_j}}{N_i} \qquad (4)$$

where $u_i \in U$ and $N_i = |U_i|$ represents the number of u_i's neighbors.

The more the types of the mobile services are used and the greater the amount of the usage is, the greater the influence of the user in mobile social network is. The formula that is used to calculate the usage of the mobile network services is as follows:

$$\overline{V}_{u_i,S}$$

$$= \frac{N_{S_{u_i}}}{N_S} \qquad (5)$$

$$* \sum_{s_k \in S_{u_i}} \left(a_1 * \frac{L_{u_i,s_k}}{\sum_{u_j \in U} L_{u_j,s_k}} + a_2 * \frac{T_{u_i,s_k}}{\sum_{u_j \in U} T_{u_j,s_k}} \right)$$

where $u_i \in U$ and S_{u_i} represents the set of the mobile network services used by u_i; $N_{S_{u_i}} = |S_{u_i}|$ represents the types of the mobile network services used by u_i; L_{u_i,s_k} represents the duration that u_i used s_k; and T_{u_i,s_k} represents the times at which u_i used s_k.

The formula that is employed to calculate the influence of the user is as follows:

$$I_{u_i} = \lambda_1 * C_{u_i} * \overline{V}_{u_i} + \lambda_2 * \overline{V}_{u_i,S} \qquad (6)$$

where $u_i \in U$, λ_1 and λ_2 represent the weights of the different influences, respectively, and $\lambda_1 + \lambda_2 = 1$.

3.2. The Influence between Users. When calculating the influence between users, consider not only the interaction behavior, but also the similarity of the user's preferences and the influence of the user. The steps that calculate the influence between users are as follows.

(1) The Influence between Users Is Based on Interaction Behavior. The influence of the user is depicted macroscopically, and it only considers the mobile users that the target user interacts with, while the influence between users analyzes the influence between two mobile users microscopically and concretely. In addition, the interaction behaviors under the different contexts have different impacts on the influence between users. For example, the user usually interacts with the other user for work during a workday, while he will interact with family or friends on the weekend [26]. Therefore, it is necessary to distinguish the influences under different contexts. The quantification formula of the interaction behavior under various contexts is as follows:

$$V'_{u_i,u_j,C_r} = n_{u_j} * \sum_{w_l \in W} \left(a_1 * \frac{L_{u_i,u_j,w_l,C_r}}{\sum_{u_q \in U_j} L_{u_q,u_j,w_l,C_r}} + a_2 \right.$$
$$\left. * \frac{T_{u_i,u_j,w_l,C_r}}{\sum_{u_q \in U_j} T_{u_q,u_j,w_l,C_r}} \right) \qquad (7)$$

where $u_i, u_j \in U$, $j \neq i$, $C_r \in C$; V'_{u_i,u_j,C_r} represents the quantification value of interaction behavior between u_i and u_j under C_r; L_{u_i,u_j,w_l,C_r} represents the duration for which u_i interacts with u_j under C_r using w_l; and T_{u_i,u_j,w_l,C_r} represents the times at which u_i interacts with u_j under C_r using w_l.

The calculation formula of the influence between users based on interaction behaviors is as follows:

$$I'_{u_i,u_j} = \sum_{C_r \in C} \beta_r * V'_{u_i,u_j,C_r} \qquad (8)$$

where $u_i, u_j \in U$, $j \neq i$; β_r represents the weight value of the C_r.

(2) Learn the Mobile User Preference. In the mobile network, the explicit user preferences are few, so the proposed method needs to learn the user preferences by analyzing the mobile user's behavior in relation to the context. The goal is to map the user's usage of mobile services relying on integers of 1 to

5, and the distribution of obtained preferences is consistent with Pareto's law.

The user's usage of the mobile network services under the context is as follows:

$$V_{u_i,s_k,C_r} = a_1 * \frac{L_{u_i,s_k,C_r}}{\sum_{s_k \in S} L_{u_i,s_k,C_r}} + a_2 * \frac{T_{u_i,s_k,C_r}}{\sum_{s_k \in S} T_{u_i,s_k,C_r}} \quad (9)$$

where $u_i \in U, s_k \in S, C_r \in C$; L_{u_i,s_k,C_r} represents the duration for which u_i used s_k under C_r; and T_{u_i,s_k,C_r} represents the times at which u_i used s_k under C_r.

The value of the user's preferences will increase when the user's usage of the mobile network services increases. When the value of the usage is larger than some value, the growth of the user's preferences slows down and gradually tends toward a constant value, which is in line with the characteristics of the logarithmic function with a base bigger than 1. Hence, the logarithmic function is employed to calculate the user's preferences. The calculation formula of the user's preferences is as follows:

$$P'_{u_i,s_k,C_r} = \log_2 \left(b + V_{u_i,s_k,C_r} \right) \quad (10a)$$

$$P_{u_i,s_k,C_r} = round \left(\frac{P'_{u_i,s_k,C_r} - P'\min}{P'\max - P'\min} * 5 \right) \quad (10b)$$

where $u_i \in U, s_k \in S, C_r \in C$; $round()$ represents the rounding function; $P'\min$ and $P'\max$ represent the minimum and maximum of the user's preferences obtained by the formula (10a); and b is the parameter, and $b \geq 1$. Additionally, b is set according to the Pareto's law.

(3) The Influence between Users Is Based on the Similarity of the User's Preferences. The Pearson correlation coefficient is employed to calculate the similarity of the user's preferences. When calculating the similarity, it not only considers the impact of the context but also considers the order in which the user's preferences occurred. If u_1 used the mobile network services and always lagged behind u_2, then u_1 is impacted by u_2, but u_2 is not affected by u_1. Hence, it is necessary to consider the order in which the user's preferences occurred when calculating the influence between users based on the similarity of the user's preferences. The calculation formula of the similarity is as follows:

$$\text{sim}_{u_i,u_j}$$
$$= \frac{\sum_{C_r \in C} \beta_r * \sum_{s_m \in S_{u_i,u_j,C_r}} P'_{u_i,s_m,C_r} * P'_{u_j,s_m,C_r}}{\sqrt{\sum_{C_r \in C} \beta_r * \left(\sum_{s_m \in S_{u_i,u_j,C_r}} P'^2_{u_i,s_m,C_r} * \sum_{s_m \in S_{u_i,u_j,C_r}} P'^2_{u_j,s_m,C_r} \right)}} \quad (11)$$

where $u_i, u_j \in U, j \neq i$; S_{u_i,u_j,C_r} represents the set of the mobile network services that u_i used before u_j under C_r; and P'_{u_i,s_m,C_r} is as follows:

$$P'_{u_i,s_m,C_r} = P_{u_i,s_m,C_r} - \overline{P_{u_i,C_r}} \quad (12)$$

where $\overline{P_{u_i,C_r}}$ represents the mean of the user's preferences under C_r; the formula is as follows:

$$\overline{P_{u_i,C_r}} = \frac{\sum_{s_m \in S_{u_i,u_j,C_r}} \beta_r * P_{u_i,s_m,C_r}}{\left| S_{u_i,u_j,C_r} \right|}. \quad (13)$$

The formula that is used to calculate the influence between users based on the similarity of the user's preferences is as follows:

$$I''_{u_i,u_j} = \text{sim}_{u_i,u_j} * \frac{\left| S_{u_i,u_j,C_r} \right|}{\left| S_{u_i} \right|}. \quad (14)$$

According to the definition of the similarity, it shows that the similarity is asymmetrical; that is, $\text{sim}_{u_i,u_j} \neq \text{sim}_{u_j,u_i}$.

According to the foregoing analysis, the calculation formula of the influence between users is as follows:

$$I_{u_i,u_j} = \lambda_3 * I_{u_i} + \lambda_4 * I'_{u_i,u_j} + \lambda_5 * I''_{u_i,u_j} \quad (15)$$

where $u_i, u_j \in U, j \neq i$; λ_i represents the weight of different influences, and $\lambda_3 + \lambda_4 + \lambda_5 = 1$.

3.3. The Prediction of Mobile User Preference. In this section, the improved CF is employed to predict mobile user preference. The procedure is as follows:

(1) Select the top-K most influential users for the target user according to the obtained influence between users.

(2) Mobile user preference is predicted according to the preferences of selected K users. The formula for predicting mobile user preferences is as follows:

$$\hat{P}_{u_i,s_q,C_r} = round \left(\overline{P_{u_i,C_r}} + \frac{\sum_{u_j \in U_{i,K}} I_{u_j,u_i} * \left(P_{u_j,s_q,C_r} - \overline{P_{u_j,C_r}} \right)}{\sum_{u_j \in U_{i,K}} I_{u_j,u_i}} \right) \quad (16)$$

where $u_i \in U, C_r \in C$; $s_q \in S_{i,C_r}$, S_{i,C_r} represents the set of mobile network services that u_i did not use under the context C_r but his top-K most influential users had used; and $U_{i,K}$ represents the set of the top-K most influential users of u_i.

4. Experimental Results and Analysis

This section introduces the used data set, experimental steps, experimental results, and the analysis.

4.1. The Data Set. The simulation experiment is executed in two data sets: (1) the reality mining of mobile users collected by the MIT Media Lab (RM data set), which includes the interaction behavior and the corresponding context (location, time, etc.) of the 94 smart phone mobile users from September 2004 to June 2005 [27]; (2) the data set integrated using the RM data set and the data set of MovieLens (RMM data set), which includes 6,040 mobile users, according to specific rules [12].

TABLE 1: The Division of Time (date).

date	Monday~Friday	Saturday and Sunday
context	workday	weekend

TABLE 2: The Division of Time (time).

Time	00:00~5:59	6:00~11:59	12:00~12:59	13:00~17:59	18:00~23:59
context	night	morning	noon	afternoon	evening

TABLE 3: The rules for determining the location context.

	night	morning	noon	afternoon	evening
workday	at home	workplace	workplace, at home or elsewhere	workplace	workplace, at home or elsewhere
weekend	at home	at home or elsewhere	at home or elsewhere	at home or elsewhere	at home or elsewhere

The RM data set includes the original context information, such as the date, time, base station information, and around-phone information obtained by Bluetooth. Hence, before performing the experiment, the location context (at home, workplace, elsewhere) is obtained using statistical analysis and reasoning according to the rules given in Tables 1, 2, and 3. The main basis of setting the rules is as follows: users usually rest at home at night (00:00~5:59); during the workday, the user usually will work at the workplace, while at noon, the user may go to the workplace, home, or elsewhere to eat or be entertained; on the weekend, the user may be at home or elsewhere for rest or entertainment.

Since the proposed algorithm in the paper considers the order in which user preferences occurred, the leave-one-out method is employed to select the training and test sets. In the paper, the data of the first 5 months is selected as the training data set, and the data of the sixth month is selected as the test data set.

4.2. Evaluation Method. The F-score is employed to evaluate the accuracy of the obtained social relationships or mobile user preferences; the formula is as follows [5, 28]:

$$F = \frac{2 * Q * R}{Q + R} \quad (17)$$

where Q represents the precision and R represents the recall, and their calculation formulas are as follows:

$$Q = \frac{N_{tr}}{N_{tr} + N_{fr}} \quad (18)$$

$$R = \frac{N_{tr}}{N_{tr} + N_{fn}} \quad (19)$$

where N_{tr} represents the number of obtained accurate social relationships or mobile user preferences; N_{fr} represents the number of obtained false social relationships or mobile user preferences; and N_{fn} represents the number of omitting social relationships or mobile user preferences. When using the F-score for evaluation, only the value of F can be used to

evaluate the obtained results; the values of F, Q, and R can also be used to evaluate the obtained results, such as in [28]. In this paper, the latter is employed to evaluate the obtained results. The greater the values of F, Q, and R, the better the obtained results.

Root-mean-square error ($RMSE$) is employed to evaluate the accuracy of predicted mobile user preferences; the formula is as follows:

$$RMSE = \sqrt{\frac{1}{N_p} \sum_{u_i \in U} \sum_{C_r \in C} \sum_{s_q \in S_{i,C_r}} \left(P_{u_i, s_q, C_r} - \widehat{P}_{u_i, s_q, C_r} \right)^2} \quad (20)$$

where P_{u_i, s_q, C_r} represents the real user's preferences obtained with formula (10a) and (10b), $\widehat{P}_{u_i, s_q, C_r}$ represents the mobile user preferences predicted by the proposed method; and N_p represents the number of predicted user's preferences.

4.3. The Experimental Steps. The benchmark method is the traditional CF, and the comparison methods include several improved CF methods. The experimental steps follow. In step (2)~step (6), the improved CF is employed to predict user preference, where K is set to $round(\omega * N_u)$, ω is set to 0.1, and if $K > 100$, K is set to 100. The difference in step (2)~step (6) is that the influence is different when using the improved CF.

(1) Determine the values of a_1 and $V_{threshold}$. In this step, simply compute the value of V_{u_i, u_j} when a_1 is set to different values in the training set of the RM data set. Thus, a_1 is set to the values in [0, 1] and its step size is 0.1. When $a_1 = 0$, it only considers the impact of the times of usage. When $a_1 = 1$, it only considers the impact of the duration of the usage. Additionally, $V_{threshold}$ is set to the values in [0, 1], and its step size is 0.1. When $V_{threshold} = 0$, it implies only if there is interaction behavior between users, it accounts for a social relationship between users in the physical world. However, it might introduce some noise data, such as harassing or dialed phone calls. When $V_{threshold}$ is too large, it is very stringent for the determination of the user's social relationship, and the accuracy will increase, but it might lose part of the social relationship, resulting in a drop in the recall rate.

The *F*-score of the edges in the constructed mobile social network is employed to evaluate the results. The mobile social network will be constructed based on the optimum values of $V_{\text{threshold}}$ and a_1.

(2) Determine the value of θ. In this step, consider the impact of network topology when predicting the user's preferences. First, compute C_{u_i} in the mobile social network constructed by step (1), and then predict user preferences according to C_{u_i}. When computing C_{u_i}, θ is set to the value in $[0, 1]$, and its step size is 0.1. When $\theta = 1$, it denotes the impact of acquaintances and strangers, which are not distinguished between; while when $\theta = 0$, the impact of the strangers is not considered.

The *F*-score and *RMSE* of the predicted preferences are employed to evaluate the results. According to the experimental results, C_{u_i} is computed where θ is set to the optimum value.

(3) Determine the values of λ_1 and λ_2. In this step, consider the influence of the user when predicting the user's preferences. First, compute $\overline{V}_{u_i,S}$ in the training set of the RM data set, where a_1 is set as the optimum values obtained by step (1). Then, compute I_{u_i} by fusing the $\overline{V}_{u_i,S}$ and C_{u_i} obtained in step (2). Finally, predict the user's preferences according to I_{u_i}.

Due to $\lambda_2 = 1 - \lambda_1$, the setting of parameters is more simplified to set the value of λ_1. Thus, λ_1 is given the values in $[0, 1]$, and its step size is 0.1. The *F*-score and *RMSE* of the predicted preferences are employed to evaluate the results. According to the experimental results, I_{u_i} is computed where λ_1 and λ_2 are set to the optimum values.

(4) Determine the value of β_r, which is the determination of the weight of the context instances. It needs to compute I'_{u_i,u_j} when β_r is given the different value in the training set of the RM data set. It then predicts the user's preferences based on I'_{u_i,u_j}. The date context includes two kinds of context instances, the time context includes five kinds of context instances, and the location context includes three kinds of context instances. Hence, the number of all context instances is $2 * 5 * 3 = 30$. In (8): ① if it does not consider the impact of the context, the weights of all context instances are equal; that is, $\beta_r = 1$ and $r = 1, 2, \ldots, 30$; ② if it considers the impact of the context instances, the number of the parameters is 30, β_r is set to the values in $[0, 1]$, and its step size is 0.1. The genetic algorithm is employed to select the optimum parameters of β_r. The adaptive function of the genetic algorithm is set in formula (20).

The *F*-score and *RMSE* of the predicted preferences are employed to evaluate the results. According to the experimental results, I'_{u_i,u_j} is computed where β_r is given optimum values.

(5) Determine the value of b. In this step, compute the user's preferences when b is given different values in the training set of the RM data set. Thus, b is given the value which makes the preference more consistent with Pareto's law.

(6) Determine the values of λ_3, λ_4, and λ_5, that is, the weight of each influence when fusing the obtained influence. In this step, first, compute I''_{u_i,u_j} where β_r is given the optimum values according to step (4), and b is given the

optimum value according to step (5); then, compute I_{u_i,u_j} by fusing I_{u_i}, I'_{u_i,u_j}, and I''_{u_i,u_j}. Since $\lambda_5 = 1 - \lambda_3 - \lambda_4$, simply determine the value of λ_3 and λ_4. Similarity, the genetic algorithm is employed to determine the values of λ_3 and λ_4, and the adaptive function of the genetic algorithm is given in formula (20). Thus, λ_3 is given the values in $[0, 1]$, and its step size is 0.1; λ_4 is set to the values in $[\lambda_3, 1]$, and its step size is 0.1.

The *F*-score and *RMSE* of the predicted preferences are employed to evaluate the results. Additionally, I_{u_i,u_j} is computed where λ_3, λ_4, and λ_5 are given the optimum values according to the experimental results.

(7) Determine the value of K, which is the number of the nearest neighbors. In the step, first, rank the I_{u_i,u_j} obtained in step (6) by descending order, and select the top-K nearest neighbors. Next, predict the given user's preferences according to the preferences of the selected nearest neighbors. Additionally, K is set to $round(\omega * N_u)$, and ω is set to 0.05, 0.1, 0.15, 0.20, and 0.25, respectively. If $K > 100$, K is set to 100. The experiment is only executed on the RM data set. Since the RMM data set includes too many users, K is set to 100 when the experiment is executed in the RMM data set.

The *F*-score and *RMSE* of the predicted preferences are employed to evaluate the results, and K is given the optimum values according to the experimental results.

(8) Compare different prediction methods. Due to considering the context information in the proposed method, the context is considered in all compared methods. The compared methods include the traditional CF, which considers the context information (CCF); the CF using the matrix factorization (MFCCF); the CF considering the user trust (TCCF), where the method in [11] is used to compute the trust; the method based on TIG algorithm in [1] (C-TIG); the method based on the k-shell decomposition method [4] (C-kSD); and the proposed method in the paper (PM).

The experiment is exacted on the RM data set and RMM data set. The *F*-score and *RMSE* of the predicted preferences are employed to evaluate the results.

4.4. Experimental Results and Analysis. (1) The impact of a_1 and $V_{\text{threshold}}$ will be examined. The experimental results are shown in Figures 1 and 2.

Figure 1 shows that when $a_1 = 0.5$ and $V_{\text{threshold}} = 0.1$, the constructed mobile social network is the best; in most instances, when $V_{\text{threshold}}$ is set to 0.1, the experimental results are better, especially when $a_1 = 0.5$; only when $a_1 = 0.1$ or $a_1 = 0.6$ and $V_{\text{threshold}}$ is set to 0.2, the experimental results are better. The reason is as follows: ① when $V_{\text{threshold}}$ is small, it is loose for the restriction of the interaction behavior between users when judging whether there is social relationship, so we can get many accurate social relationships, and the recall is higher, but it also introduces excess relationships simultaneously, which makes the precision very low. Thus, the value of F is low. For example, when $V_{\text{threshold}} = 0$, the obtained accurate social relationship is 69, but the obtained excess social relationship is 129, so the precision is low. ② When $V_{\text{threshold}}$ increases, the restriction becomes very stringent. The obtained accurate social relationship decreases, so the

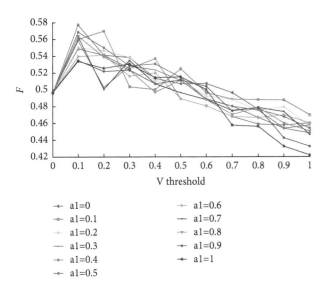

FIGURE 1: The comparison of the obtained results when a_1 and $V_{\text{threshold}}$ are given different values.

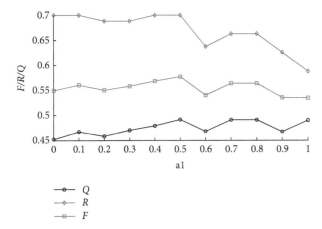

FIGURE 2: The comparison of the obtained results when a_1 is given different values and $V_{\text{threshold}} = 0.1$.

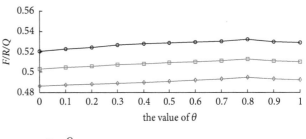

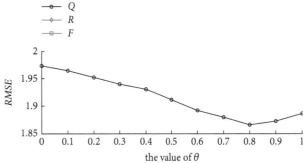

FIGURE 3: The comparison of the obtained results when θ is set to different values.

TABLE 4: The weight of the different context instances.

parameter	value	parameter	value	parameter	value
β_1	0	β_{11}	0	β_{21}	0
β_2	0	β_{12}	0	β_{22}	0
β_3	0.8	β_{13}	0	β_{23}	0
β_4	0	β_{14}	0	β_{24}	0.5
β_5	0	β_{15}	0	β_{25}	0
β_6	0	β_{16}	0.5	β_{26}	0
β_7	0	β_{17}	0.5	β_{27}	0
β_8	0.3	β_{18}	0	β_{28}	1
β_9	0	β_{19}	0.2	β_{29}	0
β_{10}	0	β_{20}	0	β_{30}	1

recall reduces. However, the excess social relationship also decreases with the increasing of $V_{\text{threshold}}$, which improves the precision. Hence, the value of F also is improved. ③ When $V_{\text{threshold}}$ is larger, the obtained accurate social relationships are fewer, so the recall is lower, which makes the value of F also lower. Therefore, the determination of $V_{\text{threshold}}$ is to compromise in the precision and recall and to make the value of F the best.

According to the above analysis, in the following experiment, $V_{\text{threshold}}$ is set to 0.1.

Figure 2 shows that ① when $a_1 \leq 0.5$, the change in R is not obvious, and when $a_1 > 0.5$, the value of R reduces; ② the value of Q meets the relationship of the convex function with a_1 substantially, and the value of Q is best when $a_1 = 0.5$; ③ similarly, the value of F meets the relationship of the convex function with a_1 substantially, and the value of F is best when $a_1 = 0.5$.

This is because the user's influence is not only impacted by the interaction duration but by the interaction times. When $a_1 = 0$, it only considers the influence of the interaction times, without considering the impact of the interaction duration, so it loses or reduces the impact of the interaction behavior; when $a_1 = 1$, it only considers the influence of the interaction duration without considering the impact of the interaction times. Hence, a_1 is set to 0.5 in the following experiment.

(2) The impact of θ will be examined. The experimental results are shown in Figure 3. The experiment shows that when $\theta = 0.8$, the obtained results are the best. This indicates that the impact of the stranger is smaller than that of the acquaintance.

(3) The weight of the different context instances are shown in Table 4.

Table 4 shows that the different context instances have different impacts on the influence. This is because there are different user behaviors under different context instances. For example, the user usually spends weekends with family or

TABLE 5: The learned preference when b is set to different values.

b	N_L	μ	b	N_L	μ
1	6150	41.64%	**100**	**5095**	**45.65%**
10	5217	45.16%	**200**	**5091**	**45.65%**
20	5149	45.47%	300	5091	45.63%
30	5130	45.54%	400	5092	45.60%
40	5121	45.54%	**500**	**5087**	**45.65%**
50	5114	45.54%	600	5089	45.63%
60	5108	45.58%	700	5093	45.61%
70	5103	45.60%	800	5088	45.62%
80	5101	45.61%	**900**	**5084**	**45.65%**
90	5098	45.63%	1000	5085	45.64%

N_L represents the number of the learned preferences.
μ represents the percentage of the learned preferences in [2 4].

TABLE 6: The weight of the different factors when fusing the influence.

parameter	λ_1	λ_2	λ_3	λ_4	λ_5
weight	0.4	0.6	0.2	0.3	0.5

friends, so the behavior under these contexts (e.g., weekend, at night, at home, or elsewhere) has a greater impact. The user spends workdays in the office with colleagues, and the contacts are usually clients or colleagues due to the work.

(4) The optimal value of b and the experimental results are shown in Table 5. The number of learned preferences by the linear function is 5,089, and the percentage of the learned preference in [2 4] is 45.61%.

Table 5 shows that when $b \leq 200$, the number of learned preferences declines and the percentage of the learned preferences in [2 4] increases with the increase of b. When $b > 200$, the results of the learned preferences decrease and the percentage of the learned preferences in [2 4] did not change much. When $b = 100$, the percentage of the learned preference in [2 4] is the same as when $b = 200$, and the number of obtained user preferences is more. Hence, in the paper, b is set to 100.

In addition, compared with the results obtained by the linear function, when $b > 70$, the results obtained by the logarithmic function are better, except when $b = 400$ and $b = 700$. This indicates that the logarithmic function is superior to the linear function when $b > 70$.

(5) The impact of λ_i is discussed. The obtained optimal values are shown in Table 6.

Table 6 shows the following: ① The user's behavior of using mobile network services plays a more important role than the network topology in the influence of the user. This is because a smart phone is not just a communication tool, and it can provide a wide range of applications, such as games, music, news, and shopping. Therefore, unlike before, the current influence of the user needs to be measured from many aspects, including traditional communication behavior, interactive behavior, and usage behavior of APP. ② The similarity of user preferences has the most impact on

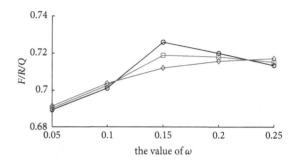

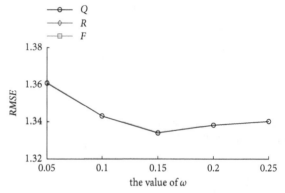

FIGURE 4: The comparison of the obtained results when ω is set to different values.

the influence between users; next is the interaction behavior; and the influence of the user has the least impact. This is because the user finds it easier to accept the view of users who have similar preferences to his, which is the basic idea of the recommender system based on CF [29]. Second, it is the influence from an acquaintance. Even though there are no similar preferences, to a certain extent, the target user may accept some views of acquaintances. The influence of the user measures influence macroscopically, such as through celebrities and leaders. The target user may be impacted by those users in some respect.

(6) The impact of K will be discussed.

Figure 4 shows that when ω is set to 0.15, the obtained results are the best. The reason is that when ω is small, although these selected nearest neighbors have very similar preferences with the target user, the selected nearest neighbors are fewer and the predicted preferences are not overall collected, so the accuracy is lower; when ω is large, although the predicted preferences are very wide overall, it introduces some excess preferences. Hence, the recall increases with the increase of ω, but the precision increases first and then falls, and the RMSE falls first and then increases.

In summary, the K is set to $round(0.15 * N_u)$, which means K is set to 14 in the RM data set.

(7) We will examine the comparison of results obtained by different prediction methods. The results are shown in Figures 5 and 6.

Figures 5 and 6 show the following:

The results obtained by the proposed method are both the best in the RM data set and RMM data set, followed by the TCCF, MFCCF, CCF, C-TIG, and C-kSD.

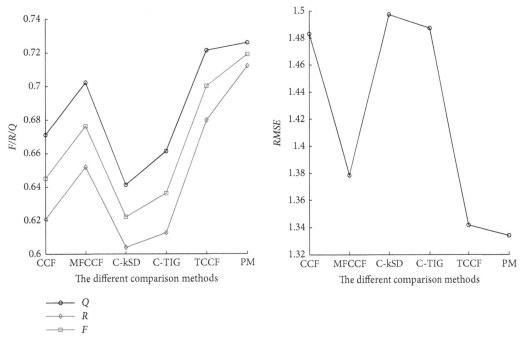

FIGURE 5: The comparison of the results obtained by different prediction methods in the RM data set.

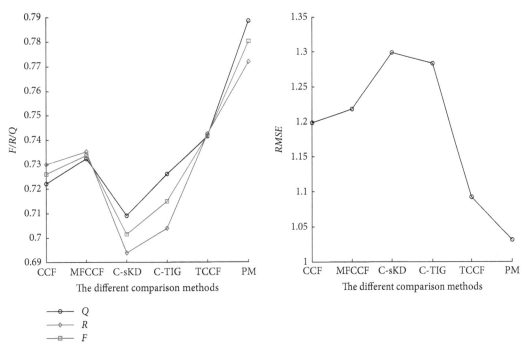

FIGURE 6: The comparison of the results obtained by different prediction methods in the RMM data set.

① The results obtained by the C-kSD are the worst. When calculating the influence, it only considers the network topology and measures the influence according the user's role in the mobile social network. The method mainly measures the influence of the user. Hence, this method cannot find the accurate nearest neighbors for the target user and leads the accuracy of the predicted mobile user preference to be lower. With respect to the C-kSD, not only does the C-TIG method

consider the network topology, but it considers the interaction behavior and dynamic of the user's behavior when calculating the influences. Therefore, compared with the results obtained by the C-kSD, those obtained by C-TIG are better.

② The results obtained by the CCF are superior to those obtained by C-TIG. This is because CCF considers the similarity of user preferences, while C-TIG considers the network topology and the interaction behavior incomplete.

According to the results obtained by experimental step (6), we know that the similarity of user preferences plays a more important role in influence than the network topology and the interaction behaviors. Hence, the experimental results are consistent with results obtained by experimental step (6).

③ Compared with the results obtained by CCF, those obtained by MFCCF improved by 4.84% in F and reduced by 0.1048 in the *RSME* in the RM data set, as well as improving by 1.06% in F and reducing by 0.0199 in the *RSME* in RMM data set. This is because using this method, MFCCF alleviates the sparsity problem by matrix factorization and improves the accuracy of the obtained similarities of user preferences. Hence, the selected nearest neighbors are more accurate, and the accuracy of the predicted mobile user preferences is better.

④ The results obtained by TCCF are superior to those obtained by the MFCCF. The reason is that the TCCF introduces the trust information into CCF, and it considers the impact of the users who have similar preferences to the target user and whom the target user trusts. Not only does the introduction of the trust alleviate the sparsity problem, but it can find more accurate nearest neighbors for the target user.

⑤ The results obtained by the proposed method are the best. Compared with the CCF, the value of F improved by 11.46% and the *RSME* reduced by 0.1494 in the RM data set, and the value of F improved by 7.47% and the *RSME* reduced by 0.1673 in the RMM data set. The proposed method considers the impact of many factors, including the similarity of user preferences, the influence of the user, the interaction behaviors between users, the context information, and the order in which user preferences occurred. Hence, this method can find more accurate nearest neighbors for the target user compared with the other methods, and the accuracy of the predicted user preference is the best.

5. Conclusion

Due to the characteristics of the mobile network, the mobile user wants to get personalized mobile network services timely, anytime, and anywhere. How to obtain accurate user preferences has become a hot issue. User preferences will be impacted by other users, such as family, friends, or users who have similar preferences to those of the target user.

In the paper, a prediction method of user preferences is proposed. To improve the accuracy of the predicted user preferences, the proposed method considers the impact of many factors, including the similarity of the user preferences, the influence of the user, the interaction behaviors between users, the context information, and the order in which user preferences occurred. The experimental results show that the proposed method is superior to the existing methods in the accuracy of predicted user preferences. In addition, according to the experimental results, we can conclude that the similarity of user preferences plays the most important role in the prediction of user preferences; next is the user interaction behavior, and the user's behavior has the least impact on user preferences.

In the paper, the propagation and the dynamic of the influences are not considered. In addition, the public data, which include mobile user behavior and context information, are few, and the MIT is the only data set. However, the mobile users included in the data set of MIT are few. In future works, we will seek the newest data set to verify the proposed method.

Acknowledgments

This research was supported by the National Natural Science Foundation of China (NSFC) (Grants nos. 61402331, 61702367, 61402332, and 61502338) and the Research Plan Project of Tianjin Municipal Education Commission (2017KJ035 and 2017KJ033).

References

[1] Z. P. Liu and D. C. Pi, "Mining social influence of nodes from mobile datasets," *Journal of Computer Research and Development*, vol. 50, pp. 244–248, 2013.

[2] L. B. Chen, S. J. Li, and G. Pan, "Smartphone: pervasive sensing and applications," *Chinese Journal of Computer*, vol. 38, no. 2, pp. 423–438, 2015.

[3] Z. H. Huang, J. W. Zhang, C. Q. Tian, S. L. Sun, and Y. Xiang, "Survey on learning-to-rank based recommendation algorithms," *Journal of Software*, vol. 27, no. 3, pp. 691–713, 2016.

[4] P. Brown and J. Feng, "Measuring user influence on twitter using modified k-shell decomposition," in *Proceedings of the 5th International AAAI Conference on Weblogs and Social*, Media, Barcelona, Spain, 2011.

[5] J. Cossu, N. Dugue, and V. Labatut, "Detecting Real-World Influence through Twitter," in *Proceedings of the second European Network Intelligence Conference (ENIC)*, pp. 83–90, IEEE, Karlskrona, Sweden, September 2015.

[6] S. Räbiger and M. Spiliopoulou, "A framework for validating the merit of properties that predict the influence of a twitter user," *Expert Systems with Applications*, vol. 42, no. 5, pp. 2824–2834, 2015.

[7] X. Hu, T. H. S. Chu, V. C. M. Leung, E. C.-H. Ngai, P. Kruchten, and H. C. B. Chan, "A Survey on mobile social networks: Applications, platforms, system architectures, and future research directions," *IEEE Communications Surveys & Tutorials*, vol. 17, no. 3, pp. 1557–1581, 2015.

[8] X. Liu, C. Aggarwal, Y. F. Li, X. N. Kong, and X. Y. Sun, "Kernelized matrix factorization for collaborative filtering," in *Proceedings of the SIAM Conference on Data Mining*, American Statistical Association, Miami, Florida, USA, 2016.

[9] L. H. Wu and W. F. Chen, "Personalized Recommendation Based on Trust and Preference," *Applied Mechanics and Materials*, vol. 713-715, pp. 2288–2291, 2015.

[10] C. C. Wu and M. J. Shih, "A context-aware recommender system based on social media," in *Proceedings of the Conference on Computer Science, Data Mining Mechanical Engineering (ICCDMME*, Bangkok, Thailand, 2015.

[11] X. Hu, X. W. Meng, Y. J. Zhange, and Y. C. Shi, "Recommendation algorithm combing item features and trust relationship of mobile users," *Journal of Software*, vol. 25, no. 8, pp. 1817–1830, 2014.

[12] H. Geng, X. W. Meng, and Y. C. Shi, "A mobile user preference prediction method based on trust and link prediction," *Journal of Electronics Information Technology*, vol. 35, no. 12, pp. 2972–2977, 2013.

[13] X. D. Wu, Y. Li, and L. Li, "Influence analysis of online social networks," *Chinese Journal of Computer*, vol. 37, no. 4, pp. 735–752, 2014.

[14] D. Huang, Y. Du, and Q. He, "Migration algorithm for big data in hybrid cloud storage," *Journal of Computer Research and Development*, vol. 51, no. 1, pp. 199–205, 2014 (Chinese).

[15] J. M. Sun and J. Tang, "A survey of models and algorithms for social influence analysis," *Social network data analytics*, pp. 177–214, 2011.

[16] D. Wei, X. Deng, X. Zhang, Y. Deng, and S. Mahadevan, "Identifying influential nodes in weighted networks based on evidence theory," *Physica A: Statistical Mechanics and its Applications*, vol. 392, no. 10, pp. 2564–2575, 2013.

[17] A. Muruganantham and G. Meera Gandhi, "Ranking the influence users in a social networking site using an improved TOPSIS method," *Journal of Theoretical and Applied Information Technology*, vol. 73, no. 1, pp. 1–11, 2015.

[18] G. F. Zhu, Y. Yang, Z. R. Zhou, Z. Y. Ying, and F. J. Han, "A method of calculating the influence of micro-blog users based on domain," *Journal of Southwest University (Natural Science Edition*, vol. 36, no. 3, pp. 145–151, 2014.

[19] E. Bakshy, D. Echles, R. Yan, and I. Rosenn, "Social influence in social advertising: evidence from field experiments," in *Proceedings of the 13th ACM Conference on Electronic Commerce*, p. 4, ACM, Valencia, Spain, 2012.

[20] J. X. Mao, Y. Q. Liu, M. Zhang, and S. P. Ma, "Social influence analysis for micro-blog user based on user behavior," *Chinese Journal of Computer*, vol. 37, no. 4, pp. 791–800, 2014.

[21] I. Verenich, R. Kikas, M. Dumas, and D. Melnikov, "Combining propensity and influence models for product adoption prediction," in *Proceedings of the 2015 IEEE/ACM International Conference on Advances in Social Networks Analysis and Mining*, ACM, France, Paris, 2015.

[22] A. Tommasel and D. Godoy, "A novel metric for assessing user influence based on user behaviour," in *Proceedings of the 1st International Workshop on Social Influence Analysis, Buenos Aires*, Argentina, 2015.

[23] I. Anger and C. Kittl, "Measuring influence on Twitter," in *Proceedings of the 11th International Conference on Knowledge Management and Knowledge Technologies*, ACM, Graz, Austria, 2011.

[24] M. Cataldi, M. Nupur, and M. A. Aufaure, "Estimating domain-based user influence in social networks," in *Proceedings of the 28th Annual ACM Symposium on Applied Computing*, ACM, Salamanca, Spain, 2013.

[25] J. Guo, Y. N. Cao, C. Zhou, P. Zhang, and L. Guo, "Influence weights learning under linear threshold model in social networks," *Journal of Electronics Information Technology*, vol. 36, no. 8, pp. 1804–1809, 2014.

[26] Y. C. Shi, X. W. Meng, Y. J. Zhang, and M. Xiao, "A trust calculating algorithm based on mobile phone data," in *Proceedings of the Global Communications Conference*, IEEE, Los Angeles, USA, 2012.

[27] N. Eagle, A. Pentland, and D. Lazer, "Inferring friendship network structure by using mobile phone data," *Proceedings of the National Acadamy of Sciences of the United States of America*, vol. 106, no. 36, pp. 15274–15278, 2009.

[28] Z. Bu, Z. Wu, J. Cao, and Y. Jiang, "Local Community Mining on Distributed and Dynamic Networks from a Multiagent Perspective," *IEEE Transactions on Cybernetics*, vol. 46, no. 4, pp. 986–999, 2016.

[29] C. D. H. Nguyen, N. Arch-Int, and S. Arch-Int, "A semantically hybrid framework of personalizing news recommendations," *International Journal of Innovative Computing, Information and Control*, vol. 11, no. 6, pp. 1947–1963, 2015.

18

An Improved Artificial Bee Colony Algorithm in LoRa Wireless Communication System for Efficient Multimedia Transmission

Yan Song,[1] Lidong Huang ⓘ,[1] Panfeng Xu,[1] Lili Li,[1] Min Song,[2] and Yue Long[1]

[1]College of Physics, Liaoning University, Shenyang, China
[2]College of Information, Shenyang Institute of Engineering, Shenyang, China

Correspondence should be addressed to Lidong Huang; 4031731893@smail.lnu.edu.cn

Guest Editor: Kai Wang

Video streaming communication networks will be a very important way to send multimedia information anytime and anywhere, and the construction of the network base station which transmits signals is crucial in future. However, there is a contradiction between the power consumption of LoRa nodes and the real-timeliness of mesh network. In order to solve the contradiction, this article aims to combine the mesh network of LoRa wireless communication system with an improved artificial bee colony algorithm. Specifically, an artificial bee colony algorithm, which is based on RBF radial basis neural network trained with random gradient method, is designed. Simulation results show that the proposed algorithm solves the contradiction between power consumption and real-timeliness effectively. When using this improved network system structure to send multimedia information, it shows obvious superiority in terms of the high efficiency and real-timeliness of multimedia transmission.

1. Introduction

With the development of wireless communication network technology, the advantages of intelligent productions of wireless communication are widely accepted, such as low cost and good scalability [1–3]. These productions have been paid more and more attention by the society [4, 5]. Moreover, the transmission of multimedia information is getting larger and more global. Video streaming and other high-capacity media transmission technologies require better wireless networks architecture [5, 6].

The LoRa technology solves the problem of long distance and low power consumption successfully. Compared to other wireless transmission technologies, LoRa has the advantages of longer transmission distance and lower consumption [5–7]. However, the existing wireless transmission technology cannot meet the real-time monitoring effect of wireless network under the conditions of low power consumption and long distance. In the existing methods, there is a mesh network architecture that minimizes the number of devices, which greatly reduces the cost of base station establishment [8, 9]. At the same time, it is very convenient to deploy the equipment [10–12]. The mesh network architecture is very stable, and it is not affected by a single node. When a near node fails or is disturbed, the packet will be transferred automatically to the alternate path for transmission. Moreover, it has flexible structure and advantages in terms of overloading and communication load balancing [13–15]. This kind of mesh network reduces the interference of the adjacent user wireless network when transmitting data, and its efficiency of information transmission has been improved greatly.

To a certain extent, the mesh network reduces the power consumption and achieves the coverage of a larger area, but it cannot completely solve the contradiction between the power consumption and real time of LoRa wireless network [16–19]. Some additional interference or space extension may result in loss of signal transmission capability. We consider adopting the basic artificial swarm algorithm. There is still a problem that the wireless network layout may be optimized correspondingly [20, 21], but the effect of optimization is not obvious enough and it converges slowly. When looking for the optimal solution in space, there may be a deviation. Moreover, the traditional method in the algorithm will affect the convergence speed of the optimal solution greatly. Therefore, this existing method cannot deal with the contradiction between power consumption and real time [11, 16, 22], which is an obstacle to the multimedia information transmission. To fill this gap, the paper proposes an improved algorithm to solve the problem.

The contributions of this paper are listed as follows: an artificial bee colony algorithm based on RBF radical basis neural network (RBFABC) is designed to resolve this problem, and this algorithm can solve the contradiction between power consumption and real-timeliness [14, 17, 23]. Furthermore, this design not only improves the traditional way of selecting and updating the honey sources in basic artificial swarm optimization algorithm, but also enables the algorithm to converge towards the optimal solution. Moreover, the convergence speed of the proposed algorithm is much higher. The improved algorithm not only ensures the real-time performance of wireless network [14, 16, 24], but also reduces the power consumption of wireless network. In brief, the improved algorithm overcomes technical obstacles in the field of multimedia wireless network, and it has great significance to the development of wireless transmission technology.

The rest of this paper is organized as follows: Section 2 introduces the basic artificial swarm algorithm. Section 3 presents the system model. Section 4 proposes the RBFABC algorithm. Section 5 performs simulations to verify the effectiveness of the proposed algorithm. Section 6 concludes this paper.

2. Basic Artificial Swarm Algorithm

As everyone knows, bees have special behavioral patterns for finding honey sources [17, 18]. In general, the process of searching for honey sources is divided into three parts: looking for the honey sources; updating the honey sources; selecting the best honey sources [14, 25, 26]. The algorithm flow is shown in Algorithm 1.

In this algorithm, the leader bees have a memory function, which can save the information of the honey sources. Moreover, the leader bees share the honey sources information with orientation bees. According to their dance of the leader bees, the orientation bees determine which direction to go. The observation bees are responsible for searching nectar around the hive, and the leader bees search for honey sources [27, 28]. We define some variables to represent them [16, 17, 23]. Firstly, a series of original honey sources are initialized randomly. $X = (X_1, X_2, X_3, \ldots, X_n)$ represents n honey sources [18, 19, 25]. The position of the m-th honey source is $X_m = [X_{m1}, X_{m2}, X_{m3}, \ldots, X_{mn}]$ ($m = 1, 2, 3, \ldots, n$), which are potential solutions to the problem [26, 27]. Then the fitness of honey sources are evaluated by the following formula:

$$fit_m = \begin{cases} \dfrac{1}{1 + f_m} & f_m > 0 \\ 1 + |f_m| & f_m < 0 \end{cases} \qquad (1)$$

where f_m represents the target function value of m-th solutions. After that, the location of n honey sources updates in a certain way. The process is described as follows.

```
Init X_mn, N, C = 1
input initial population
set the total number N
while (iter < = maxcycle)
        V_ij = X_ij + ∅_ij(X_ij − X_kj)
        apply the greedy selection process
        P_i = fit / (Σ_{k=1}^{N} fit_i)
        if f_m >= 0 then
            fit_m = 1 / (1 + fit_m)
        else
            fit_m = 1 + |fit_m|
        end if
        if P_{m+1} < P_m then
    X_mn = X_min + rand(0, 1)(X_mn − X_min)
        end if
        memorize the best position so far
        C = C + 1
        until C = maximum cycle number
end while
output the optimal solution
end
```

ALGORITHM 1: The program diagram of the artificial swarm optimization algorithm.

$$X_m^n = X_{min}^n + \text{rand}\,(0, 1)\left(X_{max}^n - X_{min}^n\right) \qquad (2)$$

If the honey sources are better, we will select the better one instead of the old one; otherwise keep the old one. If all the leader bees finished searching, the honey sources information will be transmitted to the observation bees [4, 13]. Then the observation bees choose leader bees according to the fitness value [28, 29], and the selection probability is described as follows:

$$P_m = \frac{fit_m}{\sum_{i=1}^{n} fit_m} \qquad (3)$$

$$U_{ij} = X_{ij} + r_{ij}\left(X_{ij} - X_{kj}\right) \qquad (4)$$

where X_{ij} represents the location of honey sources, U_{ij} represents the nearby location of X_{ij}, r_{ij} represents the random number within (-1, 1), P_m represents the selective probability, and fit_m represents the fitness of honey sources. If the searching process is over, the honey sources information will be transmitted to the leader bees. Then the leader bees choose a direction according to fitness of honey sources. If this honey source is not replaced after finite loops, it will be abandoned. Finally the leader bees will look for the new honey sources.

3. System Model

In order to achieve the effect of algorithm optimization, we analyze the parameters of network architecture and establish the mathematical model of wireless network. As shown in Figure 1.

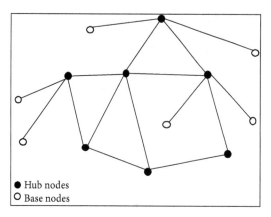

FIGURE 1: Mesh network model.

Beyond that, this paper combines the central function with the improved algorithm. In wireless mesh networks, a small amount of wireless devices can be required to cover a large range [8, 11, 15]. In other words, it is very convenient to create a mathematical model of wireless network [16–18]. The correlation signal transmission capability function of network nodes created is described as follows.

$$c_m = w_1 \alpha_{m1} + w_2 \alpha_{m2} + w_3 \alpha_{m3} + w_4 \alpha_{m4} + w_5 \alpha_{m5} \quad (5)$$

$$w_1 + w_2 + w_3 + w_4 + w_5 = 1 \quad (6)$$

The signal coverage range of nodes are related to the performance of the node (α_{m1}), the location of deployment (α_{m2}), the signal coverage (α_{m3}), the band width (α_{m4}), and the anti-interference capability (α_{m5}). The above factors have different effects on the signal coverage capability of nodes, and w is used to reflect the degree of influence of factors [7]. Under ideal conditions, the relationship between the transmitting power consumption and propagation distance of nodes is described as follows:

$$P = s + k \lg d + k \lg f \quad (7)$$

where P represents transmission power, d represents coverage range, f represents transmission frequency, s represents initial effective distance, and k represents effective radiofrequency factor [7, 16, 18]. In order to balance the relationship between power consumption and real time, the mathematical model is established as follows:

$$T_m = \frac{C_m}{C_{max}} \quad (8)$$

$$P = s + k \lg d T_m + k \lg f \quad (9)$$

where T_m represents the signal coverage capability after quantization, C_m represents the signal coverage capability of nodes, and C_{max} represents the maximum ability of nodes signal coverage.

4. RBFABC Algorithm

Although the artificial bee colony algorithm works well, there is still a problem of slow convergence rate in solving the

problem of nodes optimization. At the same time, the choice of roulette in the original algorithm may make the algorithm fall into the local optimum. Therefore, in each iteration, there will be an error with the newly generated solution due to each local optimum. Because of the limitation of adaptive value, the speed of the algorithm convergence is affected. The gradient method, which is in the RBF radial basis neural network algorithm, is used to deal with the updating factors [10, 21, 25, 26]. Thus we improve the updating factors of honey sources by the RBF. Firstly, within a specified range, a series of original nodes locations are initialized randomly. $X = (X_1, X_2, X_3, \ldots, X_n)$ represents n honey sources. The position of the m-th honey source is described as follows.

$$X_m = [X_{m1}, X_{m2}, X_{m3}, \ldots, X_{mn}] \quad (10)$$

This is a potential solution to the optimization process [9, 11]. The degree of honey source is estimated by the instantaneous error function [24–27], as follows:

$$
\begin{aligned}
J(n) &= \frac{1}{2} |e(n)|^2 \\
&= \frac{1}{2} \left| y_d - \sum_{k=1}^{N} w_k(n) \emptyset \left\{ x(n), c_k(n) \right\} \right|^2
\end{aligned}
\quad (11)
$$

where $w(n)$ represents the weighted value of the impact factors, $c_k(n)$ represents the center of the radial basis function, and $\delta_k(n)$ represents variance [27, 28].

When the instantaneous error is less than the specified error, the current honey sources are selected as the target honey sources. Moreover, the formula of searching for honey sources is described as follows.

$$y_m = \sum_{k=1}^{N} w_{mk} \left[s + k \lg \| x(n) - c_k(n) \|^2 + k \lg f \right] \quad (12)$$

$$w(n+1) = w(n) - \mu_w \frac{\partial}{\partial w} J(n) \quad (13)$$

$$c_k(n+1) = c_k(n) - \mu_c \frac{\partial}{\partial c_k} J(n) \quad (14)$$

$$\delta_k(n+1) = \delta_k(n) - \mu_\delta \frac{\partial}{\partial \delta_k} J(n) \quad (15)$$

During the updating process [22, 23, 26], $w(n+1)$, $c_k(n+1)$, and $\delta_k(n+1)$ will be updated according to the network correction equation. If these honey sources are not replaced, the position will be reserved. Then the leader bees continue to search for new honey sources. Finally, the new honey sources will be searched as a substitute of position by the improved updating formula. This process is shown in Algorithm 2.

The general steps of the RBFABC algorithm are as follows: initializing a series of original nodes location; searching for the position of some new nodes around the initialized nodes; calculating the instantaneous error value of the position of the new nodes; selecting the better nodes [6, 7, 27]; generating some new nodes around the better nodes by the updating formula; selecting better nodes with instantaneous

Init $X_{mn}, N, C = 1$
input initial population
set the total number N
while (iter <= maxcycle)
    produce new solutions
$$y_m = \sum_{k=1}^{N} w_{mk} \left[s + k \lg \|x(n) - c_k(n)\|^2 + k \lg f \right]$$
    apply the greedy selection
$$J_n = \frac{1}{2}|e(n)|^2 = \frac{1}{2}|y_d - y_m|^2$$
    if (J_n <= fitness) then
$$w(n+1) = w(n) - \mu_w \frac{\partial}{\partial w} J(n)$$
$$c_k(n+1) = c_k(n) - \mu_c \frac{\partial}{\partial c_k} J(n)$$
$$\delta_k(n+1) = \delta_k(n) - \mu_\delta \frac{\partial}{\partial \delta_k} J(n)$$
    end if
memorize the best position so far
    $C = C + 1$
    until C = maximum cycle number
end while
output the optimal solution
end

ALGORITHM 2: Program diagram of the RBFABC algorithm.

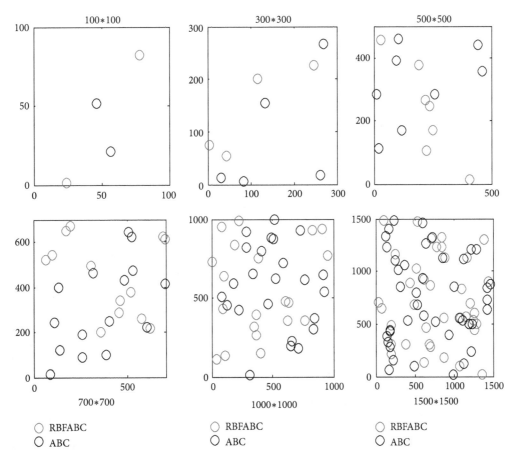

FIGURE 2: Node distribution under the same area.

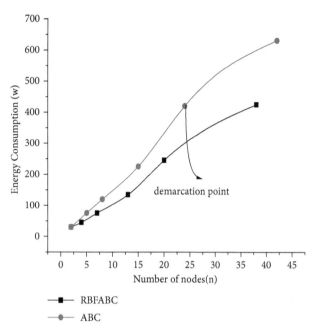

FIGURE 3: Power consumption diagram corresponding to different nodes.

TABLE 1: Optimization results of the two algorithms in certain scenarios.

Scene area (m²)	ABC (n)	RBFABC (n)
(100 ∗ 100)	2	2
(300 ∗ 300)	5	4
(500 ∗ 500)	8	7
(700 ∗ 700)	15	13
(1000 ∗ 1000)	24	20
(1500 ∗ 1500)	42	32

error values; judging whether there are points which need to be abandoned, and if so, these nodes are converted to the alternate nodes; searching for new nodes which are based on the formula [27, 28, 30]; storing the location of optimal nodes so far; evaluating whether the location of nodes meet the stopping condition of optimization, and if so, outputting the most appropriate node, otherwise going back to the second step [29, 30].

5. Simulation Results

Under LoRa wireless communication system, the contradiction of power consumption and real time is well solved, which is of great significance to the development of wireless networks. When using the improved algorithm to optimize wireless communication network, the effect of real time can be optimized to the best. Moreover, the number of nodes is the least. On the one hand, the LoRa wireless network can achieve good communication in a certain area, and, on the other hand, it can meet the requirements of real time and lower power consumption [8, 20, 23].

In order to show the effect of wireless network nodes optimized by the improved artificial colony algorithm, we select different scene areas to test the two kinds of algorithm. Under the same conditions of external influence, we keep the initial parameters of two kinds of algorithm the same in each scenario. Furthermore, the scene with an area of 100\300\500\700\1000\1500 square meters is tested and the power consumption is not limited. In these different areas, the distribution of nodes will have a very intuitive simulation effect, as shown in Table 1.

From Table 1, the improved algorithm is very efficient. Moreover, the proposed algorithm can use fewer nodes to cover the same area. Above all, the improved algorithm distributes the nodes more evenly in the same space. In a certain area, the distribution of nodes corresponding to the two kinds of algorithm is shown in Figure 2.

Figure 2 shows that, under different areas, the improved algorithm uses fewer nodes. At the same time, the real-time effect of the improved algorithm is better. In general, the improved algorithm obviously has fewer iterations, higher updating speed, and higher convergence speed. What is more, the wireless network realizes the full coverage of the network with fewer nodes by the improved algorithm. Not only that, we also find more advantages of the improved algorithm after deeper analysis of the power consumption. In different scenes, the power consumption of different number of nodes is shown in Figure 3.

Figure 3 shows that the RBFABC algorithm is obviously lower than the ABC algorithm in terms of power consumption, which shows the superiority of the improved algorithm in wireless network. In most cases, as the area of the scene increases, both the power consumption and the number of nodes also increase. However, we draw a conclusion from Figure 3 that as the number of nodes increases, the power consumption is controlled to a lower level by the improved algorithm. In summary, the RBFABC algorithm solves the contradiction between power consumption and number of nodes better in wireless network.

Correspondingly, to show the superiority of the improved algorithm, a great deal of experiments are done to test the power consumption. For the convenience of data comparison, we still take the scenario area of 100\300\500\700\1000\1500 square meters to test. In the case of certain power, the optimized spatial nodes distribution is shown in Figure 4.

It can be concluded from Figure 4 that, under the same power, the RBFABC algorithm is obviously better than the ABC algorithm in terms of the distribution of the wireless network. Beyond that, fewer nodes cover a wider range by the RBFABC algorithm. To show the superiority of the improved algorithm, we do more tests. Under the same power consumption, the specific number of nodes is shown in Table 2.

According to the data in Table 2, we can draw a conclusion that the RBFABC algorithm is better than the ABC algorithm in terms of optimization effect. Beyond that, the relationship between iteration number and optimal solution is shown in Figure 5.

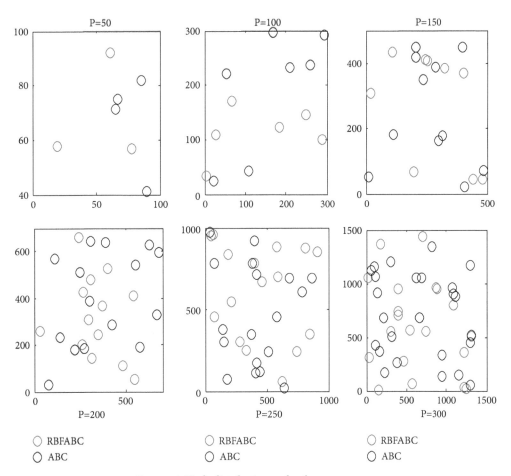

FIGURE 4: Node distribution under the same power.

TABLE 2: Optimization results under a certain power.

Power consumption (w)	ABC (n)	RBFABC (n)
(50)	4	3
(100)	7	6
(150)	11	9
(200)	15	13
(250)	18	16
(300)	25	20

TABLE 3: Comparison of multimedia data transfer speed.

Number of nodes (n)	ABC (kb/s)	RBFABC (kb/s)
(5)	200	180
(10)	400	350
(15)	620	560
(20)	810	780
(25)	980	850
(30)	1200	990

Figure 5 shows that the improved algorithm can find the optimal solution faster. Therefore, the improved algorithm has more advantages for the optimization of wireless network nodes. Moreover, in a certain area, when the number of network nodes is the same and other factors are consistent, the multimedia data transmission speed which is optimized by two kinds of algorithms is shown in Table 3.

From Table 3, the improved algorithm is obviously superior to the original algorithm in terms of transmission speed. As the number of nodes increases, the data transmission speed becomes faster and faster. In order to display the data visually, the comparison of speed trend is shown in Figure 6.

It is seen from Figure 6 that the RBFABC algorithm is faster than the ABC algorithm in terms of multimedia data transmission speed. Moreover, as the number of network nodes increases, the data transmission speed gap is bigger and bigger. In general, the RBFABC algorithm is better than the ABC algorithm. Above all, the real-time performance of the system is greatly improved. In addition to these, we do a lot deeper analysis. Under the same number of network nodes, the comparison of network delay is shown in Figure 7.

It can be concluded from Figure 7 that, under the same network nodes, the RBFABC algorithm is obviously lower than the ABC algorithm in terms of network delay. On the other hand, we compare the maximum data load of the single data transmission in the network system. The analysis results of two kinds of algorithm are shown in Figure 8.

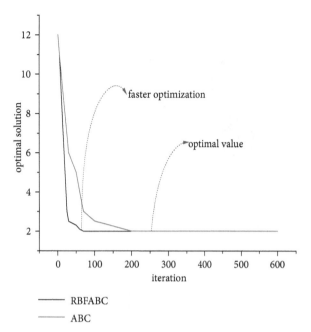

FIGURE 5: The relationship between iteration number and optimal solution.

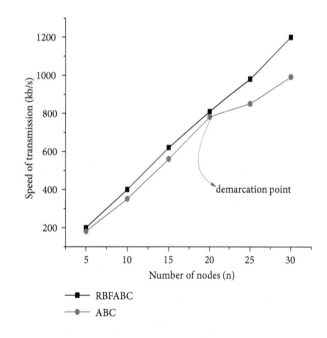

FIGURE 6: Comparison of speed trend.

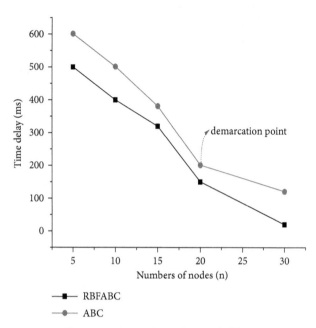

FIGURE 7: Comparison of network delay.

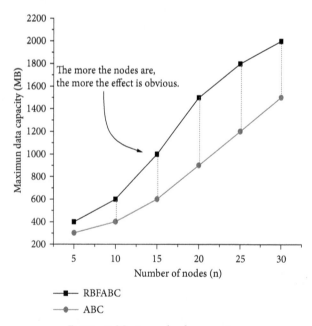

FIGURE 8: Maximum load comparison.

It is seen from Figure 8 that the RBFABC algorithm is significantly higher than the ABC algorithm in terms of the maximum data load of the single data interaction. In general, the improved algorithm has more advantages.

6. Conclusion

In this paper, to resolve the contradiction of base station establishment in LoRa wireless communication systems between the power consumption of LoRa nodes and real-timeliness of the mesh network, we have proposed a novel RBFABC algorithm which achieves better performance by embedding RBF radial basis neural network training with random gradient method. Extensive simulations have been conducted and the results have shown the obvious superiority of the RBFABC algorithm in terms of the high efficiency and real-timeliness of multimedia transmission.

Acknowledgments

This work was supported by Intelligent Manufacturing Project of the Ministry of Industry and Information Technology: Industrial Internet Data Mutual Recognition Research–Low-Power Message Distribution, the National Natural Science Foundation of China under grants 71602124 and 61773187, and Liaoning Provincial Natural Science Foundation of China under grant 20170540662.

References

[1] K. Wang, H. Yin, W. Quan, and G. Min, "Enabling collaborative edge computing for software defined vehicular networks," *IEEE Network*, vol. 32, no. 5, pp. 112–117, 2018.

[2] H. Shah, T. Herawan, R. Naseem, and R. Ghazali, "Hybrid Guided Artificial Bee Colony Algorithm for Numerical Function Optimization," in *Advances in Swarm Intelligence*, vol. 8794 of *Lecture Notes in Computer Science*, pp. 197–206, Springer International Publishing, Cham, 2014.

[3] Q. Pan, M. F. Tasgetiren, P. N. Suganthan, and T. J. Chua, "A discrete artificial bee colony algorithm for the lot-streaming flow shop scheduling problem," *Information Sciences*, vol. 181, no. 12, pp. 2455–2468, 2011.

[4] S. kuchlin and P. Jenny, "Automatic mesh refinement and parallel load balancing for Fokker-Planck-DSMC algorithm," *Journal of Computational Physics*, vol. 363, pp. 140–157, 2018.

[5] X. Ma, S. Xu, F. An, and F. Lin, "A Novel Real-Time Image Restoration Algorithm in Edge Computing," *Wireless Communications and Mobile Computing*, vol. 2018, Article ID 3610482, pp. 1–13, 2018.

[6] P. Wang and B. Henz, "Efficient approaches to resource allocation in MIMO-based wireless mesh networks," in *Proceedings of the 14th Annual Wireless Telecommunications Symposium, WTS '15*, vol. 39, pp. 1–7, USA, April 2015.

[7] F. Lin and X. Lü, "QoS guaranteed pre-pushing scheme in peer-assisted streaming network," *China Communications*, vol. 11, no. 14, pp. 111–117, 2014.

[8] J. Wellons and Y. Xue, "The robust joint solution for channel assignment and routing for wireless mesh networks with time partitioning," *Ad Hoc Networks*, vol. 13, pp. 210–221, 2014.

[9] H. Chaoui, M. Khayamy, and O. O. Okoye, "Adaptive RBF Network Based Direct Voltage Control for Interior PMSM Based Vehicles," *IEEE Transactions on Vehicular Technology*, 2018.

[10] W. Zhuang and M. Ismail, "Cooperation in wireless communication networks," *IEEE Wireless Communications Magazine*, vol. 19, no. 2, pp. 10–20, 2012.

[11] J. Si, H. Huang, Z. Li, B. Hao, and R. Gao, "Performance analysis of adaptive modulation in cognitive relay network with cooperative spectrum sensing," *IEEE Transactions on Communications*, vol. 62, no. 7, pp. 2198–2211, 2014.

[12] M. Benedetto, K. Johansson, and M. Johansson, "Industrial control over wireless networks," *International Journal of Robust & Nonlinear Control*, vol. 20, no. 2, pp. 119–127, 2018.

[13] C. M. Stefanovic, "LCR of amplify and forward wireless relay systems in general alpha-Mu fading environment," in *Proceedings of the 2017 25th Telecommunication Forum (TELFOR)*, pp. 1–6, Belgrade, November 2017.

[14] D. Prasad, V. Koneri, and K. Shivakumar, "Mitigating wireless network interface card energy consumption in mobile devices," *Research & Technology in the Coming Decades*, vol. 2014, no. 1, pp. 103–114, 2014.

[15] E. Aivaloglou and S. Gritzalis, "Hybrid trust and reputation management for sensor networks," *Wireless Networks*, vol. 16, no. 5, pp. 1493–1510, 2010.

[16] J. Wu, X. Qiao, Y. Xia, C. Yuen, and J. Chen, "A low-latency scheduling approach for high-definition video streaming in a heterogeneous wireless network with multihomed clients," *Multimedia Systems*, vol. 21, no. 4, pp. 411–425, 2015.

[17] M. Ghaderi, D. Goeckel, A. Orda, and M. Dehghan, "Minimum Energy Routing and Jamming to Thwart Wireless Network Eavesdroppers," *IEEE Transactions on Mobile Computing*, vol. 14, no. 7, pp. 1433–1448, 2015.

[18] S. Dasgupta, G. Mao, and B. Anderson, "A New Measure of Wireless Network Connectivity," *IEEE Transactions on Mobile Computing*, vol. 14, no. 9, pp. 1765–1779, 2015.

[19] X. Cheng, Q. Wang, Q. Wang, and D. Wang, "A high-reliability relay algorithm based on network coding in multi-hop wireless networks," *Wireless Networks*, pp. 1–10, 2017.

[20] Y. E. Sagduyu, Y. Shi, A. Fanous, and J. H. Li, "Wireless network inference and optimization: Algorithm design and implementation," *IEEE Transactions on Mobile Computing*, vol. 16, no. 1, pp. 257–267, 2017.

[21] J. Liu and X. Wu, "Supervision and control based on rbf neural network," *Computer Knowledge Technology*, vol. 2018, pp. 1–13, 2018.

[22] H. Qin, L. Shen, C. Sima, and Q. Ma, "RBF Networks with Dynamic Barycenter Averaging Kernel for Time Series Classification," in *Artificial Intelligence*, vol. 888 of *Communications in Computer and Information Science*, pp. 139–152, Springer Singapore, Singapore, 2018.

[23] P. Wang, "The Application of Radial Basis Function (RBF) Neural Network for Mechanical Fault Diagnosis of Gearbox," *IOP Conference Series: Materials Science and Engineering*, vol. 269, pp. 012–056, 2017.

[24] J. Dong and L. Chen, "The nonlinear integral sliding mode of RBF neural network algorithm is used to control the motion trajectory error of the manipulator," *Chinese Journal of Construction Machinery*, vol. 2018, no. 17, pp. 11–22, 2018.

[25] Y. Ma and C. Na, "Switch fault diagnosis system based on cost sensitive RBF neural network," *Railway Computer Application*, vol. 2018, no. 13, pp. 45–53, 2018.

[26] H. Du, E. Zhao, K. Guo, and H. Zhing, "Safety monitoring model of dam service based on genetic algorithm and RBF neural network," *Journal of China Three Gorges University*, vol. 2018, no. 18, pp. 15–27, 2018.

[27] D. Zaborski, W. Grzesiak, and M. Szewczuk, "An application of radial basis function (RBF) networks to daily body weight gains prediction in the indigenous Harnai Sheep of Pakistan," *Publication Preview Source Biotechnologia Problemy Wyzwania Sczecin Poland*, vol. 14, no. 18, pp. 67–87, 2018.

[28] D. Karaboga and B. Akay, "A modified Artificial Bee Colony (ABC) algorithm for constrained optimization problems," *Applied Soft Computing*, vol. 11, no. 3, pp. 3021–3031, 2011.

[29] D. Karaboga, B. Gorkemli, C. Ozturk, and N. Karaboga, "A comprehensive survey: artificial bee colony (ABC) algorithm and applications," *Artificial Intelligence Review*, vol. 42, pp. 21–57, 2014.

19

Enhancing the Security of Customer Data in Cloud Environments using a Novel Digital Fingerprinting Technique

Nithya Chidambaram,[1] Pethuru Raj,[2] K. Thenmozhi,[1] and Rengarajan Amirtharajan[1]

[1]School of Electrical & Electronics Engineering, SASTRA University, Thanjavur 613401, India
[2]Global Cloud Center of Excellence, IBM India, Bangalore 560045, India

Correspondence should be addressed to Rengarajan Amirtharajan; amir@ece.sastra.edu

Academic Editor: Yifeng He

With the rapid rise of the Internet and electronics in people's life, the data related to it has also undergone a mammoth increase in magnitude. The data which is stored in the cloud can be sensitive and at times needs a proper file storage system with a tough security algorithm. Whereas cloud is an open shareable elastic environment, it needs impenetrable and airtight security. This paper deals with furnishing a secure storage system for the above-mentioned purpose in the cloud. To become eligible to store data a user has to register with the cloud database. This prevents unauthorized access. The files stored in the cloud are encrypted with RSA algorithm and digital fingerprint for the same has been generated through MD5 message digest before storage. The RSA provides unreadability of data to anyone without the private key. MD5 makes it impossible for any changes on data to go unnoticed. After the application of RSA and MD5 before storage, the data becomes resistant to access or modifications by any third party and to intruders of cloud storage system. This application is tested in Amazon Elastic Compute Cloud Web Services.

1. Introduction

Cloud computing which is the next stage of Internet evolution ensures scalability and elasticity of the system. If the consumers and businesses are provided with Internet access, they can directly access their personal files from any corner of the world without installation. This technology enables fruitful computing by incorporating data storage, processing, and bandwidth [1]. In the cloud the data always is roaming, and in such a case the data privacy and tamper-resistance are not guaranteed. Even data can be accessed by the third party. There is a need for focusing on preventing data leakage, notification for security accident, and security incident audits. With the available conventional methods such as firewalls, security policies, and Virtual Private Networks (VPN) cloud security needs to be enhanced to get a tamperproof fertile service from it.

Security is governed by its three important aspects of confidentiality, integrity, and availability, which are the building blocks in constructing a highly secured system. These aspects ensure the security of the data, hardware, and software resources. Integrity checks data tampering. Availability is to ensure the users can use them at any time and at any place and, also, guarantee that resources for processing data and also services are available [2]. Mission critical systems availability is achieved by business continuity plans (BCPs) which are used to ensure redundancy. Confidentiality is defined as providing access only to well-authorized persons. If an unauthorized person is able to access the data, then the loss of confidentiality occurs. It can happen in both the ways either by electronic means or by the person. If the loss takes place through the communal issue, then it is called physical confidential loss. If the loss occurs while the clients and servers are not encrypting their communications, then it is known as an electronic confidential loss. RSA is chosen to achieve confidentiality [3]. Depending on the parameters called confidentiality, integrity, and availability of the consumer data it can be classified and identified as sensitive data or not.

Security and privacy are the main keys to the achievement of cloud computing and at the same time they are the most challenging issues. Recording the ownership and the data log history leads to efficient data forensics. In a cloud system, confidentiality on the sensitive documents stored is improved by the provenance scheme called digital fingerprinting [4]. Digital fingerprint images of the users are processed to provide highly secure cloud computing. Hash value or message digest is simply a number formed from a text or string which will be smaller than the text. It is generated by a well-defined formula such that the probability of the two strings generating the same hash values is extremely low.

Hash values are used to ensure unmodified data which in turn result in a secured system. The sender generates the hash value of the message, encrypts it, and sends it along with the message. The receiver then decrypts both the message and the hash and generates another hash from the decrypted message. If both the hashes are the same, then it shows that the data is not modified during the transmission. Hash generates a 128-bit digest for the message articulated in the form of text. The MD5 approach is proposed for the same.

This paper contains 4 more sections. Section 2 is all about the literature work on the area of cloud security issues and cryptographic countermeasures. In Section 3, there is the proposed architecture for achieving the data confidentiality together with integrity verification. Section 4 encompasses the outcome of the methodology. Section 5 is the conclusion of this paper.

2. Related Work

Cloud is a shared and automated environment, which offers various services to the user. Services from the cloud are software, hardware, storage, and so forth. Based on the demand from the user cloud is scalable and chargeable too. The best part in the use of cloud is access to your concealed data from anywhere at any point in time with reliability. Because of this characteristic any organization can get into cloud particularly for the storage of data offered as storage as a service by Cloud Service Provider (CSP). In this circumstance unauthorized access needs to be blocked and also impenetrable security is needed for the data stored in the cloud. Security taxonomy for cloud and the noncloud data center is alike. Based on the domain the security frameworks are deployed.

Cryptographic techniques are used to prevent the data [5]. Nowadays medical field also transformed into e-field which means that patient records are stored in the database. Telemedicine field needs support of cloud computing where exactly mobile medicine is possible. Whenever people need to get any suggestion from a physician at any time it is possible through the cloud. But the major challenge is patient privacy; there is a need to protect data from the malicious insiders [6]. Even in business sectors also, malicious insiders who are the employees of the organization as well as the real threats to the data that belong to the organization are there. Account or service hijacking is nothing but a critical area of cloud that can be accessed [7].

Generally, in the cloud, three different elements are under threat, namely, architecture, compliance, and privacy. A data security issue comes under the privacy facet, where cryptographic algorithm always supports protecting the privacy of data available in the cloud [8]. Multilevel and factor approach

is needed considering the brewing data security breaches in cloud infrastructures so hybrid encryptions can be adopted [9]. Access control of data is also one of the major issues in the cloud. If the access permission limit is set by the central authority then the trustworthy component is questionable and also not viable. The client needs an assurance that there is no collusion attack also when the data stored in the cloud is based on the identity of the data owner [10].

In addition confidentiality, integrity, and availability (CIA) factors of data are being compromised. CIA can be fortified using cryptography schemes. Symmetric, asymmetric, and hashing algorithms together contributed CIA to data. SSL (Secure Socket Layer) encryption for data confidentiality as well as MAC (Message Authentication Code) for verifying integrity of data is used to ensure CIA together with well-defined access privilege of data placed in the private or public sector of cloud [11]. Even though the owner of data is defining private or public data, the location of data in cloud is unknown and also data is in roaming state. Because of this reason integrity of data must be verified periodically [12].

Currently, data is managed and processed by a mixture of service providers so equally risk factors also increased such as unauthorized access of user sensitive data by different sectors, including service providers. So right from selection of service providers for the respective services till cryptographic techniques for protecting data from the service provider are the responsibility of the user [13, 14].

3. Proposed Methodology

This proposed model is to improve the cloud data security by incorporating various cryptographic techniques. To provide airtight confidentiality, encryption and decryption modules are added. In addition integrity of data is also verified using message digest. This is purely client side security, considering client in the cloud environment. This approach is also a reversible process. The encryption algorithm here cannot be broken easily including the popular dictionary attack. Brute force attack is also difficult to perform. The main reason for making this algorithm client side is to have the self-satisfaction and to ensure security for the clients of the cloud. Even though cloud is not trustworthy using this proposed method data can be stored in the cloud firmly. The proposed architecture is shown in Figure 1.

Data Privacy Module. Public Key Cryptography RSA is being used. In Public Key Cryptography the key for both the encryption and decryption process must be a different key. Here public key for encryption and by private key decryption is done. So this can be an appropriate algorithm for the cloud environment.

RSA: Key Generation Module

Pseudo Code. Consider the following:

(1) Select two random prime numbers which should be distinct. Assign variables to the prime numbers (*a* and *b*). Both should have similar bit length.

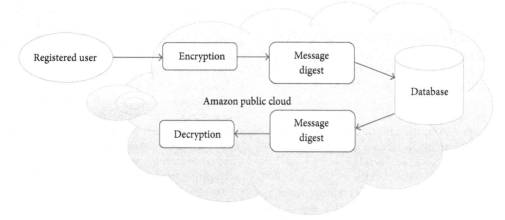

FIGURE 1: Proposed architecture.

(2) Calculate $n = ab$, where n is the number used as the modulus for private and public keys. Key length is equal to "n" length.

(3) Now calculate $\psi(n) = (a - 1)(b - 1)$.

(4) Select an integer K_e. It should satisfy $1 < K_e < \psi(n)$. GCD of p and $\psi(n)$ should be equal to 1; that is, K_e and $\psi(n)$ are coprime. Now K_e is the public key component.

(5) Compute K_d such that $K_d \cdot K_e \equiv 1(\bmod\, \psi(n))$. K_d is the private key exponent. It should be kept secret.

(6) K_e and n are announced to the public for encryption.

(7) For decryption, ciphertext, K_e, and modulus n are used. By using q and $\psi(n)$ decryption key is calculated called private key K_d and must be kept secret.

Message Digest Generation. MD5 hash function algorithm has been used for the purpose of generating the message digest. The MD5 message digest algorithm generates 16-byte hash value in text format as 32-digit hexadecimal number. MD5 has been employed in a variety of areas, mainly used to check the data integrity in the cryptographic domain. Cryptographically strong digest algorithm generates a nearly unique digital fingerprint value from any source string [14]. Small change in the message leads to the predominantly different hash. MD5 even produces a hash for zero-length string.

Pseudo Code. Consider the following:

(1) The input message is divided into blocks of 512 bits. If the total number of bits is not the multiple of 512, then the padding of bits will be done.

(2) Padding is done in the following format:

First, single bit "1" is appended to the end and zeros are padded to make message length as 64 bits less than the multiple of 512.

(3) The last block represents the original message length.

(4) The MD5 algorithm utilizes 4 chaining variables of 32-bit length.

FIGURE 2: EC2 dashboard in Amazon Web Services (AWS).

(5) There are four main functions which use the above state variables and input message to produce the message digest. The functions are as follows:

$$F(B, C, D) = (B\ \&\ C)\ |\ (\sim B\ \&\ D),$$

$$G(B, C, D) = (B\ \&\ D)\ |\ (C\ \&\ \sim D),$$

$$H(B, C, D) = B \wedge C \wedge D,$$

$$I(B, C, D) = C \wedge (B\ |\sim D).$$

Note: &, |, $\wedge$, and $\sim$ denote bitwise AND, OR, XOR, and NOT operations, respectively.

The above four functions are applied to all the individual 512-bit blocks. Finally, the digest is stored in the variables A, B, C, and D.

4. Results and Analysis

Various services to the registered users are offered by Amazon Web Services (AWS). In this proposed approach, EC2 service is used after registering in AWS. A remote machine was launched with the help of the Amazon EC2 service for the required configuration as shown in Figure 2.

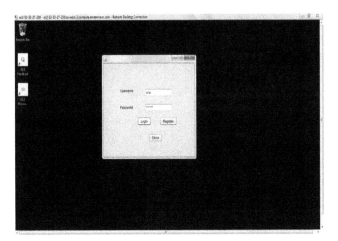

FIGURE 3: Application run on remote machine.

FIGURE 4: Registration.

The process is carried out in seven steps:

(1) User login with registered credentials.

(2) Encryption.

(3) Message digest generation.

(4) Saving the encrypted file.

(5) Retrieving the encrypted file.

(6) Checking integrity using message digest.

(7) Decryption.

4.1. User Registration. Using remote desktop connection, the remote machine was accessed and the developed application was implemented using JAVA platform as shown in Figure 3.

After giving username and password register request should be made. Before inserting the username and password in the database, a check is run in the database for any account with the mentioned username. This step is done to ensure unique usernames for every account as this column acts as the primary key in the database table. After logging into the database using the username and password, a message will be displayed as shown in Figure 4.

4.1.1. User Login. A user has to register with the system database to become eligible to store data. This prevents unauthorized access. While registering the user has to select a username and password which had not been taken before and can set any password of his choice as shown in Figure 5. After registering with a valid username, it allows the user to do the desired task in the future such as selecting the file from the drive for the encryption process.

4.1.2. Saved in Database. Figure 6 shows the username and the entered password's hash function, which is stored on the server. The entered password will be converted into its hash value using the MD5 algorithm.

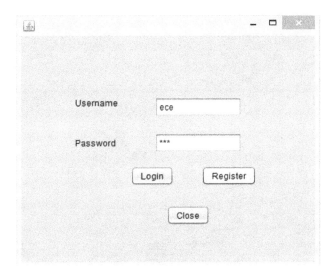

FIGURE 5: Login.

FIGURE 6: Login details in database.

4.2. Selecting a File. As a next step the user can select the file to be stored in the cloud. The file must be encrypted to maintain its confidentiality using RSA. From Figure 7 it is clear that the user can select a file by browsing and then encrypt it.

4.3. Encrypt and Save. Once the file is selected the user needs to click the encrypt button to encrypt the file using RSA

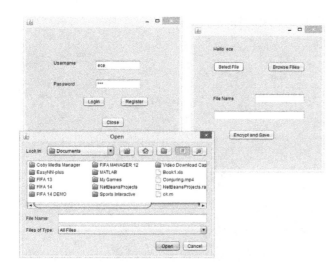

FIGURE 7: Selecting a file.

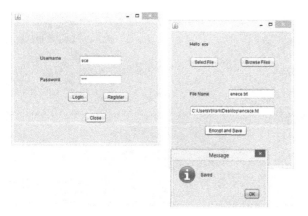

FIGURE 8: Encryption.

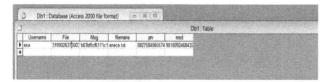

FIGURE 9: File in database.

algorithm and message digest function. After encryption, the file is saved in the database available in the cloud as shown in Figure 8.

4.3.1. Saved in Database. Now in the next database, along with the username, hash function of the password, file data (encrypted), keys used for encryption and decryption are saved as shown in Figure 9.

4.4. Decryption. Supposing that the user needs to view the file saved under the login provided, the user can select the file and download it to the specified place. The message digest is generated and at the same time it is being verified for ensuring

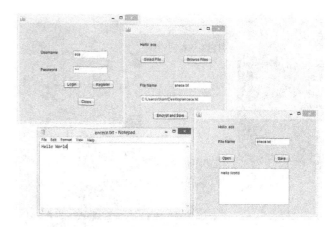

FIGURE 10: Decryption and saving the file.

the file integrity. The downloaded file is decrypted one as shown in Figure 10.

4.5. Performance Analysis. In this proposed method public key infrastructure (RSA) is used where two different keys are used one for encryption and the other for decryption. To break the crypt system factoring "n" is needed, where n is the product of two large primes. RSA system is difficult to hack because guessing of two large prime numbers in the key space is complex.

With MD5 algorithm faster avalanche effect is achievable; that is, small change in the message leads to the predominantly different hash. MD5 even produces a hash for zero-length string.

Here the length of hash is 128 bits, so, for birthday attack, 264 random documents need to be tried [14].

In this proposed approach both RSA and MD5 features were combined together so complexity increased towards hacking. So, compared with the available literature, the maximum level of privacy with tamper-resistance for file storage in the cloud was achieved.

The proposed approach is compared with the existing system based on functions and the findings were shown in Table 1.

5. Conclusion

Thus, we have designed a secure file storage system which incorporates authenticity, ingenuousness, and confidentiality. It is implemented in almost everything which required granting permission to only authorized credentials. The password is stored in the database as a message digest. This kind of password storage is really tamperproof. The encryption process makes the data secure; it prevents readability by unauthorized personnel and also establishes a framework to remove imposture. The system has been designed in such a way that this one-way hash function, if even cracked, will lead to getting encrypted data only. The application of hash function makes it impossible for any changes on data to go unnoticed. After the application of RSA and MD5 before

TABLE 1: Performance analysis.

Functions	Guo et al. (2013) [9]	Han et al. (2013) [10]	Sheu et al. (2014) [1]	Park (2015) [4]	Proposed approach
Identification & authentication	No	Yes	No	Yes	Yes
Authorization	No	Yes	No	Yes	Yes
Confidentiality	Yes	Yes	No	Yes	Yes
Integrity	No	No	Yes	No	Yes
Antiattack capability	Weak	Medium	Weak	Medium	Strong

storage, the data becomes resistant to access or modifications by any third party and to the storage system.

Competing Interests

The authors of the paper do not have a direct financial relation with the commercial identity mentioned in their paper that might lead to competing interests for any of them.

References

[1] R.-K. Sheu, S.-M. Yuan, W.-T. Lo, and C.-I. Ku, "Design and implementation of file deduplication framework on HDFS," *International Journal of Distributed Sensor Networks*, vol. 2014, Article ID 561340, 11 pages, 2014.

[2] Y. Sun, J. Zhang, Y. Xiong, and G. Zhu, "Data security and privacy in cloud computing," *International Journal of Distributed Sensor Networks*, vol. 2014, Article ID 190903, 9 pages, 2014.

[3] S. Iyer, "Cyber security for smart grid, cryptography, and privacy," *International Journal of Digital Multimedia Broadcasting*, vol. 2011, Article ID 372020, 8 pages, 2011.

[4] S. B. Park, "Security requirements for multimedia archives," *Advances in Multimedia*, vol. 2015, Article ID 956416, 5 pages, 2015.

[5] S. Balasubramaniam and V. Kavitha, "A survey on data encryption tecniques in cloud computing," *Asian Journal of Information Technology*, vol. 13, no. 9, pp. 494–505, 2014.

[6] C.-L. Chen, T.-T. Yang, and T.-F. Shih, "A secure medical data exchange protocol based on cloud environment," *Journal of Medical Systems*, vol. 38, no. 9, article 112, 2014.

[7] D. Zissis and D. Lekkas, "Addressing cloud computing security issues," *Future Generation Computer Systems*, vol. 28, no. 3, pp. 583–592, 2012.

[8] N. Gonzalez, C. Miers, F. Redígolo et al., "A quantitative analysis of current security concerns and solutions for cloud computing," *Journal of Cloud Computing*, vol. 1, no. 1, pp. 1–18, 2012.

[9] P. Guo, L. Su, L. Ning, and G. Dan, "Hybrid encryption algorithms in cloud computing," *Information Technology Journal*, vol. 12, no. 14, pp. 3015–3019, 2013.

[10] J. Han, W. Susilo, and Y. Mu, "Identity-based data storage in cloud computing," *Future Generation Computer Systems*, vol. 29, no. 3, pp. 673–681, 2013.

[11] J. Li, J. Li, Z. Liu, and C. Jia, "Enabling efficient and secure data sharing in cloud computing," *Concurrency Computation Practice and Experience*, vol. 26, no. 5, pp. 1052–1066, 2014.

[12] S. K. Sood, "A combined approach to ensure data security in cloud computing," *Journal of Network and Computer Applications*, vol. 35, no. 6, pp. 1831–1838, 2012.

[13] S. Tan, L. Tan, X. Li, and Y. Jia, "An efficient method for checking the integrity of data in the cloud," *China Communications*, vol. 11, no. 9, pp. 68–81, 2014.

[14] B. Schneier, *Applied Cryptography: Protocols, Algorithms, and Source Code in C*, John Wiley & Sons, 2nd edition, 2001.

20

Low-Light Image Enhancement based on Guided Image Filtering in Gradient Domain

Xiankun Sun,[1,2] Huijie Liu,[2] Shiqian Wu,[3] Zhijun Fang,[2] Chengfan Li,[1] and Jingyuan Yin[1,4]

[1]*School of Computer Engineering and Science, Shanghai University, Shanghai, China*
[2]*School of Electronic and Electrical Engineering, Shanghai University of Engineering Science, Shanghai, China*
[3]*School of Machinery and Automation, Wuhan University of Science and Technology, Wuhan, China*
[4]*Earthquake Administration of Shanghai, Shanghai, China*

Correspondence should be addressed to Xiankun Sun; xksun@sues.edu.cn and Jingyuan Yin; 1061233142@qq.com

Academic Editor: Fabrice Labeau

We propose a novel approach for low-light image enhancement. Based on illumination-reflection model, the guided image filter is employed to extract the illumination component of the underlying image. Afterwards, we obtain the reflection component and enhance it by nonlinear functions, sigmoid and gamma, respectively. We use the first-order edge-aware constraint in the gradient domain to achieve good edge preserving features of enhanced images and to eliminate halo artefact effectively. Moreover, the resulting images have high contrast and ample details due to the enhanced illumination and reflection component. We evaluate our method by operating on a large amount of low-light images, with comparison with other popular methods. The experimental results show that our approach outperforms the others in terms of visual perception and objective evaluation.

1. Introduction

Video surveillance is now widely used in various fields, like public security, transportation, and so on. The surveillance systems are required to perform not only in day time but also in night time. However, the videos captured in some situations such as dark place or night are very poor so that the objects can hardly be perceived by humans. Thus, it is necessary to enhance the low-light images in image processing and video surveillance.

Recently, the technique of low-light image enhancement has made remarkable progress. The commonly used methods include dark channel prior model [1, 2], neural network model [3, 4], histogram equalization (HE) [5, 6], image fusion [7, 8], wavelet domain algorithm [9, 10], and illumination-reflection model [11–14]. It is noted that the adaptability of dark channel prior model is poor in disposing the images with rich details and high brightness [2]. The design and use of neural network require domain knowledge so that the underlying neural system has good generalization. The idea of histogram equalization is to merge several bins of grayscales in order to increase contrast, but such process may yield detail

loss. The image fusion method needs multiple frame images, which is not applicable for single image frame. Wavelet transform is alternative technique for low-light image enhancement as shown in [9]. The most popular method in enhancing low-light images is to decompose images with the illumination-reflection model.

It was proposed by Land [15] that an image $J(x, y)$ can be decomposed by the reflection component $R(x, y)$ and the illumination component $L(x, y)$:

$$J(x, y) = R(x, y) \cdot L(x, y), \qquad (1)$$

where (x, y) represents the coordinates of image. Normally, the illumination component is determined by the dynamic range of the underlying image, while the reflection component is dependent on the intrinsic characteristics of the objects within the underlying image. Equation (1) is generally converted to the logarithmic domain so that the multiplication becomes addition.

The illumination component can be obtained by various methods, such as multiscale Gaussian function in [11], an improved Gaussian function in [12], and the bilateral

(a) Input image

(b) Image with halo artefact

FIGURE 1: Halo artefact.

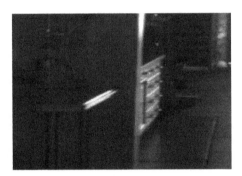

(a) Input image

(b) Image with gradient reversal

FIGURE 2: Gradient reversal.

filtering-based method in [14]. The key idea behind the Gaussian function is to use a low-pass filter as shown in (2). In the equation, $F(x, y)$ represents a center-around function, which is also a low-pass filter, and the symbol $*$ represents the convolution. Then, the reflection component can be obtained from (3) with the illumination component.

$$L(x, y) = F(x, y) * J(x, y), \qquad (2)$$

$$\lg[R(x, y)] = \lg[J(x, y)] - \lg[L(x, y)]. \qquad (3)$$

While calculating the illumination component and the reflection component of an image, what is most important is edge preserving and making the flat region smooth. The Multiscale Retinex (MSR) algorithm in [11] processes each color channel individually and then removes the illumination component to keep reflection component. Such processing is liable to color distortion. In addition, the method cannot achieve edge preserving and easily yields halo artefact as shown in Figure 1(b). Bilateral filtering (BLF), proposed by Tomaci and Mabduchi [16], is a good method for edge preserving and eliminating halo artefact. It was pointed out in [17] that the BLF may result in gradient reversal as shown in Figure 2(b). Accordingly, guided image filter (GIF) [17] and its variants, that is, weighted guided image filter (WGIF) [18] and guided image filter in gradient domain (GDGIF) [19] were proposed to achieve good edge preserving.

In this paper, we present a new method for low-light image enhancement, which mainly contributes to the following three aspects: (1) In order to effectively cope with the halo artefact and gradient reversal, the proposed method uses the illumination-reflection model and selects the GIF in gradient domain characterized by smoothness and edge preserving to estimate the illumination component; (2) the proposed method works on HSI color space to eliminate color distortion; (3) the illumination component and the reflection component are enhanced by nonlinear sigmoid and gamma transforms, respectively, to improve image contrast and enhance image details.

The remainder of the paper is organized as follows: Section 2 depicts the proposed low-light image enhancement algorithm. Section 3 demonstrates experimental results, followed by conclusion drawn in Section 4.

2. The Proposed Approach

The proposed method for enhancing low-light images consists of the following steps:

(1) Converting the low-light image from RGB color space to HSI color space

(2) For intensity (illumination) layer, estimating the illumination component with guided image filter in

gradient domain, followed by extracting the reflection component

(3) Enhancing the illumination component with a nonlinear sigmoid transform

(4) Enhancing the reflection component with a nonlinear gamma transform

(5) Taking the antilog of the sum of steps (3) and (4) as the enhanced intensity layer

(6) Converting the new HSI image back to RGB, which produces the final enhanced image

2.1. Guided Image Filter in Gradient Domain.

GDGIF [19] and WGIF [18] are both the improvements of the guided image filter. Basically, the output image q_i is a linear transform of guided image g_i in a square window M_k centered at the pixel k:

$$q_i = a_k g_i + b_k, \quad \forall i \in M_k. \tag{4}$$

In (4), guided image g_i can be input image p_i itself. The pixel i is located in the window M_k of length $(2r + 1)$, in which r is filter radius. a_k and b_k are linear coefficients in pixel k. For GIF, WGIF, and GDGIF, the larger value of a_k implies better edge preserving. On the contrary, if the value of a_k is much closer to 0, the filters have good smoothing performance in flat regions.

According to the gradient-domain optimization framework in [20], the task of filtering an image means converting one input image p_i into the final image q_i, which can be expressed as an energy function $E(a_k, b_k)$ including the zero-order data cost function $E_d(i)$ and first-order gradient cost function $E_g(i)$ terms:

$$E(a_k, b_k) = \sum_{i \in M_k} \left(E_d(i) + E_g(i) \right), \tag{5}$$

$$E_d(i) = \left(a_k g_i + b_k - p_i \right)^2, \tag{6}$$

$$E_g(i) = \varphi(i) \left\| \nabla q_i \right\|^2, \tag{7}$$

where $\left\| \nabla q_i \right\|$ is gradient magnitude; $\varphi(i)$ is gradient weight constraint. In (4), the gradient magnitude of q_i is $\left\| \nabla q_i \right\| = a_k$.

2.1.1. Guided Image Filter.

In the guided image filter [17], $\varphi_1(i) = \varepsilon$, the expressions of a_k and b_k can be obtained according to (4)–(7) shown as follows:

$$a_k = \frac{(1/|w|) \sum_{k:i \in M_k} g_i p_i - \mu_k \overline{p_k}}{\sigma_k^2 + \varepsilon}, \tag{8}$$

$$b_k = \overline{p_k} - a_k \mu_k,$$

where μ_k is the mean of image g_i in the window M_k, and σ_k^2 is the variance of image g_i in the window M_k, $|w|$ is the total pixel number in window M_k, and $\overline{p_k}$ is the mean of image p_i in window M_k. ε is a regularization parameter, which controls the trade-off between edge preserving and smoothness. As ε is generally fixed ratherthan spatially varying in filtering process, halo artefact is unavoidable in edges.

2.1.2. Weighted Guided Image Filter.

Li et al. [18] proposed the WGIF, where a spatially varying gradient weight constraint $\varphi_2(i) = \varepsilon / \Gamma_{g\_k}$ was added in (7).

$$\Gamma_{g\_k} = \frac{1}{N} \sum_{i=1}^{N} \frac{\sigma_{g,1}^2(k) + \lambda}{\sigma_{g,1}^2(i) + \lambda}, \tag{9}$$

where Γ_{g_k} is a single-scale edge-aware weighting, which is defined by using local variances in 3×3 windows, $\sigma_{g,1}^2(k)$ is the variance of guided image g_i in the 3×3 window, N is the number of image pixels, λ is a small constant and its value is $(0.001 \times L)^2$, and L is the dynamic range of the input image. The expressions of a_k' and b_k' in the WGIF can be obtained according to (4)–(7) as shown below:

$$a_k' = \frac{(1/|w|) \sum_{k:i \in M_k} g_i p_i - \mu_k \overline{p_k}}{\sigma_k^2 + \varepsilon / \Gamma_{g\_k}}, \tag{10}$$

$$b_k' = \overline{p_k} - a_k' \mu_k.$$

It is noted that the edge-aware weighting Γ_{g_k} is spatially varying in the WGIF; that is, Γ_{g_k} is larger than 1 when the pixel k locates in the edge area, and Γ_{g_k} is smaller than 1 when the pixel k locates in the flat area. As a result, a_k' is closer to 1 than a_k in the GIF, which implies that WGIF has the better edge preservation than GIF.

WGIF can reduce the halo artefact to some extent. However, both the GIF and the WGIF filters have no explicit constraints to cope with edges. Both cannot preserve edges well because image filtering is performed on edges, which definitely smoothed the edges [19, 21].

2.1.3. Guided Image Filter in Gradient Domain.

Kou et al. [19] proposed the guided image filter in gradient domain (GDGIF), by adding an explicit first-order (gradient domain) edge-aware constraint $E_e(i)$ to gradient-domain equation (5) shown below:

$$E(a_k, b_k) = \sum_{i \in M_k} \left(E_d(i) + E_g(i) + \phi E_e(i) \right), \tag{11}$$

$$E_e(i) = \alpha \left\| \nabla q_i - \nabla p_i \right\|^2,$$

where $E_e(i)$ is edge-aware constraint. The aim is to perceive the changes in local neighbourhoods so that the similar filtering is performed in the similar regions. α is a weight value, ∇q_i and ∇p_i represent the gradient values of output image q_i and input image p_i.

In the GDGIF, a multiscale edge-aware varying spatially gradient weight constraint $\varphi_3(i) = \varepsilon / \widehat{\Gamma}_{g\_k}$ is added in (7). The energy function of GDGIF is shown in (12), in which the

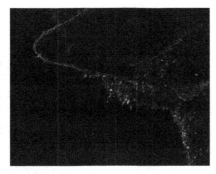

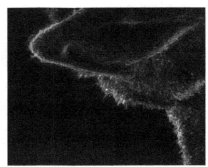

(a) Original image   (b) Edge results by Γ_{g_k} (c) Edge results by $\widehat{\Gamma}_{g\_k}$

FIGURE 3: Comparison of $\widehat{\Gamma}_{g\_k}$ and Γ_{g_k}.

second item is the combination of the first-order gradient cost function $E_g(i)$ and the edge-aware constraint $E_e(i)$.

$$
\begin{aligned}
& E\left(a_k'', b_k''\right) \\
& = \sum\left(\left(a_k'' g_i + b_k'' - p_i\right)^2 + \frac{\varepsilon}{\widehat{\Gamma}_{g\_k}}\left(a_k'' - \gamma_k\right)^2\right),
\end{aligned}
\tag{12}
$$

$$
\widehat{\Gamma}_{g\_k} = \frac{1}{N}\sum_{i=1}^{N}\frac{\chi_k + \lambda}{\chi_i + \lambda},
\tag{13}
$$

$$
\gamma_k = 1 - \frac{1}{1 + e^{\eta(\chi_k - \mu_{\chi,\infty})}},
\tag{14}
$$

where $\widehat{\Gamma}_{g\_k}$ is defined by local variances of $(2r+1)\times(2r+1)$ windows of all pixels; r is the filter radius. It is noted that $\widehat{\Gamma}_{g\_k}$ is a multiscale edge-aware weighting varying spatially, in which $\chi_k = \sigma_{g,1}(k) * \sigma_{g,r}(k)$. The edge-aware weighting detects the edge more accurately, and a pixel is detected as an edge pixel when the two scale variances are very large.

The comparison of $\widehat{\Gamma}_{g\_k}$ and Γ_{g_k} in WGIF of an image is shown in Figure 3. The edges of the image are detected accurately by using the multiscale edge-aware weighting $\widehat{\Gamma}_{g\_k}$ rather than using the single-scale edge-aware weighting Γ_{g_k} in WGIF.

In (14), γ_k is an edge-aware constraint to preserve edges. $\mu_{\chi,\infty}$ is the mean of all χ_i, and the value of η is $4/(\mu_{\chi,\infty} - \min(\chi_i))$. The value of γ_k is close to 1 when the pixel k locates in the edge area, and the value is close to 0 when the pixel k locates in the flat area.

The expressions of a_k'' and b_k'' in the GDGIF can be obtained according to (12)–(14), shown as follows:

$$
a_k'' = \frac{(1/|w|)\sum_{k:i\in M_k}g_i p_i - \mu_k\overline{p_k} + \left(\varepsilon/\widehat{\Gamma}_{g\_k}\right)\gamma_k}{\sigma_k^2 + \varepsilon/\widehat{\Gamma}_{g\_k}},
\tag{15}
$$

$$
b_k'' = \overline{p_k} - a_k''\mu_k.
$$

When the input image p_i and guided image g_i are the same, the GDGIF has better edge preserving and smoother

features than the GIF and the WGIF due to the following two points.

(1) When pixel k locates in the edge area, the expression of a_k'' can be computed as

$$
a_k'' = \frac{\sigma_k^2 + \left(\varepsilon/\widehat{\Gamma}_{g\_k}\right)\gamma_k}{\sigma_k^2 + \varepsilon/\widehat{\Gamma}_{g\_k}}.
\tag{16}
$$

It is seen that the value of γ_k is 1, and the value of a_k'' is 1, which is independent of parameter ε. In fact, the value of a_k'' in GDGIF is much closer to 1 than it is in GIF and WGIF. Hence, GDGIF has the best edge preserving feature.

(2) When a pixel k locates in the flat areas, the value γ_k is close to 0, the parameter a_k'' is accordingly independent of the choice of ε. As a result, we can select larger ε in GDGIF than that in WGIF and GIF, so that better smoothing is achieved without affecting the edge preserving [19].

For example, we use GIF, WGIF, and GDGIF for image filtering by choosing the same filter radius $r = 16$ and regularization parameter $\varepsilon = 0.8^\wedge 2$. The result is shown in Figure 4. It is observed that the image filtered by GDGIF has the best edge preserving.

In summary, the GDGIF has the best edge preserving and smoothing features. As a result, we choose the GDGIF to estimate the illumination component.

2.2. Enhancing the Intensity Layer. Generally, the processing of an RGB image is to operate the R, G, and B three channels separately, which is time-consuming. In this work, the low-light image is converted from RGB color space to HSI color space. The HSI color space stems from the human visual system, using three elements of color, hue (H), saturation (S), and intensity (I) to describe the color, which is more consistent with human visual feature than RGB color space. In HSI color space, the intensity component is enhanced while the hue and saturation components are extracted without further processing.

2.2.1. Estimating Illumination Component. Based on illumination-reflection model, combined with (2), (4), and (15), we use the GDGIF to estimate the illumination

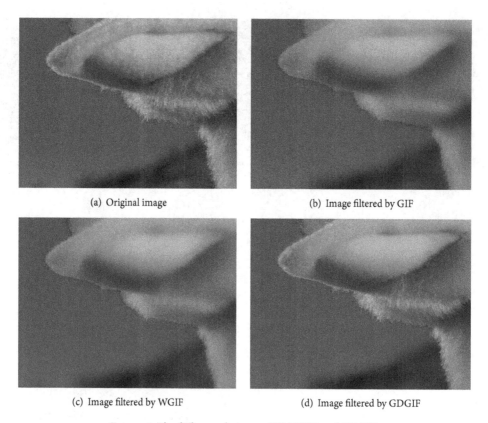

(a) Original image

(b) Image filtered by GIF

(c) Image filtered by WGIF

(d) Image filtered by GDGIF

FIGURE 4: The difference between GIF, WGIF, and GDGIF.

component $L_I(x, y)$ of intensity layer image $I(x, y)$ as follows:

$$L_I(x, y) = q(x, y) * I(x, y), \quad (17)$$

where $q(x, y)$ is represented by the GDGIF function, as shown in (4). Then the reflection component $R_I(x, y)$ of intensity layer image can be obtained according to (3) and (17) as follows:

$$\begin{aligned} r_I(x, y) &= \lg[R_I(x, y)] \\ &= \lg[I(x, y)] - \lg[L_I(x, y)]. \end{aligned} \quad (18)$$

2.2.2. Enhancing Illumination Component. Normally, the methods based on illumination-reflection model are to extract and then enhance the reflection component without considering the illumination component. Such processing leads to a lack of coordination between gray levels and yields color distortion. To cope with this problem, Wu et al. [13] proposed enhancing the reflection component together with the illumination component. Inspired by this idea, we process the illumination component by the nonlinear tensile sigmoid transform as shown in Figure 5. It is indicated in [22] that the sigmoid transform has the ability to sharpen images, highlight the local details, and stretch the image contrast.

The nonlinear tensile sigmoid transform is expressed in the following equations:

$$l_{\text{Sigmoid}}(x, y) = r_{\min} + \frac{r_{\max} - r_{\min}}{1 + e^{-a(r(x,y) - b \cdot (r_{\max} - r_{\min}))}}, \quad (19)$$

$$l_{I\_\text{out}}(x, y) = l_I(x, y) \times l_{\text{Sigmoid}}(x, y),$$

where l_{Sigmoid} is self-defined sigmoid nonlinear function, whose range is $[0, 1]$, $r_{\min}$ and $r_{\max}$ represent the minimum and maximum values of reflection component, respectively, and $l_I(x, y)$ and $l_{I\_\text{out}}(x, y)$ are the initial and the enhanced illumination component, respectively. It is noted that there are two important parameters a, b in which the parameter a controls how an image is enhanced and the parameter b controls the contrast enhancement. Generally, a large value of a enhances an image greatly. On the other hand, a small value of b enhances the contrast of the dark regions, and a large value of b enhances the contrast of the light regions. Figure 6 shows examples by taking different parameters. In this study, the parameters a, b are selected as 2 and 0.004, respectively.

2.2.3. Enhancing the Reflection Component. It is known that human eyes are not sensible for high brightness difference but sensible for the small difference in low intensity. Thus, gamma transform [23] is normally employed to enhance the reflection component as follows:

$$r_{I\_\text{out}}(x, y) = c r_I^{\gamma}(x, y), \quad (20)$$

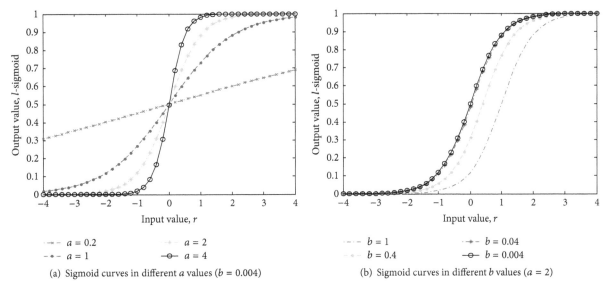

(a) Sigmoid curves in different a values ($b = 0.004$)

(b) Sigmoid curves in different b values ($a = 2$)

FIGURE 5: Sigmoid function curves.

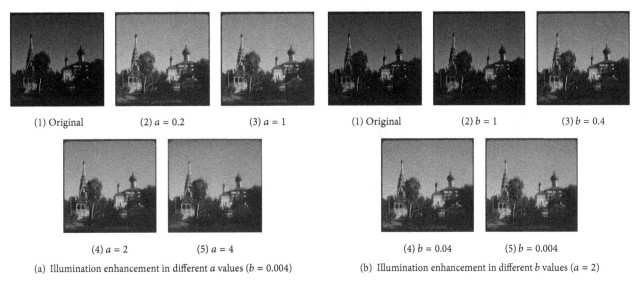

(1) Original   (2) $a = 0.2$ (3) $a = 1$

(1) Original   (2) $b = 1$ (3) $b = 0.4$

(4) $a = 2$ (5) $a = 4$

(4) $b = 0.04$ (5) $b = 0.004$

(a) Illumination enhancement in different a values ($b = 0.004$)

(b) Illumination enhancement in different b values ($a = 2$)

FIGURE 6: Illumination component enhanced by sigmoid curves.

where c is a positive constant; γ is a parameter to control the image contrast.

It is seen from Figure 7 that when γ is less than 1, the contrast in low intensities is increased. On the contrary, the contrast in high intensities is enhanced in case $\gamma > 1$. The effect of parameter c is shown in Figure 8. In this work, the parameters are experimentally selected as follows: $\gamma = 0.6$; $c = 0.3$.

2.3. Final Enhanced Image. By taking antilog of the illumination component combined with the reflection component, we obtain the enhanced intensity image. The new HSI image is made up of enhanced intensity layer, original hue, and saturation layer. Then the enhanced HSI image is converted

into RGB image to obtain the final enhanced image. The whole process is shown in Figure 9.

3. Experimental Results and Discussions

As there is no public low-light image database, we collect 20 images from the Library of Congress and Internet as shown in Figure 10. In the simulation, the parameters are predefined as follows: window radius $r = 16$, regularization parameter $\varepsilon = 0.001$, the sigmoid parameters $a = 2$, $b = 0.004$, and gamma parameters $\gamma = 0.6$, $c = 0.3$. All experiments are performed in Matlab code on Windows 7 operation system. The computer is Intel® core™ i5-4570 3.20 GHz, and the RAM is 4.00 GB. The popular algorithms such as traditional

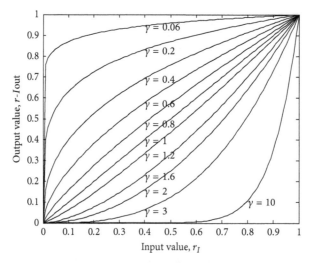

FIGURE 7: Gamma transforms ($c = 1$).

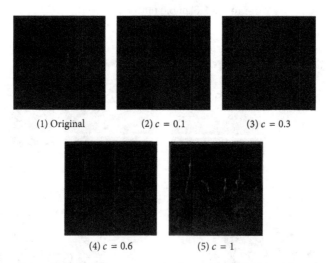

FIGURE 8: Reflection component enhanced by different c values.

MSR [11], Hao's algorithm [14], He's algorithm [17], histogram equalization (HE), improved MSR [12], and Kim's algorithm [9] are implemented for performance comparison.

3.1. Subjective Evaluation. It is observed from Figures 11 and 12 that the images enhanced by traditional MSR algorithm have obvious "white" phenomenon, which indicates color distortion. The images enhanced by Hao's method result in gradient reversal artefact as seen in red square from image 4 (white tower) in Figure 11, which indicates that the bilateral filtering has poor edge preserving property. Moreover, the resulting images by Hao's method are blurred which can be seen from images 1 (church) and 5 (the study) in Figure 11. He's algorithm also shows halo artefact which can be seen from image 1 (church), and this method cannot enhance the image contrast and brightness shown in Figure 12.

Histogram equalization algorithm can enhance image contrast, but this method misses details and enlarges noise, which can be observed from Figures 11 and 12. Improved MSR algorithm is better than the traditional MSR algorithm,

but this method causes halo artefact which can be seen from image 1 (church) in Figure 11 (highlighted box). Moreover, "white" phenomenon exists as shown in image 13 (boy), where the tire is over-enhanced and loses detailed information. Our results show that improved MSR algorithm is not effective in dealing with night images, as observed in Figure 12.

Kim's algorithm also causes color distortion, which can be seen from image 1 (church) in Figure 11, and the sky in the red square becomes gray. The enhanced images may be blurred as seen in image 1 (church), which implies that Kim's algorithm has poor edge preserving.

As seen from Figures 11 and 12, the proposed algorithm has the best color fidelity and edge preserving. Also, the enhanced images have less noise and clearer details than the one enhanced by histogram equalization algorithm.

3.2. Objective Evaluation. Currently, no standard objective metrics are proposed for enhancement assessment of low-light images. In this study, we employ information entropy

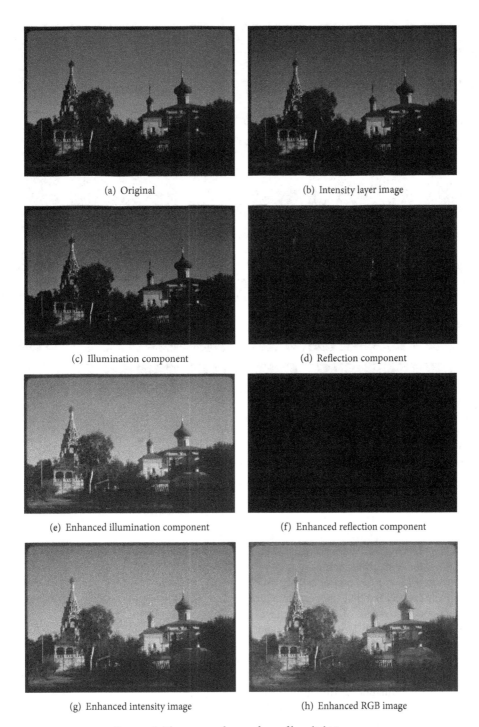

(a) Original

(b) Intensity layer image

(c) Illumination component

(d) Reflection component

(e) Enhanced illumination component

(f) Enhanced reflection component

(g) Enhanced intensity image

(h) Enhanced RGB image

FIGURE 9: The proposed procedure of low-light images.

(IE) to evaluate image details and choose the average edge intensity (AEI) to evaluate the edge preserving feature of enhanced images. The IE is defined as follows:

$$IE = -\sum_{s=0}^{L-1} P\left(r_s\right) \log_2 P\left(r_s\right), \qquad (21)$$

where $P(r_s)$ represents the probability of gray level s; L is the total number of gray levels. Larger IE indicates more

information, which implies that there are more details in the underlying image.

The AEI is defined as follows:

$$AEI = E\left(g\left(i,j\right)\right) = E\left(\sqrt{S_x\left(i,j\right)^2 + S_y\left(i,j\right)^2}\right), \qquad (22)$$

where $S_x(i,j)$ and $S_y(i,j)$ represent gradients in x and y directions on image edges. E represents expectation. In this study, Sobel operator is used for gradient computation. Larger

FIGURE 10: Datasets used in experiments.

AEI indicates good edge preserving. Also, the efficiency of the proposed method is compared with other methods.

Table 1 shows the average IE and AEI and operating time based on 20 test images. It is observed that the performance of He's method is not good in terms of IE. The images enhanced by He's method are usually dark and lose many details. Figure 13 shows the IE performances of the best three methods, that is, Hao's algorithm, Kim's algorithm, and the proposed method. It is seen that the median IE (marked by a red line) of the proposed method is the largest. The mean IE (marked by a green line) of the proposed method is 9.8% higher than Hao's algorithm and 1.8% higher than Kim's algorithm in the 20 test images.

On the other hand, it is observed from Table 1 that the improved MSR, histogram equalization (HE), Kim's algorithm, and the proposed algorithm achieve top four performances in terms of AEI. It is noted that high AEI in the histogram equalization accounts for much noise. The AEI of the improved MSR, Kim's method, and the proposed method on each individual image are shown in Figure 14. Results show that the median AEI (marked by a red line) of the proposed method is the largest, and the mean AEI (marked by a green line) of the proposed method is 26.8% higher than the improved MSR and 15.6% higher than Kim's algorithm.

TABLE 1: The average IE, AEI, and operating time (sec) on twenty images.

	Average IE	Average AEI	Average time
Original	11.057	50.756	N/R
Traditional MSR	13.439	67.485	1.77
Hao et al.'s [14]	14.091	57.838	16.289
He et al.'s [17]	11.867	61.952	0.377
HE	14.761	83.874	0.281
Improved MSR [12]	13.234	83.606	7.915
Kim et al.'s [9]	15.193	96.477	0.867
The proposed method	15.478	114.297	0.698

In summary, the proposed method achieves the best performance in terms of both IE and AEI. Furthermore,

FIGURE 11: Comparison among different algorithms.

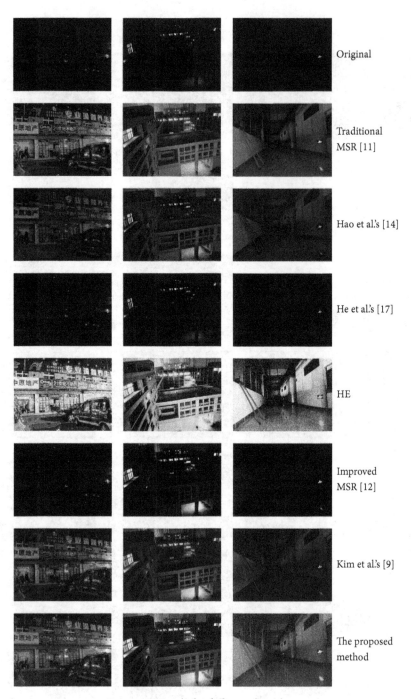

FIGURE 12: Results by different algorithms.

the proposed method is very efficient and achieves the 3rd position among the 7 methods as shown in Table 1. It is noted that He's algorithm has the worst enhanced image quality. Figure 15 shows the median operating time (marked by a red line) and the mean operating time (marked by a green line) of HE, Kim's, and the proposed method. Generally, the bilateral filtering is not as efficient as the GDGIF. The computation complexity of bilateral filtering is $o(Nr^2)$, where r refers to the window radius of bilateral filtering, and N is the number of image pixels while the GDGIF's computation complexity is

$o(N)$. In other words, the GDGIF's computation complexity is not related to the filter size. Results show that the average time by the proposed method is 59.7% higher than HE and 19.4% less than Kim's algorithm.

4. Conclusion

A low-light image enhancement algorithm is presented in the paper. By decomposing a low-light image into the illumination component and the reflection component, it

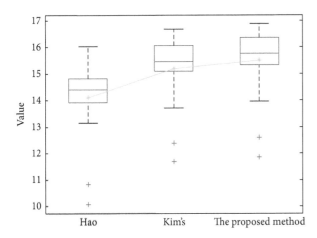

FIGURE 13: IE results by Hao's, Kim's, and the proposed method.

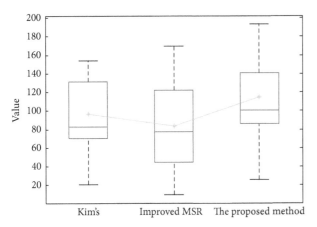

FIGURE 14: AEI results by Kim's, improved MSR, and the proposed method.

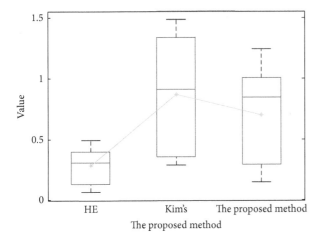

FIGURE 15: Operating time by HE, Kim's, and the proposed method.

offers a solution to expand illumination and enhances image details separately. Specifically, the illumination component is processed using guided image filter in gradient domain, followed by nonlinear sigmoid transform. The reflection component is enhanced by the gamma transform. This solution enhances low-light images and effectively avoids distortions

(for example color) and annoying artefacts (e.g., blurring, halo). Then, the final result is obtained by antilogging the sum of the enhanced two components. Experimental results demonstrate that the enhanced images by the proposed method are visually pleasing by subjective test and the performance of the proposed method outperforms the existing methods in terms of both IE and AEI assessments. Moreover, the proposed algorithm is efficient because the computation complexity is not related to filter size. The proposed method has great potential to implement in real-time low-light video processing.

Acknowledgments

This work was supported in part by the National Natural Science Foundation of China under Grant 61371190, Natural Science Foundation of Shanghai under Grants 13ZR1455200 and 17ZR1411900, the Opening Project of Shanghai Key Laboratory of Integrated Administration Technologies for Information Security (AGK2015006), the Founding Program for the Cultivation of Young University Teachers of Shanghai (ZZGCD15090), and the Research Start-Up Founding Program of Shanghai University of Engineering Science (2016-56). The authors would like to thank Se Eun Kim for sharing his code.

References

[1] A. Alajarmeh, R. A. Salam, M. F. Marhusin, and K. Abdulrahim, "Real-time video enhancement for various weather conditions using dark channel and fuzzy logic," in *Proceedings of the 2014 International Conference on Computer and Information Sciences, ICCOINS 2014*, mys, June 2014.

[2] X. Jiang, H. Yao, S. Zhang, X. Lu, and W. Zeng, "Night video enhancement using improved dark channel prior," in *Proceedings of the 2013 20th IEEE International Conference on Image Processing, ICIP 2013*, pp. 553–557, aus, September 2013.

[3] L. Tang, S. Chen, W. Liu, and Y. Li, "Improved Retinex image enhancement algorithm," in *Proceedings of the 2011 2nd International Conference on Challenges in Environmental Science and Computer Engineering, CESCE 2011*, pp. 208–212, chn, December 2011.

[4] M. Athimethphat and K. Kritayakirana, "Enhanced illumination balancing with neural network for improved degraded scanned text-photo images," in *Proceedings of the 8th Electrical Engineering/ Electronics, Computer, Telecommunications and Information Technology (ECTI) Association of Thailand - Conference 2011, ECTI-CON 2011*, pp. 983–986, tha, May 2011.

[5] G. Yadav, S. Maheshwari, and A. Agarwal, "Contrast limited adaptive histogram equalization based enhancement for real time video system," in *Proceedings of the 3rd International Conference on Advances in Computing, Communications and Informatics, ICACCI 2014*, pp. 2392–2397, ind, September 2014.

[6] Z. Rong, Z. Li, and L. Dong-Nan, "Study of color heritage image enhancement algorithms based on histogram equalization," *Optik*, vol. 126, no. 24, pp. 5665–5667, 2015.

[7] J. Xiao, H. Peng, Y. Zhang, C. Tu, and Q. Li, "Fast image enhancement based on color space fusion," *Color Research and Application*, vol. 41, no. 1, pp. 22–31, 2016.

[8] Z. Liu, E. Blasch, Z. Xue, J. Zhao, R. Laganiére, and W. Wu, "Objective assessment of multiresolution image fusion algorithms for context enhancement in Night vision: A comparative study," *IEEE Transactions on Pattern Analysis and Machine Intelligence*, vol. 34, no. 1, pp. 94–109, 2012.

[9] S. E. Kim, J. J. Jeon, and I. K. Eom, "Image contrast enhancement using entropy scaling in wavelet domain," *Signal Processing*, vol. 127, pp. 1–11, 2016.

[10] E. Provenzi and V. Caselles, "A wavelet perspective on variational perceptually-inspired color enhancement," *International Journal of Computer Vision*, vol. 106, no. 2, pp. 153–171, 2014.

[11] D. J. Jobson, Z.-U. Rahman, and G. A. Woodell, "A multiscale retinex for bridging the gap between color images and the human observation of scenes," *IEEE Transactions on Image Processing*, vol. 6, no. 7, pp. 965–976, 1997.

[12] A. B. Petro, C. Sbert, and J. Morel, "Multiscale Retinex," *Image Processing On Line*, vol. 4, pp. 71–88, 2014.

[13] S. Wu, Z. Hu, W. Yu, and J. Feng, "An improved image enhancement approach based on Retinex theory," in *Proceedings of the 2013 International Conference on Information Technology and Applications, ITA 2013*, pp. 67–71, chn, November 2013.

[14] W. Hao, M. He, H. Ge, C.-J. Wang, and Q.-W. Gao, "Retinex-like method for image enhancement in poor visibility conditions," in *Proceedings of the 2011 International Conference on Advanced in Control Engineering and Information Science, CEIS 2011*, pp. 2798–2803, chn, August 2011.

[15] E. Land, "The retinex," *American Scientists*, vol. 52, no. 2, pp. 247–264, 1964.

[16] C. Tomaci and R. Mabduchi, "Bilateral filtering for gray and color images," in *Proceedings of the Proceeding of the 6th IEEE International Conference Computer Vision*, pp. 839–846, Bombay, India, January 1998.

[17] K. He, J. Sun, and X. Tang, "Guided image filtering," *IEEE Transactions on Pattern Analysis and Machine Intelligence*, vol. 35, no. 6, pp. 1397–1409, 2013.

[18] Z. Li, J. Zheng, Z. Zhu, W. Yao, and S. Wu, "Weighted guided image filtering," *IEEE Transactions on Image Processing*, vol. 24, no. 1, pp. 120–129, 2015.

[19] F. Kou, W. Chen, C. Wen, and Z. Li, "Gradient domain guided image filtering," *IEEE Transactions on Image Processing*, vol. 24, no. 11, pp. 4528–4539, 2015.

[20] P. Bhat, C. L. Zitnick, M. Cohen, and B. Curless, "GradientShop: A gradient-domain optimization framework for image and video filtering," *ACM Transactions on Graphics*, vol. 29, no. 2, article no. 10, 2010.

[21] M. Hua, X. Bie, M. Zhang, and W. Wang, "Edge-aware gradient domain optimization framework for image filtering by local propagation," in *Proceedings of the 27th IEEE Conference on Computer Vision and Pattern Recognition, CVPR 2014*, pp. 2838–2845, usa, June 2014.

[22] O. Nuri and C. Ender, "A non-linear technique for the enhancement of extremely non-uniform lighting images," *Journal of Aeronautics and Space Technologies*, vol. 3, no. 3, pp. 37–47, 2007.

[23] A. K. Bhandari, A. Kumar, and G. K. Singh, "Improved knee transfer function and gamma correction based method for contrast and brightness enhancement of satellite image," *AEU - International Journal of Electronics and Communications*, vol. 69, no. 2, pp. 579–589, 2015.

21

Channel Estimation for OFDM-Based Amplify-and-Forward Cooperative System using Relay-Superimposed Pilots

Xianwen He[ID], Gaoqi Dou[ID], and Jun Gao

Department of Communication Engineering, Naval University of Engineering, Wuhan 430033, China

Correspondence should be addressed to Gaoqi Dou; hjgcqq@163.com

Academic Editor: Jintao Wang

For the OFDM-based Amplify-and-Forward cooperative system, a novel relay-superimposed pilot strategy is proposed, where the source pilot symbols are frequency division multiplexed to estimate the cascaded channel while relay pilot sequence is superimposed onto the top of the cooperative data stream for second-hop channel estimation. This method avoids the loss of data rate for additional pilot subcarriers but results in the interference of unknown cooperative data. To remove the interference of cooperative data during the estimation of second-hop channel, the Cooperative Interference Cancelation scheme assisted by cooperative data from direct link is proposed. We derive the approximated lower bound for the MSE of second-hop channel estimation. Simulation results are presented to validate the performance of the proposed schemes.

1. Introduction

The Amplify-and-Forward (AF) Orthogonal Frequency Division Multiplexing (OFDM)-based cooperative system has been attractive recently, due to its ability to provide broader coverage and increased reliability [1–5]. However, the AF relaying link is concatenated by dual-hop (multihop) channels, which are distinct from the point-to-point transmission link. Many applications of the cooperative systems have been studied, for example, the optimal relay selection scheme [3], the optimal power allocation and subcarrier pairing for OFDM-based systems [4], the optimal coherent combination [5, 6], etc. However, purely knowing the cascaded channel is insufficient to support the optimal design in cooperative relaying systems. In order to fully exploit the benefit of cooperative system, it is crucial for the system to acquire the reliable individual Channel State Information (CSI). As a result, the problems of dual-hop channel estimation for relaying link with a minimal cost for relay is very challenging.

In the OFDM-based transmission of AF relaying system, most channel estimation schemes are aimed at obtaining the cascaded channel [7–9] and designing special algorithms to recover the individual channels. Unfortunately, the estimation sign ambiguity exists and only flat fading channels are considered. Hence, several recent works have studied the

problems of relay-assisted channel estimation [9–13]. The pilot-based channel estimation scheme is investigated in [9], where a channel estimator is required at relay node ($\mathcal{R}$) and the quantized version of the CSI estimation of first-hop link is forward to the destination node ($\mathcal{D}$). However, it brings the increased computational complexity and additional power consumption at $\mathcal{R}$. The work in [10] proposed to reserve some subcarriers at source node ($\mathcal{S}$) to accommodate relay pilot symbols. However, the pilot subcarriers occupy the valuable bandwidth that should have been available for data transmission. In the work [11–13], the authors employ the superimposed training scheme, which preserves the spectral efficiency and reduce the computational burden for relay node. However, the performance of channel estimation in [13] is affected by cooperative data interference and the strict orthogonal constraint between source and relay training is enforced in [11, 12], which brings more complex problems including optimal sequences design and power allocation.

We consider a three-node AF-OFDM based cooperative system and propose a relay-superimposed pilot method to acquire the CSIs including the cascaded ($\mathcal{S} \rightarrow \mathcal{R} \rightarrow \mathcal{D}$) channel and the second-hop ($\mathcal{R} \rightarrow \mathcal{D}$) channel respectively. In the new method, the relay pilot sequence is arithmetically added onto the unknown cooperative data stream at relay node, which avoids the loss of data rate for additional pilot

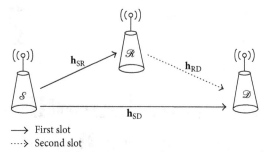

$\longrightarrow$ First slot
$\cdots\cdots\rightarrow$ Second slot

FIGURE 1: Network Model of AF Relay in three-node mode.

subcarriers but results in the interference of cooperative data in the process of estimating the $\mathscr{R} \rightarrow \mathscr{D}$ channel. To eliminate the additional cooperative interference, a Cooperative Interference Cancelation (CIC) scheme is proposed using detected symbols copy from direct channel ($\mathscr{S} \rightarrow \mathscr{D}$). We also derive the approximated lower bound for the mean square error (MSE) of second-hop channel estimation. Finally, we validate the performance of the proposed schemes with the given simulation results.

Notation 1. Superscripts H, T, $*$ denote the complex conjugate transpose, transpose and conjugate respectively. The Discrete Fourier Transform (DFT) of $N \times 1$ vector $\mathbf{x}$ is denoted by $\mathbf{X} = \mathbf{F}_N \mathbf{x}$, where $\mathbf{F}_N$ is an $N \times N$ Fourier matrix with the entry $f(k, n) = 1/\sqrt{N} e^{-j2\pi n/N}$ in row k and column n.

2. System Model

We consider a typical three-node OFDM-based cooperative system, as depicted in Figure 1, where $\mathscr{S}$ transmits data to the $\mathscr{D}$ with the assistance of $\mathscr{R}$. Moreover the direct link between $\mathscr{S}$ and $\mathscr{D}$ is available and $\mathscr{R}$ is located on the midpoint between $\mathscr{S}$ and $\mathscr{D}$. The frequency-selective fading channels between each node pairs are noted as $\mathbf{h}_{\mathrm{SD}} = [h_{\mathrm{SD},1}, h_{\mathrm{SD},2}, \ldots, h_{\mathrm{SD},L_{\mathrm{SD}}}]^T$, $\mathbf{h}_{\mathrm{SR}} = [h_{\mathrm{SR},1}, h_{\mathrm{SR},2}, \ldots, h_{\mathrm{SR},L_{\mathrm{SR}}}]^T$ and $\mathbf{h}_{\mathrm{RD}} = [h_{\mathrm{RD},1}, h_{\mathrm{RD},2}, \ldots, h_{\mathrm{RD},L_{\mathrm{RD}}}]^T$ respectively, where L_{SD}, L_{SR} and L_{RD} are channel orders. We assume the channel remains static over one OFDM block, but varies over different blocks. Individual channel taps are independent and Rayleigh distributed as $h_M(l) \sim \mathscr{CN}(0, \sigma_{M,l}^2)$ with $\sigma_M^2 = \sum_{l=1}^{L_M} \sigma_{M,l}^2$, $M = \mathrm{SR}, \mathrm{RD}, \mathrm{SD}$. Moreover, to prevent interblock interference (IBI) at both $\mathscr{R}$ and $\mathscr{D}$, a Cyclic Prefix (CP) of length $L_{\mathrm{cp}} \geq \max\{L_{\mathrm{SD}}, L_{\mathrm{SR}}, L_{\mathrm{RD}}\}$ is inserted and discarded appropriately.

We define the vector $\overline{\mathbf{P}}_s = [P_{s,1}, \ldots, P_{s,L_s}]^T$ including L_s nonzero pilot symbols with $L_s \geq \max\{L_{\mathrm{SD}}, L_{\mathrm{SR}} + L_{\mathrm{RD}} - 1\}$, and the vector $\mathbf{S} = [S_1, \ldots, S_{N-L_s}]^T$ including $N - L_s$ data symbols, where N is the total number of subcarriers. During the first time slot, the data and source pilot symbols are grouped and mapped according to the chosen modulation rule, and then $\mathscr{S}$ broadcasts the signal to $\mathscr{R}$ and $\mathscr{D}$ respectively. The transmitted signal after IDFT processing with average power P_s at source node is given by

$$\mathbf{s}_b = \mathbf{F}_N^H \mathbf{S}_b = \mathbf{F}_N^H \mathbf{\Gamma} \left[\overline{\mathbf{P}}_s, \mathbf{S} \right]^T, \tag{1}$$

where $\mathbf{S}_b = \mathbf{\Gamma}[\overline{\mathbf{P}}_s, \mathbf{S}] = [S_{b,1}, S_{b,1}, \ldots, S_{b,N}]$, $P_s = E\{\mathbf{s}_b^H \mathbf{s}_b\}/N$ and $\mathbf{\Gamma}$ is a permutation matrix. The pilot symbols are assigned by $\mathbf{\Gamma}$ in equi-spaced positions and the index set of source pilot subcarriers are denoted as $\mathscr{K}_s = \{k = \varphi + Q_s p, \ p = 0, 1, \ldots, L_s - 1\}$, where $\varphi \in [0, L_s - 1]$ and $Q_s = N/L_s$ are integers.

The received data signals at $\mathscr{R}$ and $\mathscr{D}$ can be expressed as

$$\mathbf{y}_r = \overrightarrow{\mathbf{h}}_{\mathrm{SR}} \mathbf{s}_b + \mathbf{n}_{\mathrm{SR}}$$
$$\mathbf{x}_d = \overrightarrow{\mathbf{h}}_{\mathrm{SD}} \mathbf{s}_b + \mathbf{n}_{\mathrm{SD}}, \tag{2}$$

where $\mathbf{n}_{\mathrm{SR}}$ and $\mathbf{n}_{\mathrm{SD}}$ are the Additive White Gaussian Noise (AWGN) with each entry having zero mean and variance $\sigma_{n,r}^2$, $\sigma_{n,d'}^2$. $\overrightarrow{\mathbf{h}}_{\mathrm{SR}}$ and $\overrightarrow{\mathbf{h}}_{\mathrm{SD}}$ are the $N \times N$ circulant matrices with first columns $[\mathbf{h}_{\mathrm{SR}}^T, \mathbf{0}_{1 \times (N-L_{\mathrm{SR}})}]^T$ and $[\mathbf{h}_{\mathrm{RD}}^T, \mathbf{0}_{1 \times (N-L_{\mathrm{RD}})}]^T$, respectively. Without any complicated operations, the received signal $\mathbf{y}_r$ would be amplified with the amplification factor β firstly and then the relay pilot sequence $\mathbf{p}_r$ would be superimposed onto $\mathbf{y}_r$. The relay pilot symbols are assigned in equi-spaced positions and the index set of relay pilot subcarriers are denoted as $\mathscr{K}_r = \{k = \varphi + Q_r p, \ p = 0, 1, \ldots, L_r - 1\}$, where $\varphi \in [0, L_s - 1]$ and $Q_r = N/L_r$ are integers. The amplification factor β can be denoted by

$$\beta = \sqrt{\frac{(1-\gamma) P_r}{\sigma_{\mathrm{SR}}^2 P_s + \sigma_n^2}}, \tag{3}$$

where $\sigma_{\mathrm{SR}}^2 = \sum_{l=1}^{L_{\mathrm{SR}}} \sigma_{\mathrm{SR},l}^2$, γ is relay power-allocation factor. γP_r is allocated to the relay pilot sequence and $(1-\gamma)P_r$ is allocated to the amplified received data where $0 < \gamma < 1$ and average transmitted power at relay node is denoted by P_r. The Discrete Fourier Transform (DFT) of the kth subcarrier of transmitted signal is given by

$$X_{r,k} = \begin{cases} \beta Y_{r,k} + P_{r,k} & \forall k \in \mathscr{K}_r \\ \beta Y_{r,k} & \text{otherwise}, \end{cases} \tag{4}$$

where $Y_{r,k}$ is the DFT of the received data signal at $\mathscr{R}$ on the kth subcarrier, $P_{r,k}$ is the nonzero pilot symbol. The number of nonzero pilot symbols is $L_r \geq L_{\mathrm{RD}}$ and the index set of relay pilot subcarriers are denoted as $\mathscr{K}_r$. Therefore $X_{r,k}$ is a linear combination of a relay-superimposed pilot symbol $P_{r,k}$ and relay-received signal $Y_{r,k}$, as depicted in Figure 2.

In order to avoid overlapping with source pilot symbols, the condition $\mathscr{K}_s \cap \mathscr{K}_r = \varnothing$ must be satisfied. From (4) we have the following form in time domain

$$\mathbf{x}_r = \beta \mathbf{y}_r + \mathbf{p}_r \tag{5}$$

At the second time slot, $\mathscr{R}$ forwards the signal $\mathbf{x}_r$ to $\mathscr{D}$. Afterwards, the received signal at $\mathscr{D}$ is given by

$$\mathbf{y}_d = \overrightarrow{\mathbf{h}}_{\mathrm{RD}} \mathbf{x}_r + \mathbf{n}_{\mathrm{RD}} = \overrightarrow{\mathbf{h}}_{\mathrm{RD}} \left(\beta \mathbf{y}_r + \mathbf{p}_r \right) + \mathbf{n}_{\mathrm{RD}}$$
$$= \overrightarrow{\mathbf{h}}_{\mathrm{RD}} \mathbf{p}_r + \underline{\beta \overrightarrow{\mathbf{h}}_R \mathbf{s}_b + \beta \overrightarrow{\mathbf{h}}_{\mathrm{RD}} \mathbf{n}_{\mathrm{SR}} + \mathbf{n}_{\mathrm{RD}}}_{v}, \tag{6}$$

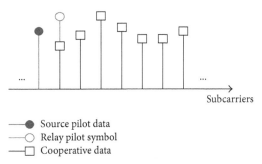

$\longrightarrow$● Source pilot data
$\longrightarrow$○ Relay pilot symbol
$\longrightarrow$□ Cooperative data

FIGURE 2: Structure of a frame with superimposed pilots in frequency domain.

where $\overrightarrow{\mathbf{h}}_R = \overrightarrow{\mathbf{h}}_{SR}\overrightarrow{\mathbf{h}}_{RD}$, $\overrightarrow{\mathbf{h}}_{RD}$ is the $N \times N$ circulant matrices with first columns $[\mathbf{h}_{RD}^T, \mathbf{0}_{1\times(N-L_{RD})}]^T$, $\mathbf{n}_{RD}$ is the AWGN with each entry having zero mean and variance $\sigma_{n,d}^2$. After DFT operation, we obtain $\mathbf{X}_d = [X_{d,1}, \ldots, X_{d,k}, \ldots, X_{d,N}]^T$ from direct link and $\mathbf{Y}_d = [Y_{d,1}, \ldots, Y_{d,k}, \ldots, Y_{d,N}]^T$ from relay link respectively in two time slots at $\mathscr{D}$. Obviously, it can be seen from (6) that three terms are included in the interference $\mathbf{v}$ for second-hop channel estimation, where the first term represents the interference of unknown cooperative data and others indicate the equivalent noise, consisting of the relay-propagated noise (the noise propagated from $\mathscr{R}$) and the local noise at $\mathscr{D}$. The first term affects the estimation performance seriously even at high SNR.

3. Channel Estimation

To eliminate the effects of cooperative data-induced interference during the estimation of the $\mathscr{R} \to \mathscr{D}$ channel, the CIC scheme is proposed. With the reliable cooperative data copy detected from direct link and the accurate estimation of cascaded channel based on the source pilot symbols, a certain operation rule is employed to remove the cooperative data-induced interference.

By selecting the source pilot subcarriers, the frequency response of the cascaded channel and direct channel can be obtained via Least Square (LS) channel estimator

$$\begin{aligned} \widehat{H}_{SD,k} &= \frac{X_{d,k}}{S_{b,k}} \quad k \in \mathscr{K}_s \\ \widehat{H}_{R,k} &= \frac{Y_{d,k}}{\beta S_{b,k}} \quad k \in \mathscr{K}_s \end{aligned} \quad (7)$$

Then the frequency-domain responses at the whole frequency pins can be obtained after linear interpolation. The CIC scheme for the estimation of the $\mathscr{R} \to \mathscr{D}$ channel is described as follows:

Step 1. Regardless of source pilot subcarriers, the equalized outputs of received data from direct channel in frequency domain can be given by

$$\check{U}_{d,k} = G_{d,k}X_{d,k} \quad k \in \overline{\mathscr{K}}_s, \quad (8)$$

where $G_{d,k} = \widehat{H}_{SD,k}^*/(|\widehat{H}_{SD,k}|^2 + \sigma_{n,d'}^2)$ is the coefficient in Minimum Mean Square Error (MMSE) equalization and

$\overline{\mathscr{K}}_s = \{0, 1, \ldots, N-1\} \setminus \mathscr{K}_s$ is assumed as complementary index set of $\mathscr{K}_s$. Let us stack the equalized results into the vector $\check{\mathbf{U}}_d = [U_{d,1}, \ldots, U_{d,k}, \ldots, U_{d,N-L_s}]$. After that, the detecting symbols are given by $\widehat{\mathbf{S}}_t = \lfloor\check{\mathbf{U}}_d\rfloor$, where $\lfloor\cdot\rfloor$ express the decision function. We finally reconstruct the transmitted signal $\widehat{\mathbf{S}}_d = \Gamma[\overline{\mathbf{P}}_s, \widehat{\mathbf{S}}_t]^T$ with permutation matrix.

Step 2. According to transmission rule, the DFT of received signal at $\mathscr{D}$ with the cooperative data interference removed is given by

$$Y_{CIC,k} = Y_{d,k} - \beta \times \widehat{S}_{d,k} \times \widehat{H}_{R,k}, \quad k \in \mathscr{K}_r \quad (9)$$

Step 3. By selecting the relay pilot subcarriers, the frequency response of the $\mathscr{R} \to \mathscr{D}$ channel can be obtained via LS channel estimator

$$\widehat{H}_{RD,k} = \frac{Y_{CIC,k}}{P_{r,k}} \quad k \in \mathscr{K}_r \quad (10)$$

The frequency-domain responses at the whole frequency pins can be acquired after linear interpolation. The channel estimation NMSE of $\mathscr{R} \to \mathscr{D}$ channel in LS criterion can be given by ($k \in \mathscr{K}_r$ and ignoring linear interpolation)

$$\begin{aligned} \text{MSE}_{RD} &= \frac{L_{RD}}{N} E\left[\left|H_{RD,k} - \widehat{H}_{RD,k}\right|^2\right] \\ &= \frac{L_{RD}}{N} E\left[\left|\frac{\beta\left(H_{R,k}S_{b,k} - \widehat{H}_{R,k}\widehat{S}_{b,k}\right) + N_e}{P_{r,k}}\right|^2\right] \\ &\approx \frac{L_{RD}}{N} E\left[\left|\frac{\beta\left(\Delta H_R S_{b,k} + H_{R,k}\Delta S_{b,k}\right) + N_e}{P_{r,k}}\right|^2\right] \\ &= \frac{L_{RD}}{N} E\left[\left|\frac{A}{B}\right|^2\right], \end{aligned} \quad (11)$$

where $A = \beta(\Delta H_R S_{b,k} + H_{R,k}\Delta S_{b,k}) + N_e$, $B = P_{r,k}$, $N_e = \beta H_{RD,k}N_{SR,k} + N_{RD,k}$, $\Delta H_R = H_{R,k} - \widehat{H}_{R,k}$ is the channel estimation error, $\Delta S_{b,k} = S_{b,k} - \widehat{S}_{b,k}$ is the symbol detecting error related to the symbol error rate (SER) p_e. For convenience, we assume that $\Delta H_R \sim \mathscr{CN}(0, \sigma_{H_R}^2)$ and $S_{b,k}$ belongs to a finite alphabet set with equally likely symbols and assume a nearest-neighbour selection when making symbol detection errors. For a given signal constellation, let there be k nearest neighbours with distance $d = |S_{b,k} - \widehat{S}_{b,k}|$, each equally likely to occur conditioned on the event that an error has occurred. We will assign zero conditional error probability to non-nearest-neighbour points.

Under these assumptions above, we have

$$|\Delta S_{b,k}| = \begin{cases} 0 & 1 - p_e \\ d & p_e \end{cases} \quad (12)$$

leading to

$$E\{\Delta S_{b,k_1}\Delta S_{b,k_2}^*\} = \begin{cases} 0 & \text{if } k_1 \neq k_2 \\ d^2 p_e & \text{if } k_1 = k_2. \end{cases} \quad (13)$$

It can be clearly denoted that random variable A is independent of B; as a result, according to (11)–(13), the MSE can be given by

$$
\begin{aligned}
\mathrm{MSE}_{\mathrm{RD}} &= \frac{L_{\mathrm{RD}}}{N} E\left[\left|\frac{A}{B}\right|^2\right] = \frac{L_r}{N} E\left[|A|^2\right] E\left[\left|\frac{1}{B^2}\right|\right] \\
&= \frac{L_{\mathrm{RD}}\left[\beta^2\left(\sigma_{H_R}^2 P_s + \sigma_R^2 p_e d^2\right) + \beta^2 \sigma_{\mathrm{RD}}^2 \sigma_{n,r}^2 + \sigma_{n,d}^2\right]}{N\gamma P_r} \quad (14) \\
&\geq \frac{L_{\mathrm{RD}}\left(\beta^2 \sigma_{\mathrm{RD}}^2 \sigma_n^2 + \sigma_n^2\right)}{N\gamma P_r}
\end{aligned}
$$

and when $p_e = 0$ and $\sigma_{H_R}^2 = 0$, we derive the lower bound of the $\mathscr{R} \to \mathscr{D}$ channel estimation with CIC method, namely, perfect CIC. However, the MSE of $\mathscr{R} \to \mathscr{D}$ channel estimation is independent of the number of relay pilot symbols. Consequently, to minimize the additional cooperative interference at the relay, the number of the relay pilots inserted at the relay should be kept to a minimum, while, for channel identification of $\mathscr{R} \to \mathscr{D}$ link with L_{RD} unknown parameters, the least number L_r of relay pilots with condition $L_r \geq L_{\mathrm{RD}}$ must be satisfied.

(1) Under the circumstance of reliable direct link, it is considered that the SER is nearly zero. Assume that $p_e \approx 0$, and, according to (14), the MSE can be given as

$$
\mathrm{MSE}_{\mathrm{RD}} \approx \frac{L_{\mathrm{RD}}\left[\beta^2 \sigma_{H_R}^2 P_s + \beta^2 \sigma_{\mathrm{RD}}^2 \sigma_{n,r}^2 + \sigma_{n,d}^2\right]}{N\gamma P_r}. \quad (15)
$$

It is clearly noted that MSE of second-hop channel estimation in CIC scheme is related to performance of cascaded channel estimation and equivalent noise.

(2) Under the circumstance of reliable relay link, it is considered that the cascaded channel estimation is approximately perfect. Assume that $\sigma_{H_R}^2 \approx 0$, and, according to (14), the MSE can be given as

$$
\mathrm{MSE}_{\mathrm{RD}} \approx \frac{L_{\mathrm{RD}}\left[\beta^2 \sigma_R^2 p_e d^2 + \beta^2 \sigma_{\mathrm{RD}}^2 \sigma_{n,r}^2 + \sigma_{n,d}^2\right]}{N\gamma P_r}. \quad (16)
$$

It is clearly noted that MSE of second-hop channel estimation in CIC scheme is related to SER of direct link and equivalent noise of relay link.

4. Diversity Combining

After the CSIs are obtained by (7) and (10), diversity combing can be performed for received data signals from $\mathscr{S} \to \mathscr{D}$ and $\mathscr{S} \to \mathscr{R} \to \mathscr{D}$ links, respectively. With the pilot terms on relay pilot subcarriers removed, the received signal from $\mathscr{S} \to \mathscr{R} \to \mathscr{D}$ link is refreshed by

$$
\overline{Y}_{d,k} = Y_{d,k} - \widehat{H}_{\mathrm{RD},k} \times P_{r,k}, \quad k \in \mathscr{K}_r. \quad (17)
$$

For $k \in \overline{\mathscr{K}}_s$, we define $\mathbf{U}_{d,k} = [X_{d,k}, \overline{Y}_{d,k}]^T$ and the MMSE coefficients are given by

$$
\mathbf{W}_{d,k} = \left[\widehat{\mathbf{H}}_{d,k} \widehat{\mathbf{H}}_{d,k}^H + \mathbf{N}_{d,k}\right]^{-1} \widehat{\mathbf{H}}_{d,k}, \quad (18)
$$

where $\mathbf{N}_{d,k} = \mathrm{diag}\{\sigma_{\mathrm{SD},k}^2, \sigma_{R,k}^2\}$ is the noise variances of the $\mathscr{S} \to \mathscr{D}$ and $\mathscr{S} \to \mathscr{R} \to \mathscr{D}$ links with $\sigma_{\mathrm{SD},k}^2 = \sigma_{n,d'}^2$ and $\sigma_{R,k}^2 = \beta^2 |\widehat{H}_{\mathrm{RD},k}|^2 \sigma_{n,r}^2 + \sigma_{n,d}^2$. With $\widehat{\mathbf{H}}_{d,k} = [\widehat{H}_{\mathrm{SD},k}, \beta\widehat{H}_{R,k}]^T$, the output of MMSE equalization is given by

$$
\breve{D}_{d,k} = \mathbf{W}_{d,k}^H \mathbf{U}_{d,k} \quad k \in \overline{\mathscr{K}}_s. \quad (19)
$$

Let us stack $\breve{D}_{d,k}$ of set $\overline{\mathscr{K}}_s$ into a $(N - L_s) \times 1$ vector $\breve{\mathbf{D}}_d$, and the detected symbols are derived as $\widehat{\mathbf{S}} = \lfloor \breve{\mathbf{D}}_d \rfloor$.

5. Simulation Results

In this section, we consider the randomly generated and uncorrelated frequency-selective channels with $L_{\mathrm{SD}} = L_{\mathrm{SR}} = L_{\mathrm{RD}} = 4$. It is assumed that data symbols are constructed by QPSK modulation and other simulation parameters are chosen as $N = 128$. For channel identification $L_s = 8, L_r = 4$ is chosen to minimize the SER. Furthermore, we select the equispaced and equipowered pilot symbols as the optimal design. The average transmitted power at the source and relay nodes is set to $P_s = P_r = 1$, and the SNR between $\mathscr{S}$ and $\mathscr{R}$, the SNR between $\mathscr{R}$ and $\mathscr{D}$, the SNR between $\mathscr{S}$ and $\mathscr{D}$ are defined as $\mathrm{SNR}_r = P_s/(d_{\mathrm{SR}}^2 \sigma_{n,r}^2)$, $\mathrm{SNR}_d = P_r/(d_{\mathrm{RD}}^2 \sigma_{n,d}^2)$, and $\mathrm{SNR}_{d'} = P_s/(d_{\mathrm{SD}}^2 \sigma_{n,d'}^2)$. Moreover $d_{\mathrm{SR}} = d_{\mathrm{RD}} = 1$ and $d_{\mathrm{SD}} = 2$ are assumed.

The power-allocation factor γ determines the proportion of the average power that the relay allocates to the relay-superimposed pilot sequence. For the given P_r, the more power the relay allocates to superimposed training, the less it allocates to the received data signal. With the simulation results for different parameters γ, we find that there is a tradeoff between the symbol detecting and the estimation accuracy of second-hop.

We plot the normalized MSE (NMSE) performance of channel estimation and the SER performance of relay link versus the parameter γ for several $\mathrm{SNR}_r = \mathrm{SNR}_d = 10, 15,$ and 20 dB, respectively, in Figures 3 and 4. With γ increasing, the estimation performance of $\mathscr{R} \to \mathscr{D}$ channel improves. Meanwhile, with γ increasing, the less average power is allocated to cooperative data and SER performance is decreasing. As a result, it is desired to choose a value of γ not decreasing the SER and obtain the acceptant channel estimation of second hop. It can be seen that the SER curve is relatively flat for a range (approximately $0.1 \leq \gamma \leq 0.3$) which includes the optimal value.

We compare the proposed CIC scheme (denoted as "proposed" in Figures 5–7) with the SP scheme in [13] (denoted as "SP" in Figures 5–7) and the subcarriers-reserved scheme in [10] (denoted as "SR" in Figures 5–7) in terms of channel NMSE and SER and effective throughput in the same simulation environment. Simulation parameters would not be changed and the relay pilot-to-data power ratio γ is set to 0.1.

As shown in Figure 5, the channel NMSE of the CIC scheme performs much better than that of SP scheme and has a certain performance gap with the lower bound. Although CIC scheme would remove the cooperative data-induced interference effectively, the channel estimation error

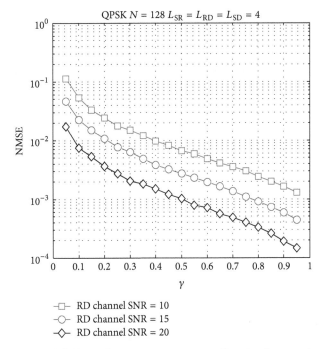

FIGURE 3: NMSE performance versus power-allocation factor at the relay.

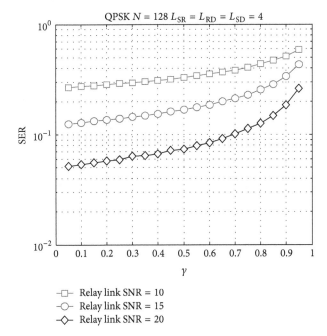

FIGURE 4: SER performance versus power-allocation factor at the relay.

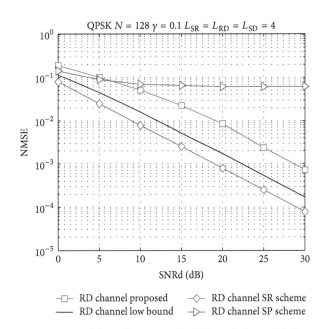

FIGURE 5: MSE of channel estimates for different links with different schemes.

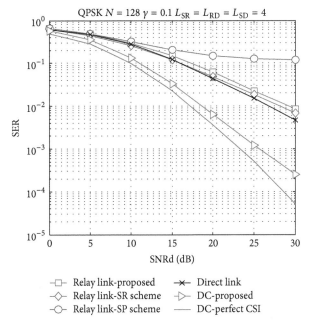

FIGURE 6: SER for different links with different schemes.

and symbol detecting error still certainly affect the NMSE performance. However, CIC scheme performs worse than subcarriers-reserved scheme, it is because that redundant cooperative data interference and relay-propagated noise restrict the improvement on the performance of second-hop channel estimation in CIC scheme while the channel estimation in SR scheme is affected only by local noise.

It is clearly denoted in Figure 6 that the detecting performance of relay link in CIC scheme behaves much better than that in traditional SP scheme and approaches the performance of SR scheme. Moreover the SER after diversity combining in CIC scheme is much better than that of direct link, which denotes that detection performance is enhanced after diversity combined with relay link.

In Figure 7, we compare effective throughput of different scheme. We define the effective throughput $r_{\text{Eff}} = f_s \xi (1 - \text{SER})$ (kBd), where the sampling period of symbol $T_s = 25\,\mu s$, transmission rate $f_s = 40\,\text{kBd}$, $\xi = N_d/N$, and SER

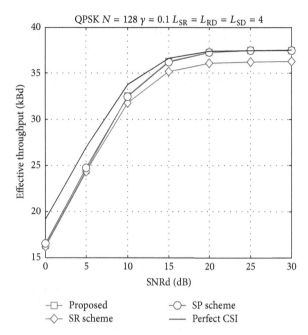

QPSK $N = 128$ $\gamma = 0.1$ $L_{SR} = L_{RD} = L_{SD} = 4$

- □ Proposed
- ○ SP scheme
- ◇ SR scheme
- — Perfect CSI

FIGURE 7: Effective throughput of different schemes.

denotes the SER after diversity combining and N_d denotes the number of subcarriers with transmitted data. As is depicted in Figure 7, the effective throughput of CIC scheme and traditional SP scheme is superior to that of SR scheme. It is because we employ the relay-superimposed pilot sequence which saves the valuable bandwidth. In conclusion, considering the simulation results proposed above, the channel estimation method using relay-superimposed pilot sequence with CIC scheme has much more superiority than others.

6. Conclusions

In this paper, we proposed a novel relay-superimposed pilot method to acquire the individual CSIs in a three-node AF-OFDM-based cooperative system. Moreover, with the help of cooperative data copy from direct channel, the interference of unknown cooperative data during the estimation of second-hop link is removed with the CIC scheme. With numerous simulation results, we derive the optimal power-allocation factor and explore that the performance of the presented scheme depends on the quality of the $\mathscr{S} \rightarrow \mathscr{D}$ link. Moreover the detection performance and effective throughput are enhanced with CIC scheme.

Acknowledgments

This work was supported by National Natural Science Foundation of China (Grant no. 61302099) and also supported by China Postdoctoral Science Foundation (Grant no. 2015T81107).

References

[1] J.-C. Lin, H.-K. Chang, M.-L. Ku, and H. V. Poor, "Impact of Imperfect Source-To-Relay CSI in Amplify-And-Forward Relay Networks," *IEEE Transactions on Vehicular Technology*, vol. 66, no. 6, pp. 5056–5069, 2017.

[2] M.-L. Wang, C.-P. Li, and W.-J. Huang, "Semiblind channel estimation and precoding scheme in two-way multirelay networks," *IEEE Transactions on Signal Processing*, vol. 65, no. 10, pp. 2576–2587, 2017.

[3] K. Singh, M.-L. Ku, and J.-C. Lin, "Power Allocation and Relay Selection in Relay Networks: A Perturbation-Based Approach," *IEEE Signal Processing Letters*, vol. 24, no. 9, pp. 1328–1332, 2017.

[4] Y. Li, W. Wang, J. Kong, and M. Peng, "Subcarrier pairing for amplify-and-forward and decode-and-forward OFDM relay links," *IEEE Communications Letters*, vol. 13, no. 4, pp. 209–211, 2009.

[5] C. Xue, Q. Zhang, Q. Li, and J. Qin, "Joint Power Allocation and Relay Beamforming in Nonorthogonal Multiple Access Amplify-and-Forward Relay Networks," *IEEE Transactions on Vehicular Technology*, vol. 66, no. 8, pp. 7558–7562, 2017.

[6] S. Abdallah and I. N. Psaromiligkos, "Semi-blind channel estimation with superimposed training for OFDM-based AF two-way relaying," *IEEE Transactions on Wireless Communications*, vol. 13, no. 5, pp. 2468–2477, 2014.

[7] F. Gao, T. Cui, and A. Nallanathan, "On channel estimation and optimal training design for amplify and forward relay networks," *IEEE Transactions on Wireless Communications*, vol. 7, no. 5, pp. 1907–1916, 2008.

[8] Z. Zhang, W. Zhang, and C. Tellambura, "Cooperative OFDM channel estimation in the presence of frequency offsets," *IEEE Transactions on Vehicular Technology*, vol. 58, no. 7, pp. 3447–3459, 2009.

[9] O. Amin, B. Gedik, and M. Uysal, "Channel estimation for amplify-and-forward relaying: Cascaded against disintegrated estimators," *IET Communications*, vol. 4, no. 10, Article ID ICEOCW00000400001000120700001, pp. 1207–1216, 2010.

[10] L. Mingliang, J. Zhang, Y. Zhang, and Y. Liu, "A channel estimation scheme for amplify-and-forward ofdm relay networks," in *Proceedings of the 70th Vehicular Technology Conference Fall (VTC '09-Fall)*, pp. 1–5, IEEE, Anchorage, Alaska, USA, September 2009.

[11] F. Gao, B. Jiang, X. Gao, and X. Zhang, "Superimposed training based channel estimation for OFDM modulated amplify-and-forward relay networks," *IEEE Transactions on Communications*, vol. 59, no. 7, pp. 2029–2039, 2011.

[12] B. Zahedi, M. Ahmadian, K. Mohamed-Pour, M. Peyghami, M. Norouzi, and S. Salari, "Pilot-based individual forward and backward channel estimation in amplify-and-forward OFDM relay networks," in *Proceedings of the IFIP Wireless Days (WD '11)*, Niagara Falls, Canada, October 2011.

[13] H. Zhang, D. Pan, H. Cui, and F. Gao, "Superimposed training for channel estimation of OFDM modulated amplify-and-forward relay networks," *Science China Information Sciences*, vol. 56, no. 10, pp. 1–12, 2013.

22

Prior Knowledge-Based Event Network for Chinese Text

Yunyu Shi,[1] **Jianfang Shan,**[2] **Xiang Liu,**[1] **and Yongxiang Xia**[1]

[1]*School of Electronic & Electric Engineering, Shanghai University of Engineering Science, 333 Longteng Road, Songjiang District, Shanghai, China*
[2]*School of Information, Qilu University of Technology, 3501 Daxue Road, Changqing District, Jinan, China*

Correspondence should be addressed to Jianfang Shan; sjfshan@163.com

Academic Editor: Hyo-Jong Lee

Text representation is a basic issue of text information processing and event plays an important role in text understanding; both attract the attention of scholars. The event network conceals lexical relations in events, and its edges express logical relations between events in document. However, the events and relations are extracted from event-annotated text, which makes it hard for large-scale text automatic processing. In the paper, with expanded CEC (Chinese Event Corpus) as data source, prior knowledge of manifestation rules of event and relation as the guide, we propose an event extraction method based on knowledge-based rule of event manifestation, to achieve automatic building and improve text processing performance of event network.

1. Introduction

Text representation is an important issue in natural language processing, such as information retrieval and text classification. An appropriate representation not only can reflect text semantic, theme, and structure but also can improve the computational efficiency. In recent years, there is a tendency to use richer text representations than just keywords-based and concepts-based ones in the field of text information processing.

Event originated from cognitive science often appears in the literature of philosophy, cognitive science, linguistics, and artificial intelligence. It has been widely used in the computational linguistics as well as information retrieval and various NLP applications, which plays a special and important role in understanding text semantic. It not only contains specific correlations among a group of text elements but also indicates logical dependencies of things and attracts more and more attentions of researchers. Cognitive scientists believe that event is not only the basic unit of human cognizing and understanding objective world but also storage cell of proposition memory [1]. Most of the current natural language processing technologies lay particular stress on the theory of grammar structure, while ignoring the importance

of semantic understanding, especially event semantic understanding [2]. Event-based text representation conforms to the rules of human cognition and natural language understanding.

Seen from present literature on event-based text representation we have consulted, there are the following main problems:

(1) The research on event-based text representation is still in its infancy; the thinking of event network is just beginning to blossom that it is necessary to be further explored.

(2) The operations and applications on event network need to be raised and further researched.

Against the shortcomings of current traditional text representation, the paper takes event as feature item of text and proposes an event-based text representation method. Event is regarded as semantic unit of text, and the events are connected by certain types of relations in the text, and these events imply correlations of linguistic units in the text by making the linguistic units (word, concept, sentence, etc.) as certain elements of event. It no longer regards text as an aggregation of independent words; consequently, the problem of "a bag of words" in classic text representation is solved. Event network not only keeps semantic information of text and presents events and relations between events but also reflects importance and dynamic behavior of events. Compared to a traditional text representation, event network can express the higher granularity of semantic meaning, closer to the reality and easier for computers simulating text understanding and memorizing of human. It will provide new technology and method for semantic-based text information processing.

The paper is organized as follows: Section 2 introduces the related work. Section 3 constructs event network of Chinese texts in the field of emergencies. Section 4 evaluates the representing effect of event network. In Section 5, the formal definition of event network model for Chinese text is generalized by inducting and abstracting the instances of event network, and then the advantages of the model are analyzed. Finally, we summarize the paper and give an outlook of the future study.

2. Related Work

2.1. The Shortcoming of Traditional Text Representation. In the fields of information retrieval and natural language processing, the traditional text representation models mainly include the following: Boolean model [3], VSM (vector space model) [4, 5], BOW (bag of words) [6], LSI (latent semantic index) [7], LDA (latent Dirichlet allocation) [8], probability retrieval model [8], N-gram model [9], and language model [10].

Semantic information of text is composed of two parts: text component term (word, concept, sentence, etc.) and relationships between terms. Traditional text representation ignored the value of the order and relationships of the component terms on semantic expressing and assumed that the terms are independent, while, in fact, the semantic meaning of text is related to not only component terms and their frequency but also assembly rules and the order of terms, which means that the word-to-word and sentence-to-sentence relationships have an effect on text semantic. The same terms with same frequencies may express different semantic, such as the two following text snippets "Tom gave Mary a book as birthday gift" and "Mary gave Tom a book as birthday gift"; traditional text representation cannot express the difference between them [11]. Text representation based on word unit or concept unit will miss the information of relationships between terms, which will loss semantic meaning of text and result in failing to reflect higher level of semantic information. From the view of event semantic understanding, the above two text snippets express two different events.

In various texts, such as novel, opera, biography, and news reports, that contain many events, traditional text representation did not pay enough attention to event or represent event and relations appropriately. From the perspective of semantic understanding, linguists think that text is not only a group of attributes and concepts but also a describer of a series of events in a higher granularity; according to the thinking, these texts should be regarded as a group of events related by some relations, which is much closer

to the laws of human cognition and understanding. From the perspective of formation of text, elementary language units (word, concept, sentence, etc.) form sentence by certain linguistic rules and sentences form a sequence of sentences or paragraph and then form text and express some semantic meaning and theme. Taking event as semantic unit of text and text component term as event-element only solves the problem of "a bag of words" but also expresses the higher level of semantic information.

2.2. Event-Oriented Text Representation. (Although the definitions of event are not unified in different applications, most of them emphasize two kinds of event attributes, action (verb or gerund) and characteristics of action (participant, location, time, etc.), so most researches are centered on verb and attributes of verb. In the paper, attribute of event is called event-element or element for short.) Looking from the current literature we have consulted, little research has been done on event-oriented text representation; the related work mainly includes the following.

Feng [12] proposed incident threading to represent English news reports at sentence level. The texts that describe the occurrence of a real-world happening are merged into a news incident, and incidents are organized in an incident threading by dependencies of predefined types. However, it does not do well in representing Chinese texts.

Glavaš and Šnajder [13] proposed an event-based text representation; however it only has temporal relation. Zhao-Man and Zong-Tian [14] proposed event lattice to represent narrative texts based on concept lattice. In the lattice, text is the object, event is the attribute, and binary relation is used to judge whether an event belongs to a text. Although lattice has precise mathematical properties, its describing power is weak, lacking the ability to express luxuriant relations. And obviously the event lattice has no meaning to one text. It is more suitable to represent inclusion between a group of texts and events than relations between events in a text.

Jian-fang and Yun-yu [15] expounded the thinking of event-based text representation in the paper named "The Research on Event-Oriented Text Representation." This paper discussed the feasibility and adaptability of event-based text representation for Chinese news reports at genre and arrangement of text. However it oversimplified relations between events, resulting in the fact that its representing power is weak. Thus there are still many issues need to be further studied.

Extracting events is the most important thing of event-based text representation. The three main approaches of extracting events are data-driven [16], knowledge-driven [17], and hybrid [18]. The accuracy is about 70 percent according to ACE (Automatic Content Extraction). The paper uses prior knowledge-guided approach.

3. Constructing Event Network of Chinese Text in the Field of Emergencies

Our experimental corpora, CEC (Chinese Event Corpus), are collected from Internet, the texts of which can be divided into five categories: earthquake, fire, traffic accidents, terrorist

TABLE 1: Statistics of annotated texts.

Text	300
Event	3977
Relation	2023
Coverage of text	85%

attack, and food poisoning according to the classification system of news report about emergency event [19]. Up to now, there are 500 texts in CEC, and 300 ones of them are human annotated event and relations. Some rules have been discovered based on the annotations using mining technology. KBR-EM (knowledge base of rule of event manifestation) has been constructed on CEC.

Verb plays an important role in semantic understanding; it is also core of event. As long as there is verb, it will involve maker and/or receiver of action, and certain regular collocation relationships will be established between action and involved entities; based on this, language would form various basic syntactic configurations and then explain construction of statement and relationship of vocabulary, and so forth. By annotating event on CEC, we find that event corresponds to verb or gerund, and 83% of these verbs or gerunds involve one or two entities, and arrangement of different text typology could affect the layout of events. The relations between events in text are as follows: some are contained in verb of sentence, some are expressed by conjunction (many conjunctions of text virtually show nontaxonomic relation between events, such as "because, therefore" indicates causation), and some are implied in the order of events (such as following relation); the experiment shows that two events will appear successively in text with great probability if there is a relation between them in reality. Our experiments show that events and relations meeting the above findings can cover 85% of entire text. Furthermore, following and causation are the largest number of relations, accounting for 81% of total relations. Statistics of the annotation are displayed in Table 1, where coverage of text is the ratio of event-contained sentences to total sentences. Thus it can be seen that event-based text representation will express text information appropriately.

The guidance of the KBR-EM modified the existing NLP tools (such as tokenizer, part-of-speech tagger, syntactic analyzer, and HowNet), and all of the programs are implemented in Java. Text is processed with word segmentation and POS tagging, syntax analysis and grammatical component tagging, identifying sentence and sentence components, and corresponding sentence or sentence components to event or event elements, regarding verb and gerund as trigger of event. and removing stop-using verbs, such as high-frequency verbs (be, do, have, etc.) and subjective verbs (feel, believe, etc.). Such events belong to stop-using events that are triggered by stop-using verbs; furthermore, stop-using events also include future events and negative events that are triggered by future-tense and negative-form verbs, respectively. Stop-using events should not be included in event network of text. Trigger-associated major components of action are other elements (time, place, subject/predicate-participant, etc.) of the event.

For the identified events, use electronic dictionary and ontology and make concept-climbing after mapping trigger of event into concept. Cluster event and generate event hierarchy by clustering based on the above climbed result, and taxonomic relations between events will be identified. According to the conjunction and other syntactic components of sentences where events are extracted from, consult the findings on relations mentioned above and identify nontaxonomic relations between events.

After identifying events and relations, event network is constructed as follows. Events in the text are arranged in a special directed graph. A named edge from event A to event B means that there is a relation between them in the text, either taxonomic (A is a B, forming multi-inheritance-allowed inheritance diagram) or nontaxonomic, such as causation (A leads to the happening of B), following (A precedes B in time), and composition (A is a part of B). And if there is more than one relation between event A and event B, then one relation is linked to one edge.

4. Experiment and Evaluating Representing Effect

Representing effect could measure whether a text representation method can represent information of original text appropriately and properly. The paper evaluates representing effect of event network with event recall rate (ER), event precision rate (EP), relation recall rate (RR), and relation precision rate (RP).

To compare between events and relations, the paper specifies some rules as follows:

(1) Two events are identical if and only if corresponding event elements are identical that are contained in the individual event.

(2) Two relations are identical if and only if corresponding items are identical that are contained in the individual relation tuple. For taxonomic relation $Is_{-a}(e_u, e_l)$, where e_u is superevent or upperevent, e_l is subevent or lower-event. For directed nontaxonomic relation $r\langle e_1, e_2 \rangle$ and undirected nontaxonomic relation $r(e_1, e_2)$, where r is name of the relation, e_1 and e_2 are two events that are connected by the relation

Evaluating on event set of event networks of texts in the field of emergency, as shown in Figure 1, the average recall rate and precision rate are 82% and 88%, respectively. Evaluation of relation set is shown in Figure 2; the average recall rate and precision rate are 76% and 85%, respectively. Compared with previous method [15], the method constructs event network from tagged corpus with events, causation, and following relations, the resulting event network added another adjacent relation and event-element-shared relation. Its event recall and precision rate will be higher, and events contained in the event network can be viewed as complete and correct in theory. According to the findings described in Section 3, nontaxonomic relation recall rate should be at least 81%. However, there are large amount of redundancy

TABLE 2: Comparison for event network and incident threading.

	ER	EP	Event F_measure	RR	RP	Relation F_measure
Event network	82%	88%	84%	76%	85%	80%
Incident threading	41%	98%	58%	18%	92%	30%

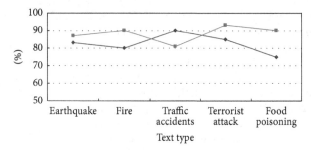

--•-- Event recall rate

--■-- Event precision rate

FIGURE 1: Evaluation of event set.

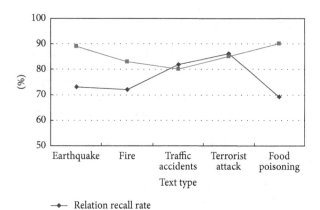

--•-- Relation recall rate

--■-- Relation precision rate

FIGURE 2: Evaluation of relation set.

and error in adjacent and event-element-shared relation; for example, adjacent relation could actually be following or with no meaningful relation, and event-element-shared relation is too general to specify a relation. So relation precision rate of this method is far inferior to the paper.

Incident threading [12] did well in representing preprocessed grouped English news texts; however, it is less suitable for Chinese text than event network. Evaluating the two representation methods is shown in Table 2.

5. Event Network Model for Chinese Text

An event network contains one or more events that are connected by relations. Events in the network are arranged in a graph, and two events are directly connected by one or more directed/undirected edges (the number of edges depends on the number of relations between the two events) and have some relations. The text representation method is called event network. Though constructing event networks of a large number of texts, we discover that event network is

different from general directed digraph. There is information on its each node and each edge, and multiple edges may exist between two nodes. The formal event network model is defined as following by generalizing and abstracting instances of event networks.

Definition 1 (event network). The tuple EN $= (E, R \diamond (R_T, R_{NT}))$ is called event network that meets the following conditions:

(1) $E = \{e\}$ is nonempty node set, called **event set**.

(2) $R \diamond (R_T, R_{NT})$ is edge set, called **relation set**.

R includes taxonomic relation R_T and nontaxonomic relation R_{NT}. Taxonomic relation $R_T = \{Is_{-a}(e_u, e_l) \mid e_u \in E, e_l \in E\}$ forms multi-inheritance-allowed inheritance diagram, where e_u is superevent and e_l is subevent. R_{NT} forms special graph structure, including directed $R_{NT} = \{r\langle e_1, e_2\rangle \mid e_u \in E, e_l \in E\}$ and undirected $R_{NT} = \{r(e_1, e_2) \mid e_u \in E, e_l \in E\}$, where the relation between event e_1 and e_2 is named as r.

Event network can be seen as directed graph. It not only keeps semantic information of text and represents events and relations between events but also reflects importance, dynamic behavior, and state changing of events. Compared with traditional text representation such as VSM, the salient advantage of event network is that it implies correlations among linguistic units of the text in its events, which not only solves the problem of "a bag of words" but also inflects the higher granularity of semantic meaning. Meanwhile relations link events together that can express logical dependencies of things and reflect the occurrence and development process of event.

Event network is a directed graph with information on its nodes and edges. Using all information, various calculations can be done on it by considering some properties of directed graph; for example, an event network can be clustered according to the similarity of events, partitioned into hierarchical structure with different threshold value, and reduced according to importance of event or can keep some other properties. The similarity of texts can be calculated according to the matching of their individual event network; some knowledge can be obtained through mining frequent and simultaneous event elements in multiple event networks. These calculations must meet not only properties of graph but also meaning of information on nodes and edges of event network, so the unique properties and special computation model of event network need to be researched. Establishing abstract operations on event network, some problems will be solved by mathematical methods, which are a kind of good form for semantic calculation and will support event-based text information processing.

6. Conclusions and the Future Work

The paper introduced requirement of event-based text representation. The formal event network model for Chinese text is defined by abstracting instances of event network on CEC texts. The difference between event network and traditional text representation is that event network keeps semantic information of text, no longer regards text as an aggregation of independent words, and solves the problem of "a bag of words." In addition, it reflects relations among events, importance, and dynamic behavior of event. Our experiments demonstrate the feasibility, adaptability, and advantage of event network as a text representation method.

In the future work, we will study computations on event network by using graph theory, clustering, formal concept analysis, granular computing, and so forth, considering particularity of the model. In this way, various applications of text will be solved by mathematical methods. Theoretical model and method support for present text information processing based on semantic meaning will be provided.

Acknowledgments

The work is supported by Science and Technology Innovation Project of Chinese Ministry of Culture (2015KJCXXM19) and Foundation for University Youth Teachers of Shanghai (ZZGCD15002).

References

[1] P. Yun-he and W. Geng, "An introduction to intelligent-computing oriented memory theory," *Journal of Computer Research and Development*, vol. 31, pp. 37–42, 1999.

[2] L. Zhong, *The theory of BSCM presented and the implementing of the natural language understanding studied*, East China Normal University, 2004.

[3] R. Baeza-Yates and B. Ribeiro-Neto, *Modern Information Retrieval*, Addison-Wesley-Longman, 1st edition, 1999.

[4] G. Salton, A. Wong, and C. S. Yang, "A Vector Space Model for Automatic Indexing," *Communications of the ACM*, vol. 18, no. 11, pp. 613–620, 1975.

[5] D. D. Lewis, "Evaluation of phrasal and clustered represen- tations on a text categorization task [A]," in *Proceedings of the Fifteenth Annual International ACM SIGIR Conference on Research and Development in Information Retrieval*, pp. 37–50, 1992.

[6] Bag-of-words model [DB/OL], http://en.wikipedia.org/wiki/Bag_of_words_model.

[7] T. K. Landauer and M. L. Littman, "Fully automatic crosslan- guage document retrieval using latent semantic indexing," in *Proceedings of the Sixth Annual Conference of the UW Centre for the New Oxford English Dictionary and Text Research*, pp. 31–38,

Waterloo Ontario, 1990, http://www.es.duke.edu/~mlittman/docs/x-lang.ps.

[8] M. David and Y. Blei Andrew, "Latent Dirichlet allocation," *Journal of Machine Learning Research*, vol. 3, pp. 993–1022, 2003.

[9] T. Chew Lim, S. Sung Yuan, Y. Zhaohui et al., *Text Retrieval from Document Images Based on N-Gram Algorithm*, http://citeseer.nj.nec.com/400555.html.

[10] J. Ponte and W. Croft, "Language Modeling Approach to Information Retrieval," in *Proceedings of SIGIR1998'*, pp. 275–281.

[11] J.-F. Shan, Z.-T. Liu, J.-F. Fu, and Z.-M. Zhong, "Important event extraction of Chinese document based on small world model," in *Proceedings of 2009 IEEE International Conference on Intelligent Computing and Intelligent Systems, ICIS 2009*, pp. 146–150, chn, November 2009.

[12] A. Feng, *Events Threading*, University of Massachusetts, 2008.

[13] G. Glavaš and J. Šnajder, "Event graphs for information retrieval and multi-document summarization," *Expert Systems with Applications*, vol. 41, no. 15, pp. 6904–6916, 2014.

[14] Z. Zhao-Man and L. Zong-Tian, "Events-based Text Similarity Computing," *Journal of Guangxi Normal University (Natural Science Edition)*, vol. 27, no. 1, pp. 149–152, 2009.

[15] Sh. Jian-fang and Sh. Yun-yu, "Research on event network for Chinese text," in *Proceeding of the Interna-tional Symposium on Information Technology Convergence, ISITC2016*, pp. 473–482, Shanghai, China, 2016.

[16] M. Okamoto and M. Kikuchi, "Discovering volatile events in your neighborhood: Local-area topic extraction from blog entries," *Lecture Notes in Computer Science (including subseries Lecture Notes in Artificial Intelligence and Lecture Notes in Bioinformatics)*, vol. 5839, pp. 181–192, 2009.

[17] E. Minkov, "Event extraction using structured learning and rich domain knowledge: Application across domains and data sources," *ACM Transactions on Intelligent Systems and Technology*, vol. 7, no. 2, article no. 16, 2015.

[18] S. Kuptabut and P. Netisopakul, "Event extraction using ontology directed semantic grammar," *Journal of Information Science and Engineering*, vol. 32, no. 1, pp. 79–96, 2016.

[19] Y. Li-ying, L. Hong-juan, and Z. Yong-kui, "The research on classification system of emergency news corpus," in *Proceeding of the monograph of the 25th academic annual conference of Chinese Informatics Association, frontier of Chinese information processing*, Tsinghua University Press, Beijing, 2006.

Permissions

List of Contributors

Xianwen He, Gaoqi Dou and Jun Gao
College of Electronic Engineering, Naval University of Engineering,Wuhan 430033, China

Yang Yu, Jucheng Yang, Jiangang Huang and Xiangbo Zhang
College of Computer Science and Information Engineering, Tianjin University of Science and Technology, Tianjin, China

Xiaofei Zan
School of Computer and Information Technology, Beijing Jiaotong University, Beijing, China

Mingfu Li, Chien-Lin Yeh and Shao-Yu Lu
Department of Electrical Engineering, School of Electrical and Computer Engineering, College of Engineering, Chang Gung University, Guishan District, Taoyuan City 33302, Taiwan

Mingfu Li
Neuroscience Research Center, Chang Gung Memorial Hospital, Linkou, Guishan District, Taoyuan City 33305, Taiwan

Xiaojie Duan, Dandan Chen, Jianming Wang, Meichen Shi, He Zhao, Ruixue Zuo, Xiuyan Li and Qi Wang
Tianjin Key Laboratory of Optoelectronic Detection Technology and Systems, School of Electronics and Information Engineering, Tianjin Polytechnic University, Tianjin 300387, China

Qingliang Chen
Tianjin Chest Hospital, Tianjin 300000, China

Guo X. Hu, Zhong Yang and Jia M. Han
College of Automation Engineering, Nanjing University of Aeronautics and Astronautics, Nanjing 211106, China

Guo X. Hu
School of Software, Jiangxi Normal University, Nanchang 330022, China

Lei Hu
School of Computer Information Engineering, Jiangxi Normal University, Nanchang 330022, China

Li Huang
Elementary Education College, Jiangxi Normal University, Nanchang 330022, China

Wei Lu, Dandan Yu and Minghe Huang
School of Software, Jiangxi Normal University, Nanchang 330022, China

Bin Guo
Information Office, Jiangxi Normal University, Nanchang 330022, China

Christian Di Laura, Diego Pajuelo and Guillermo Kemper
School of Electrical Engineering, Peruvian University of Applied Sciences, Lima 33, Peru

Fang Sun, Wei He and Ran Li
School of Computer and Information Technology, Xinyang Normal University, Xinyang 464000, China

Dongyue Xiao
School of Electrical and Electronic Engineering, Nanyang Institute of Technology, Nanyang 473000, China

Ran Li
School of Computer and Software, Nanjing University of Information Science and Technology, Nanjing 210003, China

Ruoshui Liu, Jianghui Liu, Jingjie Zhang and Moli Zhang
Information Engineering College, Henan University of Science and Technology, Luoyang 471003, China

Lina Shi, Dehui Kong and Shaofan Wang
Beijing Key Laboratory of Multimedia & Intelligent Software Technology, Faculty of Information Technology, Beijing University of Technology, Beijing 100124, China

Baocai Yin
Faculty of Electronic Information and Electrical Engineering, Dalian University of Technology, Dalian 116024, China

Fuguo Zhang, Yehuan Liu and Qinqiao Xiong
School of Information Technology, Jiangxi University of Finance & Economics, Nanchang 330013, China

Fuguo Zhang
Research Institution for Information Resource Management, Jiangxi University of Finance & Economics, Nanchang 330013, China

Tong Yi and Chun Fang
School of Information Management, Jiangxi University of Finance and Economics, Nanchang 330013, China

Ivaylo Atanasov and Evelina Pencheva
Technical University of Sofia, 8 Kliment Ohridski Boulevard, 1000 Sofia, Bulgaria

Debajyoti Pal and Tuul Triyason
IP Communications Laboratory, School of Information Technology, King Mongkut's University of Technology Thonburi, Bangkok 10140, Thailand

Bingyu Ji, Ran Li and Changan Wu
School of Computer and Information Technology, Xinyang Normal University, Xinyang 464000, China

El Hassane Khabbiza, Rachid El Alami and Hassan Qjidaa
LESSI Laboratory, Department of Physics, Faculty of Sciences Dhar El Mahraz, SidiMohammed Ben Abdellah University, Fez, Morocco

Yancui Shi, Jianhua Cao, Congcong Xiong and Xiankun Zhang
Institute of Computer Science and Information Engineering, Tianjin University of Science & Technology, Tianjin, China

Yan Song, Lidong Huang, Panfeng Xu, Lili Li and Yue Long
College of Physics, Liaoning University, Shenyang, China

Min Song
College of Information, Shenyang Institute of Engineering, Shenyang, China

Nithya Chidambaram, K. Thenmozhi and Rengarajan Amirtharajan
School of Electrical & Electronics Engineering, SASTRA University,Thanjavur 613401, India

Pethuru Raj
Global Cloud Center of Excellence, IBM India, Bangalore 560045, India

Xiankun Sun, Chengfan Li and Jingyuan Yin
School of Computer Engineering and Science, Shanghai University, Shanghai, China

Xiankun Sun, Huijie Liu and Zhijun Fang
School of Electronic and Electrical Engineering, Shanghai University of Engineering Science, Shanghai, China

Shiqian Wu
School of Machinery and Automation, Wuhan University of Science and Technology,Wuhan, China

Jingyuan Yin
Earthquake Administration of Shanghai, Shanghai, China

Xianwen He, Gaoqi Dou and Jun Gao
Department of Communication Engineering, Naval University of Engineering, Wuhan 430033, China

Yunyu Shi, Xiang Liu and Yongxiang Xia
School of Electronic & Electric Engineering, Shanghai University of Engineering Science, 333 Longteng Road, Songjiang District, Shanghai, China

Jianfang Shan
School of Information, Qilu University of Technology, 3501 Daxue Road, Changqing District, Jinan, China

Index

Printed in the USA
CPSIA information can be obtained
at www.ICGtesting.com
JSHW052023301024
72690JS00004B/147